Fluid Geographies

Fluid Geographies

WATER, SCIENCE,
AND SETTLER COLONIALISM
IN NEW MEXICO

K. Maria D. Lane

The University of Chicago Press   CHICAGO AND LONDON

The University of Chicago Press, Chicago 60637
The University of Chicago Press, Ltd., London
© 2024 by The University of Chicago
All rights reserved. No part of this book may be used or reproduced in any manner whatsoever without written permission, except in the case of brief quotations in critical articles and reviews. For more information, contact the University of Chicago Press, 1427 E. 60th St., Chicago, IL 60637.
Published 2024

33 32 31 30 29 28 27 26 25 24   1 2 3 4 5

ISBN-13: 978-0-226-29482-7 (cloth)
ISBN-13: 978-0-226-83395-8 (paper)
ISBN-13: 978-0-226-29496-4 (e-book)
DOI: https://doi.org/10.7208/chicago/9780226294964.001.0001

Library of Congress Cataloging-in-Publication Data

Names: Lane, K. Maria D., author.
Title: Fluid geographies : water, science, and settler colonialism in New Mexico / K. Maria D. Lane.
Description: Chicago : The University of Chicago Press, 2024. | Includes bibliographical references and index.
Identifiers: LCCN 2023046516 | ISBN 9780226294827 (cloth) | ISBN 9780226833958 (paperback) | ISBN 9780226294964 (ebook)
Subjects: LCSH: Water-supply—New Mexico—Management—History. | Water rights—New Mexico—History. | Water—Law and legislation—New Mexico—History. | Water resources development—New Mexico—Case studies. | Water resources development—Government policy—New Mexico—History. | Settler colonialism—New Mexico. | Traditional ecological knowledge—New Mexico.
Classification: LCC HD1694.N6 L36 2024 | DDC 363.6/109789—dc23/eng/20231113
LC record available at https://lccn.loc.gov/2023046516

Dedicated to Robin and Kris Doyle

Contents

List of Illustrations * ix
Acknowledgments * xi

ONE
Introduction: Historical Geographies of the Present * 1

TWO
Settlement: Colonialism in the Aridlands * 23

THREE
Expertise: Settler Politics and the New Water Management * 51

FOUR
Law: Envisioning an Expert Water Agency * 73

FIVE
Knowledge: Science for Settlement's Sake * 91

SIX
Dispute: Navigating Environmental Knowledge in the Courtroom * 116

SEVEN
Displacement: Geographies of Power in an Irrigated Landscape * 141

EIGHT
Conclusion: Settler Colonialism and its Aftermath * 204

Notes * 213
Bibliography * 251
Index * 273

Illustrations

Figures

Figure 2.1   Environmental geography of New Mexico * 25
Figure 2.2   Early peoples in New Mexico, 1100–1540 CE * 28
Figure 2.3   Spanish colonial presence in New Mexico, 1598–1821 * 30
Figure 2.4   Anglo settlement in New Mexico, 1846–1910 * 42
Figure 6.1   Water disputes in the Chama–Rio Grande valley, 1900–1912 * 127
Figure 7.1   Location of water disputes discussed in narratives * 142
Figure 7.2   Map of Rio Las Truchas valley at the juncture of the Rio Grande * 150
Figure 7.3   Map depicting breakwaters and wing-dam * 151
Figure 7.4   Survey to show the direction of the current of the Rio Grande from La Joya station to the town of La Joya, 2 November 1909 * 189

Tables

Table 6.1   Documents found in New Mexico district court records, Chama–Rio Grande study area, 1900–1912 * 124
Table 6.2   Coding categories used to analyze New Mexico district court records, Chama–Rio Grande study area, 1900–1912 * 125
Table 6.3   Breakdown of court participants, New Mexico district court records, Chama–Rio Grande study area, 1900–1912 * 128
Table 6.4   Breakdown of court participants (by county), New Mexico district court records, Chama–Rio Grande study area, 1900–1912 * 129
Table 6.5   Overview of litigants, New Mexico district court records, Chama–Rio Grande study area, 1900–1912 * 131

Table 6.6   Breakdown of litigants, New Mexico district court records, Chama–Rio Grande study area, 1900–1912 * 132

Table 6.7   Breakdown of dispute topics, New Mexico district court records, Chama–Rio Grande study area, 1900–1912 * 133

Table 6.8   Argumentation strategies used in water-related cases, New Mexico district court records, Chama–Rio Grande study area, 1900–1912 * 137

Table 6.9   Breakdown of environmental issues, New Mexico district court records, Chama–Rio Grande study area, 1900–1912 * 139

Acknowledgments

It took a long time to research and write this book, and a world of people and institutions helped along the way. The National Science Foundation provided funding for early archival research, and the University of New Mexico funded the final stages through writing support courtesy of Advance at UNM and a publication subvention provided by the College of Arts and Sciences Office of Research. In the intervening years, many research assistants helped tackle a variety of tasks, including Molly Blumhoefer, Natali Cáceres Arteaga, Jared Massegee, Jennifer McCabe, Brandon Morgan, Molly Padgett, Laura Paskus, Hayley Pedrick, John Schwarting, Jordan Stone, and Jeremy Work. Special thanks to Brandon Morgan, who contributed considerable research as a Ph.D. student and has continued to check in about the book's progress despite his own increasing commitments as a history professor and department chair.

For assistance in the early stages, I thank Ian Manners and Diana Davis for their moral support and Dick Nostrand for his generous encouragement. I thank Paul Matthews for introducing me to the legal geographies of New Mexico water policy and for supporting a crucial grant proposal that helped me launch the project. I also thank the anonymous reviewers of that 2007 NSF proposal for important conceptual contributions.

For direct research support, I thank Polly McCord of the New Mexico Office of the State Engineer Library as well as Elena Perez-Lizano at the New Mexico State Records Center and Archive. I also offer my utmost gratitude to the Interlibrary Loan staff at the University of New Mexico, who have been supremely helpful and patient, despite occasionally egregious borrower behavior on my part.

I'm grateful to several people at the University of Chicago Press: Christie Henry (now at Princeton) for originally inviting the project, Mary Laur and Rachel Kelly Unger for their years of patience, and Susannah Engstrom for dragging me out of a pandemic funk and convincing me to bring the manuscript down the home stretch. Three anonymous reviewers provided critical feedback that helped me improve the final manuscript, and I'm especially grateful to the press for agreeing to commission multiple reviews from non-settler scholars.

For intellectual engagement that helped me develop numerous ideas for the book, I credit presentation audiences at the American Association of Geographers; the Southwest Division of the American Association of Geographers; Florida International University; University of Delaware; University of Maryland, Baltimore County; Idaho State University; Trinity College; Dartmouth; and the Universidad Central de Ecuador. Special thanks to Garth Myers and colleagues at Trinity; to Kate Hall and Garrett Nelson, then at Dartmouth; and to all the participants at Challenging Canada 150. I also thank in aggregate the attendees of the Sixteenth International Conference of Historical Geographers in 2015 in London, whose enthusiasm helped renew my commitment to scholarly life at a time when it had faltered.

For encouraging words about the reality of writing while carrying an administrative load, and for sharing smart ideas about irrigation and identity, I thank Eric Perramond. For reliable sanity checks on many occasions, I thank my favorite coeditor of all time, Arn Keeling. For long-distance writing companionship during the pandemic, I'm grateful to Michaela Buenemann and Yolonda Youngs. And for setting an inspiring example of how to wrestle with settler positionality and responsibility, I am indebted to Kirsten Greer.

The University of New Mexico is a wonderful place to work, and I've benefited from interaction with many astute mentors through the years, including Pamela Cheek, Maya Elrick, and Julia Fulghum. Our campus is filled with smart, critical scholars who dig deep into New Mexico topics; it is truly a privilege to read their books, attend their presentations, and sit alongside them on committees. I'm especially grateful to Sam Truett, whose intellectual honesty makes him stand out among many wonderful people on campus, and to Myrriah Gómez, who motivated me to read authors I'd overlooked and to reread others I hadn't read carefully enough.

In my home department, Geography and Environmental Studies, everyone on the faculty is above average and good-looking. I'm grateful to literally everyone in GES for their collegiality, which provides a cornerstone for my scholarship and professional well-being. Special thanks to John Carr (now at University of New South Wales) for a critical conversation about legal-geography methods during a six-hour journey over back roads to Las Cruces, to Chris Duvall for taking over department chair duties and immediately instructing me to finish the book, to Sean O'Neill for helping me find the draft manuscript and associated digital files after I "misplaced" them during a computer transition, and to Ronda Brulotte for a string of morning text messages that helped me keep going after missing every conceivable deadline. Endless gratitude to Mindy Morgan for many perfectly timed latte runs, and to Marygold Walsh-Dilley for providing detailed and honest critique (by hand!) on the entire manuscript.

Our department also hosts the world's most creative, ambitious, hardworking, persistent, and courageous students. I am grateful to students in GEOG502 for the outlet they provided when discussing the peer-review process, and I am indebted to the honors, master's, and Ph.D. advisees who read and offered insightful feedback on numerous chapter drafts: Javier Astorga Villarroel, Natali Cáceres Arteaga, Brad Hanson, Laurel Ladwig, Desiree Loggins, Ramona Malczynski, Taressa Nield, Laura Paskus, Hayley Pedrick, Shannon Pepper, and Joe Scala. Special thanks to Laura for motivating me to change the way I think about writing and reading.

I started this project when I had a one-year-old. As I finish the final draft, that kid is halfway through high school, with two more siblings close behind. A lot else happened in the interim, personally and professionally, including intellectual side trips and one major detour into university administration. Thank you to everyone who helped with childcare and provided personal support during those difficult years in which professional intensity coincided with the constant commitments of raising a young family. Collective child-rearing isn't the norm in my culture, but many friends, teammates, and neighbors provided critical support at desperate moments, and this book absolutely would not exist without them.

For going above and beyond in all categories of support, I thank Kris and Robin Doyle. No one else in my life has made me think more deeply about place, distance, and home. This book is dedicated to them.

My own household has lived with *Fluid Geographies* longer than anyone ever expected, usually with grace. Thank you to Annie for coining "Dr. Professor Mommy" as an honorary title, complete with nameplate. Thank you to Kristina for relentless optimism and a steady stream of good books. Thank you to Simon for provocative music and other healthy distractions. And thank you, Matt, for reminding me that writing a book is just like laboring to deliver a baby: at the moment you declare it to be well and truly impossible, you're actually very close to the end.

Like every child that makes its way into the world, this book is imperfect. It reflects my own faults of intellect and ambition, and I fret often about the yawning gap between a book describing injustice and the more important work of actually doing something about it. To those scholars who find *Fluid Geographies* lacking and seek to remedy its inadequacies: I look forward to reading and learning from your work. To those who will never read this sentence because they ignore academic publications in favor of doing the hard work: I honor you, and I invite all readers to do the same.

1

Introduction

HISTORICAL GEOGRAPHIES OF THE PRESENT

It's hard to ignore water histories in New Mexico. When I first settled in Albuquerque in 2006, it seemed like half the streets in my new neighborhood were ripped up for a massive pipeline installation. According to the newspapers, the city was pursuing a major transition: connecting the municipal water supply from groundwater to river water for the first time. I learned that Albuquerque had over-pumped its aquifer since the 1960s, depleting geologic layers under the city until some neighborhoods began slowly sinking. Reporters and engineers hailed the new pipeline as a perfect solution; relying on river water instead of groundwater would give the aquifer a chance to recover.

I got caught up in the excitement. I happily detoured around closed roads on my ride to work. I checked worksite progress on my evening walks. I duly noted the Water Authority's mailers explaining that the taste and appearance of tap water might change when the new system started operating.

But it also seemed a bit curious. Every utility hole cover installed above the new pipe sections commemorated the tricentennial anniversary of Albuquerque's 1706 founding as a Spanish *villa*. It made me wonder: was this really the first time a three-hundred-year old desert city had connected its municipal water supply to the major river running through its central valley? And did the city actually use so much water that it depleted an ancient aquifer in just a few decades? If so, did the river even have enough water to meet the municipal needs of a still-growing city with more than half a million residents? It didn't take much research to get basic answers to my questions (in order: technically yes, yes, and probably), but the investigation only raised new ones for me. Each time I maneuvered my son's stroller over the new utility hole covers to give him a better view of the workers lowering mammoth concrete sections into place, I got more curious about the historical geographies flowing between my family and the Rio Grande's many other dependents.

For centuries before Albuquerque's founding, Tiwa Puebloans had used river water for both domestic and agricultural needs throughout the middle Rio Grande valley. The first Spanish colonial villages followed their example by digging community ditches in the 1600s and 1700s. But Anglo newcomers arriving in the late 1800s strained the valley's ditch systems and reoriented urban growth outside the floodplain. By the middle of the twentieth century, the city had largely left the valley behind, climbing eastward into the foothills of the Sandia Mountains. During this time, the floodplain became almost unrecognizable to Indigenous and Spanish-descended residents thanks to channelization, water impoundment, and irrigation intensification. These generational residents fiercely protected the agricultural land uses that anchored them to long cultural histories in the valley, even when new infrastructure functionally ended the Rio Grande's seasonal flood regime.

By the time I arrived in 2006 the City of Albuquerque had invested half a century into a network of groundwater wells to support the influx of settlers chasing military- and energy-focused jobs. An unexpectedly swift depletion of the aquifer, however, reduced the viability of groundwater pumping. By the 1990s attention had turned back to the river as a water source, but ditches and canals wouldn't be enough. Albuquerque would need a water treatment plant, a massive pipeline system, pump stations, and a whole lot of water. Most of that water would come from the other side of the Continental Divide, thanks to a small allocation for Albuquerque in New Mexico's original share of the 1922 Colorado River Compact.

When the taps at my house began to flow with river water in 2008, my family was on the receiving end of a highly engineered journey that lifted water out of tributaries to the San Juan River (itself a tributary of the Colorado River), sluiced it through the Azotea Tunnel and under the Continental Divide in northwestern New Mexico, dumped it into a creek tributary of the Rio Chama, and propelled it through a series of dams and reservoirs until it reached the Chama's confluence with the Rio Grande. At the confluence, this "San Juan–Chama water" joined water arriving from the Rio Grande headwaters after traveling its own gauntlet of dams and reservoirs through southern Colorado into New Mexico. The commingled waters then made their way to Albuquerque, where a low dam guided them into a diversion facility on the north end of town. There pumps raised water out of the Rio Grande, funneled it through a treatment plant, and forced it uphill. It traveled through concrete pipes that eventually connected to my house, 8.3 miles away from and 305 feet above the intake structure. It tasted fine.

As an aridlands newcomer, I marveled at the knowledge, the coordination, and the structures that made it possible for me to fill a cup with cold water on demand in the high desert. And as a historical geographer with an interest in science and technology studies (STS) and the geographies of science, I enthusiastically set out on a quest to understand the scientific origins of this sociohydrologic complex. But everywhere I looked for scientific histories, I found instead stories of power, inequality, and conflict.

I soon realized there is nothing simple or innocent about workers installing a pipeline and stamping it with text announcing Albuquerque's tricentennial milestone. The new water pipeline emerged as a celebrated engineering solution to a significant problem (land subsidence) that stemmed from an earlier engineered solution (groundwater pumping) to a different thorny problem (rapid population growth), which existed only because of earlier engineering projects (channelization and impoundment) that had fundamentally changed the landscape of the Rio Grande valley. Even more interesting to my historical-geographer's eye: the cyclical unmaking and remaking of landscapes through water engineering appeared to be the defining feature of Anglo-American settlement in New Mexico.

The robust literature on New Mexico's history of European settlement, colonial violence, and Indigenous dispossession suggests that we worry less about science per se than about the mutual constitution of science and colonialism. Through big infrastructure, new agencies, and knowledge politics, Anglo water engineering repeatedly marginalized existing residents of the Rio Grande valley while simultaneously transforming the ecology of the Rio Grande. The historical record challenges us to understand settler colonialism as a key driver of environmental-knowledge politics, of environmental policy, and of state investment in science and engineering. Not only in the past, but also in the present.

The Fluid Geographies Project

This project tackles Cole Harris's incisive question to historical geographers—"how did colonialism dispossess?"—by exploring the introduction of "scientific" water policy to New Mexico.[1] For centuries before and throughout the nineteenth century, New Mexico's Indigenous, Spanish, and Indo-Hispano farming communities produced and applied environmental knowledge: they maintained irrigation infrastructure, prepared for seasonal changes in water flow, controlled flood damage, and organized community efforts to ensure productive harvests.² After the 1848 Treaty of Guadalupe Hidalgo included New Mexico in the massive cession of Mexican lands to the United States, however, Anglo settlers began to arrive in droves and put intense pressure on many communities' long-standing methods for understanding aridity and predicting environmental conditions. Land claims, economic upheaval, and changing demographics pushed environmental-knowledge production into a combative and conflict-oriented mode dominated by the court system, where the deck was stacked in favor of the new Anglo arrivals.

Animated by Harris's question, *Fluid Geographies* takes a closer look at the production of environmental knowledge and policy in New Mexico. The book uses a fine-grained analysis of legislative texts, administrative records, and court cases to investigate the origin story of New Mexico's modernist water-management system. These settler archives show that modernist water policy both reflected and constructed a racialized understanding of scientific expertise. New Mexico's settler water agency discredited nonwhite water managers as unscientific and inexpert while simultaneously lauding white irrigators and engineers who often displayed significant hydrologic and environmental ignorance. In the face of a racialized management philosophy, subsistence irrigators from Indigenous and Indo-Hispano backgrounds found it increasingly difficult to protect their customs, bodies of knowledge, and landscapes. Settler science enacted its colonial power quietly, often without courting the fierce resistance that attends more violent forms of colonialism. It supported regimes of commercial extraction that laid waste to New Mexico's waters and environments, yet it remains prominent today as the dominant mode for engaging with water policy and official decision-making.

I didn't write this book to naturalize settler power or to justify its insidious persistence. My goal is to show that technoscientific water management led by engineers is a culturally specific policy approach based in structures of Anglo dominance. Other approaches to water management have other politics and are grounded in other logics. This book takes no stance on who should be in charge of water management in New Mexico. It insists, however, that we acknowledge the politics of water science and engineering, both historically and in the present. And if we accept that modernist water management is political, we accept that it can change.

Indigenous scholars are leading the effort to outline alternate paths, often focusing on the foundational role of knowledge politics in not only enabling settler ecologies but also protecting Indigenous sovereignty.³ Despite the ways this scholarship foregrounds environmental damage and settler policies that "crept up on Native people and their land,"⁴ it remains essentially hopeful. Indigenous scholars and their allies show that uncritical acceptance of modernist scientific knowledge hinders new environmental approaches that could be built on a foundation of multiple forms of knowledge.[5] And they argue that reconciliation will remain elusive as long as the structures of colonial disadvantage persist.[6] The inverse is also true: an honest and critical view of settler environmental knowledge may open our eyes to other, decolonial possibilities for the management of environments and waters.

The Indigenous critical theorist Jodi Byrd argues that decolonization is possible only through a different kind of theoretical stance, one that is derived not from poststructural theory but from Indigenous theory.[7] This book offers a precursor to that step, providing a detailed critique of the racialized disadvantage encoded in New Mexico's water-management policies, institutions, and technologies. It explores the complex power dynamics that both constrained and emerged from modernist water-management structures during New Mexico's territorial period. And it identifies a precise new way of talking about settler knowledge structures and their weak points. I offer *Fluid Geographies* in solidarity with other thinkers working to imagine new environmental futures that supersede the reclamation era and its colonial injustices.

Frameworks

Fluid Geographies examines communities in conflict, technologies that remake landscapes, and environmental changes that influence political decision-making. It investigates modernist thinking that arrived in New Mexico closely on the heels of the railroads, when new ways of knowing water, understanding aridity, and valuing nature arrived with Anglo-Americans in the nineteenth century. Small tributaries, intermittent streams, irrigation canals, field-side ditches, and the great river itself felt the impact, as environmental policy based on settler science helped legitimize the dispossession of Indigenous and *Nuevomexicano* communities throughout the Rio Grande watershed.

The book explores this complex transition through numerous stories: about the management of community conflict, about the persistence of communal water management in the face of political change, about the far-reaching environmental impacts of modernist infrastructure, and about the role of engineering in destabilizing natural and social systems. Almost all of these stories consider the dynamics of racial and ethnic relations in an area of geopolitical transition. Together, they show that differing understandings of phenomena such as aridity, flooding, and hydrology emerge from different knowledge foundations. Decisions about how to resolve a conflict or address an environmental issue vary depending on whether the decision-makers prioritize cultural teaching, eyewitness observation, scientific measurement, cartographic survey, engineering expertise, legal custom, or some other means of establishing knowledge. By examining these underlying knowledge commitments, I hope to deepen our understanding of environmental and political change.

Fluid Geographies asks readers to look at a range of stories and to consider the role of modernist water-management policy in displacing non-Anglo peoples and communities in New Mexico. To this end, the book relies on several academic disciplines. Interdisciplinary scholarship on settler-colonial studies helps place New Mexico's stories within the wider context of the United States' dispossession of Indigenous and Nuevomexicano communities. Scholarship on the geographies of science points toward the deep importance of place in knowledge-making and worldmaking. Debates in the fields of human-environment geography and legal geography inform critical decisions about the methodology used in this research. All of these frameworks contribute to a historical geography of science and dispossession in New Mexico.

SETTLER COLONIALISM

In this book, most of my attention and many of my arguments revolve around the foundational role of settler colonialism in structuring U.S. society and policy. Settler colonialism differs significantly from the extraction-oriented colonialism that drove European imperial expansion around the globe starting in the sixteenth century. Whereas "franchise" colonies such as Peru or India revolved around resource extraction and labor exploitation, "settler" colonies focused instead on taking control of land from the original inhabitants.[8] In the colonies that became the United States and New Zealand, for example, settlers focused on "making a territory their permanent home while continuing to enjoy metropolitan living standards and political privileges."[9] In the process, settler colonists dispossessed Indigenous people, displaced them from their homelands, and established structures of perpetual disadvantage that persist into the present. Scholars of settler colonialism examine its complex dynamics and legacies from multiple disciplinary angles, considering economic, legal, military, cultural, social, political, and environmental dimensions.

The North American settler colonies (now Canada and the United States) provide clear examples of settler colonialism's foundations and continuation. Most visibly, European settlers in North America engaged in a violent process of removal that continuously pushed Indigenous peoples off their lands ahead of an ever-shifting frontier. Genocide and ethnic cleansing constituted the most extreme removal methods but went hand in hand with legal institutions and discourses of rationality that justify dispossession and racial superiority.[10] By rejecting collective land ownership and nonsedentary-community boundaries, courts allowed Anglo and other European settlers to lay enduring claim to possession of nearly an entire continent.[11] In addition to military and legal actions, settlers introduced new commercial economic systems that disrupted regional trade and devoured the autonomy of Indigenous people, pushing them into wage labor as they lost their land base. Economic intrusion thus paired dispossession with economic dependency.[12]

A considerable body of literature in the humanities and social sciences argues that settler colonialism's dispossession extends far beyond the legal, military, and economic aspects of land transfer.[13] More broadly, displacement disrupts "language, culture, family, lifestyles, [and] identities, as well as gender and generational relationships."[14] Through numerous programs for "social improvement, all perpetrated in the name of 'civilisation' and 'progress,'" settler societies created a fundamental opposition between the racialized identities of white settlers and nonwhite others.[15] Settler narratives continually reinforce this racial opposition and contort history to erase Indigenous presence while engaging in nation-building projects premised on whiteness.[16] When Indigenous peoples push back with narratives that resist racialization—by focusing on political sovereignty rather than racial identity—they are typically rendered invisible or illegitimate within a dominant settler culture.[17] As a result, non-Indigenous peoples rarely notice or acknowledge the structures and institutions that exist all around us to dispossess Indigenous people.[18] The enduring dynamic of the settler state, then, is a pernicious displacement structure that perpetuates itself by fading into the background.[19]

Geographers have contributed to this conversation by exploring conceptualizations of space, property, and territoriality in both Indigenous and settler societies.[20] Critical historical geographers focus specifically on the role of new knowledge forms and concepts in founding the settler state. Early settler administrations in North America, for example, relied on a conceptualization of land as *empty* and inviting to settlers, yet also *bounded* to constrain Indigenous people. Private property—as a knowledge construct and legal concept—allowed settlers to reorganize Indigenous territory as unclaimed land and to marginalize Indigenous communities as premodern entities incapable of territorial control.[21] Settler governments also made regulatory decisions based on a "spatial politics of governmental knowledge" that exalted scientific authority while disregarding Indigenous knowledge.[22] In a process of "colonial unknowing," settlers rejected Indigenous understandings of space and environment that were based on notions of kinship, collectivism, and intimate relations between humans and nonhuman entities.[23] The new settler states were built instead on Enlightenment philosophies of individualism, humanism, and white supremacy. These ideals became deeply intertwined with modernist forms of scientific knowledge and authority, and with devastating environmental change.[24]

I rely on this scholarship to examine the legal and political contexts in which modernist water policy emerged in New Mexico. *Fluid Geographies* argues that water policy provided key contributions to structural, racialized dispossession via social and environmental impacts. In the process, the book goes beyond the settler-Indigenous dichotomy that animates much of the literature on settler colonialism. Recent scholarship on New Mexico and the U.S. Southwest has begun to expand the definition of settler colonialism, using an intersectional lens to highlight complex and fluid cultural geographies that evolved at the intersection of multiple colonial power structures.[25] Nuevomexicano peoples and communities exemplify this multidimensional fluidity: they first entered the region as violent colonizers, returned after Indigenous rebellion with an assimilationist commitment to *mestizaje* (multiracial identity), and later became colonial objects themselves under the thumb of dispossessive U.S. law and policy.[26] We cannot explain settler colonialism and its ongoing impacts without looking carefully at these shifts in positionality. *Fluid Geographies* argues that modernist water policy participated directly in the erasure, elision, and simplification of complex identities. In the process, it created new hydrologic histories interwoven with settler colonialism as a racialized sociopolitical structure.

GEOGRAPHIES OF SCIENCE

Scholarship in science and technology studies (STS) has shown persuasively that producing knowledge is never a neutral act or a reflection of truth. Rather, it is always about power: "the ways in which we know and represent the world (both nature and society) are inseparable from the ways in which we choose to live in it."[27] Empire-building, for example, relied on certain kinds of scientific knowledge, such as geography and cartography, and simultaneously generated resources and legitimacy for those same sciences in specific places at specific times.[28] The modern states that emerged from European empires were thus entangled with the rise of modern sciences, each reinforcing and making the other possible in a process of "coproduction."²⁹

STS and its predecessor fields have long excluded nonscientific knowledge from analysis, but recent scholarship takes a broader stance.³⁰ We now recognize that science is only one part of "the whole of humanity's epistemic development" and must be contextualized alongside other knowledge forms, including "negative" forms such as ignorance, failure, and imprecision.³¹ To study the coproduction of knowledge and power, STS scholars examine how objects and ideas are defined and organized, how identities and institutions are created to uphold knowledge and power, and how discourses and representations create and reinforce specific views about knowledge and governance.³² The most recent scholarship also sees science as necessarily part of debate, advocacy, and politics.³³

The geography of science literature adds to this scholarship by urging scholars to address these topics within a spatial framework. David Livingstone wrote the foundational pieces calling for attention to the spatiality of scientific production (sites), of scientific institutionalization (regions), and of scientific legitimization networks (circulation).³⁴ Space-aware STS scholars responded to this call, and historical geographers and their STS colleagues have now richly explored the "spatiality of scientific practice and of knowledge circulation" at key points in the history of modern science.³⁵ Contemporary geographers also increasingly use these concepts to examine scientific practices that challenge social boundaries and remake social relations.³⁶ Departing from historical geographies of science, this scholarship is more likely to use political economy and class formation in framing the geographies of science, or to bring postcolonial and feminist theory to bear.³⁷

Both historical and contemporary geographers focus on the spatial scales of knowledge. Modern science has achieved significant cultural and political authority because of its apparent "placelessness" and universality. Yet foundational scholarship in STS showed that even universal truth claims can be localized in certain practices that facilitate the mobility, stability, and combinability of knowledge.³⁸ Geographers have built on this argument, showing that all scientific practice is locally situated and that "the dominant conception of universal rationality" should be replaced "with notions of the local geographies of knowledge."³⁹

Fluid Geographies applies these concepts to modernist water policy in New Mexico, demonstrating that environmental claims can be traced to specific actions, individuals, places, and politics. Its chapters delve deeply into the contestations, negotiations, and power plays that produced hydrologic knowledge in a racially stratified U.S. territory. The book shows that modernist water policy for New Mexico was never placeless or based in objective science. It was based from the beginning in a racialized political project centered on remaking both environments and social relations.

HISTORICAL GEOGRAPHIES OF SETTLER SCIENCE

Fluid Geographies draws on insights from the literatures of both environmental and social relations. It reviews the increasing prevalence and authority of scientific knowledge in New Mexico during a time of Anglo settler encroachment in order to develop a historical geography of water science and engineering in a settler-colonial context. Environmental knowledge is a recent topic in the literature on settler colonialism, and nonscientific knowledge is a recent topic in the literature on geographies of science. This book therefore offers an opportunity to build on the scholarship in both fields.

Environmental science emerged from the cradle of Anglo settler colonies such as the United States and Canada.[40] Settlement created new ecologies in places where settlers engaged in intensive extraction activities, such as forestry, grazing, agriculture, irrigation, trapping, fishing, and mining.[41] Although the new "settlerscapes" became quickly degraded, settlers pressed ahead with extensive overdevelopment throughout North America, in the apparent belief that modern science and technology would help them overcome environmental obstacles.[42] Commercial extraction led instead to inevitable environmental catastrophe—deforestation, soil degradation, flooding, salinization, the collapse of fisheries, poisoned waters— which settlers then paradoxically blamed on Indigenous communities that had rarely seen such phenomena before the arrival of European settlers.[43] Settlers targeted "traditionalist" Indigenous communities because they rejected settler science and remained committed to knowledge forms that centered environmental relations instead of profit-oriented extraction.[44] Environmental science thus became a tool of "colonial ecological violence" by allowing settlers to address environmental disaster without taking responsibility for it.[45] In the process, settlers engaged in mass landscape alterations that displaced generations-old Indigenous ecologies, disrupted Indigenous subsistence strategies, and undermined Indigenous communities' "social resilience as self-determining collectives."[46]

Together, environmental change and management became deeply implicated in conflicts over sovereignty, identity, and territoriality in the North American settler colonies. This held true for the western colonies that overlapped and displaced the northernmost Spanish settler colonies in what became the American Southwest. Today, environmental-management issues continually reemerge in the United States and Canada as political flash points where the racist, militaristic, and violent overtones of settler territoriality are both reproduced and challenged.[47] Settler infrastructures such as dams, canals, mines, and fences can become political objects that help define settler-indigenous relations.[48] And many celebrated environmental conservation projects simply maintain the settler-colonial order when they work to address environmental catastrophes caused by settler extraction but negate Indigenous sovereignty and knowledge in the process.[49]

In the twenty-five years since the anthropologist Patrick Wolfe amplified the insights of Native American and Indigenous Studies scholarship by declaring settler colonialism to be "a structure, not an event," scholars have debated the implications of his statement.[50] If we see colonialism as an event, we can declare it to be in the past and discount its role in ongoing "post"colonial violence and politics. But if settler colonialism is a structure, it will continue inflicting damage on our societies as long as its structural integrity remains intact. Scholars in decolonial and Indigenous studies have pressed beyond this second insight, arguing that colonial structures indeed persist, as does indigeneity in many forms.[51]

Knowledge forms that enable ongoing colonial displacement therefore deserve heightened scrutiny, including primarily science. Many promising historical-geographical works focus on settler knowledge in Canada, with less critical geographic attention focused on the United States.[52] Following the work of "New West" historians, scholars certainly recognize American westward expansion as a settler-colonial process.[53] But scholarship exploring the American West's cultural conflicts, fraught identity politics, and disadvantaged Indigenous communities tends to focus on military violence or cultural and legal disenfranchisement.[54] Less prominent are the scientific contours of settler colonialism, although a few excellent works have productively explored conflicts between scientific management and political interests in environmental management.[55] Not coincidentally, these works largely focus on the American Southwest, where the environmental legacies of two different European settlement efforts intersect with complex racial and identity politics.[56]

Fluid Geographies focuses on New Mexico, specifically considering the role of settler environmental knowledge produced through engineering agencies, personnel, and projects. I have argued elsewhere that insights from geographies of science should also be applied to engineering.[57] As a key agent of modernity, engineering has tremendous power to conjure not only material infrastructures but also social networks, landscape transformations, and geopolitical narratives.[58] State support for specific forms of engineering creates a "sociotechnical imaginary" that coproduces technical knowledge with specific, powerful visions for social and environmental change.[59] *Fluid Geographies* draws from and contributes to this literature by illuminating the spatial geographies of water policy development, application, and impact in late territorial New Mexico.

Methods in Human-Environment Geography

In taking up the geographies of modernist water science and engineering in New Mexico, *Fluid Geographies* interrogates the human-environment relations brought into being by the settler-colonial project. To put settler knowledges and practices into context alongside those they displaced, the book relies on methodological cues from a few different strands of human-environment geography.

Human-environment geographers explore the links between science, technology, and environmental policy in several different ways. Most notably, the subfield of political ecology looks at the causes of environmental change by using political economy as an explanatory framework for field-based empirical research on structures and institutions.[60] Political ecology usually focuses on contemporary issues, but a small field of historical-political ecology takes a "field-informed perspective on the past" that includes "an explicit linkage between social justice and the management of natural resources."[61] Although this historical branch mimics the larger subfield's focus on economic structures and institutions, some scholars push historical work to center the knowledge structures that define expertise and legitimate certain types of data.[62] The historical-political ecologist Diana Davis has urged political ecologists to foreground the colonial roots of neoliberal management approaches by showing that today's scientific resource management often relies on foundational data sets and approaches generated during colonial regimes.[63] Historical-political ecology can therefore "illustrate the insidious and pernicious effects of the institutionalization of colonial/imperial environmental knowledges/narratives" in today's "postcolonial" natural resource–management regimes.[64]

The work of some poststructural scholars intersects with these concerns from the angle of hybrid geographies. Their scholarship is far more concerned with discourses, narratives, and knowledge than with neoliberal and capitalist frameworks as drivers of environmental change. Hybrid geographies focus on the coproduction of environments and knowledge, both as historical context for contemporary concerns and as historical scholarship in its own right. Numerous good examples that focus specifically on water reveal a complex intertwining of environmental technologies, management institutions, knowledge structures, and social inequalities.[65] This scholarship calls our attention to the existence of "socionatures"—hybrid landscapes—that challenge modernity's insistence that "environment" and "nature" are categories separate from humans.[66]

Important work in both of these fields unfortunately tends to marginalize biophysical explanation. Political ecologists focus on "our always-politicized interactions with the biophysical environment" through an almost exclusive reliance on social theory and explanation, while often ignoring actual material ecologies.[67] Hybrid geographers similarly discuss the integration of natural and social domains, but their insights come almost exclusively from a human-geography standpoint.

To address these shortcomings and confront questions about how we produce environmental knowledge, a recent effort has crystallized around the subfield of critical physical geography (CPG).[68] CPG spurs critical human geographers to engage in producing science while also asking physical geographers to critique their own scientific practice. CPG comprises a broad topical range, but "its common characteristic is deep engagement with both theories of power and physical science, using integrative explanatory frameworks to better illuminate the coproduction of sociobiophysical systems."[69] The resulting aspiration—to produce integrative and interdisciplinary work that is simultaneously descriptive, analytical, and transformative—offers a compelling intersection with historical-geography research on past environments and environmental sciences.[70]

I have argued that a historical CPG could productively consider the influence of physical geographies on past environmental-knowledge production.[71] We cannot focus solely on historical actors' social and theoretical commitments if we hope to grasp the fundamental intertwining of human and environmental geographies at multiple scales in the past. We must consider imperial and colonial reactions to specific environmental conditions, and also how those reactions reflected and justified specific forms of knowledge based on technical expertise.[72]

Finally, this book also brings methods to bear from legal geography, a growing subdiscipline that focuses on how law and space are coproduced.[73] Not only does law affect material and social spaces, but space and social relations also affect the development of law itself.[74] The founding scholarship in legal geography often focused on cities and social relations, with minimal attention to environmental control and policy. One early compilation, however, showed that changing ideas about settlement, environment, and resource use have contributed to an increasing reliance on science in American law.[75] Law, like science, claims to be a truth-*seeking* institution. Yet both institutions are better understood as institutions that bring truth *into being*. Through law and science, worlds are made—material conditions are created, and social relations are produced—under an authoritative institutional banner.[76]

Legal geographers have increasingly called for attention to the environmental dynamics of legal world-making, given that American law—and English law, from which it is derived—is rooted in a dualistic Enlightenment concept of humans as separate from nature.[77] Their ongoing conversations about law, resources, and the modern state reflect the multiple strands of human geography discussed above, with some scholars relying on political ecology while others turn to hybrid geographies and new materialism.[78] Critical legal geography can also be drawn into conversation with settler-colonial studies when it provides a close reading of legal texts, legislation, and litigation that normalize disadvantages for certain communities.[79] Attention to legal practices of litigation and adjudication thus provides a method for understanding environmental-knowledge politics: "The legal process, emerging legal discourses, and the adjudicated result disrupt past legalsocial relations and remap how people, either individually or collectively, relate to each other and themselves."[80] Some of these insights have already been applied to historical geographies of extractive colonies, and I apply them here specifically to a settler-colonial domain.[81]

Fluid Geographies makes use of these varied methodological insights by focusing on the production of certain forms of environmental knowledge within New Mexico's water-management structures and policies in the late territorial era. In reviewing the environmental claims present in legal statutes, agency reports, and court disputes, the book foregrounds a critical understanding of the agents and discourses through which physical geographies of water became established, credible, and powerful. And it reveals the political context in which engineers and policymakers performed their scientific work. The analytical and interpretive methods used in *Fluid Geographies*—each of which is described in more detail in individual chapters that tackle different subjects—work together to provide a fine-grained view of water science and water engineering at a transitional moment that foreshadows the present.

A Note on Terminology

For those unfamiliar with the history and historiography of New Mexico, some of the terms used to identify people in this introduction may feel uncomfortable. Contemporary New Mexico traffics in a tricultural mythology that elides considerable diversity.[82] Hence this short note to explain how and why certain terms appear in this book; none is used accidentally or without care.

First, I use the term "Indigenous" to refer broadly to numerous distinct nations that resided in New Mexico long before Europeans arrived. I use "Indigenous" rather than "Native American" or "American Indian" to align with an emerging consciousness of global indigeneity and in solidarity with decolonial initiatives. In places, I differentiate between "Pueblo" peoples, who lived in culturally distinct agriculture-focused communities, and "nomadic" or "pastoralist" peoples, who engaged in varied subsistence activities spanning substantial geographic extents. In many cases, I refer to these Indigenous nations by name—for example, Pueblo of Isleta or Navajo Nation—to provide specificity for historical episodes. And in some cases I use multiple names for a single nation, reflecting the increasing modern use of Indigenous nations' own names and place-names, even though imposed colonial names are more likely to appear in the historical or legal records consulted in this study—for example, Navajo rather than Diné, and Santo Domingo Pueblo rather than Kewa Pueblo.

Second, I use the term "Anglo" or "Anglo-American" to refer broadly to the white-racialized settlers who arrived in New Mexico from elsewhere in the United States, starting in the early 1800s. During the periods of Spanish and Mexican control in the Southwest, the term *norteamericano* dominated as shorthand to distinguish white European Americans from the Spanish settlers who had arrived in New Mexico centuries earlier.[83] During the territorial period, the terms "Anglo" and "Hispano" emerged to distinguish these same groups within a bureaucratic lexicon. Both terms encapsulated racial meanings, with "Anglo" referring specifically to white settlers of English or British origin and "Hispano" referring to white settlers of Spanish origin. (See the detailed discussion of "Hispano" identity below.) I rarely use the term "white" in this book, relying most often on "Anglo" to denote a specific group of white settlers who appear often in territorial archival and institutional records. I acknowledge that the term clouds cultural, national, and class differences among nineteenth- and twentieth-century immigrants to and settlers in New Mexico, hiding their complexity behind a veil of presumed whiteness and power. I also acknowledge that New Mexico's diverse culture groups today use a variety of identity terms to refer to themselves and to one another; the ongoing bureaucratic use of "Anglo" as a socioracial identifier seeps into some groups' colloquial use, but that does not mean it is an undisputed or widespread term.[84]

Third, I use the term "Nuevomexicana/o" to denote a broad collection of individuals and communities with distinct claims to Spanish heritage. As discussed in chapter 2, New Mexico's Spanish speakers have a complex cultural history that challenges academic notions of settler colonialism. This book is not a work of cultural studies, but it relies on a vast, smart literature that explores shifting identity categories through the lenses of regional, ethnic, and cultural studies.[85] During the Spanish colonial period, different terms emerged to refer to colonists in different areas of what is today the U.S. Southwest: *Californio*, *Nuevomexicano*, and *Tejano*. These place-based identity terms recognized cultural distinctions among colonists without implying any racial identity. In Spanish New World colonies, in fact, there was always a recognition that multiple races coexisted in complex social hierarchies. Throughout the Spanish colonies, *mestizos* (people with both Spanish and Indigenous heritage) were always most numerous, but colonial culture recognized many other racial identities as well.[86] The first Spanish colony in New Mexico included Indigenous, Spanish, mestizo, and African people, and New Mexico has a documented legacy of intermarriage similar to that in other Spanish colonies in the Americas.[87] Over the centuries, a cacophonous cultural geography has emerged throughout the Rio Grande watershed on the basis of intermarriage, coercion, political alliance, and conflict among different towns and villages. Scholars have devoted considerable attention to the fraught prospects of identifying New Mexico's Spanish-speaking peoples with a single, meaningful identity term.[88] Some authors use the general term "Indo-Hispano" to capture the racial and cultural mixing elided by settler narratives.[89] Others prefer regional or colloquial terms such as *manitos*, *morenos*, or *norteños* to refer more specifically to identity and belonging in northern New Mexico.[90] Many young people also now identify as Chicana/o in solidarity with a broader cultural-political movement that claims Mesoamerican origin, and New Mexico writers have helped articulate the intersections of Chicana/o and Nuevomexicana/o identity.[91] Other general terms such as "Hispanic" and "Latina/o" are used infrequently by Nuevomexicanas/os in comparison with regionally specific terms. Nonetheless, interracial identity (*mestizaje*) has long been central to the identity of Spanish-speaking communities, and many Spanish-speaking New Mexicans now use the term "Nuevomexicana/o" as a broad identifier of regional, historical, and interracial character.

Older academic publications in both geography and history often use the term "Hispano" to refer to this same broad group of interracial Spanish speakers. I have not followed their lead, because this generic usage both ignores the complexity described above and overlooks the term's historical meaning. After New Mexico became part of the United States, Anglo territorial officials commonly used the terms "Mexican" or *mexicano* to refer to mixed-race Spanish speakers who remained in or moved to New Mexico. Around 1900, however, Anglo territorial leaders began to refer to elite Nuevomexicanas/os as "white" and started using the term "Hispano" to essentialize their Spanish-European heritage.[92] Territorial officials hoped this shift in terminology would make New Mexico more palatable to U.S. congressional leaders, who were considering whether the territory deserved statehood within a nation premised on whiteness as its central social characteristic.[93] "Hispano" worked in tandem with other identifiers such as "Spanish," *rico*, and *patrón* to designate upper-class whiteness against the foil of terms like "Mexican," *nativo*, and *vecino*, which denoted lower-class brownness.[94] Although Anglo officials and bureaucrats have used "Hispano" since the turn of the twentieth century, it has never enjoyed widespread cultural salience among Spanish speakers. Only Nuevomexicano elites were ever likely to embrace the "Hispano" identity, claiming the whiteness and status it implied in a specific historical context.[95] The word is now appropriate mainly as a historical term to designate Nuevomexicano elites who strategically denied their own lived experience of mestizaje in response to Anglo bureaucratic goals.

Furthermore, I acknowledge the inadequacy of *all* these terms and of the tricultural myth in New Mexico. Important groups are completely excluded by these identifiers, including historical and contemporary residents of New Mexico. Most notably, people of African descent are unnamed and ignored in the tricultural myth, despite the presence of Africans in the first Spanish expeditions to New Mexico, as settlers in the first Spanish colonies in New Mexico, and as founders of African American farming communities during New Mexico's territorial period.[96] Over the last century, people have settled in New Mexico from a wide variety of geographic and cultural origins, only to find themselves unrecognized within the tricultural story told in museums, histories, and tourist brochures.[97] All of the terms identified above function as social and political markers. They reflect the structure and impact of a political-racial hierarchy in which individuals and communities construct their own sense of place and belonging in relation to other groups. This book does not focus on the deep complexities of identity formation processes in New Mexico, but it does trace settler colonialism's dependence on racialization as the basis of power in New Mexico, especially focusing on how that racialized power was coproduced with environmental knowledge.

Finally, a note on the use of non-English words and names. I have attempted to correctly reproduce the spelling and diacritics of all non-English words. For non-English words other than names or place-names, I use italics at first use to indicate the word's non-English origin. In subsequent use I drop the italics to indicate words that enjoy regular contemporary usage in New Mexico. This includes words that refer to ethnicity, to irrigation infrastructure, and to landscape. For the specific term Nuevomexicano, I use the masculine singular form whenever using it as an adjective. When it is a noun, I use the common constructions Nuevomexicana/o (singular) and Nuevomexicanas/os (plural) to be grammatically inclusive, unless the referent individual(s) are known to be wholly identified by one gender.

On Complicity

My research shows how the scientific policies, values, and structures that Anglo-American settlers brought to New Mexico disrupted and displaced communities of non-Anglo races and ethnicities. But I myself am a beneficiary of the ongoing settler-colonial structure, along with hundreds of other University of New Mexico faculty members and tens of thousands of other Albuquerque residents who arrived in the modern era. How do I account for my own complicity in the structure I critique?

Writing this book has made me revisit virtually everything I ever learned in my career as a settler scholar.

I returned to the work of thinkers who raised early cautions about archival work being inherently complicit with colonialism.[98] I reread arguments about the importance of historical geographers' being modest with theory and sensitive with empirical work, of reading against the archival grain for unintentionally recorded phenomena.[99] I sat with numerous cautions about well-intentioned efforts that serve only to reinforce colonial structures.[100] I engaged with Indigenous thinkers' critical struggles to decolonize both thinking and methodology in historical scholarship and science studies.[101]

These works implore us to tread carefully and with humility, to use the incompleteness of historical records as an analytical lens, to look for complexity and messiness in archives that invent institutional organization only after the fact, and to focus on embodied practices despite the difficulty of accessing them through paper archives. They forced me to question methodological choices, confront my use of archives, struggle with my inability to speak for others, and consider my failure to seek or find the most meaningful voices and materials. They also reinforce the difficulty and the challenge of engaging in historical scholarship that stands against displacement, and not for it.

I am under no illusion that this book, or my broader research agenda, has the power to right a long legacy of colonial wrongs. But I remain optimistic that settler scholarship can be part of a reparative effort. Most consequentially, my research shows that scientific and rational approaches to resource development started from places of grave uncertainty. Anglos entering the newly minted New Mexico territory did not take possession of water immediately or easily. They had to negotiate and accommodate, fight and manipulate. By tracing and understanding one process through which Anglo settlers gained power—modernist water management—this book illuminates a path toward unraveling and challenging the structures of that power. And none too soon. With the U.S. Southwest forecast as an epicenter of climate-change impacts, and New Mexico itself at the precipice, it is beyond time to engage deeply with alternative environmental futures.[102] It is time to forge new relationships that allow meaningful thinking, together, about the realities of persistence in a changing landscape.

At its core, this book is haunted by my own misgivings about whether writing an academic book is a meaningful way of working for change in the world. Academic books, like scientific programs, are good at explaining but bad at storytelling. We know that stories are the best tool we have for making sense of the world, for figuring out who we are, and for imagining the relations we want to build. The most important stories in New Mexico center on the complexities, identities, and achievements of peoples whose place-based perspectives have persisted over centuries and generations, despite recent traumas inflicted by aggressive settlement and commercial development. But those are not my stories to tell. This book turns the lens on a dominant yet unexamined story from my own Anglo cultural tradition. It's a story about how science and settlement and whiteness and Americanness exist only alongside, and because of, one another.

Structure of the Book

Chapter 2 provides a historical and geographical overview of lands, waters, and communities in what is today known as New Mexico. Ancient civilizations once dominated the wider region, using a variety of irrigation techniques to maintain productive agriculture even in areas marked by high aridity and minimal precipitation. As these large civilizations waned, small agricultural pueblos emerged throughout the Rio Grande watershed, connecting a network of agricultural, pastoral, and nomadic communities across multiple ecological regions. The chapter describes Spanish entry into the region as the first episode of settler colonialism, in which Spanish settlers displaced thousands of people through direct and indirect violence. Two hundred fifty years later, Anglo-Americans brought a new phase of settler colonialism to the region, afflicting not only the Indigenous communities that had already absorbed Spanish impacts but also Nuevomexicano communities themselves descended from colonial ancestors. This chapter highlights the importance of water management to each phase of settler colonialism, tracing different displacement and dispossession impacts on Indigenous and Nuevomexicano communities.

Chapter 3 focuses on the emergence of U.S. water-management policies and bureaucracies in the nineteenth century. Relying on historical and policy scholarship, it situates water management within the broader Progressive Era effort to claim and control new territory in the American West via environmental policy. The chapter links rationalistic, science-based management policy to the settler-colonial project, showing that governance of lands and waters became synonymous with governance of racial minorities. Focusing on water management, the chapter traces the rise of "reclamation" policy, which relied on scientific expertise and engineering efficiency. It shows how new conceptions of expertise privileged politically elite Anglo-Americans as water managers, even in regions where Anglos were newcomers. The chapter thus sets the stage for an argument that the rise of science-based and engineering-led bureaucracies for water management enacted settler-colonial power and contributed to displacement of non-Anglos in New Mexico.

In chapter 4 I transition to a more detailed examination of U.S.-era water governance in New Mexico, diving into the legislative creation of its centralized water agency. Starting in the opening years of the twentieth century, New Mexico developed new water laws at the territorial level to encourage, authorize, and control water development projects that "made room" for Anglo settlers. Using legislative texts as evidence of an effective governance vision, the chapter shows that territorial officials worked hard to enact federal resource-management philosophy while also struggling with New Mexico's unique settlement history and water-related cultural history. I argue that the increasing legislative focus on expertise and rational resource quantification reflects an increasingly determined attempt to enable Anglo settlement and displace or disadvantage existing Indigenous and Nuevomexicano communities.

Chapter 5 shows that the new water agency created for New Mexico in 1905—the Office of the Territorial Irrigation Engineer—enacted its legislative mandate in specific ways that enabled American settler colonialism in a fraught cultural context. Using the agency's detailed biennial reports and hydrologic surveys as primary sources, the chapter resurrects and reexamines the agency's own vision of its mission, expertise, primary activities, and contributions to the citizenry and government of territorial

New Mexico. The agency professed a strong commitment to principles of rationalization but struggled to enact them in the practical management of water resources. It focused more on economic and demographic concerns than on hydrology, devoting itself to data development in support of settlement expansion.

Chapter 6 examines an intersection point where scientific expertise, water policy, and environmental knowledge came together: the courtroom. It begins by reviewing New Mexico's legal traditions and providing historical context for shifting approaches to water disputes under different colonial and national regimes. Attention then turns to nearly two hundred cases from eight New Mexico counties in the Rio Chama–Rio Grande corridor between 1900 and 1912. Using descriptive statistics, the chapter shows that plaintiffs and defendants used different approaches to make their arguments, and court personnel such as judges and referees sought different forms of resolution. The spatial geography of these differences reflects specific colonial contexts, in which different forms of knowledge carried different weights. But throughout the study area, Anglos dominated the court system and engaged in litigation much more often than non-Anglos.

Chapter 7 focuses on a subset of fourteen disputes, providing detailed narrative summaries for each. These cases provide a close view of the mediation of environmental knowledge, the tactical deployment of science and expertise, and the upheaval of ethnic relations in response to increased Anglo settlement. District court records reveal clearly how and where hydrologic knowledge and environmental management contributed to the displacement and dispossession of non-Anglo residents in New Mexico. They also show that the territorial court system itself participated in the process of American settler colonialism. Even when struggling to resolve questions about hydrologic conditions, proper irrigation practices, and legitimate water rights, judges consistently supported irrigation development projects, often at the expense of long-standing subsistence-oriented water users.

The concluding chapter makes a final case for viewing water management in New Mexico as part and parcel of a settler-colonial project. It views structural control of water knowledge as a fundamental building block for early Anglo water administration, and it considers the contemporary relevance of the book's historical-geography analysis. New Mexico's current human and environmental geographies are directly related to the early incarnations of Anglo settler colonialism, when new settlers struggled to consolidate power over material resources and sought statehood as part of the U.S. federal polity. Environmental knowledge was then an effective tool for displacement and dispossession, and it remains a key aspect of ongoing settler-colonial structures. At a moment of U.S. reckoning with environmental crisis and racial injustice, the chapter considers the possibility of moving toward a water policy that leaves colonial legacies behind.

✳ 2 ✳
Settlement

COLONIALISM IN THE ARIDLANDS

As my favorite airport T-shirt helpfully clarifies, New Mexico is "not new" and "not Mexico." This chapter tries to fill in a few geographical details that don't sell as well in the tourist shops. Environmentally, the chapter focuses on conditions that influence water use and management. Historically, it details two layers of European colonization and their violent intersection with both Indigenous peoples and one another. The first colonists—the Spanish—entered the Rio Grande valley from the south in the late sixteenth century and wrested control of Indigenous lands and bodies in a precarious effort to produce wealth. In a second wave, Anglo-American settlers entered New Mexico from the north in the nineteenth century, first as commercial merchants and later as farmers and natural-resource speculators who displaced Indigenous and Nuevomexicano peoples simultaneously. In both cases, the trajectories of settlement intersected with water management, fundamentally altering human geographies over the course of three centuries.

It is difficult to narrate histories of displacement without relying on the voices of those who caused it. Anglo voices are critical to understanding the structures, meanings, and power vectors of settler-colonial laws, agencies, and officials. But they cannot fully describe the broader context that shaped and limited the colonial project itself. Scholarly reconstructions of Indigenous communities that predated the Spanish, for example, systematically ignore or exclude information preserved by nonelites and conveyed through oral tradition.[1] Historians often use archaeological analysis or fragmentary Spanish colonial documents to understand the Indigenous geographies that shaped early colonialism, but neither approach typically engages Indigenous histories on their own terms. Nuevomexicana/o and Indigenous scholars have proved highly adept at accessing historical voices that foreground cultures of resistance and resilience. To the extent possible, I have relied on these scholars' guidance to understand the impacts and limits of settler-colonial power.

New Mexico's Environments

The modern boundaries of New Mexico bear no clear relation to the contours of any cultural or physical geographic zone. The state's northwest corner excises a portion of the Colorado Plateau—homeland of the ancestral Puebloans, the Diné, and the Hopi. Its northern boundary bisects not only the southernmost spurs of the Rocky Mountains but also the headwaters valley of the Rio Grande. Its eastern boundary lops off a ragged edge of the Llano Estacado and western Great Plains, where the Comanches built a powerful empire. The state's southern boundary arbitrarily crosses the Chihuahuan Desert and the basin and range lands long dominated by Apache nations. Its western boundary cuts through the midst of the Mogollon Mountains complex and traces a straight line that ignores the Continental Divide's meandering route to its east.

For all the ways New Mexico's nearly rectangular boundary is dissociated from the region's historical physical and human geographies, however, its borders do mark a few meaningful and distinctive characteristics. As figure 2.1 shows, the modern state is centered on the upper watershed of the Rio Grande, which links cool, mountainous northern highlands with increasingly warm elevated basins and ranges in the south. The river's north–south corridor runs through a sometimes wide riparian zone of fertile floodplains and contains the great majority of surviving communities descended from ancestral Puebloans. The river also served as the primary northward vector for early Spanish colonial settlement, resulting in a high density of Spanish-descended communities in its northern valleys and southern floodplains. The much later establishment of New Mexico as an American territory likewise revolved around key sites in the Rio Grande watershed.

Climatically, New Mexico is distinct from the plains of Texas and the lowlands of Arizona. Its vast land area spans a large climatic range from north to south, but aridity is a dominant condition throughout. Average annual precipitation across the state is fifteen inches, with some highland areas receiving upward of three feet of precipitation per year while the drier zones get only eight to ten inches annually. Precipitation comes primarily at two times of the year, with roughly half of the annual precipitation falling in seasonal winter storms and the remainder concentrated in late-summer downpours associated with a monsoonal wind pattern. Most of New Mexico has large daily and annual temperature ranges owing both

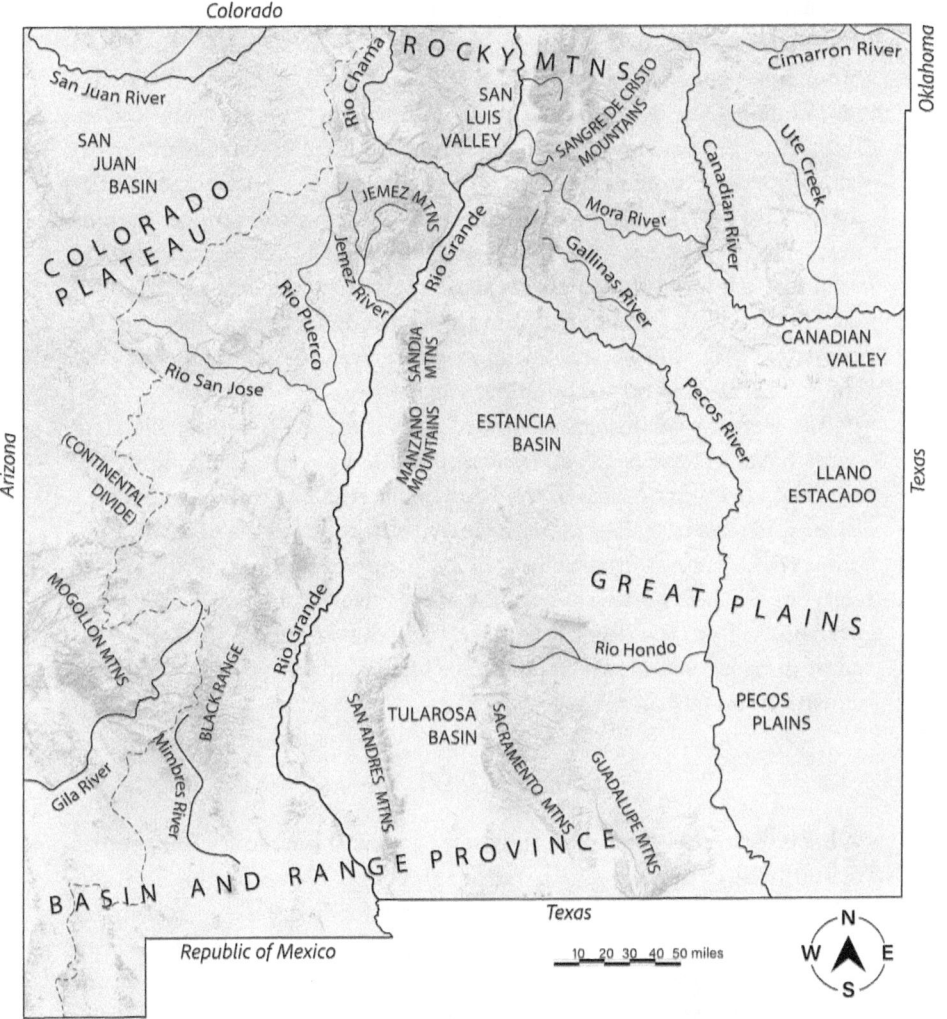

FIGURE 2.1 Environmental geography of New Mexico
Map by Maria Lane. Source data: Jerry Williams, *New Mexico in Maps*, 2nd ed. (Albuquerque: University of New Mexico Press, 1986). Shaded relief: Resource Geographic Information System (RGIS)

to the prevalence of dry air and to the low atmospheric pressure at high elevations. The northern mountains are marked by severely cold winters and cool summers, while the southern lowlands have mild winters and long, hot summers. Overall, New Mexico's temperature variations are most directly determined by elevation, creating a highly variable landscape of microgeographies that defy easy generalization.

Vegetative ecozones vary with elevation- and climate-driven patterns that change drastically from the southeastern lowlands to the north-central mountain heights. Broadly speaking, conifer forests blanket well-watered mountain highlands, and scrub grasslands dominate arid lowland basins. But significant patches of montane shrub, montane grassland, and riparian vegetation dominate different topographical areas. Historically, settlements have been found across these ecozones, with strong concentrations in valleys, floodplains, and other places where water can be captured and used for farming. While New Mexico's hydrology revolves around both winter snowpack and summer rains, spring snowmelt provides the most consistent irrigation water, while monsoon-driven summer rains bring the annual threat of torrential flooding.

The largest river system in New Mexico is the Rio Grande. The state contains all but the headwaters section of the upper river, including the complete tributary basins of the Rio Chama, the Rio Salado, the Jemez River, and the Puerco River. New Mexico also contains the headwaters of other river systems—the Canadian, Red, and Pecos Rivers in the northeast, and the Gila River in the southwest—as well as the fertile floodplain portions of both the Pecos (southeast) and the San Juan (northwest). In all of these areas, water resources have historically proved the definitive constraint on human settlement.

Early Indigenous Geographies

What is today the American Southwest was once home to ancient peoples in multiple locations. Basketmaker peoples began domesticating corn and other crops an estimated 3500 years ago, eventually developing sedentary civilizations that engaged in trade networks reaching east to the Gulf of Mexico, west to the Pacific Ocean, north into the Great Plains, and south into the population centers of Mesoamerica.[2] In the lower basin of the Salt and Gila Rivers (in today's southern Arizona), the Hohokam began work probably fifteen hundred years ago on an extensive canal system, with which they irrigated sculpted waffle gardens and produced a substantial food surplus.[3] In the upland headwaters of the Gila and Mimbres Rivers (in today's southwestern New Mexico), early Basketmaker hunter-gatherer groups developed by 1000 CE into the sedentary Mogollon culture, whose people lived on small farmsteads reliant on highland precipitation.[4] On the Colorado Plateau, the Chaco Phenomenon—an interlinked and regionally influential network of farming hamlets centered on Chaco Canyon—also emerged by 1000 CE. These small farms generated significant food surpluses by using checkdams, gravel-mulched fields, terracing, and rock-lined ditches to support water harvesting and flood irrigation along intermittent streams throughout the San Juan Basin.[5]

All of these civilizations depended on the control and management of water, and they all experienced a precipitous decline in the centuries just before Europeans arrived in the Americas. We do not have definitive explanations for these declines, but the archaeological record confirms that the massive Hohokam civilization was greatly reduced by 1100 CE, and Spanish explorers found only the remnant Pima and Papago (Tohona O'odham) peoples in the Salt River basin in the early sixteenth century. Chaco Canyon was also abandoned shortly after 1100 CE, and a new agricultural center arose in Mesa Verde (today just east of the Four Corners intersection of the borders of New Mexico, Arizona, Utah, and Colorado) before it too was abandoned by 1300 CE. From both Chaco and Mesa Verde, migrants moved into smaller villages along the mesas of the Colorado Plateau and the valleys of the Rio Grande after the thirteenth century. The Mogollon settlements lasted slightly longer, with a final major center collapsing in 1450 CE and driving some descendant groups northward into the Rio Grande valley, where they joined other communities fused from multiple cultural groups.[6]

By the fifteenth century, as many as 150 small Pueblos were thriving across and beyond the Rio Grande watershed in a patchwork geography of intermingled language groups. Adapting ancient agricultural traditions for the conditions of their specific environments and locations, these egalitarian communities engaged in a range of subsistence and economic activities. Some of them combined irrigated and dry farming (e.g., the Zuni), others mixed agriculture with hunting and gathering (e.g., the Taos), and still others pursued both agriculture and trade with Plains societies (e.g., Pecos). Throughout the valleys of the upper Rio Grande watershed, villages commonly used flood-irrigation methods, and water management became a basis for social organization and ceremonial life.[7] In general, the Pueblos were small, independent communities organized with farmsteads surrounding a central town.[8] Although each Pueblo constituted an autonomous village, regional political links emerged through mutual dependency within and beyond the watershed.[9] Within the Rio Grande valley system, Pueblos sometimes consolidated to fend off Plains raiders before returning to their own communities. Regionally, the Pueblos were linked to extensive trading networks that allowed cultural exchange across multiple different linguistic groups when nomadic peoples overwintered in the Pueblos or when Pueblo dissidents moved to external groups for residence.[10]

In terms of irrigation, the Pueblos implemented a wide variety of water-

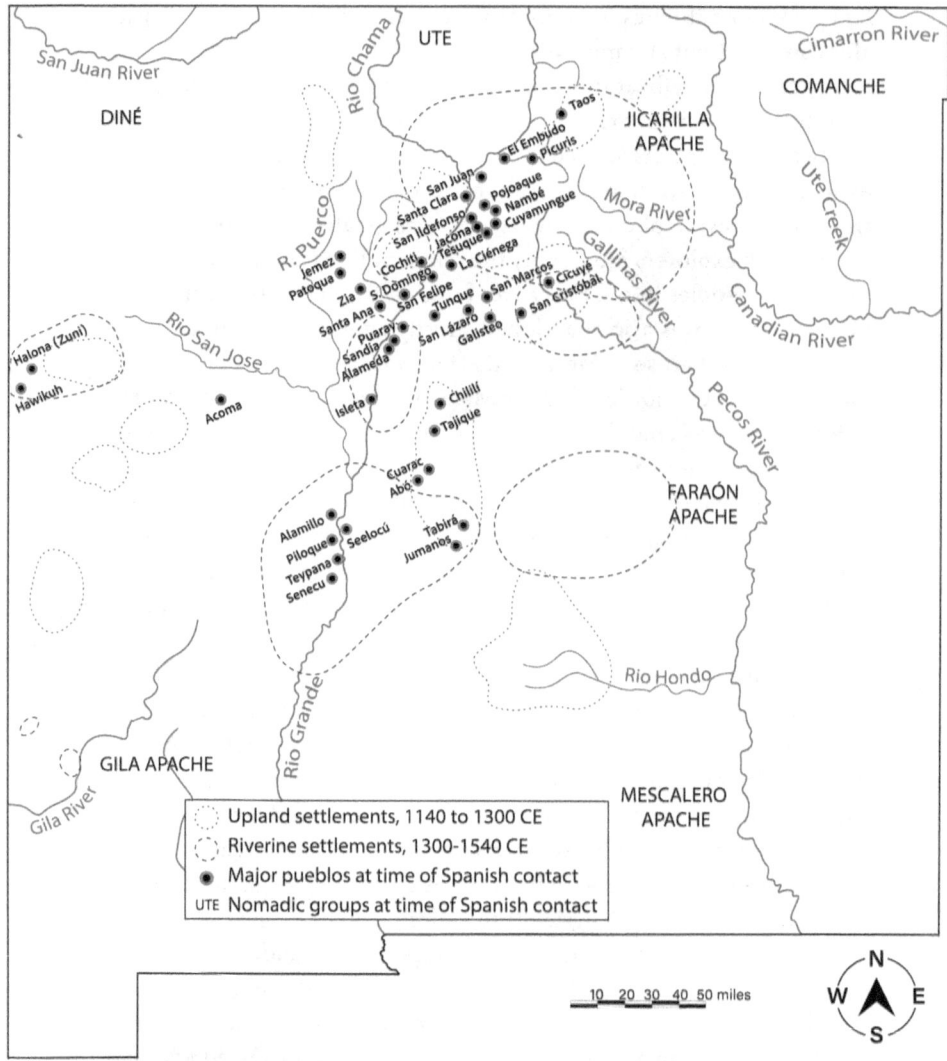

FIGURE 2.2 Early peoples in New Mexico, 1100–1540 CE
Map by Maria Lane. Source data: Williams, *New Mexico in Maps*

management practices to harness water from both running streams and seasonal floods. The uplands hosted the oldest irrigation systems, where precipitation was most frequent and abundant. The floodplain of the Rio Grande's main stem contained the least-developed irrigation infrastructure because of its dense vegetation and its flood-prone nature.[11] Depending on the water source, Pueblo irrigators used different technologies to bring water to agricultural land, including diversion canals from running waterways, checkdams on periodic or ephemeral streams, and even, in some areas, standing reservoirs.[12] Without any concept of private ownership, Pueblos maintained these structures through communal effort, although most farming was conducted through kinship or clan groupings. Water use "apparently was a prescriptive right based on the principle that as long as tracts were kept productive in this manner, the kinship group would continue undisturbed in its right of use."[13] Throughout their irrigated valleys, Pueblo communities produced a surplus of maize and other crops, which early Spanish explorers reported with admiration.[14]

Across the Colorado Plateau, where the ancestral Puebloans had once thrived, nomadic Diné groups also practiced some agriculture by the fifteenth century. The Diné became increasingly linked with the Pueblo communities as they took up pastoralism and absorbed Pueblo refugees.[15] Other itinerant groups (Apaches in the south and west, Comanches in the east, and Utes in the north) practiced comparatively little agriculture, but they were closely linked to the Pueblo communities. Through trade and raiding, nonsedentary groups gained access to the Pueblos' agricultural wealth as well as to goods and cultural exchange across vast areas of the southern plains and Rocky Mountains.[16]

Spanish Settler Colonialism: The Entrada

Spanish colonial agents entered this complex cultural geographic domain from the south, first as explorers and then as settlers. In 1540 Vázquez de Coronado's expedition in search of mineral resources found numerous Indigenous communities in the Rio Grande valley. Expedition reports confirmed that these communities were well stocked with grain, textiles, ceramics, and other items procured through regional trade. The explorers exploited this surplus almost immediately, forcing Pueblos to give up food and robes to support a Spanish winter camp near the modern location of Albuquerque, then releasing Spanish cattle into Pueblo fields, where they ate and damaged valuable pasturage. Confronted for their offenses, the Spanish attacked and burned Pueblo villages, forcing survivors to flee the valley in harsh winter weather.[17] The Coronado expedition thus presaged the exploitative, oppressive, and violent colonial posture the Spanish would assume in New Mexico.

More than five decades later, Juan de Oñate received approval from the Viceroyalty of New Spain to lead the first official settlement *entrada* (entry) into New Mexico. He mustered six hundred colonists in a racially mixed group to carry the banner for colonial New Spain into the upper Rio Grande valley.[18] Oñate and his entourage targeted the confluence of

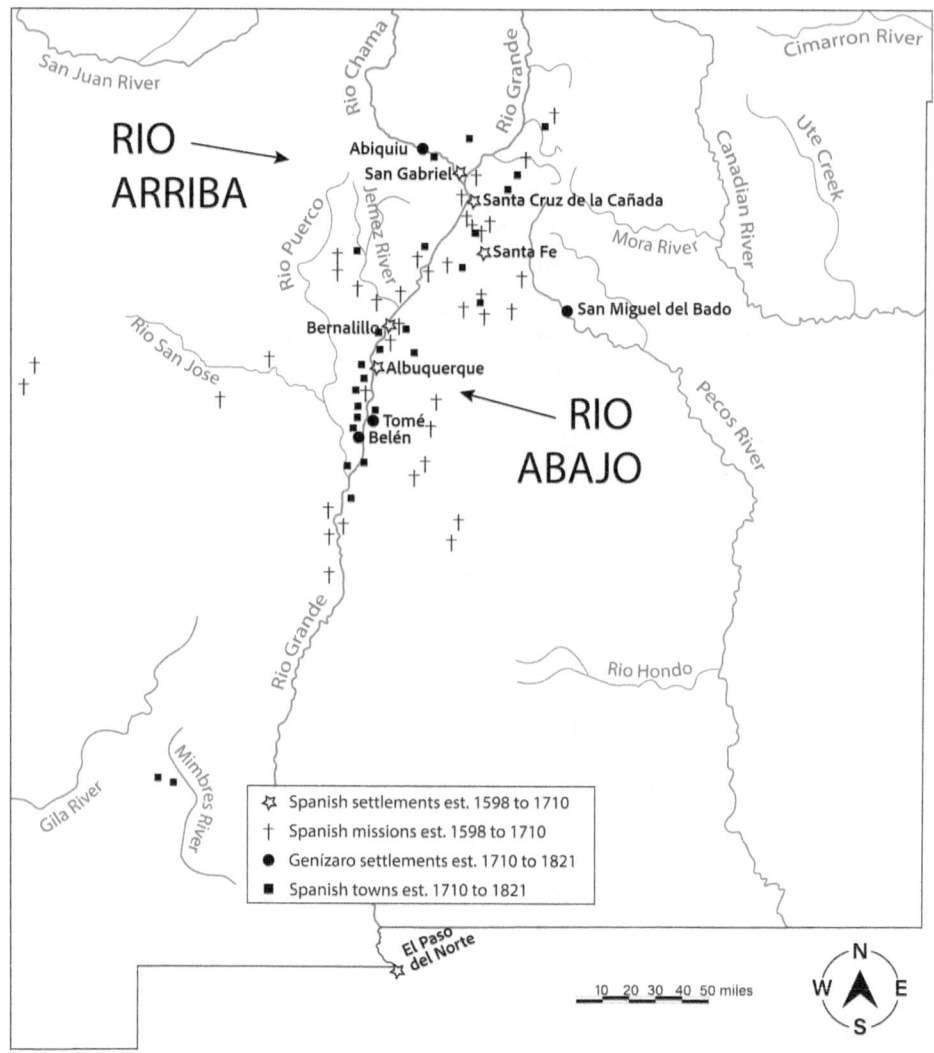

FIGURE 2.3 Spanish colonial presence in New Mexico, 1598–1821
Map by Maria Lane. Source data: Williams, *New Mexico in Maps*

the Rio Grande and Rio Chama as a settlement destination, based on reports that area villages enjoyed large food surpluses.[19] Arriving at the confluence in 1598, Oñate declared Spanish authority and immediately appropriated land, labor, and food from Ohkay Owingeh Pueblo (which Oñate renamed "San Juan"). The colonists began constructing dwellings alongside the main village, conscripted fifteen hundred Indigenous laborers to dig an irrigation ditch, and helped themselves to food supplies from the Pueblo's granary.[20] After one winter, Oñate moved the colony across the river to Ohkay Owingeh's sister village, Yunque Owingeh (which he renamed "San Gabriel"), apparently taking direct possession of the entire village and forcing its few residents out.[21]

During that first year, while the colonists at San Juan built infrastructure to support their families, farms, and ambitions, Oñate and his lieutenants explored the wider region for trade routes and natural resources. In the process, they also announced Spanish intentions by demanding food, blankets, cotton cloth, ceramics, and loyalty from every Indigenous community they encountered. Residents at Acoma Pueblo responded to aggressive requests by killing thirteen Spanish soldiers in the winter of 1598. Oñate countered their resistance with extreme, exemplary, and retributive violence, overwhelming Acoma in an attack and then sentencing all survivors to either slavery or disfigurement.[22] When the Spanish began amputating the right foot of every adult male who had defended Acoma Pueblo, word spread quickly to New Mexico's other Indigenous communities that the new arrivals were both powerful and brutal.[23]

Oñate's barbarous domination policies, however, belied his colony's severe dependence on its Indigenous neighbors. From the beginning, the Spanish found that northern New Mexico's environment presented substantial challenges to colonization. Frequent frost limited agriculture in the confluence area and upper watershed (Rio Arriba), while periodic flooding threatened the agricultural potential of the lower river (Rio Abajo). And beyond agriculture, the landscape presented few obvious resources. Colonial settlers found no minerals and relied almost exclusively on piñon seeds and salt pans as the only commodity exports. Cottonwood groves stabilized stream banks effectively along the main river stem, but they provided inferior lumber. The best lumber, by contrast, came from piñon-juniper and ponderosa forests in the north, where agricultural conditions were difficult.[24] So the Spanish found themselves caught between the floodplains of the south and the forests of the north, in an area where productive agriculture was limited to irrigable locations near perennial streams. These locations, of course, were already inhabited.

Spanish colonial laws forbade settlement on Indigenous lands, infringement of Indigenous resources, and coercion of Indigenous labor. But the settlers at San Juan and San Gabriel violated these prohibitions from the start.[25] The first three years of Spanish settlement coincided with very dry conditions and widespread crop failures in New Mexico. Settlers survived only by taking grain supplies that Pueblos had set aside from past years' surpluses.[26] Between Spanish demands and the Pueblos' own needs, these supplies quickly dwindled, decreasing the resilience of both groups during a regional drought.[27] In the face of famine and increasing Indigenous resistance, more than half the colonists and nearly all of the women and families deserted the Spanish colony in the summer of 1601 while Oñate was away on an expedition.[28] The Spanish Crown reinforced the costly colony only reluctantly, and Oñate soon lost favor with the authorities in New Spain. He resigned in 1607 and was eventually prosecuted for undue harshness toward Indigenous peoples, mismanagement of the colony, dishonesty, and other offenses.[29]

Notwithstanding his ignoble ouster, Oñate's decade in command produced a pattern that defined the first century of Spanish settler colonialism. Colonists dispossessed Indigenous people by encroaching on their lands, extracting feudal-style tribute (*encomienda*) of food and trade goods, and coercing their labor (*repartimiento*) "for public works or personal service," often in contravention of Spanish Crown decrees.[30] Elite colonists established large estates (*haciendas*) surrounded by irrigated farm and grazing lands, and they assumed control over all trade between Pueblos and Apaches, making it illegal for Indigenous people to move freely between villages or to trade outside of Spanish-established annual fairs.[31] The Spanish took advantage of epidemic-driven population losses among the Pueblos to disperse throughout the Rio Arriba, encroaching on abandoned villages and enticing new settlers from Mexico to replace those who had defected.[32]

These tactics allowed the Spanish to establish a regionwide system of imposed control, yet they remained vulnerable in many ways. It took five decades after the 1601 defection for the Spanish to rebuild their population to the levels of the original entrada. During that same time, the Puebloan population contracted by a staggering 75 percent, removing much of the resource base and labor supply that the Spanish had relied on.[33] Throughout the seventeenth century, regular caravans carried commercial goods and positive official reports from Santa Fe to Mexico City, but the northern colony was not well. The Spanish had produced in New Mexico a feudal landholding system, and the abusive institutions of encomienda and repartimiento created slavery-like serfdom among communities that had previously enjoyed full autonomy. Constant competition between the missions and the landholding elites to control labor and mercantile wealth took an ever-increasing toll on Indigenous communities, ensuring that Rio Grande Puebloans "suffered the most devastating period of their history" from 1600 to 1680.[34]

Out of this devastation bloomed a long and strategic resistance.[35] At first, individual Pueblos or bands independently resisted Spanish offenses and impositions using strategies of accommodation, strategic conformity, refusal, secrecy, raiding, and outright attack.[36] Later, the Pueblos joined together in an Indigenous coalition that attacked Spanish settlers simultaneously in multiple locations across New Mexico in 1680. In what became known as the Pueblo Revolt, Indigenous revolutionaries burned Spanish haciendas and *ranchos* throughout the colony.[37] They killed or evicted most settlers and leaders from the upper and middle Rio Grande valley, returning immediately to autonomous rule.[38]

Efforts to reconstruct pre-Spanish life proved difficult for Indigenous communities after decades of disrupted land use, trade links, and social coherence.[39] Over a dozen years, the unprecedented Indigenous coalition unraveled. The Spanish colonial government, exiled to El Paso after the Pueblo Revolt, returned in 1692 after exploiting a fractured Pueblo alliance. Indigenous resistance continued, culminating in another significant Pueblo uprising in 1696, but did not succeed in dislodging Spanish colonists a second time.[40] Indigenous resistance *did* succeed, however, in changing the Spanish approach to colonization.

In post-reconquest New Mexico, a precarious coexistence developed as Spanish authorities abandoned many of the most hated colonial practices, including encomienda, regional trade restrictions, and aggressive attempts at Christianization.[41] But the new governor, Diego de Vargas, initiated "more subtle policies of colonial domination" that would come to define the cultural geography of New Mexico for centuries.[42] Authorities used large land grants to convey elite privilege on "Spanish" men, although the term had more of "a social rather than a biological connotation" given the reality that many original colonists were *mestizo* and that the 1601 desertion led to increased intermarriage.[43] Lower-class laborers typically enjoyed access to shared or communal land grants but could acquire individual property only by settling in areas most likely to disrupt repeated attacks from nomadic groups.[44] These vulnerable buffer settlements were first dominated by *genízaros*, Indigenous laborers who spoke Spanish and followed Spanish customs owing to childhood abduction, purchase, ransom, or dissidence.[45] Eventually, nonelite mestizos also moved into these buffer towns, or into Pueblo villages where decreasing populations made extra land available to settlers.[46] Throughout this culturally and racially mixed region, New Mexicans experienced a spectrum of culturally defined disadvantage between the two poles of Spanish elitism and Indigenous marginalization.

In the larger colonial context of New Spain, New Mexico functioned purely as a military buffer meant to protect the silver mines in Mexico's southern interior from Indigenous interference and to mitigate rising Indigenous resentment.[47] The northern colony produced virtually no wealth for New Spain and contained less than 1 percent of the Spanish colonial population in the New World.[48] In the Rio Arriba and Rio Abajo settlement areas, particular complexes of social stratification, subsistence agriculture, and water management created a distinct mestizo subculture that persisted over time in New Mexico. Nuevomexicano culture emerged within a triangular core marked by the villas of Santa Fe, Albuquerque, and Santa Cruz. In the core area, Nuevomexicano villas and Indigenous pueblos coexisted in an intertwined spatial arrangement that fostered cultural mixing as well as knowledge exchange for practices in water management and subsistence agriculture.[49]

Acequia Culture

Over the course of two centuries, Spanish colonists established small irrigation systems throughout the Rio Arriba modeled on the medieval *acequia* (ditch) systems of southern Spain. Over time, acequia irrigation came to define colonial land use and governance in the upper Rio Grande watershed, creating a patchwork of small rural communities that developed locally specific practices based on informal custom. The Spanish preference for acequia irrigation both influenced and was influenced by Indigenous irrigation norms, reflecting the broader context of cultural exchange and mestizaje in New Mexico.[50]

New Mexico's acequia traditions derive from Roman and Moorish irrigation in the Iberian Peninsula, where a culture complex combining small-scale irrigation technologies and cooperative social structures supported productive agriculture in a semiarid climate.[51] As practiced in New Mexico, acequia irrigation starts with an in-stream diversion (*presa* or *atarque*) of brush, rock, earth, timber, or other materials at a point upslope of the fields to be irrigated. The diversion raises water levels high enough to flow into a primary ditch (*acequia madre*) that then makes its way downhill through a valley parallel to the original stream, using smaller branching ditches (*contra acequias*) to route water toward individual fields. At fields' edges, irrigators use wooden headgates (*compuertas*) to allow water into small lateral ditches (*sangrias*) on a managed schedule. The *sangrias* then connect back to an outlet ditch (*desagüe*) that returns excess water to the river downstream of the irrigated area.

In a traditional New Mexico acequia community, *parciantes* (those who hold water rights) are permitted to use water for domestic consumption and for irrigation, subject to the oversight of an elected *mayordomo* (ditch manager, based on the Spanish medieval *acequiero* or ditch superintendent) and commissioners. In return for their water right, parciantes bear a responsibility to contribute to the maintenance of the acequia and uphold the rules governing its use. Although acequia water is considered the free property of everyone, water users work cooperatively to maintain ditches and other infrastructure, through either levies or individual labor, typically in proportion to the amount of land they irrigate.[52] In times of drought or in cases of dispute, the mayordomo or the heads of household make decisions about how to allocate water fairly.[53]

Small acequia systems worked best first in the Rio Arriba, where tributary streams ran through narrow canyons to small areas of flat, open land. Focusing on the original settlement region, Spanish settlers built four hundred community irrigation ditches between 1598 and 1846 to irrigate 55,000 acres in small tracts, usually less than ten acres. These systems did not contain storage or reservoir components; they were based purely on the diversion of running streamflow into ditches dug by hand with simple wooden tools.[54] Spanish settlers often started by using Indigenous ditches before expanding to other areas or reusing abandoned ditches from Indigenous communities.

After the reconquest, settlers who moved into the Rio Abajo (now commonly known as the middle Rio Grande valley) were forced to use the main stem of the Rio Grande for irrigation, since its tributaries were mostly ephemeral and often ran dry. The wide floodplain of the middle Rio Grande valley provided extensive irrigable land, but it also presented considerable water-management challenges. Spring floods could easily wipe out brush or rock diversions, while late-summer lulls in water flow could drop water levels below the ditch intakes. By 1846 the Rio Abajo contained one hundred acequias serving 140,000 acres, which was ten times the land area per acequia system in the Rio Arriba.[55] In addition to the scale difference, water management defined community relations differently in the upper and middle watersheds of the river. In the Rio Arriba, individual acequias were self-contained within their own valleys and rarely had relations with other acequia communities. In the Rio Abajo, where the river was more variable, communities more frequently needed to work together in response to flooding and other natural hazards.[56]

Getting water efficiently from the ditch to individual fields required substantial coordination during the Spanish colonial period, as irrigators could not simply water whenever they wanted. Mayordomos played an important role in controlling the timing of water distribution to ensure a full head of water pressure "to push the water at right angles down the field" of each irrigator when it was his turn.[57] When water supplies ran low, mayordomos typically turned to a few different approaches. Supplying water *por necesidad* (by necessity) might mean prioritizing irrigation of food gardens over animal pasturage, or permanent crops like orchards over annual crops like beans. Supplying water *por tandas* (in turns) involved a complex rotation through individual fields to deliver limited water volumes with sufficient pressure to make sure it would flow into the ditch. Finally, a mayordomo might decide to provide water *por derecho* (by right), giving larger tracts more irrigation time or prioritizing seniority among rights holders.

In colonial New Mexico, each community had its own local norms and governed its own water. New Mexico was subject to Spanish law, but it was so peripheral to New Spain's power centers that the mandates of local geography, climate, and politics usually prevailed over strict legal interpretation of colonial rules.[58] Local norms were not necessarily perceptible to outsiders, producing "a remarkable patchwork" of acequia management practices.[59] Despite local variation, most systems were based on two standard principles: local control and discretionary authority of individual leaders.[60] The goals were to provide everyone with enough water for a good crop and to prevent pollution of the water or degradation of the irrigation infrastructure. To wield effective discretionary authority, mayordomos needed to be both decisive and equitable, in accordance with local norms. This critical basis for village governance in New Mexico was passed down through generations as local tradition and not as formal legislation.[61]

Acequias did not gain full legal status in New Mexico until 1895, yet they carried deep cultural importance as the foundation for Nuevomexicano communities. The establishment of every Spanish colonial community began with the building of the acequia and the church; these two institutions became linked in "a basic ritualistic Catholicism that emphasized the holiness of irrigation activities."[62] Community governance also intertwined strongly with the acequia institution. In a handful of large villas and towns, the *cabildo* (municipal council) formally managed the acequia madre, often appointing an individual as mayordomo. In rural areas consisting solely of dispersed ranchos, however, the mayordomo constituted the only local government institution in the early colonial period. Later in the colonial period, three-person acequia commissions were added alongside the mayordomo, and these four individuals constituted the sum total of formal governance in rural irrigated communities.[63]

Spanish colonial approaches to irrigation—as a technology, object of ritual, and institution of governance—also influenced Indigenous irrigation norms in many areas of prevalent cultural and spatial contact. Most fundamentally, Pueblo irrigators developed a more intensive focus on ditch irrigation to the exclusion of other irrigation practices. In a process Sylvia Rodríguez calls "acequiazation," the Spanish commitment to ditch irrigation appropriated much of the available water in a drainage area, precluding many other forms of irrigations the Pueblos had used before Spanish colonists arrived.[64] The Spanish also introduced new irrigation-dependent crops, such as wheat, vegetables, and fruit trees, alongside Pueblo cultivars with variable drought tolerance—corn, beans, squash, melon, cotton, and tobacco. By the nineteenth century most Pueblos had adapted to a new way of life in irrigation as in all else: honoring ancient traditions and teachings while also operating within the Spanish world and building on Spanish customs.[65]

Over time, acequia management "became a process of mutual exchange whereby local indigenous knowledge of the hydrological and microclimatological environments joined with an imposed regime of ditch construction, regulation, utilization, and maintenance."[66] Pueblo communities adopted Nuevomexicano traditions, such as adding a mayordomo position for ditch management, and Nuevomexicano communities adopted a more communal approach from their Pueblo neighbors.[67] The result was similar to what happened elsewhere in the Americas: Spanish settlers did not simply transplant European society to New Mexico but rather initiated a process of interconnection between Spanish formal institutions and folk lifeways and culture.[68] Over the centuries, acequia systems matured and expanded throughout northern New Mexico, relying on cultural hybridity and water sharing to foster autonomy and self-sufficiency among nonelite mestizo communities.[69]

Transitions To and From Independence

In 1821 Mexico gained independence in a wave of revolutions that swept Spain's American colonies. The sovereignty transition affected New Mexico in only minor ways at first, but it set the stage for a second, devastating wave of settler colonialism. Administratively, New Mexico remained distant from and inconsequential to the new center of power in Mexico City. New Mexico's top-level officials were still appointed by the central government, but the local *alcalde* (magistrate) position changed from an appointed seat to an elected office, which had the effect of focusing political control on local priorities.[70] Indigenous communities became more active in local politics at this time, as the Mexican government stopped recognizing race as a basis of distinction and status and granted full rights to Indigenous people and genízaros who had previously been marginalized by law. The free Mexican state thus "brought an exuberant involvement on the part of Pueblo Indians and villagers in the larger political process in which they were suddenly equal citizens."[71]

Under Mexican sovereignty, water management remained largely unchanged from Spanish colonial precedents. New Mexico's village communities continued to build acequia infrastructure, elect mayordomos, and resolve disputes according to customary norms with minimal formal legal expression. In Nuevomexicano villages, disputes rarely found resolution through formal law or through denial of water. Instead, local decisions enforced sharing and community-based allocation to benefit the community as a whole.[72] The social distance between those authorized to resolve conflicts and those beholden to their decisions, however, began to widen dramatically during the period of Mexican independence. The removal of Spanish authorities allowed wealthy patrones in New Mexico to consolidate power over landless vecinos who found subsistence agriculture increasing difficult in the face of external conflict with Indigenous groups and internal conflict among liberal and conservative patrones.[73] As large landholders developed a tenuous symbiosis with vecinos who provided labor on their lands, as well as political support for their factional contests with one another, they "exacerbated [class differences] to a point that ultimately fractured the community."[74] This divide would only grow as the century went on.

Geopolitically, the independent Mexican government changed its stance toward the westward-expanding United States. It reversed the long-standing Spanish colonial policy of maintaining a closed northern border and instead embraced strategic economic connections with the young nation. American trappers and traders operating on the western fringes of the United States were well connected to commercial brokers in Kansas City and St. Louis, and a series of new wagon routes through the southern plains connected these established trade centers with Santa Fe after 1821. The new Santa Fe Trail promised lucrative opportunity to traders on both ends, but it was also vulnerable to raiding, particularly as a powerful Comanche coalition took control of the southern plains.[75] To protect against the threats of Indigenous resistance and power, New Mexico's governors encouraged settlement expansion after 1821, doling out land grants as an incentive to create farming and ranching buffers. Some of those grants included Pueblo lands that had never been patented or documented (or for which no documentation survived), again reducing the Pueblos' land base despite their newly equal social status.[76] From the 1820s to the 1840s, Nuevomexicano settlement expanded well beyond the original core area as settlers ventured northwest into the San Juan Basin and east down the Pecos River valley.[77]

In welcoming trade with the United States, New Mexico opened the door not only to commercial merchants, but also to Anglo settlers. That door would never close. Beginning almost immediately after Mexican independence, the Santa Fe Trail became a vector for demographic and political change, bringing an influx of Anglo traders and craftsmen whose aggressive mercantile interests set the stage for U.S. political control.[78] Early economic changes led quickly to a marked wealth disparity.[79] Indigenous and Nuevomexicano villagers did not participate in the new cash economy and acquired very few of the newly available trade goods. As Anglo elites gained more wealth, Nuevomexicano patrones also leveraged wealth for themselves, while vecinos found themselves increasingly working the land of others. When Nuevomexicanas/os and Pueblos organized a revolt in solidarity against elites in 1837, it was already too late to reverse the changing economic tide, which had devalued subsistence agriculture, increased debt servitude, introduced a cash economy, and created massive wealth for a small number of Nuevomexicano landholders and Anglo settlers.[80]

At the same time the Santa Fe Trail introduced U.S. commercial interests to New Mexico, the larger westward movement of U.S. settlers announced aggressive territorial intent across northern Mexico.[81] When Anglo settlers in Texas seceded from Mexico in 1836 with encouragement from the United States, international hostilities erupted quickly. New Mexico played a key role in the conflict.[82] The U.S. Army launched its military offensive against Mexico in 1846 via Santa Fe, which it entered with confidence, knowing that both Anglo and Nuevomexicano elites wanted to prevent any disruption of the Santa Fe trade.[83] Promptly after seizing New Mexico's capital city, the U.S. Army took control of New Mexico's government and implemented a system of territorial laws, while troops continued west to California and south into the heart of the Mexican republic. In an 1847 uprising, Nuevomexicanos targeted both Anglo and Nuevomexicano officeholders in the unwelcome American government, provoking retributive violence in return.[84] Soon afterward a racial reorganization began to take shape. Anglos exploited social fractures in the multiracial Mexican territory in two ways. First, they encouraged Nuevomexicano elites to embrace their white Spanish heritage as a way of currying favor with Anglo officials. Second, they posited strict new distinctions between Nuevomexicano and Pueblo peoples, who had long lived side by side within a complex racial hierarchy recognized by the Spanish and Mexican governments.[85]

In 1848 the Mexican-American War ended in victory for the United States, and the Treaty of Guadalupe Hidalgo legitimized a massive cession of Mexican lands to the United States. Although the treaty contained provisions to protect the property and rights of Mexican citizens who opted for American citizenship, it became instantly problematic. Before ratification, the U.S. Senate removed a treaty article providing for the protection of land and property rights, and the Senate also changed wording about the timeline for when cession lands would be admitted to U.S. statehood. In the process, they defied treaty negotiators' intentions and briefly imperiled the end of the war.[86] And when all was said and done, the Treaty of Guadalupe Hidalgo left New Mexico hanging out to dry in territorial status for more than six decades.[87] Residents obtained a "hollow federal citizenship" that afforded no opportunity to elect territorial leaders. In the absence of democracy, presidentially appointed territorial leaders either participated in or failed to stop a stunning dispossession of lands and waters, either using the treaty as justification or ignoring its text with impunity.[88]

Anglo-Americans and the New Settler Colonialism

Having entered New Mexico in small numbers after Mexican independence, Anglo-Americans ended the century in a position of almost total control. Early Anglo traders and commercial operators confined themselves to towns along the Santa Fe Trail and Camino Real when Mexico first opened the region to U.S. commerce.[89] But by the first decade of the twentieth century, Anglo-Americans dominated New Mexico's territorial government, controlled rangeland and farmland throughout the eastern and southern parts of the state, held consolidated political power in urban centers along the Rio Grande, and enjoyed significant economic advantages. Anglos converted the territorial economy from barter-based subsistence to cash-based extraction, linking New Mexico to the industrial production centers and urban markets of the eastern United States. This second layer of settler colonialism displaced Indigenous and Nuevomexicano residents simultaneously, although the two groups experienced largely divergent impacts.

Nuevomexicano elites could be forgiven for thinking their control was durable in the early territorial period. For a couple decades after 1848, they dominated local elected positions and seats in the territorial legislature, and they watched the number and spatial extent of Nuevomexicano communities expand, while only small numbers of Anglos entered the unfarmed plains of northeastern and eastern New Mexico.[90] But the control implied by this expansion was illusory. In the first half century of U.S. control, Nuevomexicano elites were systematically excluded from the highest-level appointed positions in New Mexico, all of which went to Anglos.[91] Furthermore, the small size of the early Anglo population obscured the force of its commercial presence. In the larger effort to connect New Mexico to the U.S. economy, Anglo mercantilists enjoyed a significant advantage because they had access to cash. Pueblos and vecinos who did not hold or control cash, on the other hand, eventually found their communities and ways of life upended.[92] New railroad connections in the 1880s sounded the economic death knell for subsistence-oriented and land-based communities. Not only did the rail system provide a commercial link to markets far beyond the regional economy, but it also created an easy way for more and more settlers to enter the territory.

By century's end Anglos were encroaching on Nuevomexicano lands in the Pecos and Mesilla valleys, arriving in numbers sufficient to shift the balance of political power in the territorial government (fig. 2.4).[93] In these later years the elected assembly was divided between Anglo and Nuevomexicano representatives. Anglo lawmakers generally supported territorial officials' economic-development initiatives, while Nuevomexicano lawmakers sought to protect Nuevomexicano communities and negotiate new conflicts emerging from the influx of new Anglo settlers.[94] As a whole, the late territorial government spent its energy on opening new lands to settlement, controlling the Indigenous population, and promoting irrigated agriculture as the basis for a modern economy. Together these priorities served to increase Anglo control and dominance while displacing existing residents and communities in different ways.

Anglo officials pursued multiple legal and extralegal avenues to open New Mexico's lands to additional settlement. First, they worked to clarify existing land ownership in order to facilitate the sale or transfer of private property to incoming settlers. The Treaty of Guadalupe Hidalgo's negotiators had agreed on numerous provisions to protect Mexican citizens' lands under American law, but one entire treaty article addressing property rights was never ratified by the United States.[95] Anglos sought to exploit the resulting gray area to take control of extensive areas of good agricultural and forest land that Nuevomexicanas/os had believed would be protected. The legal process required to confirm Nuevomexicano land ownership deriving from Spanish and Mexican land grants (themselves based on colonial occupancy and dispossession of Pueblo lands), however, proved both tedious and challenging, owing both to missing documentation and to profound legal questions. To speed up the land claims process and reduce the delays to Anglo settlement, the federal government created a new court in 1891—the Court of Private Land Claims (CPLC)—to review land claims comprehensively throughout the territory.[96] The CPLC

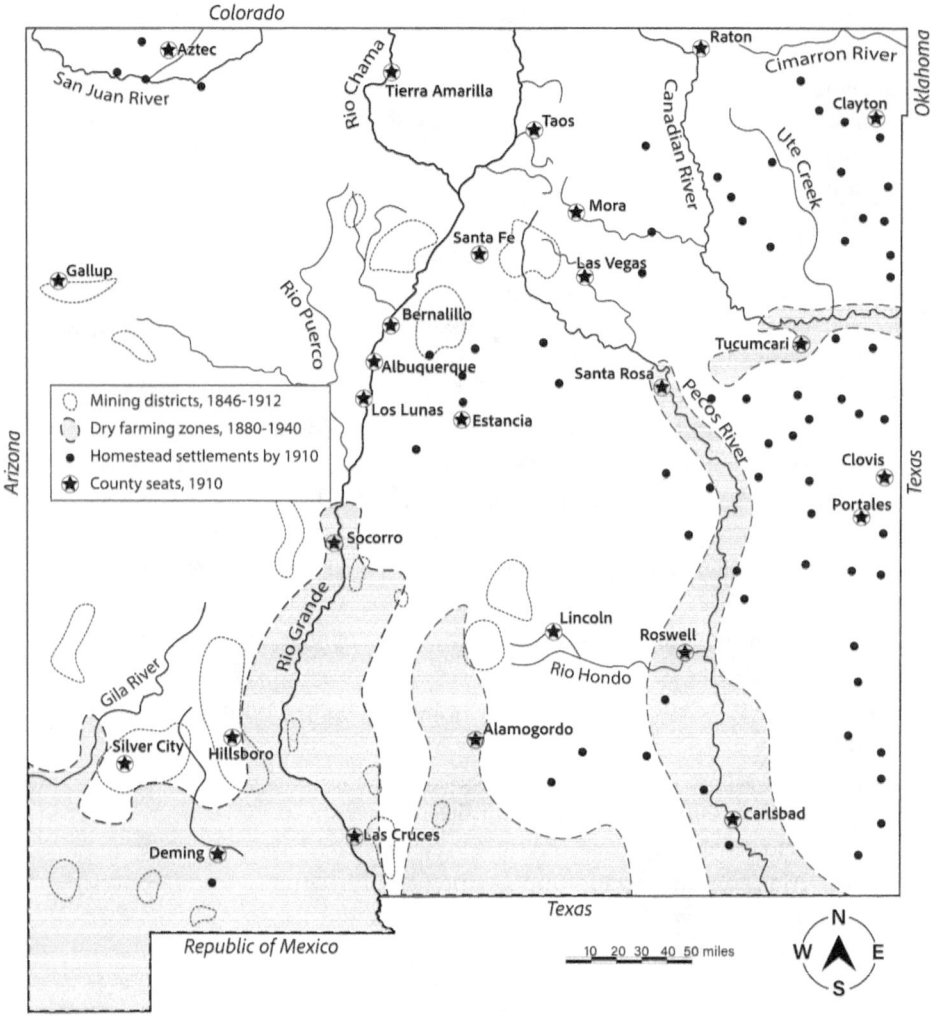

FIGURE 2.4 Anglo settlement in New Mexico, 1846–1910
Map by Maria Lane. Source data: Williams, *New Mexico in Maps*

rejected numerous Nuevomexicano land claims on the basis of technical and legal deficiencies, prioritizing a market approach to land that required strictly defined boundaries to render land as an exchange commodity.[97] It also refused to confirm most community-held grants, which many Nuevomexicano villages depended on for grazing or fuelwood gathering. Spanish and Mexican authorities had granted land both to individuals and to communities, with most of the communal land grants going to those at the low end of the social hierarchy, given that communal grants were typically located in areas subject to conflict and hostility with Indigenous groups—areas that elites did not favor as settlement sites.[98] Since U.S. law classified individual lands as private property, courts determined that communal land grants must be classified instead as public lands and turned over to the federal government. Some of those new federal lands were then made available for homestead claims; others became national forests or other managed lands.[99] In addition to their refusal to confirm commons lands, the CPLC confirmed only a small percentage of *individual* land-grant claims, despite their apparently clear protection in the Treaty of Guadalupe Hidalgo.[100] Whether management was transferred to private owners or to bureaucrats, these lands most often ended up under Anglo control.

At the same time that territorial and federal officials were sorting these legal issues, nefarious operators also took advantage of Nuevomexicano communities through trickery and outright fraud. Most egregiously, the "Santa Fe Ring"—a shadowy collective of attorneys, judges, and government officials—tricked many Nuevomexicanas/os into giving up lands by misusing power of attorney or claiming land as payment for services.[101] In the century after the Mexican cession, Nuevomexicano residents lost nearly 80 percent of their lands to outsiders.[102] The (often Anglo) perpetrators of this legal and illegal dispossession amassed astonishing levels of land and wealth, with many later ascending to higher public office.[103] Nuevomexicanas/os who lost their lands, on the other hand, could no longer engage in subsistence agriculture and were forced to join the wage economy at its lowest levels. They found themselves on the losing end of an increasingly unequal wealth divide that split largely along ethnic lines. The irreversible land losses of the 1880s and 1890s became a source of deep, enduring conflict in northern New Mexico, leaving many Nuevomexicanas/os with a bitter distrust of the Anglo-controlled American judicial system and a resentment toward Indigenous peoples, whose lands were largely protected by the same courts.[104]

Indigenous communities experienced the Anglo settlement boom very differently from their Nuevomexicano neighbors. U.S. Indian policy classified Indigenous people as wards of the state, subject to "protective" policies that mandated assimilation, spatial containment, and dependency. New Mexico's Indigenous communities experienced two aspects of this policy thrust. In the first, sedentary Pueblo communities got seemingly good treatment, as the U.S. government confirmed and protected their village lands. But this protection came at the expense of being infantilized by a federal-supervision bureaucracy that severely limited Pueblo autonomy and sovereignty over their lands and waters. Pueblos had historically moved between different settlement areas in response to changing environmental conditions or political alliances, but U.S. policy hardened their recognized boundaries and forbade Pueblo individuals or leaders to sell or buy land without explicit government permission.[105] Federal Indian policy thus eliminated Indigenous people's ability to respond strategically to changing economic conditions. Federal policy also removed Pueblo children from their homes to be educated in boarding schools designed to suppress Indigenous cultures and promote assimilation to Anglo norms.[106]

Although federal Indian policy existed ostensibly for the benefit of Indigenous people, it was based in a fundamentally racist belief that Indigenous people were too ignorant to govern themselves.[107] So it should be no surprise that this "protective" policy was easily manipulated to benefit the Anglo settler state that created it. When Anglo commercial ventures needed access to Pueblo land for ditches, railroads, and other infrastructure, for example, the courts quickly approved condemnations. In supporting Anglo encroachment efforts while simultaneously preventing the Pueblos from making decisions on their own behalf, courts ensured that the Pueblos were damned if they relied on their assigned agents for protection and damned if they didn't.[108] In New Mexico, the U.S. government consolidated responsibility for the affairs of nineteen Pueblos in the hands of a single Indian agent, making clear the Pueblos' low priority within a growing bureaucratic state.[109]

For itinerant Indigenous groups, who were not recognized as holding land or having boundaries, the U.S. government took a different tack. In response to raids and attacks carried out by mobile bands of Apaches in the southwest, Comanches in the east, and Diné in the northwest of New Mexico, the federal government mandated either sedentarization or outright extermination, both carried out by the U.S. military.[110] In the 1860s the U.S. army called up six thousand soldiers in New Mexico for Civil War duty. When those militias were no longer needed to fight the Confederate Army, the U.S. Army turned them instead against Indigenous groups.[111] Militias quickly targeted Apache bands in southern and western New Mexico, meeting fierce resistance with murderous state force until only small bands remained.[112] In 1864 the U.S. Army force-marched almost ten thousand Diné from their lands on the Colorado Mesa to a containment area in eastern New Mexico. Apaches captured in other operations had already been sent to the same location, Bosque Redondo, where government officials expected them all to settle down and become farmers in the Pecos River valley. The sedentarization experiment resulted in abject failure: Bosque Redondo became a de facto concentration camp that produced nothing but conflict and suffering. The U.S. Army abandoned its containment efforts after a few years, but Indigenous groups did not fare well after returning home. The U.S. government established new reservation lands for the Diné in the Four Corners, but it did little to impede continual Anglo encroachment on this land.[113] Government policy also confined Apache bands to small reservation boundaries that curtailed their movements to make way for Anglo settlers. After closing Bosque Redondo, the U.S. Army turned its attention to the Comanches in the east and the Utes in the northwest, using military force to eliminate or reduce populations, which were then confined to reservation lands too small to allow them to continue their nomadic lifeways. These violent, genocidal policies are now recognized as vital underpinnings of Anglo settlement throughout the U.S. West.[114]

By the 1890s Anglo settlers had gained the upper hand in New Mexico. The earlier expansion of Nuevomexicano villages was over. The Pueblos found themselves constrained by law; the Apache and Diné, by military force. New commercial institutions had closed the door on barter-based regional trade and flung open a new door to large-scale speculation in agriculture and resource extraction. Increasing numbers of Anglo settlers arrived every year by railroad, gaining land through federal distributions or by purchasing it from individual owners. Many of the sellers were Nuevomexicano villagers caught in the difficult transition to a cash economy, unable even to maintain flocks of sheep—a traditionally robust exchange commodity or "poor man's cash" in rural New Mexico—as Anglo courts dispossessed Nuevomexicano pasturage lands outright.[115] Elites in New Mexico's territorial government—both Nuevomexicano and Anglo—worked hand in hand with investors and companies to buy up land from the government and the railroads in order to create a "colonization movement," which almost exclusively targeted Anglos.[116] By century's end, the sharp increases in Anglo population had also become apparent in the makeup of the territorial legislature. The addition of new Anglo-dominated counties and the election of more Anglo legislators led to ethnic parity between Nuevomexicanas/os and Anglos in the territorial assembly, and elites from both groups strongly supported Anglo settlement and governance.[117]

American conquest initiated significant existential impacts for both Nuevomexicano and Indigenous peoples. The multi- and interracial Spanish-led expeditions that settled in New Mexico in 1598 and 1692 had entered the seventeenth and eighteenth centuries as colonists. But their descendants staggered to the end of the nineteenth century in the grip of a "double colonization" that forced them "to navigate two different racial regimes simultaneously" while also grappling with land loss.[118] Pueblo peoples likewise found themselves caught in the transition from a Mexican system that recognized their political rights to an American system that wholly disenfranchised them.[119] Equally pernicious, the new American economy indiscriminately devalued individuals of all races and ethnicities who lacked capital or commercial ambition. On the hierarchical ladder of American settler colonialism, land-based communities of both Indigenous and Nuevomexicano heritage came to occupy the same economic rung, which "engendered a new era of labor exchange and economic interdependency" between peoples who had a long history together, however contentious and competitive.[120] Anglos who could afford to acquire land embarked on commercial endeavors divorced from any place-based culture or meaning, while subsistence villages found themselves increasingly alienated despite being strongly anchored to place through culture, story, and practice. Anglo colonial structures tended to divide Indigenous and Nuevomexicano peoples, and many Indigenous activists carry a perspective that the "Spanish" will ever retain the label as colonists.[121] But many Nuevomexicanas/os believe that a new culture group was born in the valleys of northern New Mexico when the descendants of Spanish colonists embraced their interracial reality and developed new customs in a new land.[122] A long and lively debate about Nuevomexicanas'/os' indigeneity, based in a mestizo identity and homeland, continues its relevance and urgency even today.[123] Regardless of where one comes down in this debate, the historical record clearly shows that both Indigenous and Nuevomexicano communities suffered systematic dispossession during the American territorial period, and that they continue to suffer structural disadvantages into the present.

Americanization and Environmental Change

Policies aimed at increasing Anglo settlement, opening consumer markets, and supporting extractive industries contributed to a process of "Americanization" that was itself critical to territorial possession.[124] In post–Civil War national politics, New Mexico was thought "too Mexican" to join the United States, despite having a larger population and more resources than other western territories that received statehood without delay.[125] In the late 1800s a booster industry sprang up to improve the territory's statehood prospects by changing its racial complexion and introducing "American" economic and cultural characteristics. Updating tropes that had brought Anglo farmers to the Great Plains, boosters claimed that new irrigation technology would remake the aridlands into a productive gardenscape beyond anything Indigenous or Nuevomexicano farmers could have imagined. In the process, promoters marketed a mythologized version of New Mexico's cultural geography that sanitized its fraught history and cast non-Anglos as quaint, nonthreatening relics of a bygone era.[126] Marketers depicted Indigenous people as noble savages and Nuevomexicanas/os as proud inheritors of a heroic Spanish conquistador lineage, relying on invented narratives that legitimized Anglo settlement while eliding its racist and colonialist underpinnings.[127]

Americanization was only one thread in a complicated process of social formation and identity politics surrounding shifting meanings of race, ethnicity, and nationality in New Mexico.[128] But for the Anglo-dominated territorial government of New Mexico, Americanization became a central policy goal at the turn of the twentieth century. Environmental policy was one of the most useful tools for achieving that end. In the late nineteenth century the U.S. Congress passed numerous laws designed to transfer public lands to individual ownership. Through multiple incarnations—the Homestead Act, the Preemption Act, the Desert Land Act, the Timber Culture Act, the Carey Act, and the Morrill Act—these laws focused on a single objective: providing economic incentives that would draw settlers from the U.S. east and midwest to newly acquired territories in the west. No single law perfectly achieved this goal, as it proved impossible to simultaneously satisfy competing political interests while also accounting for differences between homesteaders and speculators, between arid and nonarid lands, and between lands suitable for agriculture versus other forms of resource extraction. Once enacted, however, these laws all led to increased Anglo settlement and increased exploitation of resources in the western states. New Mexico was no exception.

New Mexico's Anglo-led territorial government supported commercial resource extraction: large-scale irrigated agriculture in the central and eastern valleys, grazing in the central and eastern grasslands, commercial forestry in the northern mountains, and copper mining in the southwest. Throughout the Rio Grande valley, the new extraction orientation led to significant environmental change, putting pressure on non-Anglo communities beyond the land dispossessions they had already experienced. In the Rio Arriba, for example, new commercial operators quickly exploited their access to former Nuevomexicano commons lands by clear-cutting entire forests for railroad ties and by stocking sheep and cattle on fragile grasslands near new railroad connections. When a huge irrigation project was built in Colorado's San Luis Valley in the 1880s, it compounded these impacts by detaining enough of the river's flow to change the downstream flood cycle. Decreased hydrologic flows (caused by the irrigation project) and increased amounts of sediment flow (caused by deforestation and overgrazing) quickly led to massive sedimentation throughout the middle Rio Grande valley. The middle valley was already characterized by aggradation—sediment deposition that continually adds new layers to a floodplain—but the upstream projects pushed the river's hydrology into an extreme aggradation regime. Sediment deposits in the middle valley formed tall riverside levees that easily contained the river during dry spells but suffered disastrous breaching during sediment-heavy floods of increasing magnitude. As with other rivers afflicted by severe aggradation, annual floods often changed the course of the river, making it difficult for agricultural settlements to persist within the floodplain. In 1884 the Rio Grande devastated its middle valley, damaging everything in its path between Albuquerque and El Paso and causing the permanent abandonment of several towns. The river flooded again in 1885, 1886, 1889, 1891, and 1897 when it "rampaged along its entire course through New Mexico."[129] Over the next three decades New Mexico had eleven more regionally damaging floods as a result of the Rio Grande's aggradation, and the middle valley's floodplains additionally began to suffer from salinization as the rising riverbed prevented excess irrigation water from returning to the main channel.[130]

Speculators made plenty of money during this time. Anyone who had cash could either purchase lands at lower risk for flooding and salinization or hire engineers to solve the problem.[131] They invested in flood-control infrastructure alongside irrigation infrastructure, increasing agricultural yields and sustaining ever-larger populations, all at the expense of the environmental resource base upon which production depended.[132] But the environmental changes devastated subsistence irrigators who relied on the productivity of their lands for basic survival. Longtime Pueblo and Nuevomexicano irrigators in the middle Rio Grande valley suffered considerably. They had no income and could not afford to fix flood damage, did not have the capacity to build major infrastructure themselves, and did not participate in the cash economy that could have produced funds to support big infrastructure. Stuck with increasingly saline soils that they could not afford to irrigate, many small irrigators found they had no way to produce a good harvest.[133]

The Anglo settler state, on the other hand, benefited over time from the environmental degradation its own resource exploitations produced. Not only did environmental change drive non-Anglo irrigators off their farmlands and force them to join a wage economy controlled by Anglos, but it also became a justification for Anglo environmental management. When the new government's policy led to overgrazing, that same government used overgrazing as an excuse to take control of Indigenous rangeland.[134] When the new government incentivized speculative timber extraction that led to deforestation, that same government used deforestation as an excuse to prohibit Nuevomexicano woodcutters from accessing the northern forests.[135] And when the new government advocated large-scale irrigation projects that disrupted the Rio Grande flood cycle and led to devastating flooding, that same government used the floods as an excuse to introduce new expert-led water-management bureaucracies.[136]

In all of these cases, the new settler-colonial government explicitly viewed the communal land- and resource-management practices of subsistence-oriented smallholders as a primary cause of environmental degradation. New agencies for resource management—such as the Forest Service, the Soil Conservation Service, and the Reclamation Service— relied on individualistic and profit-centered paradigms for nature-society relations. They displaced actors while also holding them responsible for their own marginalization, poverty, and displacement.[137] New Mexico's emerging environmental bureaucracies were thus central to the production of a racial-social order that both reflected Anglo dominance and used environmental management to retain that dominance.[138]

Conclusions on Water and Colonialism

New Mexico's colonial histories have always intertwined with water management. The Spanish emphasis on ditch irrigation over other communal irrigation techniques, for example, decreased Pueblos' resilience to drought. But the Spanish presence in New Mexico did not disrupt village-level social organization and in fact amplified the sociocultural significance of water management in ways familiar to Indigenous communities. The new Anglo government, by contrast, preserved almost nothing. Instead, it introduced a new economy that threatened virtually every aspect of Pueblo survival and produced "intense, chronic rural poverty" that afflicted Nuevomexicano communities as well.[139] Anglo settlement placed the land-based cultural foundations of Nuevomexicanas/os under considerable strain, and it is no coincidence that the acequia—"the main force that established a distinct place, defined the community's boundaries, and sought to maintain harmony with the natural environment"— persists as a focal anchor for those working to preserve Nuevomexicano identity, knowledge, and cultural landscapes.[140]

Starting in 1848, the American settler-colonial regime began a broad conquest of peoples, environments, philosophies, and economies. In contrast to Nuevomexicano and Pueblo communities that held local villages and subsistence lifeways as the center of their cultural focus, early Anglo settlers focused on individual profit, which linked them culturally to a broad national pursuit of commercial progress. New territorial laws contradicted acequia logic, burdened rural ditch governance, and incentivized large-scale corporate irrigation. The rise of commercial agriculture separated noncommercial farmers from their lands while simultaneously degrading rivers, floodplains, and their wider watersheds. Non-Anglo groups reacted to displacement and marginalization with sociopolitical movements that spurred powerful identity formation, yet it is clear that the Anglo settler-colonial framework continues to erase the visibility and agency of both Indigenous and racialized non-Indigenous communities.[141]

On 6 January 1912 New Mexico's territorial-era elites achieved their goal: New Mexico was admitted to the United States as its forty-seventh state. Resource extraction and intensive agriculture anchored the new state's economy. These industries remain important pillars of New Mexico's economy today, despite the aching depletion of forests, grasslands, minerals, and watersheds. Anglo settlement has grown considerably in the century since statehood, and recent efforts toward social and environmental justice have not stemmed the continual marginalization of Nuevomexicano and Indigenous communities.[142] Looking back, many historians fault the territorial-era land grabs—especially the alienation of land grants that should have been protected by international treaty—as the primary driver of ongoing displacement and inequity in New Mexico. In the remainder of this book, however, I show that water management provided the keystone for a broader structure of dispossession.

3

Expertise

SETTLER POLITICS AND THE NEW
WATER MANAGEMENT

Individual Anglo settlers did not invent scientific water management. It emerged from a broader federal approach to natural resources in the interior west. As the U.S. government consolidated control over massive stretches of territory in the late nineteenth century, it hurried to implement policies that would wring commercial profits from new lands. Time-tested approaches from the eastern United States, however, proved useless in the arid west, spurring new debates about how best to manage lands and waters. Over several decades, the federal government attempted, and then discarded, multiple policy approaches in a chaotic legislative process that agreed on little other than the need to spur settlement. But by century's end, federal policy had coalesced around the Progressive Party's modernist vision for remaking the environmental and cultural geographies of the nation through science and technology. As Progressive politicians rose to power, they embraced an environmental governance philosophy that separated humans from nature, lauded science as the premier knowledge form, and prioritized engineering expertise as the basis of governance. These commitments took center stage in the Progressives' marquee policy program: "reclamation" of arid western lands through irrigation and settlement.

Although Progressive policy based in modernist science pretends to operate in a sphere of complete neutrality and objectivity, it is deeply colonial. In this chapter I argue that the Progressive commitment to expertise—the embodiment of authoritative knowledge in specific individuals—constituted one of the most powerful tools in the settler-colonial project. Under the Progressives' modernist governance framework, resource-management "experts" wielded extensive power to remake landscapes and communities. Invariably they used this power to benefit Anglo settlers. The program for aridlands reclamation, for example, unleashed intense environmental impacts across New Mexico and the wider west that disadvantaged long-standing agricultural communities. At the same time, the reclamation program delegitimized the hydrologic knowledge and agricultural practices of both Indigenous communities and Spanish colonial descendants. Expert-led laws, agencies, and administrative procedures thus accomplished the dirty work of settler colonialism more effectively and less noticeably than violent military action. This chapter links colonial displacements to the rise of expertise at the core of the reclamation program. We begin in a narrow canyon of the upper Rio Grande watershed.

Embudo, New Mexico

In December 1888 the U.S. government launched a major new government science program in New Mexico. The goal: to measure surface-water flow across the entire western United States. The reason: to help organize and direct settlers to lands with profitable irrigation prospects. The problem: no one had ever attempted a stream-gauging project of continental magnitude. The solution: train engineers in stream-gauging techniques before deploying them across the arid watersheds of the western United States. The location: Embudo, a Nuevomexicano village and whistlestop between the San Juan and Culebra ranges of northern New Mexico.

The Embudo camp was organized in a hurry. John Wesley Powell, director of the United States Geological Survey (USGS), had secured a last-minute congressional appropriation in October 1888, and he needed to spend the money immediately. With winter looming, Embudo was one of only a few western sites where the river was unlikely to freeze. The tiny village also enjoyed a stop along the Denver and Rio Grande narrow-gauge railroad, making it reasonably accessible for camp equipment and personnel. USGS archives contain no information about whether local residents or leaders were consulted regarding the location of the camp.

A small group of trainees—"men of good education and high general intelligence"—began arriving at the Embudo depot in early December.[1] The trainees had engineering backgrounds, but none had any experience with stream gauging. One of them had lived in the western United States; the others were entirely unfamiliar with the variable nature of river flow in arid regions. Powell assigned a young graduate student from MIT, Frederick Newell, to run the camp as an instructor. Newell was twenty-six years old and had never conducted stream gauging. He nonetheless launched the camp in mid-December, supervising a daily routine of meteorological observations, streamflow measurements, water sampling, and calculation of the river's changing sediment load and channel movement. Newell was assigned to teach the engineers basic stream-gauging techniques on the Rio Grande, then send them on short expeditions to practice techniques and collect additional data on nearby streams.[2]

In many ways the camp was a bust. Despite Embudo's selection as a "southern" site, the location was frigid. Equipment froze even during the day, and at night the men desperately abandoned their army-issue cots for pits dug into the ground or nearby dirt cliffs. (Although the official camp documentation contains minimal references to interaction with local peoples and locales, Newell's personal journal reported that he purchased and distributed "Mexican blankets" and "Navajo blankets" to camp attendees in January.[3]) They began work without the most essential tool of stream gauging, a current meter, because none could be secured on short notice. At first they improvised by building a raft and hanging a rope across the river to take minimally accurate water velocity measurements using chip floats. They improvised other scientific methods as well, using tomato cans as survey markers and commandeering the cook's bread pan to make amateur evaporation measurements.[4] In general, money and other provisions arrived late or not at all, compounding the difficulties of equipment failures or losses. When the camp goat devoured the only air thermometer, for example, they had no choice but to slaughter it in a "sacrifice ... to that sterner divinity, Science."[5]

The Navy finally shipped a surplus current meter to Embudo, but it turned out to be too big and unwieldy to use in the Rio Grande. A different model sent from Denver was equally useless. In fact, none of the current meters then in use in the United States was suitable for a river like the upper Rio Grande. At low flow, the river was too shallow to allow a current meter to be suspended below the gauging raft. But after a storm, the river raged too high for the engineers to safely deploy any raft-based equipment at all. In one particularly scary incident at Embudo, two engineers fell into raging waters while trying to take measurements, losing valuable equipment and records. (Both men survived.) Throughout the spring of 1889 one of the Embudo engineers, J. B. Williams, made repeated trips to a machine shop in Denver to design more useful current-meter prototypes. The group in New Mexico also experimented with automatic gauges that could be fitted to a rod or cable, sparing individuals the danger of entering the channel on a raft or boat.[6]

In technical terms, the camp was successful in teaching engineers how to conduct stream gauging. Through trial and error, trainees learned how to measure streamflow under a variety of conditions. Scientifically, however, the camp had only mixed success. Embudo engineers successfully calculated the Rio Grande's overall average volumetric flow, or "discharge," based on their current measurements at different points in the channel. But they were not able to achieve the goal of developing "rating curves"—computations of the mathematical relationship between the river's height ("stage") and its discharge—owing to equipment inadequacy and failure. The computation of rating curves was critical to the larger project of determining the total amount of water available across the western United States. USGS leadership found it frustrating that the camp could not achieve this goal.[7]

The camp ended in April 1889. When it concluded, some of the trainees quit, some were fired, and the remaining eleven (including the director, Newell) were assigned as "Hydrographers" to scattered sites across the western United States. Powell urgently asked Congress for more money to conduct stream gauging during the 1889 summer irrigation season and then again in spring 1890 to support ongoing irrigation projects. In their new remote western posts, the Embudo-trained engineers collectively took on the daunting task of initiating the world's most massive stream-gauging program. Few of them had sufficient equipment or facilities, however, and they continued the improvisations that had been standard at Embudo. One engineer soon resigned because of health issues; another drowned when his meter-suspension raft was caught in a fast current. And barely a year after the field school had ended, the entire gang was decommissioned by Congress. Political winds had turned against Powell, and the Irrigation Survey lost its entire funding allocation. J. B. Williams took his own life soon after hearing the news.[8]

Powell had envisioned that many hydrologic field schools would be established across the west, but the Embudo camp turned out to be the first and last. The vision of an expert-led science and engineering program to support irrigation, however, lived well past Powell's political downfall. Before the Irrigation Survey was suspended in August 1890, Embudo trainees had managed against the odds to establish functional gauging stations in many western watersheds. Newell kept them running throughout the 1890s with piecemeal funding for basic maintenance and operation, and stream gauging got new life when it was included in the 1902 Reclamation Act.[9] This major piece of legislation established a financial model and governance paradigm to support irrigation engineering across the western states and territories.

Federal Policy takes a "Progressive" Approach

To understand how a dozen young men from the eastern United States secured the foundation for a regionwide scientific program in the west, we must first review the federal political context. As the United States adjusted to the pressures of industrialization after the Civil War, the Progressive Party became a dominant voice advocating comprehensive policy reform. The staggering impacts of immigration, urbanization, labor strife, and economic depression increased throughout the 1890s, raising fears that the country "was on the verge of class warfare and revolution."[10] Progressives argued that these problems were too big to leave in the hands of local governments and too urgent to wait for inefficient and stalemate-prone legislatures to act. They proposed concentrating power at the executive level in expert-led bureaucratic agencies that could implement far-reaching reforms.[11] Progressives promised that government would become vastly more efficient, reliable, and useful if its bureaucracies could operate on the basis of scientific knowledge.[12] The Progressives' position was a radical departure from the democratic and antistatist traditions of the country, but they believed desperate times called for desperate measures.[13]

The new government bureaucrats looked a lot like the men who had been invited to Embudo, and Newell himself eventually rose high in the ranks of the federal government as a scientific leader. But the Embudo camp attendees hardly seemed to be models of scientific expertise. They were uniformly ignorant about stream gauging, and they struggled to produce valid measurements both during and after a comically unprepared seasonal field camp in New Mexico. A small camp expedition investigated the irrigation infrastructure of "mostly Indians and Mexicans" in the local area but did nothing to incorporate local knowledge into the stream gauging program[14]—this despite the fact that the Embudo Valley was home to a thriving acequia community that had successfully managed water for crop cultivation for centuries.[15] Nonetheless, the Embudo camp attendees fit the bill for the Progressive Party's new agenda in U.S. resource management: they were college educated, they were men, they had skills in math and engineering, and they were white.[16] As the Progressive Party rose to power, these characteristics came to define the new face of resource management.[17] Despite technical ignorance and a lack of place-based knowledge, white men ascended into decision-making positions because of a general association with scientific rationalism and a willingness to engage in technical training. Even when field-based training was truncated or incomplete, the Progressives lauded it as evidence of expertise and used it to displace other knowledges and practices for resource management.

Progressives first applied scientific and bureaucratic solutions to the eastern urban centers, but they soon began to look westward. Politicians claimed the remote West was an obvious solution to overcrowding, where migrants from "worn-out, unprofitable" eastern and southern farms could simply start over.[18] With government support to establish new farms in the west, they wouldn't need to give up rural agriculture for urban shift work in the growing eastern cities.[19] Progressives also believed that agricultural settlement would promote the assimilation of Indigenous populations across the West.[20] By investing in these priorities simultaneously, Progressives argued, the western United States could be converted from an economic wasteland into a productive engine for a nation then emerging onto the global stage.[21]

In turning attention to the western region, Progressives merged urban social reform goals with a program for rural environmental conservation. They sounded alarm bells about the depletion of forests, soils, mineral resources, and waters, arguing that the United States could not prevail in the geopolitical competitions of the globalizing world without a natural base for commercial growth. "Conservation" became synonymous with careful management and development of natural resources to support broader goals, such as settlement and industrial growth. The figurehead of Progressivism, Theodore Roosevelt, actively championed natural resources as the foundation of the United States' imperial goals.[22] As president from 1901 to 1909, he presided over the creation of national forests, parks, monuments, and reserves to conserve the nation's resources and apply them to both continental and global expansion. Environmental control was part and parcel of the Progressive reform program, and the conservation of western resources "became inseparable from geopolitical competition in an imperial world."[23]

After decades of shrinking federal government, the Progressives ushered in a new era of federal expansion based on modernist environmental control. Politicians began to embrace resource management as a central element of modern governance.[24] As in other "environmental-management states," resource managers wielded a discourse of high modernism, ascribing superiority to humans over nature and lauding landscape transformation as a reflection of successful state-building.[25] Big dams and other water-control infrastructures became essential to the "creation stories" or master narratives that connected Anglo-Europeans to places they had only recently encountered in the western United States. These same narratives ignored the region's Indigenous and Mexican inhabitants and emphasized a second creation story—one that explained the role of modernity at the center of white European presence.[26]

The Progressives' program for environmental control reflected a fundamental prioritization of scientific and technical expertise. Claiming a need to eliminate inefficiencies in government, Progressives rejected piecemeal policy development by the many hands of local government, individuals, corporations, and courts.²⁷ They especially disdained local knowledge as a basis for government policy. To conquer western wildlands and make them productive, Progressives wanted to make decisions on the basis of scientific data and maps. The U.S. Congress had funded multiple scientific expeditions to the western United States after the Civil War, but data collection was uncoordinated, with multiple surveys competing against one another. Progressives proposed putting these same scientists and engineers into government to lead a coordinated, centralized, science-driven bureaucracy.

The Progressives didn't invent science or modernity. They were simply the first political party in the United States to build a successful platform and governing structure on the principle of rational, expert control. Progressives claimed that scientific and technical experts had a unique ability to apply objective criteria, to deploy rational logic, and to avoid politics.²⁸ In proposing that decisions should be made by engineer-bureaucrats rather than by politicians, the Progressives denied the existence of politics among scientists and engineers. It was a shrewd political argument. Their powerful platform changed the face of public service and shifted control of resource governance into the hands of experts.

As a world-making project, Progressivism was riddled with contradictions, especially in its conservation programs. Ostensibly meant to preserve rural life and prevent social decline, Progressive Era conservation policy instead alienated families from agrarian lifeways, either by reorienting rural workscapes toward large-scale commodity production or by labeling rural lands as "wilderness" to satisfy an urban fantasy that separated humans from nature.²⁹ The Progressive rallying cry of "efficiency" likewise created a paradoxical expansion of government institutions, personnel, and policies that led to wasteful bloating. And the quest for expert-led decision-making did not make governance more rational. In fact, it was completely *ir*rational to install resource managers who had little knowledge of the resources or places they were expected to manage. The veneer of scientific objectivity made a virtue of this ignorance, however, since it allowed managers to pretend their decisions were made at a distance from local political concerns. In reality, though, Progressivism simply traded one form of politics for another, replacing complex local decision-making with a racially charged federal commitment to "placeless" science and modernity.³⁰

Over time, many Progressive resource-management programs led to social disintegration and environmental catastrophe. The new expert class of government bureaucrats was overwhelmingly white, which provoked ethnic tensions, exacerbated racial divisions, and often led to violence. Social disruption also went hand in hand with environmental disaster. Scientific management of western forests for commercial extraction, for example, led eventually to the spectacular collapse of fire-adapted landscapes. Anglo managers used fire suppression to maximize yield in the short term, but it was a poor long-term replacement for Indigenous subsistence forestry practices, which relied on stand thinning to moderate fire damage without disrupting natural burn cycles.[31] Many western forests soon succumbed to insect epidemics, species transition, and megafires, ills that still plague today's western forest managers.[32] In hindsight, we know that Progressive approaches to resource management did not achieve their stated intention of conserving natural resources for the good of all. Instead, Progressive policy led to widespread degradation of natural systems for the commercial benefit of the very few.

At the heart of these failures lay the Progressives' commitment to expertise as the core of governance. Expertise based in scientific rationality was nothing but a cloak for the displacement of local resource managers, the racial politics at the heart of settlement expansion, and the government's sanction of environmental exploitation and social exclusion. Progressive reform was ostensibly about pushing back against the damaging social effects of unfettered capitalism and aggressive industrialization, but it did not reject or in any way undermine the structures of settler colonialism that underlay capitalism.[33] Instead, Progressive forms of environmental governance strengthened the political project of market-oriented settler colonialism.[34]

Reclamation Science and Policy

The hapless engineers at Embudo probably did not think of themselves as pawns in a high-stakes power grab. It is more likely they saw stream-gauging work the same way the public did: as part of a noble effort to civilize the western region through "aridlands reclamation." The Progressives' centerpiece program for irrigation and water management enjoyed immense visibility that spurred many easterners to migrate westward. Despite its publicity and popularity, however, federal reclamation encapsulated many of the central contradictions of U.S. Progressivism. Reclamation was expected to create an "irrigated Eden" that preserved critical rural pieces of the social fabric while also increasing the commercial productivity of family farms and generating wealth for the nation.[35] Instead, it produced a stunning transfer of wealth from federal coffers into private hands, remaking the West's landscapes and communities in highly uneven ways.[36] The construction of high-profile dams and other infrastructure came to symbolize a national transformation based on technological power and scientific expertise.[37] But these technical achievements masked an aggressive phase of settler colonialism that displaced and lowered the self-sufficiency of non-Anglo communities across the western United States.

The scientific work of U.S. reclamation originated in 1888, when Congress authorized the Irrigation Survey and launched the stream-gauging program at Embudo. Observation of hydrologic conditions was an age-old practice, but scientific hydrology was at that time fairly new.[38] Systematic deployment of stream-gauging instruments and methods had never been attempted on a continental scale. Nor had it been optimized for arid basins, where relatively small stream channels flashed between trickling and raging flow levels over short time scales.[39] Powell planned to install gauging stations on a few representative streams and then use those stations' data to create rating curves that could predict the flow of all other western streams. Thus, Embudo trainees were expected not only to obtain individual expertise in stream gauging, but also to develop systematic and replicable techniques for measurement and estimation across the West. Despite making some technical advances, the Irrigation Survey never evolved into a robust regional scientific program, and its congressional discontinuation in 1890 indicates that it was a political failure. What happened?

First, there were simply too many variables. It was not possible to develop rating curves that reliably accounted for the almost infinite conditions in "exposure, slope, soil, vegetation, temperature, seasons, ground moisture, and precipitation, and all the interrelations among them."[40] Second, the challenges of taking direct measurements were legion, even for a few sample sites. Engineers found themselves constantly adapting to local conditions, with no hope that there would ever be enough money to provide the equipment or develop the expertise needed for every location. Third, and most important, Powell's scientific program impeded the settlement effort. Powell insisted on withdrawing lands from "public entry"—making them off-limits to settlement claims—until they were mapped and measured by the Irrigation Survey. This existential threat to land offices and to the progress of westward settlement prompted Congress to withdraw funding from the Irrigation Survey, despite legislators' earlier enthusiasm for Powell's scientific work.[41]

But this setback for government hydrography did not last forever. In the summer of 1890, when Newell wrote to Embudo-trained hydrographers with instructions to "turn over their equipment, mules, and horses to the nearest topographic field parties," he was already making plans for continued stream gauging. Newell got himself transferred to the USGS

Topographic Survey, where he managed to piece together and redirect enough funding each year to keep stream gauging alive through the 1890s. Like Powell, Newell believed in the scientific mission of stream gauging, and he wanted to see it continue. Unlike Powell, he shrewdly perceived the political peril of supporting a scientific program that impeded settlement. Newell took a different political tack. He put less energy into modeling entire drainage basins and more into communicating streamflow data to lawmakers and the public. Newell believed that the regular publication of hydrography would convince both engineers and legislators that "the extreme irregularity" of the western streams required that they be tamed behind reservoirs.[42] His strategy worked, and his publications helped generate consensus for a massive federal investment in dams, storage reservoirs, and canals. In 1901 Nevada Senator Francis Newlands sponsored a comprehensive water-management bill, and in 1902 it passed Congress as the Reclamation Act, with strong support from Progressive backers, including President Theodore Roosevelt.[43]

Consistent with the broader Progressive political platform, the Reclamation Act incorporated both social reform and resource conservation. It created a new science-based agency within the Hydrographic Branch of the USGS and charged it with enabling efficient and rational development of water supplies throughout the sixteen states and territories of the western United States. Newell was appointed the first director of the new U.S. Reclamation Service, which quickly began to build dams and canals in multiple locations. Legislation charged the agency with building infrastructure for "the optimal exploitation of the nation's resources" as well as rationalizing the administration of settlement and land distribution.[44] It linked these responsibilities in a cyclical way. Anywhere the Reclamation Service installed dams and irrigation infrastructure, it then distributed newly irrigable land to settlers. By collecting filing fees and direct land payments, it then raised proceeds to support the building of new projects in other locations. The entire venture was thus premised on a continual flow of new settlers to public lands.[45]

In order to accomplish its multipart mission, the Reclamation Service needed employees with expertise in both engineering and public administration. Unlike the hiring process that had brought Newell himself into the USGS alongside other "good men" just over a decade prior, the new process required applicants to prove their qualifications through a civil service examination.[46] Hiring by examination didn't change the fact that the Service hired almost exclusively young white men from the eastern United States. But it did create an expectation that government irrigation projects would be led by qualified experts. Reclamation engineers gained a reputation for being "objective, impartial [and] unswayed by 'get rich quick' motives."[47] Newell rose to prominence as an ideal Progressive leader who coached his staff to consider legal and commercial forces alongside their technical and design work.

Make no mistake: the Progressive focus on expertise arose purely to serve colonial ends. Reclamation boosters and bureaucrats embraced expert-led irrigation as an engine of settlement, a symbol of progress, and a critical tool for remaking the nation.[48] The Progressive political platform valued the environmental work of conservation—taming wild rivers and turning fertile soils to productive use—primarily for its abilities to generate profit and enable Anglo settlement. Roosevelt himself stated, "The settlement of the great arid West by the makers of homes is the central object, both of the irrigation and the forest policy of the United States."[49] Newell agreed, arguing in a book on irrigation principles that engineers should "derive satisfaction" from the way their work provided "foundations upon which are built agricultural communities, villages, lines of railroad, and the whole social fabric."[50] Juxtaposed against earlier references to the primitive irrigation works of "native inhabitants" and "early Spanish settlers," who merely redirected water instead of building infrastructure to store it, his words referred specifically to a social fabric woven from the *Anglo* group, not from Indigenous communities or Nuevomexicano villages. The reclamation program displaced Indigenous and Nuevomexicano customs with Anglo-led management and knowledge focused on scarcity, extraction, and colonialism.

President Roosevelt saw engineers and scientists as key to his imperial vision, both at home and abroad. They allowed him to claim that American empire was focused on providing modernization and democratization to its subjects, rather than fostering the inequalities and abuses inherent in typical assertions of imperial power. Roosevelt was especially keen to promote scientific conservation as evidence of American global leadership. Newell predicted in 1900 that the western states and territories would eventually host as much population as was then contained in the entire United States, declaring that "dead and profitless deserts need only the magic touch of water to make arable lands that will afford farms and homes for the surplus of people of our overcrowded Eastern cities."[51] Newell and other American engineers, hydrologists, and irrigation advocates remained in constant conversation with their counterparts in other settler nations, especially Australia, to exchange ideas about technology and policy.[52] And the Roosevelt administration "fostered broader international exchange on ideas of irrigation" through irrigation congresses and travel-exchange programs, thus creating a "crisscrossing imperial circuitry of knowledge" that provided the political logic for western settlement.[53] The western reclamation effort thus reflected a shrewd reincarnation of an old impulse to displace those in the path of Anglo settlement.

Despite its high profile, the Reclamation Service was not entirely successful. Few of its early projects panned out financially, and cost overruns quickly undermined plans to use early proceeds to fund additional construction.[54] The agency spread itself too thin, starting too many projects in too many places, which made it impossible to experiment with different approaches, learn from mistakes, or even provide basic resources to every project.[55] But it enjoyed widespread support among legislators and the public, based on a central belief "that government scientists and engineers could manage the nation's streams and public lands more democratically than politicians."[56]

Progressives stuck with reclamation despite its failures because it achieved a fundamental settler-colonial objective: displacement. Construction projects tore up or inundated inhabited lands. Legal maneuvers stripped non-Anglos of possession and usufruct rights to both land and water. Most destructively, the Reclamation Service's new standards for expertise devalued non-Anglos' knowledge and management customs, relegating them to the status of petitioners rather than knowledge holders. Irrigation-based societies had maintained water-management technologies and customs in the southwestern United States for hundreds of years, but Progressives rejected any knowledge that did not include a concept of efficiency or an orientation toward profit. Absent those concepts, the agricultural civilizations of the southwestern United States were characterized as empty "wastelands," while the young Embudo camp attendees who'd never before set foot in the region enjoyed commendation as "experts."[57]

Looking back, we can see that reclamation was afflicted by the same contradictions as the broader Progressive movement. It utilized a rhetoric of high-minded rationality, but it was fundamentally beholden to local interests and settler politics. It relied on a powerful and authoritative engineering persona, but very few of its engineers had any experience with arid landscapes. And it claimed to operate in the broad public interest, although its vision was dominated by an Anglo-led social hierarchy. How did these many contradictions go unnoticed or unremarked during reclamation's heyday?

Progressivism's key public aspect—creation of an efficient and expert-led bureaucracy—cloaked its underlying commitment to a costly and inefficient process of displacement. The reclamation program itself was linked to a global imperial network "replete with racist sentiment" that identified white men as the only plausible experts.⁵⁸ So although reclamation fell short of Newell's promise to irrigate tens of millions of acres, it succeeded in opening the door to a radical remaking of the western United States. Large-scale agriculture and other extractive industries created a domain for Anglo settlement in the midst of areas already long inhabited and irrigated by non-Anglos. In the process, they ensured that the rationalization of resources and policy would benefit Anglo settlers more than any other ethnic or racial group.

Reclamation's Uneven Impacts

By design, reclamation projects disrupted both environmental and human geographies within their prescribed watersheds. Also by design, reclamation managers ensured that projects' calculated impacts would land in uneven ways. Overall, Anglo settlers were most likely to benefit from federal irrigation projects, even when they failed. And non-Anglos were most likely to bear the burdens and costs of environmental disruption and human displacement, even when projects succeeded.

Throughout the western United States, reclamation projects fundamentally altered hydrologic regimes by taking all possible water from a project area and applying it to irrigation. Newell counseled engineers to capture the entire flow of streams in their project areas and to consider remnant downstream water "as an indication of poor management or imperfect control."⁵⁹ Irrigation engineers' faithful adherence to this guidance caused extensive disruptions throughout the targeted river ecosystems. Big dams and canals changed rivers' channel geometry, reduced natural aggradation and levee height, decreased delta size, ended seasonal flow variations, choked riparian forests, and afflicted entire floodplains with salinization and other soil degradations. These costly environmental changes inflicted the most pain on generational Indigenous and Nuevomexicano agricultural communities, whose inhabitants could not easily move away from dangerous or despoiled areas surrounding the new irrigation projects. Conversely, the changes benefited newly arrived Anglos, who could choose where to make homestead claims and avoid the ruined lands.

Reclamation engineers' bid to use every last drop of water also created a double whammy of scarcity and inflexibility for existing communities. With all extra water flowing into the new projects, subsistence irrigation often became impossible in places where Indigenous or Nuevomexicano communities had been farming for generations.⁶⁰ This scarcity, in turn, removed literally all resilience from the system. Without excess water in the reclamation-controlled watershed, subsistence communities had no way to adapt to disturbances like drought, lower-than-usual snowpack, decreased monsoon activity, or meager runoff.

Reclamation's obsession with efficiency had negative impacts on Anglo settlers too. Farmers transplanted from humid eastern regions had no experience with arid landscapes. Their learning curve was exacerbated by engineered water scarcity, which left absolutely no room for error and turned their chances into a crapshoot. Furthermore, water rights were strictly quantified to limit applicants to the *minimum* amount of water necessary for any given crop, as determined by climatic and soil conditions. With no extra water available to offset the inevitable inefficiency of new settlers, reclamation necessarily led to crop failures in every single project area. Many farmers in the first settler generations failed in New Mexico, forcing them to go deeply into debt, sell their lands, and/or become tenant farmers.

All of these failures led toward one common outcome: land abandonment. And every time land was abandoned, speculators took the opportunity to purchase land at a discount. This allowed a relatively small number of (mostly Anglo) speculators to concentrate extensive land and water rights into large commercial operations, typically with financial support from Anglo investors from the eastern United States or the United Kingdom. At a macro scale, then, the costs of reclamation were largely borne within the region, while benefits accrued outside the region. Failed projects proved most costly, producing massive environmental disruptions without generating any significant financial benefits. But even successful projects extracted a toll in both environmental and human terms.

The Reclamation Service pursued five irrigation projects in New Mexico soon after the agency's 1902 creation. Federal investment focused primarily on the lower Pecos River valley, where private irrigation had already enabled a wave of Anglo settlement. The journalist-turned-booster William Smythe predicted that "civilization" and "new institutions" would "sprout from the soil" around Carlsbad alongside new reservoirs, canals, and artesian wells.[61] He contrasted Anglos' engineering commitment to market-oriented agriculture with the "scattered" and "petty" ditches maintained for subsistence agriculture by "Mexican peons" and "town-building Indians" elsewhere in New Mexico.[62] Yet Smythe's rhetoric belied the failure of nearly all of the Reclamation Service projects in New Mexico. The Hondo Creek project, for example, became an embarrassment and object lesson for Service engineers when a reservoir meant to irrigate ten thousand acres failed to materialize. Project engineers had situated the dam in a natural depression, where water could simply leak underneath instead of rising behind it. That project was abandoned after an exorbitant waste of federal dollars.[63] The nearby Carlsbad Project was taken over by federal authorities only because a private irrigation scheme failed catastrophically, with floodwaters repeatedly overtopping its two dams and destroying one of them. The Secretary of the Interior claimed it was necessary "to purchase this collection of wrecks . . . in order to save from destruction an entire community" downstream of the spotty infrastructure.[64] The federal infrastructure solved the problem at significant cost, but it seemed no cost was too high when Anglo settlement was on the line, no matter how small the acreage served.

The Rio Grande Project—the biggest and most successful reclamation project in New Mexico—also introduced deleterious effects. The project was meant to reinvigorate Anglo settlement in southern New Mexico, satisfy legal-compact obligations to deliver water to Mexico and Texas, and regulate hydrologic extremes in a valley where irrigation had become highly precarious. By building dams in southern Colorado, Anglo settlers had unintentionally disrupted seasonal flood cycles far downstream.[65] In southern New Mexico, farming became almost impossible: "Often the river was dry for months at a time, and when a freshet came, it usually washed out the temporary dams of rock and brush."[66] The Rio Grande Project endeavored to resolve this problem with a major Rio Grande dam a hundred miles north of the New Mexico–Texas–Mexico border, along with supporting dams in tributary valleys. Completed in 1916 after twelve years of construction, the massive concrete structure at Elephant Butte was one of the Reclamation Service's most celebrated early dams. Its reservoir was hailed at the time as the world's largest artificial lake, highlighting the agency's technical engineering capabilities and making clear the stakes for settlement in southern New Mexico.

But as water began flowing through canals and laterals meant to serve 100,000 acres of cultivated fields, subsistence irrigators in southern New Mexico experienced immediate destabilization. Farming in the Rincon and Mesilla Valleys had typically used flood-irrigation techniques that relied on sediment-rich waters flowing through communal ditches. Water captured behind Elephant Butte dam was instead sediment free, and many farmers found it difficult to adjust their irrigation volume ratios, which led to widespread waterlogging and salinization.[67] Adjusting to the new environmental realities while also struggling to pay the new taxes and maintenance fees imposed by Reclamation, both Anglo and Nuevomexicano farmers lost or were forced to sell their lands. In the end, the new buyers were almost universally Anglos, making Elephant Butte Dam and the Rio

Grande Project one of the premier tools enabling the rapid expansion of Anglo settlement in southern New Mexico.[68]

Reclamation for Non-Anglos

The Reclamation Service was not the only, or even the first, federal agency to build irrigation infrastructure in New Mexico. The Bureau of Indian Affairs (BIA), which also relied on Progressive philosophy and politics, originally took direct responsibility for irrigation projects on Indigenous lands through its Indian Irrigation Service (IIS). The IIS began installing irrigation infrastructure on tribal lands in the 1890s with a dual objective: to increase the agricultural potential and independence of Indigenous communities, and to provide reliable wage labor to Indian men that would help them assimilate into the broader economy and society.[69]

Outwardly, the IIS appeared similar to the eventual Reclamation Service: it received federal funding and enjoyed federal authority to evaluate, authorize, design, and construct irrigation projects. In reality, the two agencies were drastically different. The BIA never received appropriation amounts anywhere near the millions sent to the Reclamation Service. IIS positions did not require training in engineering, and the agency was "no match for the Reclamation Service in numbers or talent."[70] In fact, IIS employees "received the lowest salaries of any in governmental service."[71] Overall, the IIS suffered from a complete lack of planning or coordination. Most projects were managed not by engineers but by Indian agents who typically hired local Anglos to fill contract roles as "engineers," regardless of any design or construction experience. As a result, "the dilatory BIA irrigation program always lagged behind the better-financed Anglo projects; it built Indian irrigation projects so slowly that the initial stages of the projects became dilapidated before the latter stages were begun; the agency's construction schedule was slower than the rotting wood and rusting metal that characterized Indian irrigation projects."[72] Federal prescriptions paradoxically held Indigenous communities hostage to modernist standards and expectations for irrigation engineers while simultaneously ensuring they would receive no experts capable of helping them meet those standards. In essence, the IIS prevented New Mexico's agriculturalists from continuing their traditional irrigation practices but provided useless infrastructure as a replacement. It was the worst of both worlds; furthermore, IIS failures were always held against Indigenous communities and never against the agency.

The lack of money and technical expertise was only part of the problem for the IIS. Even when they succeeded, IIS projects usually resulted in persistent disadvantage to New Mexico's Indigenous communities. As was true for many programs in the early BIA, IIS policy reflected cultural ignorance and disregard.[73] Efforts to build dams and foster cash cropping on Zuni and Navajo lands ended in disaster, even though both areas had long histories of productive agriculture. Why did they fail? First, IIS programs focused on crops rather than livestock, the traditional agricultural mainstay for both Zuni and Navajo communities. IIS agents offered programming and education to men rather than to women, the ones who held traditional responsibility for subsistence agriculture.[74] Second, IIS programs focused on commercial rather than subsistence agriculture, which required expertise in unfamiliar activities such as buying, selling, and timing business transactions. Finally, IIS managers expected Zuni and Navajo men to provide manual labor for dam-building in return for wages that would help teach "the virtues of thrift and careful money management."[75] Wages turned out to be poor motivation. Many of the intended laborers were busy with subsistence-oriented priorities; others considered it futile to build permanent dams instead of customary brush diversions that could be replaced easily after flooding.[76] Indigenous men showed up to work when it suited them, frustrating construction managers and Indian agents endlessly. Policymakers had expected irrigation projects to provide a natural path to assimilation, pushing Indigenous people into the cash economy and into the real estate market. Virtually none of their projects succeeded.

The laughably inane failures of the IIS provide textbook examples of settler hubris and cultural ignorance, and we might be tempted to view them as examples of settler colonialism's frailty. But the IIS was a very small cog in a vast and devastating machine. Even as IIS managers wasted federal dollars on a fruitless civilizing mission, the machinery was still grinding away at Indigenous sovereignty. By promoting small irrigated farms on tribal lands as a way of strengthening the nuclear family and increasing property values, irrigation programs disastrously opened Indigenous lands to Anglo interest and encroachment. The policy goal of "driving up the value of land" ostensibly intended to help Indigenous people "develop an 'instinct' for private property" while also attracting Anglos who could "serve as models of industry, self-discipline, and thrift."[77] But the pressure of arriving Anglos actually exacerbated inequalities throughout New Mexico and the West. When IIS projects failed and Indigenous farmers defaulted on their financial obligations, the result was land transfer to Anglos. When IIS projects succeeded and property values went up, the result was the same: land transfer to Anglos. Through IIS programs, Anglo settlers gained control of millions of acres of Indigenous lands. And the sale or transfer of tribal and heirship lands typically included water rights. Paradoxically, then, the IIS eventually became responsible for installing and maintaining irrigation systems that served primarily Anglo settlers.[78] The irony was complete when the new settlers began hiring Zuni and Navajo men to work their old lands, thus extracting financial profits from land, infrastructure, and labor that the federal government had originally promoted as a source of Indigenous independence.[79]

The U.S. government poured money into Reclamation Service projects with no concern for the failure of nearby IIS projects, making clear that its vision of irrigated empire was largely incongruous with the existence of Indigenous communities. And in 1907 the BIA turned over management of its biggest tribal irrigation projects to the Reclamation Service, acknowledging the extent to which they had already begun to focus on Anglo settlers.[80] Predictably, reclamation policy caused further failures among the remaining Indigenous farmers, leading to increasingly accelerated land transfer. Subsistence farming continued on both Zuni and Navajo lands, but noncommercial agriculture did not count as a "beneficial use" of water sufficient to claim or maintain a water right. Confirmation of water rights depended on building irrigation projects, which introduced financial losses that could only be covered by offering land for sale, which removed it from Indigenous ownership. Rhetoric swirled around the idea that Indigenous people simply did not have the expertise to manage their own lands and waters, but in fact "reclamation was just another scheme to escape treaty obligations and transfer control over [Indigenous] land to whites."[81] Federal policy saw irrigation as "the vital core of western development, the essential base ingredient of [a] New Eden."[82] The New Eden clearly did not include Indigenous people.

A third major group in New Mexico—Nuevomexicano agriculturalists—occupied a liminal space. Some of the largest landowners, who became known as Hispanos, moved into elite roles aligned with Anglo commercial producers. Others became marginalized in exactly the same ways as their Indigenous neighbors, through Anglo encroachment and land loss. But the federal government did not recognize Nuevomexicanas/os as a special group, and no BIA-like agency was created with even a nominal mission of protecting Nuevomexicano interests. In the face of devastating marginalization, Nuevomexicano communities held tight to the acequia—"the main force that established a distinct place, defined the community's boundaries, and sought to maintain harmony with the natural environment"—as a foundation for political action and cultural preservation.[83] In both northern and southern New Mexico, acequia landscapes and customs became "sources of identity, manifestations of political competence, and foundations for effective civic life."[84]

Maintenance of acequia systems also allowed Nuevomexicano communities to claim and demonstrate crucial expertise in water management, environmental knowledge, and governance.[85] Acequias were too small to support commercial agriculture, and their continued existence challenged many aspects of the Anglo settlement project in New Mexico. But Nuevomexicano communities protected them ferociously, wedging them into territorial legislation through unique policy provisions that acknowledged their twin roles: water infrastructure and cultural mainstay. As federal reclamation philosophy made its way into state and territorial policy throughout the west, Nuevomexicanas/os found themselves, paradoxically, in a stronger position to protect cultural lifeways than their Indigenous neighbors. Nuevomexicanas/os had no designated protection from a federal agency, but they also were not subjected to BIA programs meant to promote assimilation to new ideas about environmental expertise.

Politics at the Heart of Expertise

Expertise served as a common thread between Progressive resource management and settler colonialism at the turn of the century. Institutional science had enjoyed rising social and political importance throughout the eighteenth century, and the Progressive Party rose to power in the United States partly by pushing for a strong federal commitment to science. But the Progressives' major innovation lay in shifting attention from scientific *work* to scientific *personnel*. Progressivism cast Reclamation Service engineers and other resource managers in the role of "missionar[ies] to society," raising an expectation that impartial experts and bureaucrats could save the nation from conflict, unrest, and degeneration.[86] For science and engineering to provide a true basis for governance, Progressives reasoned, scientific and engineering experts should wield the political authority to govern. This stance dovetailed perfectly with a new phase of settler colonialism. Expert-led environmental management provided a powerful lever for displacing non-Anglos from western lands while offering a supposedly objective and neutral approach to governance.

In the Progressive framework, only "experts" could produce legitimate knowledge. And in New Mexico, only Anglos could achieve designation as experts. Whiteness thus became a definitive marker of expertise, independent of knowledge, training, or experience. Thus, the stream-gauging field camp at Embudo should be viewed as a series of failures and shortcomings, not a pillar of knowledge and expertise. Leaders were completely ignorant of stream-gauging science, attendees were unprepared to adapt rudimentary engineering knowledge to an unfamiliar arid landscape, and the camp was marked by improvisation rather than systematic science. Camp records leave no trace of engagement with local communities, whose water-management traditions rested on centuries of observation and practice in the Rio Grande watershed. But this ignorance mattered little, because the Progressive agenda identified objective, systematic, scientific measurement *by Anglos* as the only legitimate way of producing knowledge. After a mere five months' work in Embudo—where they lost expensive equipment and spent their free time pulling complicated pranks on the leadership—camp graduates claimed the mantle of expertise. These young white men then dispersed across the western United States to enact a system of racialized privilege in water management, all the while thinking their work was perfectly objective because it was based on science.

The Anglo-led model of expert resource governance that crystallized at Embudo disadvantaged non-Anglos in important ways. First, and most directly: expert-supported Anglo settlement in the western United States pressured and displaced non-Anglos who were already living in irrigable areas. More insidiously: government support for Anglo experts simply delegitimized resource-management practices and decisions by non-Anglos. Indigenous agriculturalists were treated as if they had zero expertise, in water management or anything else, and required support from a separate federal agency. Neighboring Nuevomexicano communities, whose members had developed a rich cultural complex centered on irrigation practice and knowledge, also found themselves relegated to nonexpert status because they were not focused on commercial production and showed little interest in the cash economy. Of the major groups living in New Mexico at the turn of the century, Anglos had by far the least expertise with aridlands irrigation. Their farms failed conspicuously in many areas, yet the politics of expertise absolved them. The Progressive construction of expertise as Anglo refused to hold new settlers responsible for their failures, lauding them instead as brave souls willing to face and tame the desert with new science and new tools.

Federal projects were no more scientific or rational or likely to succeed than local projects carried out by cooperative action. The veneer of truth that bolstered the Reclamation Service's claims to expertise obscured the fact that experts are essentially always in conflict or disagreement. By claiming that science and efficiency were embodied in Anglo engineers, the Progressive government performed a classic maneuver of the environmental-management state, producing a racialized federal bureaucracy that claimed an ability to "consolidate power and produce an orderly, disciplined society."[87] Progressives used natural-resource management to expand the state's executive power and to add new tools to the long-range project of displacing non-Anglos to make room for new settlers.[88] Most of the ideas at the foundation of Progressive Era water engineering came from outside the region through a global circulation of environmental knowledge between North American engineers and their counterparts in other Anglo settlement colonies such as Australia and New Zealand.[89] In all of these settlement colonies, resource managers plied their trade to maximize profit extraction in areas previously dominated by subsistence agriculture.

Reclamation advocates claimed that science-based water management was above politics, but I argue that the commitment to science *was* its politics. Reclamation necessitated a new form of knowledge (scientific hydrology), a new structure of governance (centralized bureaucracy), and new expert personnel (water engineers). Each element had the unmistakable impact of displacing people and communities already engaged in other forms of water management. Virtually all irrigation projects in territorial New Mexico led to land abandonment and ownership transfer, disproportionately benefiting Anglos over other groups. Starting with Embudo, New Mexico, science-based policy narrated the foundation for western integration into a nation imagining itself as white.

The Aftermath

Within a few short decades the reclamation era was past its heyday. The big dams had put only a few million acres under irrigation by the mid-1930s, despite Newell's prediction in 1902 that sixty to a hundred million acres could be reclaimed in the West.[90] The political calculus changed so significantly by the 1970s that the Bureau of Reclamation (as it had come to be known) eventually began to consider the decommissioning of its own dams.[91] The changing fortunes of reclamation never led to a retreat from expert-led environmental governance. John Wesley Powell's vision of a western United States governed entirely by objective science has in fact become quite popular in recent decades. (Note: Powell was not a Progressive, and he did not support the intrusion of federal bureaucracy into local governance.[92] But he was deeply committed to Progressive ideals about science, arguing repeatedly that scientific knowledge was the only proper foundation for U.S. governance and expansion.[93]) Powell's revivalists like to claim that his backstabbing by politicians is an example of how good science can be undone by good politics.[94] The stories from this chapter should convince you instead that science *is* politics.

The lionization of science and engineering permeates resource policy at all levels in the United States today, despite the patent impossibility that perfect knowledge or objective science will ever be achieved or that it could provide a politics-free foundation for policymaking. STEM fields now enjoy such deep privilege across all educational levels that it is hard to imagine broad acceptance of any other form of knowledge. Herein lies a key challenge of modernity: expertise-based bureaucracies subvert democracy and become ends rather than means. If governance can be accomplished only by experts, who themselves control the programs and bureaucracies through which expertise is defined and attained, challenge or revision from nonexperts through an open and democratic process will never occur.[95] In tandem with this debilitating bureaucratic effect, large infrastructure from the reclamation era served as a long-lasting wedge between the fortunes of Anglo and non-Anglo communities. Across the western United States, irrigation projects created early disparities that produced compounding inequalities over time.[96] As a result, Indigenous disadvantage and Nuevomexicano marginalization continue almost invisibly in the present, perpetuating the settler-colonial conditions that originally fostered them.

The Progressive approach to irrigated agriculture changed virtually everything about water management in New Mexico. It prioritized commercial ventures over subsistence lifeways, centralized control over village-level systems, individual property rights over communal accommodation, and strict quantification of water rights over negotiated agreements that could vary based on environmental and political conditions. Large-scale irrigated agriculture intersected with other forms of resource exploitation to cause environmental change throughout the Rio Grande valley, displacing and disadvantaging many vulnerable agriculturalists. At the same time, the new government's expert-led water bureaucracy displaced Nuevomexicano and Pueblo leaders and governance structures that had anchored New Mexico's communities for centuries. In the final push for statehood, New Mexico's legislature passed its foundational 1907 water law, creating a centralized engineering office to manage water rights and quantify water use. That is the story to which I turn next.

✷ 4 ✷
Law

ENVISIONING AN EXPERT WATER AGENCY

The Progressive Party emerged in the eastern United States, but its governance vision depended on the exploitation of lands and resources in the western part of the country. As Progressive politics swept the nation at the turn of the twentieth century, western states and territories duly scrambled to fulfill their expected roles. They threw open doors to settlement and rushed to establish resource-management policies and agencies based on Progressive philosophy. One critical piece of this puzzle involved crafting water laws that would induce an irrigation-fed settlement bonanza. These new water statutes often mimicked or replicated one another, offering a one-size-fits-all prescription for expert management of water resources in support of profit-oriented settlement.

New Mexico followed this politically astute trend, but not immediately. New Mexico's early territorial laws focused on integrating Nuevomexicano and Pueblo irrigation norms within the legal framework of the United States. Later, as the number of Anglo settlers began to explode, New Mexico's legislators began adding piecemeal accommodations for profit-oriented agriculture. Not until after the passage of the 1902 federal Reclamation Act did New Mexico pass its own comprehensive water law. By 1907 it had created a powerful territorial engineering agency and a robust water-permitting process.

This chapter uses government archives and legislative texts to narrate the evolution of New Mexico's territorial-era water laws. It reveals the complex and uncertain layering of legal statutes, as the New Mexico territorial assembly struggled to protect long-standing water customs while also accommodating large-scale water projects in the first six decades after U.S. annexation. Each round of water legislation increasingly prioritized Anglo settlers over existing communities, eventually committing fully to expert-led rationalization of water management. The end stage of this statutory evolution—New Mexico's centerpiece 1907 water law—redefined water relations and codified a Progressive governance vision that remains unchanged today. Shortly after New Mexico established its water engineering agency, the U.S. Supreme Court developed new principles for understanding and codifying Indigenous water rights at the federal level, but those principles were consistent with the same colonial Progressive vision that guided New Mexico's water administration.

The Legal Foundations for Settlement

Legislators negotiate and approve individual laws within the constraints of existing legal doctrine. These broader frameworks tend to be very stable; they evolve only through lengthy processes of judicial interpretation or changing political philosophy. But there is one major exception: a change in sovereignty. When a war ends, or when two nations agree on a territorial purchase or transfer, the legal system can change in fundamental ways over a very short time. The parties spell out the transition through treaty negotiation, usually including a timeline for when and how the new sovereign's legal system will be enacted. Even the most gentle treaty, however, produces a more rapid legal transition than could ever occur organically through the political or judicial process. And so it was for New Mexico in the second half of the nineteenth century.

Upon arriving in Santa Fe as a conquering force in 1846, the U.S. Army declared a new legal code, effective immediately. Two years later Mexico ceded its northern territory to the United States through the Treaty of Guadalupe Hidalgo, which stated that property "of every kind, now belonging to Mexicans . . . shall be inviolably respected."[1] Legally, however, it was not clear how the treaty's stipulations would be accomplished. The new American legal system simply could not recognize all forms of property acknowledged by Spain and Mexico, including the traditional Spanish/Mexican "commons" and the combined land and water rights so foundational to acequia governance.[2] American law also prioritized individual rights over community rights, which challenged the communal decision-making traditions that had long defined Spanish, Mexican, and Indigenous approaches to land and water. In addition, the exceeding formality of American law clashed with the informal and customary nature of usufruct rights and water-management norms in Pueblos and Spanish settlements. Finally, it was unclear whether Indigenous rights should receive different treatment than those of other Mexican citizens.[3] Anglo settlers sometimes responded to the legal uncertainty by taking matters into their own hands, consolidating control over land grants and water rights through explicitly dispossessive tactics as they waited for authorities to reconcile these incompatible legal traditions.[4]

New Mexico was only one of many U.S. territories that scrambled to administer land claims and water rights in response to rapid Anglo settlement. In California, the gold rush prompted an entirely new legal doctrine—"prior appropriation"—that soon ruled nearly all western water claims. In contrast to the doctrine of "riparian rights," common in the wetter American east, prior appropriation used chronological order instead of geographic location to distinguish between competing water claims. Under riparian rights, those who own land along a riverbank automatically enjoy the right to use its water. But under prior appropriation, it is not necessary to own land near water. Anyone can claim a water right by building infrastructure to carry water from its source to some "beneficial" (i.e., not wasteful) use. As long as the claimant is "first in time" and does not harm any preexisting beneficial and continuous uses of the same water source, they will gain a water right that is senior to any subsequent claims. The only requirement to retain this right is to continuously use the water for a beneficial use, season after season, without violating the rights of more senior users.

The doctrine of prior appropriation emerged from the mining domain but quickly moved beyond it. Very few western lands enjoyed easy access or proximity to rivers, streams, springs, or other waters. Riparian law would have rendered most lands worthless. But prior appropriation doctrine promoted enthusiastic settlement throughout the region. Settlers and investors could reasonably claim even the most arid lands by committing labor and resources to developing irrigation infrastructure. A simple brush or rock structure was usually enough to divert water from a running stream into an earthen or reinforced ditch. With assistance from gravity or pumps, irrigation ditches efficiently moved water across stubborn landscapes, allowing settlers to establish farms, pastures, and other water-dependent operations. After the U.S. government determined that water-rights doctrine was a matter of state jurisdiction, almost all of the western territories chose prior appropriation as the legal basis for water rights.

In New Mexico, prior appropriation had a complex intersection with the existing customs of both Pueblo and Nuevomexicano communities. In some ways existing traditions could easily accommodate prior appropriation, because they already recognized a hierarchy of seniority within irrigation systems, and they also recognized continuous irrigation as the foundation of water rights.[5] But the new doctrine promoted an individualistic and commercial framework for Anglo settlement, which challenged New Mexico's long-standing water-governance customs.[6] Under Spanish and Mexican law, "the main purpose of irrigation was to create a permanent community, not to encourage individual enterprise."[7] The state retained ownership of water; individuals or communities held only *use* rights, administered by an officer of the state. Spanish and Mexican administrative officials enjoyed considerable flexibility to make changes in water-sharing arrangements, and judges resolved conflicts in the best interest of the community. In times of shortage, water managers essentially *never* entirely denied water delivery to the most junior irrigators.

Despite these fundamental differences, prior appropriation eventually replaced New Mexico's older approaches to water management, spurred both by the irrigation boom of the 1880s and by calls for modernization across the western region. Before long settlement was booming. As investors learned to rely on the new doctrine, they began pouring resources into irrigation infrastructure. Diversions expanded into dams and ditches evolved into canals, etching western landscapes with concrete evidence that the U.S. legal system supported opportunistic speculation.

Under the new Anglo-led framework, water rights became almost a competitive sport. As Donald Pisani puts it, the "welfare of the community became the product of a multitude of discrete decisions made in the marketplace, with no sense of planning and little of collective responsibility."[8] This new reality was a far cry from the communitarian traditions of New Mexico's water management.

Acequias in the Eyes of the Law

Although prior-appropriation doctrine spread like wildfire across the western United States, individual water-management statutes seeped more slowly into legislative codes. States and territories experimented with different policies through multiple statute iterations, correcting mistakes or adding new provisions each time settlement went awry or in unanticipated directions. New Mexico's tortuous legislative process lasted more than five decades before it enacted a water code to match its western neighbors, showing that irrigation development was "the story of two conflicting forces, one communitarian and the other individualistic, one centripetal and the other centrifugal."[9] At the center of these competing forces: traditional acequias.

At the time the United States declared military control in Santa Fe in 1846, New Mexico had "by far the oldest conscious tradition of water control and use in all of the present United States."[10] The long history of

Indigenous and Nuevomexicano farming throughout the valleys of the Rio Grande watershed ensured that community governance was largely synonymous with water management. Small communities were required by law to hold annual elections for the purpose of selecting an irrigation manager (mayordomo) and three commissioners responsible for the administration and oversight of water-sharing agreements for the year. As the key official in community-level water governance, the mayordomo determined irrigation schedules, made work assignments for annual ditch cleanouts, and inspected flow-control infrastructure to ensure that individual irrigators abided by their scheduled water allocations. Under Spanish and Mexican law, acequia membership, crucially, required annual labor contributions—both to clean out ditches and to shore up ditch, bridge, flume, and headgate infrastructure—ensuring that all who received water from a community ditch also contributed to its upkeep.

The traditions of membership, governance, and obligation that revolved around the acequia defined community life in Spanish-era New Mexico, and they became mainstays of cultural preservation for Nuevomexicano communities during the early U.S. territorial period.[11] Unlike what happened in other western territories, New Mexico's U.S.-era water laws first prioritized cultural traditions over federal principles for resource exploitation. The New Mexico territorial assembly of the 1850s, 1860s, and 1870s passed water laws to encode the "amalgam of Spanish and Indian law and custom which had been mutually acceptable to both cultures" over the previous three centuries.[12] Perhaps reflecting the influence of legislators' own cultural identities—primarily Nuevomexicana/o—the territorial assembly declared agriculture to be the highest-priority water use and passed laws strengthening the community acequia as the locus of water use, control, and governance.

As Anglo settlement increased across New Mexico, however, legislators began to introduce new legal concepts in the 1880s.[13] The new statutes carefully maintained existing laws' support for subsistence agriculture while twisting and extending language to additionally promote commercial farming endeavors. First, legislators recognized livestock pasturage as "a branch of agriculture," so that irrigated alfalfa farming, a common endeavor of new Anglo setters, could be prioritized in the same way as traditional subsistence cultivation. Second, they changed the definition of acequia to include springs and livestock tanks, thus requiring commissioner elections and maintenance regulations for both public and private irrigation ditches. Soon afterward legislators determined that private and public acequias should actually be treated as identical under the law. By granting equivalence to private ditches built by Anglo settlers for commercial use and public acequias used by Nuevomexicano and Indigenous communities for subsistence, the territorial assembly introduced an existential challenge to the acequia institution. In 1882 the assembly went even further, categorizing *all* acequias as private property, thus negating their customary role as public, community-based institutions.

By century's end, as national political winds shifted toward expert-led resource governance, New Mexico's legislators definitively relegated acequia traditions to the margins of territorial water policy. In 1895 they dissolved the equivalence of public acequias and private ditches, elevating private ditches with the new label of "corporations" while acequias returned to their old status as "community ditches." This new law gave commissioners fundamental authority over all ditches, transforming the mayordomo position into an operating manager or CEO. Mayordomos had long been elected on the basis of skills in community leadership, decision-making, and conflict resolution; their new technical role came as a blow to Nuevomexicano cultural norms. In the same law, legislators introduced a new punishment for water violations: denial of water. In comparison to the traditional sanction of fines, water denial constituted an extreme repercussion. It illustrated how far water policy had moved away from a water-sharing model oriented around community welfare.

Laws to Support Settlement

As they wrangled over these various acequia accommodations, New Mexico's territorial governors and legislative leaders became increasingly certain that the political path to statehood would require large-scale commercial agriculture. Engineers looked disdainfully at the community acequias dominating New Mexican watersheds at the end of the nineteenth century, labeling them wasteful and backward. Statehood boosters called for massive increases in dams, canals, pumps, and other irrigation infrastructure that would support the development of Anglo towns. They saw acequias as antithetical to the development needed to prove New Mexico's "Americanness" and fitness for statehood.

Within the statehood-obsessed political climate, legislators began to raise concerns about the difficulties of maintaining a "dualistic authority" for different irrigation frameworks.[14] When the 1882 water law allowed irrigation companies to incorporate, for example, it created a legal gray area that produced numerous conflicts between subsistence-oriented acequia communities and profit-oriented commercial farmers. The 1887 law, as another example, separated water rights from land ownership so that settlers could buy or sell water rights without complications from communal water-management expectations. Although Anglo towns expanded rapidly in the lower Pecos River valley as a result, the law exacerbated fraught ethnic relations at a time when Nuevomexicano farmers were suffering a massive loss of land ownership to Anglo settlers.

Territorial officials wanted a water-management scheme that could move past the conflicts engendered by accommodation of multiple water institutions. In 1897 new legislation created an irrigation commission tasked with evaluating development projects and analyzing the need for further legislative change. The commission's first report argued that no statutory changes were needed, noting that New Mexico's water laws were "sufficiently just, progressive, and simple" to serve territorial needs.[15] In cases of conflict, the commission argued, courts could easily interpret the legal principles at issue and find equitable solutions that "brought peace to the whole community and established firmly the rights of each claimant" across a range of unique places with diverse physical and cultural geographic conditions.[16] The commission's report thus directly contradicted emerging federal reclamation policy, which prioritized comprehensive statutory prescriptions over adjudication of disputes by slow-moving courts. (Waiting even two months for a judge to hear and rule on a case about water rights could result in a total crop loss for one party or the other.) Federal officials, such as the Reclamation Service director, Elwood Mead, and President Theodore Roosevelt even weighed in against New Mexico's position, prompting commission members to reevaluate their stance.

In 1903 two competing bills made it to the floor of the territorial legislature, illustrating New Mexico's split thinking about how to proceed. In the prior decade, water-management authority had shifted back and forth from mayordomos to ditch commissioners, while the consequences for violating acequia rules shifted from fines to denial of water. A bill proposed in 1903 (the "Ortega" bill) rejected the denial of water as too drastic a consequence and outlined a restoration of mayordomo power above commissioners' authority. The competing "Fall" bill, however, went the other direction by expanding commissioners' power and weakening the mayordomo. The bills were discussed together in both legislative chambers, and both eventually passed with amendments that split their application geographically. The Ortega bill would be limited in application to the central counties of Bernalillo, Socorro, and Sierra.[17] Those three counties returned to a strong-mayordomo system for community ditches, in keeping with the traditional authoritarian style of water governance inherited from the Spanish and Mexican periods. In all other counties, the strong-commissioner system prevailed, pushing the community ditch toward a corporate governance mode. Over the following two decades, eight counties switched from the Fall to the Ortega system, indicating strong ongoing importance for the community ditch as an institution. But legislators did not give up on the idea of a sweeping water law that would smooth its path to political incorporation as a U.S. state.

A 1905 Law Creates the Territorial Irrigation Engineer

New Mexico adopted comprehensive water legislation in 1905. The new law followed Progressive principles, consolidating authority in a new expert agency—the Office of the Territorial Irrigation Engineer. Like other Progressive policies founded on measurement, expertise, and efficiency, it superseded local approaches and variations. And like other Progressive policies in general, it served the cause of settler colonialism.

The new statute stated explicitly that science would play a foundational role in water administration. According to the 1902 Reclamation Act, modernist science alone provided the means for maximizing efficiency and making determinations about beneficial resource use. This federal philosophy made its way into state and territorial legislation across the West very quickly, primarily because the federal government withheld irrigation funding until states adopted acceptable water legislation. The U.S. Reclamation Service even drafted a model water code for the Western states to follow, including the two signature elements that eventually anchored New Mexico's legislation: a permitting system and a state engineer.[18]

Under the new system, aspiring water users in New Mexico applied for water permits from the territorial irrigation engineer, who evaluated their requests in light of (a) the total water quantity available in the stream system, (b) the amount of water already claimed by legitimate water users, and (c) the actual amount of water needed for the claimant to beneficially use the water without impeding the public good. By statute, the new territorial irrigation engineer was required to make permitting decisions based on "careful measurement" and "reasonable information" gathered in surveys, fieldwork, and mapping of hydrologic, topographic, and other geographic conditions.[19] The Act specified numerous other details for how to make permitting decisions, including units of measurement, allowable uses of surplus waters, establishment of irrigation rights-of-way via eminent domain, and requirements that maps, plans, and surveys be included with every water application. All of these provisions originated from federal philosophy that saw rational, expert management as the key to efficient resource use and exploitation.

Since detailed information on streamflow and water use in New Mexico did not exist in 1905, however, the new law's commitment to scientific management actually made water administration more complex and difficult. Permit applications required claimants to submit maps and quantitative streamflow rates, which typically meant hiring an expensive surveyor. Accurate review of the applications required the territorial irrigation engineer to survey streamflow and confirm existing water users within the relevant watershed, both of which required significant time and labor. And when water claims came into conflict, the new law obligated the courts to parse quantitative evidence and arguments. Compared to the basic principles developed through territorial legislation between 1848 and 1905, the new law's provisions clearly would prolong dispute resolution.

The 1905 water law, then, did not really streamline anything other than the consolidation of water rights for massive irrigation projects. The new law made it easy to request a water permit in areas without much preexisting irrigation. After filing a written notice of intended irrigation at county court, prospective water users could begin using water immediately. As long as they did not impede others' existing rights, water claimants faced no limits other than the amount of water available in the stream system and their own ability to use it. Aspiring large-scale irrigators thus needed only to provide quantitative evidence that a proposed new water diversion would not harm existing users and would not waste water.

In order to accurately interpret and evaluate the quantitative evidence included in permit applications, the position of territorial irrigation engineer required a very specific type of scientific expertise. In accordance with federal reclamation policy, New Mexico's legislation required that the governor appoint an engineer with "theoretical knowledge and ... practical experience and skill" in water management.[20] Among his many official duties, the engineer had to "become conversant with the water-ways and the irrigable lands of New Mexico, and her needs as to irrigation matters; furnish reasonable information ... to the newspapers for the territory upon proper request, be the locating agent, and expert engineering advisor of the land commission, [and] give special instructions to all mayordomos, or water masters, as to measurement of water so as to secure a just and uniform distribution of said water."[21] The engineer was also required to work with federal government officials on Reclamation Service projects, measure all streamflow in New Mexico, and inspect all dams holding at least ten feet of water depth. No water official in New Mexico had ever held this range of responsibilities, even across a small local area.

The 1905 water law also created a "board of control" that tasked six irrigation commissioners with regional-level water administration. The governor appointed one commissioner from each of six water divisions, which were delineated in a somewhat geometric fashion. For example, Division I was established as "that portion of New Mexico within the water-shed of the Rio Grande down to the third standard parallel north, and the first guide meridian west."[22] The expert board was empowered to act in concert with the territorial irrigation engineer to "make all adjudications of water within New Mexico, subject to review by the district and supreme courts of the territory," while each individual commissioner was also responsible for "general supervision of the administration of irrigation matters in his division."[23] Together, the commissioners could also sit as an appeals board to review decisions by the territorial irrigation engineer regarding permitting and apportionment of public waters. Although an 1897 law had seated a three-member Irrigation Commission, before 1905 members had not represented specific geographic areas, nor had they possessed the authority to make decisions or render judgments. The previous commission was in fact purely advisory.

The authority invested in these new expert-level administrative positions changed the geographic scale of water-related decision-making in New Mexico. New layers of administration at both the territorial and regional scales displaced local personnel—mayordomos and small commissions—that had long been empowered by local elections to make decisions within a single stream system or basin. By increasing the complexity of water-management tasks and expanding the geographic range in which they were meant to be conducted, the new law thus disrupted centuries of tradition and created the need for a new type of expertise: engineering.

At the same time, the 1905 law contained specific provisions aimed at *preserving* existing traditional approaches to water administration. First, the law explicitly said that "local or community customs, rules, and regulations" would not be impeded so long as "such rules or regulations have for their object the economical use of water."[24] This provision was intended to avoid unnecessary conflict with existing Nuevomexicano communities, where communal ditch management was prevalent. As long as communities could meet a basic standard of efficiency ("economical use"), they could maintain their own norms outside the view of the expert territorial irrigation engineer. Second, the law allowed local determination in implementing *new* rules and regulations in cases where a majority of users agreed to adopt "harmonious local custom or customs, in the matter of water diversion and distribution which are not detrimental to the public welfare."[25] Finally, the 1905 law recognized special status for community ditches, holding them exempt from taxation and adjudication by the board of control.[26] The law gave the board of control power to "hear, determine, or adjudicate any rights affecting community ditches or acequias," but only in cases in which a very high bar was met: consent was acquired from "all parties interested."[27]

The 1905 water code thus indicates a complicated effort to adopt federal prescriptions while also responding to unique conditions in areas where community-based irrigation had dominated daily life for centuries. It made room for limited local variations in management, but it did not allow any local adjustments to modernist engineering standards. The statute specified units of measurement, including the "second foot" and "miner's inch" for flow rates and the "acre foot" for total volume. It noted that maps and plats submitted for court adjudications must be made "on a scale of not less than one inch to the mile" and with "substantial accuracy."[28] And it barred from appointment as territorial irrigation engineer any individual without a sufficient engineering pedigree: "No person shall be appointed to the position of territorial irrigation engineer who has not had such theoretical knowledge and such practical experience and skill as shall fit him for the position."[29] As a whole, these provisions created new obstacles and disadvantages for Indigenous and Nuevomexicano irrigators because they required new forms of measurement and certification that could not be completed without paying for "expert" assistance.

New Mexico's 1905 water law enacted a centralized permitting and administration system that displaced existing small-scale irrigation systems and used "efficiency" as an excuse to introduce massive, landscape-altering irrigation projects. Yet the first territorial irrigation engineer, David White, complained that it had not gone far enough. White regularly notified the territorial government that his office needed more resources and more authority to carry out its mission. He also criticized the law as insufficiently attuned to New Mexico's unique conditions: "The irrigation law as it is today ... is but a conglomerate of laws prevailing in different States where conditions are entirely unlike those of this Territory."[30] He argued that standardization based on a federal ideal created a handicap and impeded his ability to implement the new legislation. In 1907, at the end of his two-year term, White reported that his office had accomplished virtually nothing.

The 1907 Law Creates a Water-Management Complex

Territorial legislators heard White's grousing. They also noted that federal officials declared the 1905 law insufficient to support settlement, given its accommodation of noncommercial and non-Anglo irrigators.[31] Responding to these pressures, lawmakers revised the enabling statute in 1907 to make the Office of the Territorial Irrigation Engineer a fully independent and more powerful agency.

The 1907 law renamed New Mexico's water-management agency the Office of the Territorial Engineer and expanded its powers, increased its funding, and reinforced the importance of scientific decision-making in water administration. The new law clarified that it applied to all waters, "whether such be perennial, or torrential."[32] It reaffirmed prior appropriation as the legal basis for water rights, expanded the power of eminent domain for irrigation infrastructure, and increased the severability of water rights from land rights, all of which helped facilitate the flow of eastern capital into territorial settlement and agriculture. At the same time, the act included some provisions that accommodated existing tradition and increased local authority, indicating an attempt to better fuse new principles of rational and economic quantification with existing norms for community water management.

Most fundamentally, New Mexico's 1907 water code expanded the territorial engineer's authority to act on behalf of the public interest. Whereas the initial 1905 law had upheld prior appropriation and beneficial use as the joint basis for water rights, the new law added "public interest" as a justification for water management. The law thus expanded the Engineer's power by requiring the office to serve the public interest in ways that went beyond reviewing irrigation permits as an arbiter of individual private interests. This very broad responsibility included (1) quantifying public waters, (2) evaluating existing water rights claims, (3) overseeing the appropriation process, (4) ensuring the safety of irrigation infrastructure, (5) supporting the courts in the orderly adjudication of water rights, (6) communicating information to water users throughout the territory, and (7) working with the federal government to identify reservoir sites and withdraw federally targeted waters from the state distribution process.

In consideration for this comprehensive and technically demanding workload, the 1907 law required that the territorial engineer be a "technically qualified and experienced hydraulic engineer."[33] It gave the office authority to hire a substantial technical staff and greatly expanded the Engineer's budget. It allowed him to collect fees for activities like filing permits, surveying stream basins, reviewing maps, and conducting safety inspections for irrigation infrastructure.[34] In return for this larger budget, the Engineer's portfolio expanded in terms of both workload and technical expectations. For example, the Engineer was newly required to assist counties in "making preliminary surveys and establishing systems of drainage, or any other engineering work" on top of the existing responsibility to make hydrographic surveys "of each stream system and source of water supply in the Territory, beginning with those most used for irrigation."[35]

While increasing the territorial engineer's power and responsibility, the 1907 law reduced the power of the board of control. Whereas the original 1905 board included six members appointed from six geographic regions of New Mexico, the new board included three at-large members appointed by the governor. The board maintained its role as an official appeals body, with the power to summon witnesses and compel the Engineer to "transmit or produce . . . papers, maps, plats, field notes and other data in his possession."[36] And its decisions were final unless appealed to the district court. The individual members of the board, however, no longer retained any powers to oversee water administration within their own regions.

The 1907 law did not eliminate local authority over water administration. It added a new provision for the territorial engineer to appoint "water masters" to individual water districts under certain circumstances. In cases where the majority of water users in a district made written application to the territorial engineer, he was obliged to appoint a water master who would take charge of water-management decisions.[37] The territorial engineer could also appoint a water master to any district to ensure public safety, even if water users did not make a request. Water masters received their pay from the county governments containing their district, but they reported directly to the territorial engineer on water availability, water shortfalls, and problems with water apportionment, at least annually at the end of every irrigation season.[38] Water users in each district had the power to appeal acts and decisions of the water master to the territorial engineer and, above that, to the board of control.[39] By adding this provision for water masters, the 1907 legislation created two tiers of meaningful water authority—one responsive to local priorities (the water masters) and one focused on territorial prerogatives (the territorial engineer). And it did away with the geometrical boundaries for water districts, giving the territorial engineer power to set boundaries that conformed to natural watersheds.[40]

Despite this new geography of water administration, New Mexico continued to prioritize centralized administration and expert management at the expense of local personnel. The 1907 water law allowed engineers and surveyors to enter private lands for activities associated with irrigation development and reservoir siting. This privilege applied not just to government engineers, but to *any* engineers, elevating the rights of those with technical credentials above those of other private citizens. Specifically, the statute declared that "engineers and surveyors of the United States, the Territory and of any person, firm or corporation shall have the right to enter upon the lands and waters of the Territory and of private persons and of private and public corporations" in order to carry out their work in "making hydrographic surveys and examinations and surveys necessary for selecting and locating suitable sites and routes."[41]

Often, water engineers and surveyors entered these lands with the added backing of eminent domain. The 1907 law offered broad rights for irrigation developers to take and acquire land for "the construction, maintenance and operation of reservoirs, canals, diches [sic], flumes, acqueducts [sic], pipe lines or other works for the storage or conveyance of water for beneficial uses."[42] Eminent domain could even be used simply to enlarge existing structures, or to connect infrastructure components into broader irrigation networks. To emphasize that these provisions should be used to support economic expansion, rather than simply to ensure basic water access or to improve public safety, the law explicitly noted that eminent domain should be used in the same way it could be used for "railroad, telegraph, telephone and other public uses and purposes."[43]

Overall, the 1907 law included numerous provisions meant to encourage irrigation-based settlement. It offered a new ideal protocol for the adjudication of water rights, charging the territorial engineer with surveying "each stream system and source of water supply in the Territory" and then turning over findings and "all other data in his possession" to the territory's attorney general (AG).[44] The AG, in turn, would then bring suit against water users so that the courts could conclusively determine all valid water rights. According to the legislative text, court-based adjudication would identify available waters that could then be allocated to prospective settlers.[45] In a related move, the new law allowed landowners to sever water rights from the land without losing their priority date.[46] This made it possible—and profitable—for irrigators to sell a portion of their water rights without selling all of their land. This provision incentivized long-term landholders (or their heirs) to transfer valuable water rights with early priority dates to incoming settlers, who would otherwise be disadvantaged by junior priority dates.[47]

The territorial engineer sat at the center of these settlement goals, providing and reviewing data to support the settler project. After 1907, no one in the territory of New Mexico could get a water right without applying to the engineer's office for a permit, and no one could prove an existing water right without providing information about water use and water flow to the engineer through the adjudication process. Data requirements included the "information, maps, field notes, plans and specifications . . . made from actual surveys and measurements."[48] In cases of large diversions (using more than five hundred second-feet of water) or large infrastructure (dams more than thirty feet high), the territorial engineer had a right to collect extra information on his own before considering the permit. The territorial engineer then evaluated all of this information from a technical perspective, rendering judgment on whether the public interest would be met or undermined by the proposed use.

In addition to assigning the territorial engineer this role as an arbiter of knowledge, the 1907 law gave him broad authority to compel certain actions among water users. In cases where a project would store or carry more water than the owner could beneficially use, the territorial engineer could require owners to sell the excess water rights "for a reasonable price."[49] Once the territorial engineer determined that water was available and approved a water application, he also had the power to declare an application forfeited if the owner did not make sufficient progress (completing one-fifth of the construction work within one-half of the allotted construction time), or to extend the timeline "due to physical and engineering difficulties which could not have been reasonably anticipated."[50] The territorial engineer had the power to make safety inspections, require installations or repairs to infrastructure, and instruct ditch owners to install headgates and lockable measuring devices "of a design approved by the territorial engineer" that the engineer could control himself.[51] The territorial engineer's power to compel these actions rested in his ability to void priority dates for water rights based on noncompliance. The territorial engineer also had police powers related to the protection of measurement instruments. He could arrest people for the following misdemeanors: "interfering with or injuring or destroying" gates, locks, and measuring devices; using someone else's water; wasting water; starting a diversion project without a permit; and obstructing someone else's water works.[52] Although the 1907 Act claimed to protect local customs for water management (so long as they were oriented toward "economical use of water"), nothing was allowed to impede the work or authority of the territorial engineer and water masters.[53]

Vernon Sullivan, New Mexico's first territorial engineer, worked tirelessly to expand, define, and reinforce the office's power over time. Starting in 1907, he collaborated with USGS to establish a comprehensive stream-gauging program that would fulfill the vision that began at the old Embudo camp. Like those young engineers who had suffered on the banks of the Rio Grande, Sullivan's staff went into the field to catalog, review, and track ongoing irrigation projects throughout New Mexico. Sullivan himself reviewed permit applications, made water allocation decisions, challenged overestimates in claimants' stated irrigation needs, and tried to fend off speculators to ensure New Mexico's water was put to beneficial and economic use. He saw a number of his decisions overturned by the post-1907 board of control, or by the courts, but the statute proved robust.[54]

The Question of Indigenous Water Rights

At the federal level, legal questions about Indigenous water rights began to evolve during this same time. Those evolutions did little to slow the spread of Progressive water-management norms across the American West, and they never posed a significant threat to the new settler water administration in New Mexico. In the middle decades of the nineteenth century, as the U.S. government aggressively asserted stewardship over Indigenous territory, federal bureaucrats handled questions about Indigenous water rights as administrative concerns. But a 1908 U.S. Supreme Court case, *Winters v. United States*, moved the topic into the legal realm. In *Winters*, the high court confirmed that Indigenous nations retained their water rights even when they agreed to treaties forcing them onto reservations.[55]

Although some saw the *Winters* ruling as a protection of Indigenous rights, however, it was never meant to override the prevailing logic of settler colonialism. As the critical geographer Andrew Curley argues, it is no coincidence that the first delineation of Indigenous water rights under U.S. law defined them as subject not to aboriginal control but to federal administration.[56] *Winters* emerged from the same colonial logic that supported the creation of New Mexico's Office of the Territorial Engineer: it was focused on quantifying and enclosing Indigenous rights within carefully circumscribed limits, opening them to purchase, settlement, and exchange within a commercial structure.[57] At the time it was written, the *Winters* decision did not measurably contribute to Indigenous autonomy or self-sufficiency, and decades of activism throughout the twentieth century did not produce any meaningful expansions of water rights for Indigenous nations. In fact, settler officials and politicians quickly manipulated the rights established by *Winters* to Indigenous nations' detriment, quantifying Indigenous water needs at minimal levels and withholding other federal benefits in order to pressure Indigenous leaders into legal settlements, which usually forced them to bargain with their *Winters* rights.[58] Recently, decolonial activists have challenged *Winters*' colonial premise, reframing and claiming quantified water rights as part of Indigenous resurgence and nation-building efforts.[59] But at the time of its origin, the decision did little to stem Anglo settlers' speculative commercial interests or to prevent them from commandeering waters on or near Indigenous lands.

Conclusions

During the territorial period, New Mexico's water laws evolved to support twin newcomers: large-scale irrigated agriculture and Anglo settlement. But the transition from small-scale, community-based water management to expert-led centralized administration was not easy. Over several decades, territorial officials tried to make changes "without disturbing time-honored customs," but they found it an impossible task.[60] New administrative codes based in Anglo-American law and custom largely took the place of Nuevomexicano and Indigenous approaches based on shared labor and governance. New rules assumed that technology and capital investment would prove the backbone for irrigation management, rather than mutual support and a barter economy. By the time New Mexico became a state in 1912, its approach to water administration had been transformed. Comprehensive water laws anchored a powerful governance vision based in settler colonialism.

As is often true of settler-colonial environmental policy, the introduction of new legal codes added significant complexity and complication to New Mexico's water administration. Under the Spanish and Mexican systems, an authoritative individual (the mayordomo) made decisions about how water would be shared within each shared irrigation network. This straightforward system spread responsibility across numerous legitimized individuals, each of whom operated within the constraints of shared culture and local custom. Anglo common law replaced this approach with a different simple system (prior appropriation), giving the highest priority to the first irrigators in any stream basin. But the Progressive Era brought a new philosophy that went well beyond chronology as the basis of water management. New Mexico's 1905 and 1907 water laws saddled a single political appointee with the responsibility for measuring all water flow in the territory, rationalizing water permits to maximize commercial efficiency and public benefit while simultaneously providing input to both private and public irrigation projects.

Despite ascending to absurd heights of complexity, the 1905 and 1907 water statutes effectively facilitated Anglo settlement in New Mexico. If territorial legislators intended to make irrigation investment seem "safe," from a regulatory point of view, they achieved that goal early. Investors flocked to New Mexico to build reservoirs, construct canals, and expand ditches. They came in such numbers and built so much water-storage infrastructure that one whole aspect of the engineer's mandate—administering water supply in times of shortage—went long untested. Reclamation activities developed new water supplies in virtually every watershed, stream drainage, and river basin. By the 1930s, investors additionally turned their attention to groundwater extraction, perceiving almost limitless water supplies in the Rio Grande's central valley. Progressive Era laws maximized water development and prevented water shortages for almost a century, despite the rapid influx of new settlers. Only now, as the reality of climate change looms, and as predictions crystallize around a certainty of future regional extremes of warming and drying, has the court adjudication of water rights become a truly urgent priority for New Mexico.

In today's New Mexico, many Indigenous and Nuevomexicano irrigators perceive the current administrative process of adjudication as a form of cultural imperialism enacted by the Office of the State Engineer.[61] As this chapter has confirmed, their perception is accurate. New Mexico's territorial-era environmental-management policy started from the foundational goal of enabling settlement for new kinds of people, bringing new economic and cultural priorities with them. Even when legislators crafted laws that seemed to accommodate New Mexico's unique water-related cultural history, they were making a careful calculation about how to facilitate Anglo settlement without stoking conflicts that might scare away capital investors or impede statehood. The 1907 water law promised a new agricultural era and provided a key rationale for U S statehood. In the process, it overran existing residents' sovereignty and autonomy with a redefinition of expertise that still underlies water law and management in New Mexico today.

✶ 5 ✶
Knowledge

SCIENCE FOR SETTLEMENT'S SAKE

It took decades for legislators to encode Progressive resource-management models into law, and even longer for newly appointed "experts" to fulfill their assignments on the ground. Engineers and bureaucrats had no clear guidance for how to accomplish their statutory mandates, so they experimented with different techniques to increase New Mexico's water supply, attract investors, and promote agricultural settlement. In their quest, water officials spent a lot of time producing, controlling, disseminating, and negotiating knowledge. This chapter focuses on the knowledge work of New Mexico's first formal water managers, from the Commission on Irrigation and Water Rights to the Office of the Territorial Engineer. How did these "expert" water officials perceive their responsibilities? How did they enact their authority through new positions based on expertise in hydrology, agronomy, engineering, market economics, and geography?

As described in their own words, expert water managers accepted the mantle of settler colonialism but toiled to deliver on its promises. The Progressive mandate to manage water on the basis of expert knowledge continually ran aground on the shoals of settler ignorance. In following politicians' promise of water and profit, farmers from the eastern United States ventured into an unfamiliar climate and landscape where they did not know how to succeed at farming. Water engineers thus found themselves navigating a perilous path. At first they enthusiastically aided and abetted Anglo settlers, using all available administrative and scientific resources. When the hoped-for settlement rush started to materialize, however, engineers found themselves frantically trying to steer settlers away from disaster. Along this tortuous trajectory, engineers' knowledge work both strengthened and obscured the United States' colonial grip on New Mexico.

Reading Between the Lines

Official reports provide the best resource for understanding how engineering personnel perceived their roles and defined their administrative duties against the backdrop of settler colonialism. The early Commission on Irrigation and Water Rights provided regular reports to the governor of New Mexico, as did the various offices of the territorial irrigation engineer. The governor in turn relayed these reports both to the territorial legislature and to the federal government. In a typical report, the reporting entity explains its duties, accounts for its funding, details its activities, and submits entreaties for additional resources, personnel, or authority. This chapter is based on detailed analysis of several sets of primary sources: the Commission's annual reports to the governor from 1899 to 1912, the engineer's biennial reports and hydrographic surveys from 1905 to 1911, and the New Mexico governor's annual reports to the Secretary of the Interior from 1900 to 1911, which often contained or described other officials' reports sent to the governor.[1] Throughout the text that follows, I include many exact quotes from bureaucratic missives, allowing readers to hear government officials' own words as they describe their commitment to expertise in New Mexico's specific political and cultural context.

Beyond their description of scientific practices and bureaucratic goals, official reports offer two key insights. First, the reports themselves played an inescapably political role. While accounting for their activities and costs, water managers and engineers used administrative reports to send important political messages. Reports from commissioners and engineers to the governor curried his favor in the territory's budget, for example, and reports from the governor to the Department of the Interior made the case for New Mexico's statehood at every opportunity. Second, official reports reveal that Progressive ideals for rational resource management proved difficult and often impossible to implement. Water engineers explicitly linked their technical work—hydrographic surveying, stream gauging, dam inspection, permit review, and dissemination of knowledge about aridlands cultivation techniques—to the broader goal of increasing Anglo settlement and making New Mexico more "American." Yet even as they lauded engineering with lofty language, they paradoxically painted a picture of frustration and failure. Whether surveying potential reservoir sites, evaluating water permits, measuring hydrologic flows, circulating information on irrigation techniques to farmers, supporting reservoir and canal projects on Indigenous lands, or providing information to the courts to settle water-related disputes, engineers rarely achieved their technical goals.

Reading between the lines of each report's explicit categories and topics, we find abundant "knowledge work": efforts focused on defining, producing, and legitimizing knowledge. The remainder of this chapter focuses in detail on the numerous ways officials conducted knowledge work in water administration. The most common agency activities and the most prominent report narratives reveal that water engineering intersected with knowledge in data science, engineering, geography, economics, agronomy, hydrology, and public administration. This complicated knowledge network played an important role in the settler-colonial project, lending authority to Progressive policies and displacing non-Anglos from water management to make room for new settlers. It also clouded the Progressive ideal of rational resource management, introducing endless inefficiencies that made it virtually impossible for irrigation engineers to implement a purely scientific paradigm for water management in New Mexico.

Data Science: Hydrography as a Key to Settlement

As discussed in chapter 3, the federal approach to natural resources at the turn of the twentieth century was based on Progressives' deep commitment to science and engineering. Water management, specifically, rested on a cornerstone of stream gauging and hydrographic data. So too in New Mexico. All of the work envisioned and undertaken by territorial water managers hinged directly on their ability to produce quantifiable information about New Mexico's river flows and environmental features. Land surveyors had begun mapping New Mexico's topography and cataloging its landscape features almost as soon as the United States acquired the territory in 1848. A half century later, however, there was still no parallel effort to collect comprehensive information about water supplies.

When New Mexico's territorial assembly established a Commission on Irrigation and Water Rights in 1897, the very first governor-appointed commissioners immediately identified the lack of "reliable and instructive data" as a critical issue.[2] Governor Miguel Otero, a Nuevomexicano elite who served three terms as the first Nuevomexicano governor of New Mexico, staked his political career on the pursuit of technological modernization as a path toward New Mexico statehood.[3] Unlike previous governors, who supported the territorial assembly's attempts to preserve and accommodate Nuevomexicano culture and practice in water management, Otero focused on reform as a foundation for political enfranchisement. He charged the Commission with evaluating New Mexico's water laws so they could be updated to encourage large-scale irrigated agriculture. The commissioners' first report argued, however, that "the greatest need of New

Mexico upon the subject of irrigation and water rights at the present time is not new legislation, but accurate information" about streamflow, storage capacity, and reclamation potential.[4] Underscoring the urgency they felt, commissioners decided to divert their small budget to hire a civil engineer, covering administrative and travel expenses out of their own pockets.

In their first report to the governor, commissioners made three arguments to appeal for a territory-wide data-collection program. First, they argued that a recent federal promise of agricultural land grants (through the Carey Act) had set a sale price that could never be realized in New Mexico without irrigation, and that it was impossible to determine which lands were suitable for irrigation without systematic data. Second, they predicted that ongoing appropriations of Rio Grande water would eventually overrun the source and create an interstate conflict with Colorado, which Colorado was likely to win based on its access to superior data produced by "its well-organized and liberally supported State engineering department."[5] Finally, commissioners argued that their own original mandate—to evaluate existing water law and propose new legislation—could be met only if they had access to data produced through "systematic observation and record of facts, often extending through months and years."[6]

Eventually, the Commission managed to wrangle additional funding from the governor for data-collection activities. Its 1903 report included "accurate and trustworthy" weather and crop records for the first time,[7] and it proposed a plan to use revenue from land sales and pasturage contracts "to employ a thoroughly competent engineer and all expert assistants necessary ... and in this manner gather scientific and reliable data" for the benefit of those considering reservoir projects.[8] Governor Otero highlighted the Commission's work in several reports to the Secretary of the Interior, noting that the territory of New Mexico was also working with federal engineers from the Reclamation Survey. In 1905 Otero reported that "sufficient data have been gathered and published" to determine where to build reservoirs "which at a minimum cost would benefit the greatest number of people."[9] He argued that New Mexico's improvements in data collection, recording, and circulation proved the territory's political readiness to become a state.[10]

The brand-new Office of the Territorial Irrigation Engineer, however, was less bullish about data sufficiency in that same year. Many lauded the legislature's 1905 law for its creation of an irrigation engineering office and water-permitting system, both based on scientific principles for water management. But in his very brief first report to Governor Otero after just a few months in his position, the newly appointed irrigation engineer, David White, lamented that "New Mexico has no topographical maps, and little of public use ... in a hydraulic way." He described his own "consciousness of his nudity as to data upon which to base an opinion" and identified "the collection of data [as] the first step in the line of his duties."[11] After two years running the engineering office, White was *still* worried. He reported that his office could not yet produce the data needed to "bring to New Mexico a worthy and desirable class of people" owing to handicaps to the office's independence, authority, and funding.[12] White proposed a revision to the enabling legislation that had created his office, and the territorial assembly duly passed new legislation in 1907 to restructure it.

New Mexico's second engineer thus enjoyed additional resources for data collection, but he continued to struggle with data sufficiency. In 1908 Vernon Sullivan, who took over from David White and went on to hold the position of territorial engineer for four years, characterized New Mexico's lack of hydrographic data as a serious impediment to settlement. According to Sullivan, New Mexico desperately needed more stream-gauging stations, which provided "the only sure ground upon which the Territorial Engineer can proceed in the distribution of water through application."[13] He included a report written by USGS District Engineer W. B. Freeman, who argued that "capital is not disposed to invest in power and irrigation schemes ... unless considerable is known of the flow of a stream."[14] Sullivan agreed. He pursued a comprehensive plan for compiling and integrating existing hydrographic data while also establishing a framework for "the measuring of streams and collection of general hydrographic data upon a permanent and working basis."[15] In cooperation with the USGS, Sullivan's office reestablished abandoned gauging stations, added new ones in promising areas, and reached a maintenance agreement under which the USGS provided equipment, salaries, and travel expenses for gauge readers, while the New Mexico engineer coordinated local arrangements.[16]

If Sullivan was right in 1908 when he wrote that access to systematic gauge data was critical ("the only sure ground") for ruling on water-permit applications, it was even more urgently needed for settling legal conflicts between water users under the new law. One of Governor Otero's successors, George Curry, reported to the Secretary of the Interior in 1908 that scientific data was invaluable to the courts, as judges could request hydrographic surveys from the engineer's office whenever water supply or hydrologic relations were at issue in a lawsuit.[17] To provide comprehensive data for even a small drainage basin, however, required significant time and effort. For example, in 1907 the district court requested a survey of the Hondo stream system, a small tributary of the Pecos River, to settle a dispute stemming from a railroad company's attempt to purchase all waters in the area for domestic use associated with the rail line. To comply with the court's data request, the engineer's office undertook "installation of about 150 weirs and 10 or 15 gauging stations, besides a topographical survey of the entire system."[18] Sullivan reported this work as a great success, neglecting to mention that this enormous effort returned only a meager result. To assist the court with a single lawsuit, the territorial engineer spent almost a full year completing hydrographic surveys and processing data for one small stream system that supported very few settlers. In a remarkable understatement, Sullivan noted that "the making of maps and calculations of the areas of cultivated land, the flow of water in many ditches, irrigating same, etc. from notes sent in by the field force, has occupied a great deal of time."[19]

In addition to responding to requests from the courts, the territorial engineer's office also responded to map requests from private investors and the wider public. The engineer's office relied on existing USGS topographic surveys or conducted their own fieldwork to generate maps of elevation, landforms, and crop locations along stream reaches suitable for irrigation. The U.S. Weather Bureau provided data on temperature and precipitation throughout the territory, and chemists at the New Mexico College of Agriculture and Mechanic Arts (later renamed New Mexico State University) analyzed water samples to evaluate water quality. Field staff from the engineer's office analyzed soil characteristics and talked with farmers about their water use and crop success in some areas, combining this information with detailed maps that had been collected by the USGS Reclamation Survey in federal project areas. The engineer then combined all of this information to the extent possible, with a goal of producing comprehensive maps for use in water management. As an appendix to his 1909 report, Sullivan published tables compiling all known hydrographic data for New Mexico, arguing that the territory's lack of water-supply records could be offset somewhat by compiling "scattered records or data upon the various creeks and rivers in the territory" from federal agencies into "one common form" that included estimated monthly discharge, in acre-feet, for each gauging station.[20]

Curry's successor, Governor William Mills, commended these efforts, reporting to the federal government in 1910 that "New Mexico is doing more in the line of collecting accurate, official stream-flow records than any State on the eastern slope of the Rocky Mountains."[21] The territorial engineer's report that year had asserted that only engineers could understand New Mexico's water supply because of their access to data. Claiming that "practically 90 per cent" of water supply estimates were incorrect exaggerations, "even among men who make the measurement of water a business,"[22] Sullivan aligned himself with the USGS district engineer,

W.B. Freeman, who had written that the engineer's job was to combat "chronic" ignorance among water promoters. Sullivan's office threw itself into the completion of hydrographic surveys for the Hondo and Rayado stream systems, which he reprinted in full in his 1910 report "to show the effectiveness, accuracy, methods used, facts determined, results, etc." from the two comprehensive data-collection efforts.[23]

Sullivan's 1910 report also included flow measurements from various sinkholes in the Pecos basin, water-quality data based on chemical analysis from multiple streams, and an update on efforts to improve stream gauging throughout the territory. With technical support from the USGS engineering staff in both Colorado and Washington, D.C., along with financial support from federal and territorial agencies as well as private commercial and individual sources, Sullivan proudly reported that daily records were collected at thirty different gauging stations, some of which used state-of-the art automatic gauges. By 1911 the territory had expanded its network to include a total of forty-two gauges that collected hydrographic data on dozens of principal streams.

In reporting on this work, New Mexico's engineers frequently touted the ideal of comprehensive data and cartography as having "inestimable value,"[24] but it is clear from those same reports that most of their value was political. The celebrated hydrographic surveys of the Hondo and Rayado streams are remarkable for their smallness. Their value may have been "inestimable" for the scattered settlers using Hondo and Rayado water, but what about the much larger Pecos River? Or the Canadian River? And no mention is made in any report about completing a hydrographic survey of the mighty Rio Grande. To achieve the political standard of truly "rational" water-permitting decisions or to resolve legal conflicts over water rights based on quantitative evidence, engineers needed to collect comprehensive data regarding hydrologic conditions across the *entire* New Mexico territory. That never happened. The costs of data collection and compilation at a territorial level proved insurmountable. Hydrographers grappled with only the smallest streams, only in response to court cases, and only in an area dominated by Anglo settlers.

Engineering Knowledge: Redefining Expertise

In all of his reports to the U.S. Secretary of the Interior, Governor Otero praised rational water engineering as the key tool for spurring Anglo settlement and making New Mexico an "American" territory worthy of full statehood. He compared data-driven irrigation to other evidence of economic development: improvements in public education, an increase in the number of newspapers, the establishment of churches, and the extension of rail lines and roadways. But perhaps more important, Otero and other officials used engineering expertise as a yardstick for measuring the backwardness of non-Anglo communities.

Despite their long history as irrigators in the New Mexico territory, non-Anglo farmers invariably appeared in official reports as uncivilized or untamed. Both Indigenous and Nuevomexicano irrigators typically prioritized human-made infrastructure over machine-produced structures, community subsistence over individual profit, topographically responsive design over landscape alteration, and observational knowledge over mathematical modeling. We know now that traditional irrigators possessed deep knowledge of climatic, ecological, and hydrologic conditions in New Mexico.[25] However, Anglo engineers found it easy to characterize Pueblo farmers and acequia parciantes as objects rather than subjects of the civilizing force of irrigation because non-Anglos did not cultivate engineering expertise or value Progressive water-management institutions. Official reports simply had nothing to say about Indigenous and Nuevomexicano farmers' understanding of hydrology, agronomy, ecology, and other scientific topics. Their knowledge was nearly invisible to the newcomers.

Official reports stripped non-Anglo communities of their knowledge resources, characterizing them instead as threats or inconvenient obstacles. Governor Otero's 1902 report to the Secretary of the Interior admitted that a majority of territorial residents (144,000) were of Spanish or Mexican descent and were "well scattered throughout the Territory." Along with a minority (12,700) of Indigenous residents—Pueblo people "living in village communities of their own" and Apaches and Navajos on reservations—the total number of non-Anglo residents made up about two-thirds of the territorial population.[26] Governor Otero reassured his readers at the Department of the Interior, however, that non-Anglo inhabitants were "rapidly assimilating with the newcomer" through a linguistic shift that saw "the younger generation rapidly amalgamating with the complex American [English] of Anglo-Saxon, Teutonic, Celtic, and other origins."[27] Just three years later, Otero reported that less than half of New Mexico's population was of Spanish or Indigenous descent and that the use of English was rapidly increasing. His report was forthright about the goal of New Mexico's settlement wave: "A few more decades will witness the complete amalgamation of the native people, both as to language and as to customs, with the newcomers of Anglo-Saxon origin."[28]

Governor Otero credited this demographic shift to the expansion of irrigation. He drew sharp contrasts between Anglo settlers' scientific irrigation methods and non-Anglo communities' traditional approaches, praising engineering knowledge for bringing a new dawn to a backward land. Referring to Nuevomexicano towns and villages in the upper reaches of the Rio Grande watershed, for example, the governor noted that "farmers in this valley, among whom those of mixed Spanish and Indian descent predominate, have followed traditional customs and show little energy or skill. There lands are tilled in the most laborious fashion, largely by hand, and the returns are small."[29] His report acclaimed new settlers from the eastern United States, on the other hand, for "building up new agricultural communities of considerable importance" through engineering expertise and the collection of hydrographic data.[30] Official reports thus paradoxically lauded New Mexico as one of the oldest and most promising irrigated districts in the United States while simultaneously minimizing or discrediting irrigation practices that existed before the arrival of Anglo settlers.

On Indigenous lands, water administrators classified irrigation projects as "remedial" efforts, distinct from the economic-development opportunities prized by Anglo settlers. The territorial engineer, in fact, took limited responsibility for irrigation projects outside Anglo settlement areas. The federal superintendent assigned to oversee irrigation initiatives for New Mexico's Pueblos and Jicarilla Apache reservation aggressively dismissed those communities' irrigation knowledge and infrastructure. In 1901 Superintendent John Harper reported in detail to Governor Otero about an irrigation failure at the Pueblo of San Ildefonso, where the population was "on the verge of starvation" because ditches had run dry repeatedly and ruined the crops four years in a row. Although community members had been working on a new ditch, he reported, they could never complete the project "on account of a mistaken idea of where the water would run."[31] In 1903 he had a similar story from the Pueblo of Cochiti: residents had "for centuries" been rebuilding a dam in the channel bed to raise water levels to ditch height, "but their work was never more than a partial success and often a failure" when spring freshets or summer floods damaged the dams or washed them away entirely.[32] Harper's reports repeatedly blamed a shortage of critical irrigation infrastructure on Indigenous ignorance and called for new dams and canals built by Anglo engineers.

None of Harper's assessments acknowledged that the Indigenous communities in question did not desire permanent irrigation infrastructure. By annually constructing temporary diversion structures, residents had long engaged in a labor-efficient practice of subsistence agriculture. It was only when large-scale Anglo projects began to change hydrologic regimes across numerous watersheds that this practice became unsustainable.[33] Anglo-led irrigation engineering thus actually *caused* most of the problems that federal and territorial officials used as justification for the commissioning of new formulaic engineered "solutions." In the short term, Superintendent Harper's projects were considered remedial successes, but many eventually ended as failures. The notorious Zuni Reservoir, for example, "filled with silt at a more rapid rate than any other major reservoir in the Southwest," becoming useless in just three decades and serving for many more as a federal laughingstock.[34]

Beyond the supposed infrastructure problem, federal reports also identified water governance as an area of struggle for Pueblo communities. In 1904 the U.S. Special Attorney for the Pueblo Indians of New Mexico reported to Governor Otero that he had represented Pueblo interests in a number of lawsuits, fully half of which involved water and irrigation. He indicated that friction between longtime residents and newer arrivals (both Nuevomexicano and American) revolved around water issues, and he commented on the difficulty of counseling his clients "concerning their duties toward the American and Mexican population residing in the vicinity of their pueblos and concerning the property laws of the United States and the Territory."[35] Otero's successor as governor, Herbert Hagerman, in his 1906 report to the Department of the Interior quoted an Anglo federal judge and "Indian agent" who ascribed the conflicts to the Pueblo peoples' being "unaccustomed to the constant touch of the hand of a superior government."[36] This view was common among federal Indian agents, and among Progressive elites more generally.

Governor Hagerman himself was a rare outlier who saw things differently from many of his fellow Anglo elites. He agreed that Anglos showed exceptional success in irrigated agriculture and economic development, but he also acknowledged the racial animus behind territorial water legislation. Hagerman reprinted statements in his 1906 report that identified the cause of Pueblo-involved water litigation as repeated "trespasses upon their anciently acquired water rights," especially by "native Mexican" communities that reportedly held deep prejudices against Pueblo peoples. Hagerman's report also reprinted statements pointing out the irony of New Mexico's territorial legislature's making it illegal for Pueblo Indians to vote at acequia elections when "many of the oldest and best irrigating ditches of the Territory were constructed and had been for many years in use before Caucasians had settled in the vicinity of the Indian villages."[37] Publication of these statements and others cost Hagerman politically, despite his overall support for the Progressive mission to improve efficiency in both government and resource management. During his short stint as governor he continually found himself at odds with New Mexico's wealthiest and most influential men, who convinced President Theodore Roosevelt to remove him from office unceremoniously after just one year.[38]

Hagerman's contentious views on the expertise of non-Anglo irrigators throw into stark relief the attitudes of his contemporaries, who based their approach to irrigation on deep assumptions about the superiority of Anglo engineering knowledge. According to most territorial and federal officials, the sole purpose of irrigation in New Mexico was to enable Anglo settlement. Before the Office of the Territorial Irrigation Engineer even existed, annual reports from Governor Otero to the U.S. Secretary of the Interior's office explicitly characterized irrigation work as a demographic project. He used pioneer tropes to cast irrigation as a civilizing force with the power to tame both recalcitrant landscapes and non-Anglo peoples: "First, nature, and then the Indian, only less pitiless, had to be subdued [and] to-day even the Mohave and Colorado deserts and kindred wastes have been made to yield tributes of corn and wine to the dominion of man."[39] Otero's comments echoed manifest-destiny narratives used by white Americans at that time to justify their expansion and conquest of western North America.[40] But Otero's reports elevated engineers to a more prominent position in the narrative than Anglo pioneers, lauding their technoscientific expertise: "Where the pioneer has gone and died, the engineer follows, 'opens rivers in high places,' science smiles, and the desert blooms."[41]

Geographic Knowledge: Optimizing Settlement

All places are not equal, in agricultural terms. Differences in slope, soil quality, temperature range, precipitation seasonality, and water availability influence the potential success of agricultural endeavors. Equally important to the variations in environmental geography are the lenses of the geographical imagination, which determine both how peoples conceive their belonging in certain places and how outsiders dismiss or supplant those claims to belonging by characterizing some peoples and landscapes as inherently superior or inferior. Historians of geography have shown not only that the discipline of geography was born from a colonial desire to map, catalog, and control territory, but also that the geographical imagination has proved to be one of its most useful and enduring tools.[42] In New Mexico, geographical questions—and imaginations—proved critical to the Anglo settlement project.

Different landscapes call for different decisions: whether to irrigate instead of relying on dry farming, whether to use surface water instead of drilling wells, which crops to plant, how much water to use, how best to conserve soil moisture, and many others. In accordance with a Progressive vision of engineering-led resource management, New Mexico's officials expressed an unwavering belief that every decision and aspect of agricultural production could be optimized through the "systematization of all matters pertaining to water supply and irrigation."[43] The first step, to "determine projects which at a minimum cost would benefit the greatest number of people," required an analysis of geographic suitability.[44] Anglo settlers proved largely inept at this kind of analysis, however, requiring considerable intervention from the territorial engineer. In his work to optimize settlement locations and thereby maximize economic development and commercial production, New Mexico's lead engineer circulated geographical knowledge as a method of combating ignorance among settlers.

Many farmers arriving from the eastern United States chose to settle in New Mexico's eastern plains, where irrigation water was available from the Pecos or Canadian Rivers. But others went to isolated plains or small eastern valleys entirely devoid of surface water, rolling the dice on dry farming. The territorial engineer maintained a policy "not to encourage immigration into those districts which have not been thoroughly tested," yet settlers flouted it egregiously.[45] Some were after easy homestead claims, and lands outside irrigable valleys appeared unlikely to provoke claim contestation. Others relied on politicians' and boosters' boasts that New Mexico was an agricultural wonderland. Governor Otero himself wrote in 1905 that "it has been proven by careful laboratory and field work that 8 inches of rainfall are sufficient to grow good crops, providing the water is all utilized."[46] This kind of boosterism vexed the territorial engineer because it projected scientific confidence while glossing over the grievous difficulties of using "all" water or accounting for its unpredictable timing.

During his tenure as territorial engineer, Vernon Sullivan and his staff worked frantically to direct settlement to places where irrigation was most likely to produce ample harvests. They taught settlers to consider local geographic conditions as a key element in deciding which crops to plant, how best to tend the soil for moisture conservation, and how and when to apply irrigation water. In Sullivan's eyes, soil moisture was one of the most important, least understood, and unfortunately ignored factors in maximizing agricultural productivity. "It must be remembered that the conserving of water not only means the construction of reservoirs but also the conserving of the moisture after applying it to the soil," he wrote. "The amount of water adjudicated to the specified land should not be more than necessary when the soil and water have been properly cared for."[47] His reports included extensive detail on his attempt to distribute information about the "Campbell method" of soil preparation, which required turning soil over at sufficient depth to ensure moisture would be captured and held near plants' roots without either percolating into the water table or evaporating into the desert air.[48] By focusing on this "new" method in agricultural science, Sullivan helped reinforce a perception among settlers that the knowledge held by New Mexico's traditional communities was irrelevant to modern agriculture.

Each biennial report of the territorial engineer included a catalog of completed, approved, and proposed projects, detailing the project area's soil quality, topography, climate, irrigation potential, and market access. The reports make clear that in both irrigated and dry-farming districts, the territorial engineer and his assistants spent considerable time in the field, talking to farmers, inspecting project works, and responding to queries about reservoir design, canal alignment, construction materials, and other technical issues. As Sullivan reported in 1908: "While in the field the Engineer has had occasion quite frequently to go over the ground of proposed projects and has been able ... to aid the development going on, by lessening to some extent the difficulties to be overcome which would doubtless increase the outlay of the investors."[49] Requests for expert advice usually exceeded the response capacity of Sullivan's office staff, but they claimed to offer all possible support to help agricultural investors understand geographic conditions.

New Mexico's engineering office also worked to develop new agricultural geographies, focusing on three main project types. First, engineers designated suitable reservoir sites on rivers and streams near fertile lands. By storing water for later use at times optimized for an area's crops and climate, reservoirs allowed engineers to add new lands to New Mexico's irrigation-possibility map, including major projects in the northeast (Maxwell, Springer), northwest (San Juan), and southeast (Pecos) parts of the territory. A second method of irrigation development involved extracting groundwater (then called "underflow") from aquifers, using either artesian or pump-powered wells. Territorial engineers surveyed potential groundwater sources and circulated information to settlers about how deep to dig their wells to reach water-bearing strata and how strong a pump would be needed to bring water to the surface. By treating underflow waters as a "new" resource, engineers helped expand irrigation-focused settlement to areas long thought useless for agriculture, including the Portales, Estancia, Alamogordo, and Mimbres basins. Finally, the territorial engineer helped federal officials design channel alterations for the Rio Grande, a river notorious for its powerful spring floods. By decreasing the risk of floods, New Mexico's territorial-engineering staff helped expand irrigated agriculture into the floodplain of New Mexico's most voluminous watercourse.

All of these projects shared the goal of maximizing agricultural productivity and fostering Anglo settlement. In other words, they were essential to the settler-colonial project. Governor Otero explicitly described New Mexico as a colonial landscape where profit could be accumulated through extraction. He compared New Mexico to other high-profile colonies, such as the Philippines and Puerto Rico, lauding engineers for their work across the main and tributary valleys of the Pecos, San Juan, and Canadian Rivers.[50] Otero had predicted early that engineered stream diversions, water-storage reservoirs, groundwater wells, and distribution canals would allow "capital and American energy [to be] wielded with all their concentrated power" in New Mexico.[51] Hagerman made similar statements during his term as governor, arguing that New Mexico could establish new communities superior to those even in the eastern United States, so long as settlers' own ignorance was tempered by the superior knowledge possessed by government engineers: "under Government supervision irrigation engineering will become an exact science, and many of the mistakes, over-estimates as to the capacity of water, under-estimates as to cost of construction and maintenance, and the calamitous results inevitable therefrom will be avoided."[52] In the territory of New Mexico, government engineers stood ready to help farmers get the geography right, while private investors lined up to help with infrastructure needs.

Market Knowledge: The Duty of Water

However monumental it may have seemed at the time (and however impossible it may appear in retrospect), irrigation engineers wanted to ensure that every drop of water would be used in the most efficient way possible in hopes that settlers might irrigate every possible acre of land. Their determination stemmed from pastoral visions and nationalist goals, yes, but it also rested fundamentally on a quest for profit. Sullivan reported his support for irrigation projects that linked "eastern capital and western men" in a "colonization scheme ... whereby thousands of industrious, enterprising American farmers are being settled on small tracts" that would allow them to quickly establish profitable operations.[53] He pointed to Anglo settlements in the Pecos and San Juan River valleys as successful examples of rapid settlement expansion, and he forecast an irrigation-fueled increase in New Mexico's territorial population by 200,000 farmers, "not counting the inhabitants of the towns and business centers these agricultural communities would support."[54] The governor likewise reported to the Secretary of the Interior that "enterprising men with capital to carry out plans for irrigating on a large scale" had begun blazing a path toward modern economic development.

Officials predicted a substantial difference in fortune between long-standing agricultural communities and new Anglo settlements on the basis of agronomic knowledge and commercial acumen.[55] Yet most settlers arriving from the eastern United States had knowledge of neither. Settlers who engaged in agriculture before arriving in New Mexico rarely had experience in an arid setting or under a speculative irrigation-dependent model that required much higher acreage to turn a profit. Early engineers proselytized settlers and investors, begging them to rely on science for decision-making and promising in return a financial ledger written in black ink. The territorial engineer took it upon himself to "circulate articles and place in the hands of interested settlers reports, bulletins, articles, catalogues, etc., giving data and information" about how to maximize profit for any given investment of capital.[56]

Such quasi-promotional work dovetailed with the territorial governor's and the legislature's tireless efforts to attract investors to New Mexico. When Governor Otero proclaimed in his 1905 report to the Secretary of the Interior that "the major part of [New Mexico's] wealth is latent: the bulk of its natural resources is undeveloped," he identified the Office of the Territorial Engineer as the government's best tool for accessing untapped riches.[57] Otero claimed that engineering support could help farmers increase crop yields and financial returns, easily offsetting the costs of investing in equipment or infrastructure: "From 10 to 30 acres of fruit land carefully cultivated will comfortably support any family and leave leisure for its enjoyment. Broad acreage is not what tells in irrigation farming, but the amount of intelligent effort . . . is what swells the profits."[58] It was the engineers' job to ensure "intelligent effort" among farmers, and they duly filled the role of expert for both technical questions and matters of market efficiency. When encouraging farmers to consider new ventures, such as digging wells to access groundwater or installing generators for hydropower production, for example, the territorial engineer's staff frequently provided a profit calculation that compared the costs of infrastructure investment with the income likely from increased market sales.

The Office of the Territorial Engineer jointly evaluated productivity and profitability by analyzing the "duty" of water. This term refers to a ratio of crop acreage per volume or flow rate of irrigation water. For example, if two neighboring farmers each had ditches of the same size and water volume (say, one cubic foot of water per second, or one second-foot), the ditch that irrigated the larger number of acres would be credited with a higher duty. The duty of irrigation water varies widely by crop type, soil type, elevation, climatic conditions, ditch quality, and other factors that farmer both can and cannot control. The territorial engineer's review of water-permit applications, therefore, required him to determine the proper duty of water for intended crops in specific locations. Projects proposing to irrigate thirsty fruit crops, for example, had a much lower duty than projects intending to grow a drought-resistant grass such as alfalfa. Before approving a proposed irrigation project, the engineer needed to understand its duty and adjust infrastructure requirements accordingly.

In 1908 Territorial Engineer Sullivan reported to the legislature that it was not possible to maximize duty without extensive reliance on scientific data. He determined the "highest standard for continued economical [water] use" in New Mexico was two hundred acres per second-foot. He calculated this ideal duty along the Pecos River, where private and public infrastructure investments had produced a thriving agricultural region: "This project today is one of the best managed systems, and the land owners under it the most prosperous, of any project in the West, being the result of skillful management and a careful study of local conditions."[59]

When evaluating other projects, or when providing hydrographic data to the courts, Sullivan continually made reference to the duty of water. In the Hondo Hydrographic Survey, for example, Sullivan included tables that calculated duty for 140 different ditches, revealing astonishing variations in ditch efficiency. His report to the judge who requested the survey pointed out that the Kline Ditch was incredibly efficient (irrigating 77.02 acres with less than .32 second-feet) compared to the Nicanora Ditch, "which used nearly a second foot for a little over 18 acres of land and which would have covered that area during that year, if there was no loss through seepage and evaporation, 34 feet deep."[60] Sullivan's report acknowledged that duty should be expected to vary naturally throughout the area of any stream system, but he cautioned the court that most of the variation in the Hondo basin was due to human factors: "the water was not properly handled and cared for in many, many instances. The natural human instinct to get all you can if it does not cost anything more is probably predominant in the use of water for irrigation."[61]

Sullivan suggested that the court require a minimum duty of one hundred acres per second-foot across the Hondo basin, with duty increasing to two hundred acres per second-foot in less mountainous areas with better soils. He pointed out that "some of the ditches lose more water than others, yet they could be made by proper construction to carry the water with less loss" and encouraged the court not to reward inefficient water users: "the party who neglects his ditch [should not] be entitled to more water on account of his carelessness for we certainly do not want to put a premium on shiftlessness."[62] He encouraged the court to refer to his tabulated duty calculations and to review each property's location on the topographic map before making decisions about how to adjudicate water rights. Sullivan related these same recommendations in his hydrographic survey of the Rayado stream system, pushing the court to apply a scientific perspective that prioritized efficiency: "The duty of water on different areas of irrigated land under a stream system [is] necessary in determining the amount of rights to the use of water for the specified areas, thus the data included are of inestimable value in obtaining a just adjudication."[63]

In these statements Sullivan seems to be suggesting that water rights be allocated primarily based on hydrologic or market efficiency, rather than on the legal principle of prior appropriation: "From an engineering standpoint we question whether one individual should have the right to use several times more water for a given area than another party when the natural conditions are similar simply because the one individual does not try and conserve the moisture by proper handling of the water and the cultivation of the soils."[64] This perspective did not mesh with prevailing legal norms. In a high-profile case that went all the way to the New Mexico Supreme Court, Sullivan rejected a permit application because it requested significantly more irrigation water than could possibly be put to beneficial use. He instead approved a different request for the same water, even though it had been filed later, because he determined that the later request was more aligned with the public interest, which he defined as efficient profitability. The supreme court agreed that the territorial engineer could use public interest or profitability as a basis for decision-making, but it also cautioned that the engineer could not reject an application simply because another project was cheaper or more efficient.[65] The court sent that case back to the district court for a technical review of the first permit application, without comparison to the more efficient project. The ruling thus enforced a particular form of regulatory efficiency that confounded the engineer's work to quantify, streamline, and optimize settlers' returns on investment.

Hydrologic Knowledge: The Contradictions of Anglo Settlement

And therein lies the rub. New Mexico law prioritized the settlers or speculators who first managed to irrigate new lands before anyone else arrived in the same stream basin. But almost by definition, these first arrivals were completely dependent on assistance from the territorial engineer, who couldn't be everywhere at once. Prevailing Progressive views put scientific irrigation on a pedestal, holding it up as a perfect example of the supposedly civilizing force of science and engineering. To make this rhetoric come true, engineers had a steep hill to climb. The only way to combat Anglo settlers' deplorable misunderstandings of basic hydrology and soil science was for engineers to spend most of their time on knowledge work: teaching, circulating instructional materials, and countering misinformation. Engineers accordingly invested themselves in this work to minimize the dangers of Anglo ignorance, all while keeping up a rhetorical drumbeat of praise for Anglos' natural superiority.

As soon as the Office of the Territorial Irrigation Engineer was established, in fact, its leaders parroted then-standard comments equating irrigation engineering and Anglo settlement with civilization. The first engineer, David White, wrote to the New Mexico governor in 1906 that irrigation engineering was the "only [. . .] means that we can hope to induce desirable immigration into this Territory."[66] His first official report in 1907 clarified what he meant, detailing efforts to attract "investors and homeseekers in other parts of the country, thereby bringing to New Mexico a worthy and desirable class of people."[67] White's implicit critique of Indigenous and Spanish-speaking irrigators as *un*worthy and *un*desirable became explicit in other reports that celebrated the sale of lands from owners "who seldom made good use of them" to "good farmers from the Middle and Mississippi Valley States. The latter are usually educated, intelligent, and industrious men who expect to win and do win by hard work and common sense."[68] In these and other early reports, engineers and bureaucrats breezily dismissed non-Anglo farmers as uneducated, focusing their efforts instead on attracting Anglos to New Mexico with their superior knowledge, intelligence, and common sense.

When advocating for irrigation investments to prioritize the settlement of knowledgeable Anglos, however, official reports glossed over substantial hypocrisies. Federal reports continually cast irrigation as a "new" solution that would "encourag[e] the Indians to labor and become self-supporting, rather than longer foster slothfulness and idleness by continuing the old policy of doling out annuities."[69] Yet those same reports acknowledged the Pueblos' long history as agriculturists who had practiced irrigation for generations. Engineering reports excitedly discussed the ways that irrigation investments would generate huge profits and make the desert bloom in new Anglo settlement areas. Yet they never mentioned those benefits in descriptions of irrigation projects on Pueblo lands. Officials never forecast anything beyond self-sufficiency for Pueblo irrigation. The Indian Irrigation Service's federal superintendent characterized Pueblo infrastructure projects in tepid terms, predicting only that they would raise communities "from a condition of mere existence to that of effective workers, turning the products of their labor into the channels of trade."[70]

According to official reports, Pueblo irrigation was meant to create self-supporting laborers, while Anglo irrigation was meant to create entrepreneurial leaders. Pueblo irrigation was pursued as a corrective to slothfulness, while Anglo irrigation was pursued as a means of wealth generation. And while Pueblo communities were pitied as incapable of irrigation without government intervention, new Anglo settlements were encouraged to set up private concerns as quickly as possible. The gulf between these two irrigation narratives stemmed from deep-seated assumptions about Anglos' superior knowledge and non-Anglos' ignorance and inferiority.

Rhetoric diverged substantially from reality. New Mexico's early engineers took Progressive ideals to heart, and they wanted to optimize water-management efficiency, both by preventing waste and by maximizing investment returns. But for all their commitment to scientific analysis and rational management, engineers couldn't ignore the frustrating reality that Anglo settlements failed repeatedly at most aspects of aridlands farming and wasted excessive amounts of water.

As discussed in chapter 3, reclamation-era water managers and water engineers focused obsessively on the problem of "wasted" surface waters that flow past arable lands without being used for irrigation. New Mexico's territorial engineers followed suit, working to identify the best locations for dams and reservoirs and then analyzing the efficiency of private infrastructure projects. But in the quest to eliminate waste, engineers went well beyond water; they also focused on energy, money, and potential. As described in official reports, engineers looked not only for the classic case of water flowing through a stream unused, but also for projects that under- or overused water and subverted the overall efficiency of an irrigation system.

In official analyses, New Mexico's traditional ditch systems served as a foil for modern infrastructure. In 1905, for example, Governor Otero reported to the U.S. Secretary of the Interior that areas "where irrigation has been practiced for centuries" frequently had a lower ratio of cultivated to irrigable land than the new settlement areas.[71] He chalked up the inefficiency partly to infrastructure and partly to tradition. In the Rio Grande valley, where "small farmers and the pueblo Indians" controlled most irrigation, the governor claimed that water-sharing conflicts frequently left ditches sitting idle and unused while irrigators undermined one another or disputed their water allocations. In addition, he wrote, "the ditches have no regular gates or sluices, and flooding is the only means of irrigation; consequently the use of water is extremely wasteful."[72] Otero used these denigrations to create a contrast with an imagined future based in scientific agriculture. He reassured the Secretary of the Interior that New Mexico's engineers would introduce modern technology, techniques, and systems to improve efficiency and eliminate the wastefulness of the past.

The only stumbling block to Otero's prediction became a common preoccupation for territorial authorities: New Mexico's newest irrigators were incredibly wasteful. Engineers who charged traditional irrigators with underusing available water found Anglo newcomers guilty instead of *over*use. Settlers from the eastern United States had no familiarity with aridlands farming techniques, and they often applied more water than could be taken up by a given crop type in a specific soil. Along one ditch within the Hondo stream system, for example, the second territorial engineer, Vernon Sullivan, groused about settlers' excessive water use: "the people in these valleys would have made lakes out of their farms if it had not been for the natural drainage conditions.... The soils have been so leached out by the pouring of water through them ... that they can not raise as good crops now as they should."[73] Sullivan seemed exasperated by the meager productivity in new settlement areas: "New Mexico is favored with the best climate in the world and is abundantly supplied with the most fertile soil [yet] the beneficial results obtained from the amount of water being used is less than thirty per cent of what it should be."[74] He blamed settlers' inefficiency on a "lack of general knowledge of ... how and when to irrigate, how to care for the soil and crops and what kind of crops are suited to the natural conditions."[75]

Engineering reports also complained about other forms of settler ignorance, including their misunderstanding of climatic and hydrologic seasonality. Dry farming was technically possible in some areas of eastern New Mexico, but authorities continually warned farmers not to rely entirely on precipitation for water. Settlers familiar with dry-farming techniques from the midwestern United States often ignored these cautions, only to watch crops wither and die when rains didn't arrive. As Sullivan noted in 1908, "Many of the farmers now coming into the territory ... will make failures where successes ought to have been, especially in the dry farming districts."[76] He and other engineers counseled new settlers to invest in reliable irrigation systems, despite the fact that the "largest irrigation system in the Territory, and probably in the United States"—in the Pecos valley—was plagued by dam failures.[77] Governor Otero suggested in 1905 that the government should commandeer infrastructure construction work to avoid settlers' predictable mistakes. The territorial engineer of New Mexico was not equipped to take over dam-building and canal development, but Sullivan eventually required that permit applicants submit maps and "elaborate plans" for all projects but the smallest dams and canals.[78]

In 1910 Sullivan noted that dam construction was generally "tending toward a much improved character" across New Mexico but complained about having constantly to battle new settlers' inadequate hydrologic sensibilities. Anglo settlers did not seem to grasp "the extreme fluctuation of the water level" or the seasonal likelihood that "dry streams become raging torrents and carry with the water, immense quantities of silt, owing to the friableness of the soil and the rapid fall of the river channel."[79] Sullivan expressed ongoing concern that "builders of irrigation projects do not fully appreciate the magnitude of New Mexico floods by providing ample spillway capacity in connection with their reservoir or dam."[80] To combat hydrologic ignorance and thus prevent waste, the engineer's office assumed for itself an important role: to "assist the farming class in learning proper methods with which to care for their soil and water and the kind of crops best paying and best suited for local conditions."[81] Sullivan's reports are filled with details about engineers' work to educate settlers about efficient technologies and techniques for aridlands agriculture. Sullivan himself sponsored a Trophy Cup competition "for the best article on the economical use of water" and then published the best papers in a free pamphlet intended to redress settlers' "indifferent knowledge of scientific irrigation."[82] The Atchison, Topeka and Santa Fe (AT&SF) railroad undertook a similar initiative, hiring a soil scientist to establish experimental farms in the eastern and southeastern plains and to provide informational lectures on how better to prepare soil during winter and early spring.[83]

Overall, the Office of the Territorial Engineer conceived of its job simply: attracting as many new settlers to New Mexico as possible, in concert with private enterprise. Anything that stood in the way of this goal—existing residents' traditions or new settlers' ignorance—became a problem for expert engineers to manage and clean up. Before the engineering office came into existence, Anglo settlers had relied on land boosters or irrigation speculators for resources and information, but those individuals rarely maintained long-term connections with farmers who were new to aridlands farming. The Office of the Territorial Engineer assigned to itself the job of providing a knowledge base for the new settlers. In pursuing this goal, the lead engineer did not seek out knowledge from irrigation communities with long histories in New Mexico, and he did not observe or compile techniques suitable for subsistence agriculture; he instead worked to document an entirely new approach based on engineering formulas and agronomic experiments developed for large-scale commercial farms.

Regulatory Knowledge: Fulfilling the Progressive Vision

Cleaning up or preventing waste—of water, crops, infrastructure, dollars, potential—proved to be the Progressives' most critical project in New Mexico. Waste prevention required attention to the geography of settlement locations. Waste prevention elevated scientists and engineers to positions of authority within a data-driven bureaucracy. And waste prevention created complex management goals that wove market profits into the fabric of hydrographic and agronomic science. The final step involved cleaning up regulatory and legal structures to end wasteful government practices that impeded settlement.

The first few territorial engineers' reports reflect the importance they placed on streamlining the office's administrative efficiency and reducing the paperwork burdens on farmers and investors. White spent most of his first official report complaining about bureaucratic red tape and structural hurdles that made it impossible for him to do his job. He requested and was given office space, additional funding, and a new administrative workflow in which local mayordomos would report to water commissioners who would in turn report to the territorial engineer. White's goal was to ensure a smooth flow of information and authority that settlers could rely on when applying for water permits and establishing new farms.

After him, Sullivan endeavored to improve individual components of the management structure, including office work, fee collection, correspondence, data recording, and field coordination. Sullivan especially focused on the need to reform fieldwork, which quickly chewed through the agency's meager budget as engineers moved around New Mexico inspecting dams and conducting hydrographic surveys. He created a hydrographic survey fund by collecting court fees from participants in water adjudications, which helped defray engineers' travel and equipment expenses. He also brokered agreements with the Reclamation Service and the USGS to share both equipment and personnel in the field, earning praise for his smart efforts to reduce government waste.

Sullivan's biggest challenge, however, required him to confront the inherent wastefulness of the permit application process. Progressives wanted Anglo settlement to change the racial balance in New Mexico while also pouring agricultural profits into its economy. But by linking agricultural development to market logic, the permit application process quickly became overrun by competition-induced inefficiencies. Sullivan found that "practically 90 per cent" of water-supply estimates submitted for permit evaluation were "greatly in excess of the true supply," and that "in a great many cases applications have been filed . . . for the purposes of throwing clouds upon other permits to appropriate water from the same supply."[84] To stanch the flow of bogus or wildly exaggerated permit applications, Sullivan successfully introduced a new rule in 1910 that required permit applicants to pay a cash bond within thirty days of their permit application.

The bond not only provided a new revenue stream to support engineering work but also created a financial disincentive for commercial inefficiency.

Sullivan's reports also show that he was distressed by the wastefulness and ignorance of Anglo settlers, which often landed them in a court system that had institutional efficiencies of its own. Most notably, the courts could not easily handle conflicts concerning water rights that had been established in "the usual indefinite manner" *before* the 1907 legislation was passed.[85] It was impossible for judges to apply Progressive principles for rational resource management to Spanish-, Mexican-, and early American-era county records that lacked virtually all of the quantitative details needed to establish a modern water right after 1907. Sullivan believed engineers' knowledge was superior to any other claims brought in court, even though it was impossible to participate in every case. He sent engineers to courtrooms whenever possible and tied his agency's data-collection work to court needs. At the same time, he encouraged judges and other bureaucrats to seek and value quantitative data when making judgments about water administration.

As reflected in official reports, much of Sullivan's time and energy went toward improving regulatory and bureaucratic structures so that engineers could spend their time developing data, conducting scientific measurements and research, and providing engineering advice for irrigation projects. He hoped that regulatory efficiency would reduce demands on engineers and allow the agency to take up detailed hydrographic surveys, which would theoretically make it possible for judges to comprehensively adjudicate all pre-1907 rights across New Mexico. That goal was not achieved during Sullivan's time in office, nor in the time since.

Conclusion

Knowledge work provided the dense core of New Mexico's early environmental bureaucracy. Data-production efforts provided sharp tools that displaced existing irrigators and water managers, both from their positions of authority and from their lands. Then as now, knowledge work rarely received its political due. Hidden behind the shield of rationality, data production was simply unremarkable and unremarked. Other types of knowledge work also became entrenched in the laborious duties of the Office of the Territorial Engineer and were little contested in official narratives.

As their official reports reflect, engineers perceived and enacted their official water-management duties across two primary dimensions: science and settlement. In their scientific work, engineers had clear instructions from territorial officials, from their enabling legislation, and from Progressive norms about the use of scientific expertise as the basis for natural-resource management. But they found it difficult to live up to scientific ideals, judging by constant requests for new resources. Engineers would need a vast staff and nearly limitless authority to actually survey all of New Mexico's waters, to calculate duty for every crop, and to perfectly describe irrigation conditions everywhere in the territory. Yet, given their limited funds and personnel, they couldn't complete even basic stream gauging for most watersheds.

Scientific shortcomings did not impede the settlement effort. Official reports contained nearly as much information about targeting prospective settlers as they did about technical work. The territorial engineer and his staff ultimately saw all of their work—to produce data, maximize profits, and prevent waste—as part of a larger effort to advertise New Mexico's irrigation potential and attract new Anglo settlers. As soon as settlers started arriving, engineers found their attention diverted to the problem of addressing new farmers' ignorance. But even inefficient irrigators—who settled in the wrong places, overestimated water availability, used the wrong irrigation techniques, built impermanent dams, and disputed the engineer's decisions—were counted as successes.

In the eyes of the territorial engineers, the balance between science and settlement tipped heavily toward settlement as the critical priority in New Mexico. Engineers worked hard to cultivate improved agronomic-hydrologic expertise among farmers that had been resettled from the relatively wet eastern United States. When new Anglo settlers engaged in inefficient irrigation, however, engineers did not count it against them as a disqualifying characteristic, as they did when describing non-Anglo irrigators. New Mexico's Office of the Territorial Engineer measured its own success primarily through its ability to enable Anglo settlement in a landscape with long-standing agricultural settlements.

In wrestling with inefficiency, ignorance, and data limits, New Mexico's engineering agency provided a foundation for Anglo settlement, which then opened the door for even newer institutions that also became central to the settler project. Economic transformation rested on a foundation of irrigation-generated wealth, which was then invested in English-language schools, churches, "and other civilizing influences" expected to remedy knowledge deficiencies among non-Anglos. As Governor Hagerman noted in 1906, "Very much is to be hoped from the English education of our Spanish-speaking people who, in many localities . . . have made little or no progress, while the Pecos Valley has grown from almost nothing to what it now is."⁸⁶ The governor imagined that the Pecos model would spread as its leading Anglo settlers gained sufficient political power to influence the territorial government. Engineers served as the linchpin for this effort, holding together a settler-colonial apparatus that relied on irrigation engineering to displace existing communities and recruit a new cohort of "American" settlers.

∗ 6 ∗
Dispute

NAVIGATING ENVIRONMENTAL
KNOWLEDGE IN THE COURTROOM

If engineers served as the linchpin for settler colonialism in New Mexico, judges and courtrooms provided the wheels and axle. As Anglo settlers streamed into New Mexico around the turn of the century, they confronted and created a host of complicated water problems. The court system offered a supposedly neutral venue in which individuals, communities, and corporations could resolve disputes through the rational application of universal principles. In reality, however, the new American courts in territorial-era New Mexico participated actively in the systematic disadvantaging of non-Anglo participants, especially nonelites. Even when judges were unable to answer basic questions about hydrologic conditions, proper irrigation practices, and legitimate water rights, they consistently supported irrigation development projects, often at the expense of long-standing subsistence-oriented water users.

New Mexico's district courts handled hundreds of water disputes in the late territorial period, and each case offered an intersection point where scientific expertise, water policy, and environmental knowledge came together. In this chapter I provide a statistical analysis of nearly two hundred district court case records that trace the legal geography of local water disputes in the Rio Grande watershed. The next chapter dives into narrative analysis for a small subset of these cases. Together, these two chapters show how district court archives provide a window into the social and political relations surrounding water management at a time of great change in New Mexico.

This chapter begins by reviewing New Mexico's legal-administrative structures and providing the historical context for shifting approaches to water disputes under different colonial and national regimes. It then describes the method I used to analyze historical court records from eight New Mexico counties between 1900 and 1912. The remainder of the chapter presents a statistical examination of key trends and county-specific variations in water disputes during the late territorial era. These statistics show that the resolution of water disputes often required courts to evaluate environmental claims. Disputants, witnesses, attorneys, and judges used the formalized structures and protocols of the court system to contest environmental knowledge and produce environmental truth. But court participants from different ethnic groups approached knowledge production in different ways, and water disputes unfolded differently in different places. In other words, the geography of truth is variable. Scientific reasoning was all-important when it was available to support Anglo settlers' commercial prospects, but judges didn't insist on engineering certifications or quantified data when Anglo interests weren't at stake. Most notably, when scientific surveys or evidence were presented *against* Anglo interests and those Anglo disputants couldn't muster anything scientific in reply, judges easily slipped into other modes of fact-finding and resolution-seeking. Judges sometimes conducted their own eyewitness observations or made their own environmental determinations, comfortably countering scientific evidence when necessary to support continued settlement expansion.

Dispute Resolution Structures and Practice in New Mexico

Over the last many centuries, communities in New Mexico have resolved water disputes through both custom and formal law. The following historical summary reviews the changing nature of dispute administration in what is today New Mexico during the periods of Puebloan dominance, Spanish colonialism, Mexican independence, and American territorial control. Up until the last two decades of the nineteenth century, most of New Mexico's water disputes were handled locally, in accordance with place-based political and social norms. As Anglo settlement began to accelerate just before the turn of the twentieth century, however, longstanding legal norms underwent radical change. The new settler-colonial context imposed new constraints on the contestation of water-related claims among disputants of all ethnicities.

Indigenous nations governed water use and access using a variety of communal forms before and after Spanish colonists arrived.[1] Indigenous dispute resolution also followed diverse forms and practices, often using restorative-justice techniques that have enjoyed prominence in recent decades, both within Indigenous resurgence movements and as the basis for alternative justice efforts within the U.S. legal system.[2]

Throughout the sixteenth, seventeenth, and eighteenth centuries, Spanish colonial authorities granted water rights—like land rights—to both individuals and communities, with a fundamental expectation that new water rights would not be allowed to prejudice or negatively impact existing users.[3] In many parts of New Spain, this expectation was enforced by local town councils (*ayuntamientos* or *cabildos*) that made decisions about water allocation for large community ditches and referred disputes to a local magistrate (*alcalde*) or appealed them to the provincial governor. New Mexico was unique, however, in its extensive reliance on the small community ditch, or acequia, as the primary vehicle for rural water administration. In small acequia systems, an annually elected mayordomo held responsibility not only for supervising water apportionment and delivery, but also for settling disputes. Mayordomos took charge of disputes between parciantes (individual irrigators) and between entire ditch systems, negotiating agreements with neighboring acequias and mayordomos. They typically performed these tasks on the basis of custom, common sense, and local political dynamics.

The most intractable conflicts required judicial review at a higher administrative level. Most commonly across New Spain, magistrates used the process of *repartimiento*, a form of adjudication that considered the rights and needs of all parties at once in order to determine an equitable solution based on many factors.[4] An individual's legal right to water was only one consideration. Judges also considered broad questions of equity—for litigants, other individuals, and the community as a whole—reviewing not only what would be gained for each, but what could be lost.[5] Judges' decisions typically involved a compromise aimed at minimizing harm to individuals and maximizing community welfare. To develop legitimacy for compromise-oriented settlements, judges or magistrates often used commissions of community members as observers or fact-finders to support the judicial review. This "rudimentary and informal" system relied not on lawyers or trained legal officials but on custom developed in social and political context: "Under such a system, whether the *alcalde* knew the law was not as important as whether he was considered by the community to be a fair judge. . . . Under the Hispanic system of justice, any dispute represented a wound in the community's body politic, and healing that wound was the desired outcome."[6]

The political transition to Mexican independence in 1821 had relatively little impact on either Nuevomexicano or Pueblo traditions for handling water disputes in New Mexico, despite some fundamental changes in the institutions of local governance. In the few short decades of Mexican rule (1821–48), responsibility for water disputes remained in the hands of Nuevomexicano elites, although administration changed from individual village leaders (alcaldes) to multiperson councils (ayuntamientos) and then to two new types of officials: the *juez de paz* handled local matters, and the *prefecto* held regional authority. As before, however, water disputes were defined by efforts at compromise and conciliation in a system that "responded to public opinion and recognized the importance of accepted customs in water administration."[7] In New Mexico, rural acequias remained the dominant water institution, even as Nuevomexicano farmers began moving into new areas like the Pecos valley and San Juan headwaters basin in the early 1800s. Competition for both land and water among Nuevomexicano settlers and villagers produced an increasing number of water disputes during this period. As was true in the Spanish colonial era, conflicts were resolved in accordance with local custom, typically ending in commonsense decisions that required water-sharing and used a community-based apportionment system.[8]

In the first decades after Mexico ceded its northern territory to the United States in 1848, New Mexico's approach to water disputes went largely unchanged. The first governance system under American dominion (the Kearney Code) codified existing Mexican structures for local government, with only a few adjustments to incorporate American legal customs.[9] The former juezes de paz became justices of the peace and maintained responsibility for holding mayordomo elections, hearing complaints related to acequia governance, and signing off on water agreements negotiated by users. The former prefectos became probate judges, who either heard water disputes on appeal from justices of the peace or directly handled complex disputes that involved multiple localities. Nuevomexicano elites dominated both of these offices thanks to their electoral power in the early territorial years, and they ensured that numerous traditions continued from the Spanish and Mexican periods.[10] For example, although probate judges were newly empowered under American law to seat juries, they rarely did so. Juries had never been part of the Spanish or Mexican legal system, and probate judges generally relied instead on traditional expert panels made up of a few respected individuals from the community.

Using familiar Spanish customs as "time-honored procedures for settling water issues," probate judges heard a wide range of water-related disputes. Water users often found ways to settle issues outside of court, through local agreements brokered by justices of the peace. Only the thorniest disputes went before probate judges and expert panels, typically covering a wide range of topics such as apportionment of water, work regulations, headgate management, engineering issues, and expansion of acequia systems to accommodate new lands and settlers.[11] Because probate judges wielded considerable local power and prestige, they typically resolved conflicts with finality. In the rare cases where a probate judge failed to settle a dispute, appeals were heard at the federal level, in U.S. district courts dominated by Anglo appointees.

In the final decades of the nineteenth century, however, dispute resolution began to move away from traditional Spanish custom. In tandem with the extension of railroads into New Mexico and the nationwide promotion of irrigation as a key to aridlands economic development, Anglo settlers flooded into New Mexico to claim or purchase arable land after 1870. (From 1870 to 1900 New Mexico's territorial population grew by 20 to 30 percent each year, and the census count increased by an incredible 70 percent from 1900 to 1910.) The Anglo influx changed the balance of power in territorial politics, and it changed the nature of water disputes in two ways. First, many water disputes took on new ethnic overtones in the context of settler colonialism. Although pre-American water disputes in New Mexico had often cleaved along ethnic lines between Nuevomexicano and Indigenous irrigators, the post-1870 Anglo settlement boom introduced conflicts with more complicated ethnic contours. Enabled both by new technology and by new water policy, the Anglo capitalists and entrepreneurs flooding into New Mexico had their sights set on private, large-scale, development-oriented irrigation projects. In many locations Anglo water use proved fundamentally incompatible with the communal, subsistence-oriented water uses practiced by both Indigenous and Nuevomexicano irrigators. To head off intractable conflict, the increasingly Anglo-dominated territorial legislature eventually developed legislation that centralized water administration and sidelined small communal ditches and other traditional irrigation systems.[12] Because small ditch systems had long been integral to non-Anglo community cohesion and governance, disputes over seemingly simple issues served to magnify the emerging ethnic dimensions of conflict.

Second, the administrative structures for resolution of water disputes changed fundamentally during the same period of rapid Anglo settlement. The territorial legislature passed a law in 1876 to create a three-person board of county commissioners and gave it some responsibilities that had previously been held by probate judges. This law eroded the power of a local office that had typically been filled by Nuevomexicano elites and made it increasingly likely that water disputes could not be resolved at the local level. Whenever a probate judge could not resolve a case, it moved into federal district courts that were controlled by federally appointed judges and formally trained attorneys. These positions were filled almost exclusively by Anglos, who saw their role as helping to "civilize" New Mexico by reducing the arbitrariness of Mexican law and courts.[13] District courts proved much less accessible to water users and also less responsive to local conditions and norms. Whereas local probate judges had traditionally worked to find "pragmatic solutions in keeping with community values," district judges were more likely to focus instead on formal and "legal technicalities that failed to resolve the practical issues in question, thus leading to more litigation."[14] Both Indigenous and Nuevomexicano irrigators learned how to use these Anglo-dominated structures tactically, to gain political advantages against one another or within their own communities. In the long run, however, federal courts' dedication to the development of legal principles—to stabilize private-property rights and project capital investments, for example—ended up dispossessing non-Anglos more often than not.[15] An analysis of civil disputes in the New Mexico Territorial District Court Archives illustrates many of the social, political, and environmental contours of such dispossession.

Dispute Analysis Methodology

Reading old court cases is fun, but it can also be frustrating. The fun part: legal disputes provide inherent narrative drama. A complete case record contains multiple elements that draw the researcher's interest, especially the "facts of the case"—the actions or events that caused the dispute and shaped its evolution—as well as the judge's determination of how the conflict must end. The frustrating part: court archives are often fragmentary, and it can be hard or impossible to piece together the details of a case when multiple documents are missing.

What materials are included in an ideal case record? The case begins when a plaintiff submits a complaint describing harms caused by the alleged infractions of a defendant. The defendant responds to the plaintiff's detailed list of facts, agreeing or disagreeing with each point and sometimes adding new claims of their own (counterclaims). Both plaintiff and defendant may submit various documents as evidence with their claims, including maps, contracts, photos, and other items. The case file may include documents revealing that the judge ordered participants to stop certain activities (injunction) until the dispute could be resolved, or that he called people to court to testify (summons) about various facts of the case. A few case files may also contain complete transcripts of witness testimony. The final documents in a complete case file include administrative notes about the scheduling of hearings, the judge's written order declaring his decision, and financial statements tracking receipt of any court-ordered payments.

In New Mexico's district court archives from the territorial period, almost every case file is missing one or more documents. Fortunately for the historical researcher, however, the documentation of legal claims and responses is highly repetitive; each response typically refers in detail to all points included in the prior claim. That means it is often possible to reconstruct content from a missing document simply by reviewing later documents that respond to its claims. Even a complete case file, however, presents considerable challenge. Documents refer to places that may not appear on modern maps or employ place-names no longer in common usage. Language can sometimes be difficult to follow, although thankfully most court records between 1900 and 1912 were typed rather than handwritten. Sometimes one case will refer to another, requiring cross-referencing of documents and decisions across multiple counties while taking into account that county boundaries changed over time. Understanding a case often requires numerous direct readings of the file, along with considerable external research to figure out exactly where things happened or to track down additional information about the individuals and communities involved. Research assistants helped me record and process basic details for each case, but I sat with many of these cases for a long time before I understood the full dimensions of each dispute. Eureka moments were few and far between, sometimes attained only after a short road trip to check the geometries and topographies of the site in question.

Why go to all this trouble? New Mexico's territorial-era district court records contain hundreds of cases that dealt with water issues, and all of them are held in the New Mexico State Records Center and Archives in Santa Fe. In one location the researcher can access a comprehensive legal record that reveals not only the facts of water management but also the contestation of facts and knowledge in specific social and political contexts. District court records show how different water approaches came into conflict in different ways and how new management ideals carried different weights of authority in different places, at different times, and when presented by different people. Analyzed in the aggregate, these rich materials permit a spatially aware reconstruction of the changing flows of knowledge, authority, and power.

I analyzed local water disputes in two ways, tracing the dynamics of settler colonialism both broadly and in depth. Chapter 7 contains a deep exploration of individual cases, following a north–south path to illustrate various spatial dimensions of water-management change. I know readers will thank me for limiting such detailed analysis to only a handful of cases, given the length of that chapter. But before diving into the drama of individual conflicts, the remainder of this chapter sets the stage with a broad analysis based on descriptive statistics.

Within the broader context of New Mexicans' disagreements over water, formal court cases are outliers. Most people would have handled their disputes outside the court if at all possible, using family members or local-level officials to mediate conflicts. When that didn't work, however, one side or the other initiated formal legal proceedings. Before 1900 local probate courts handled most water cases, but by 1900 water disputes had moved to federal district courts as the first resort.[16] Litigation increased, and judges scrambled to handle all their cases while making rounds through their assigned county circuits. Descriptive statistics allow us to develop an aggregate understanding of this world, even without excavating every detail of each case. By analyzing a key chronological and geographical slice of the district court archives, we get a clear view of the interactions between modernist water management, environmental claims-making, and ethnic relations in a settler-colonial context.

Chronologically, these statistics describe cases initiated or heard between 1900 and 1912. Those last twelve years of the territorial period provide a bracket around New Mexico's most critical transition in water administration, from five years before the comprehensive 1905 water law to five years after 1907's substantial statutory modification. That was a time of massive Anglo settlement and population growth in New Mexico, which led to many water disputes alongside numerous political and social changes.

Geographically, the study area includes all New Mexico counties that intersect the line of the Rio Grande, starting from its Rio Chama tributary at the Colorado border and continuing along the main stem of the Rio Grande to the Texas border. County boundaries were in flux during the territorial period (and after), and these statistics include cases from newly established counties or those that had their boundaries changed to include an intersection with the river between 1900 and 1912. By focusing on the Chama–Rio Grande system, this study excludes other important areas in New Mexico's irrigation history, including the basins of the Gila, San Juan, Pecos, and Canadian Rivers, as well as the Rio Grande headwaters upstream of the Chama confluence and many groundwater-irrigated settlements throughout the eastern plains. The central river valley nonetheless offers a substantial and meaningful perspective on New Mexico's irrigation history, since it contains a complete cross section of water-management approaches, settlement types, and cultural geographies.

Within the chronological and geographical parameters described above, this analysis does not rely on sampling; it includes every single district court case that dealt with a water issue in the study area and period. I produced this data set by combing through every box of legal records

TABLE 6.1 Documents found in New Mexico district court records, Chama–Rio Grande study area, 1900–1912

Document type	No. of case files containing document type	% of total cases containing document type (n = 187)
Complaint	155	82.9%
Injunction	28	15.0%
Defendant response	115	61.5%
Plaintiff response	49	26.2%
Witness testimony	15	8.0%
Map or survey	15	8.0%
Final ruling or decree	105	56.1%
Other*	131	70.1%

* May include summonses, injunction bonds, orders to appear in court, various forms of evidence, contracts, trial date announcements, notices of attorney change, etc.

for counties in the study area and reviewing every single case file from the study period to determine whether it related to water management in any way. For all water-related cases, research assistants helped complete the first analytical steps: cataloging extant documents and coding basic information about topics, participants, and case outcomes.

As shown in table 6.1, most individual case records were incomplete in some way, with only a handful of cases definitively containing all of the documents that had been filed at the time the case was heard. At a minimum, a complete case file necessarily contains a complaint, which initiates the case; a defendant's response, in which the accused party answers the charges; and a ruling and final decree containing the judge's decision. Table 6.1 shows that these are indeed the most common surviving documents in the archives. Other materials depend on the nature of the case. A plaintiff's response often follows up on points raised in the defendant's response to introduce new facts. And judges commonly issued injunctions when they perceived a matter of urgency and wanted to address it immediately while parties waited for a final ruling on the case. Not all cases recorded evidence or testimony, but many case files referred to records that apparently didn't survive. For almost all of the incomplete cases, I was eventually able to analyze them by piecing together missing information from other materials in the file. For a few frustrating files, the lack of documents made analysis impossible.

After collecting and deductively completing (when possible) the chronology and outcomes for all water-related case records, I also analyzed them along multiple dimensions. First, research assistants coded the primary dispute topic, with categories ranging from water rights to water-related damage. (See the first column in table 6.2 for the full list of topics.) Next, they flagged examples of environmental-knowledge production, in which disputants made environmental claims or raised environmental issues that required the court to make a ruling (second column in table 6.2). Finally, I coded the forms of evidence and argumentation that disputants used to make their cases (third column in table 6.2). Owing to the in-

TABLE 6.2 Coding categories used to analyze New Mexico district court records, Chama–Rio Grande study area, 1900–1912

Dispute topics	Disputed environmental knowledge	Argumentation and evidence
Water delivery	Surface water hydrology	Basis of argument
- quantity	- relation of tributary and main stem	- simple assertion
- timing	- seasonality of flow	- appeals to authority
- location	- flow quantity/direction	- testimony
	- headwaters source	- evidence
Water rights		
- seniority	Groundwater hydrology	Types of testimony
- abandonment	- spring source	- eyewitness
	- seepage rates	- expert
Water-related damage (flooding, drought, etc.)	- flow quantity	
		Types of evidence
- crops	Channel geometry	- sketch map/illustration
- property	- river channel shape	- scientific cartography
- infrastructure	- natural vs. manmade changes to channels	- hydrologic data
		- photographs
Water governance	- channel shape impact on flood stage flows	- legal documents
- acequia elections		
- labor/maintenance contributions	Environmental events	
- water allocation	- flooding	
	- drought	
Physical changes to water systems	- erosion	
- canal construction	Other	
- channel changes	- agronomy	
- infrastructure additions/ changes	- arability	
	- water quality	
Land ownership impacts		
- trespass		
- condemnation		

completeness of individual records, it was not possible to link the nature of argumentation to the results of the case or to develop statistics for the success rates of different approaches, but this coding helps us understand the general nature of argumentation throughout the study area and time period.

In addition to coding the cases topically and in terms of argumentation, I worked with research assistants to attempt an ethnic breakdown for the individuals who participated in each case (see table 6.3). Wherever possible, we extracted the surnames of plaintiffs, defendants, attorneys, judges, referees, probate judges, witnesses, and anyone else who participated in each case. By cross-referencing these names with historical records for New Mexico, we were able to establish a basic categorization of ethnicity and then update or correct it based on direct documentation from the case record. For example, if witness testimony referred to an individual disputant as "Mexican," we could confirm that person's ethnicity in the Nuevomexicana/o category; if a court filing labeled someone as "Dutch," we recorded that person as an Anglo. For individuals sufficiently prominent to be included in published histories (judges, some attorneys, and the occasional disputant), we used secondary sources to confirm ethnicity. This approach is imperfect, despite being the most common historical method for determining ethnicity in New Mexico's complex cultural landscape.[17] The most likely errors are (1) the misidentification of Indigenous people as Nuevomexicana/o, based on the Spanish colonial practice of assigning Spanish surnames to Indigenous individuals, families, and communities during Christian baptism, and (2) the misidentification of people from mixed Anglo-Nuevomexicano families as Anglo based on surname, although they identify with Nuevomexicano culture and custom. Owing to the probability of these errors and my inability to quantify their extent, I refrain in this chapter from making definitive claims about how different ethnic groups engaged in water disputes in the years before statehood. Instead, I use the data to provide general overviews and suggest broad trends.

Statistics: Legal Geographies across the Chama–Rio Grande Valley

For the eight counties that intersect the Chama–Rio Grande watershed, New Mexico's State Records Center and Archives contains 187 water-related cases for the 1900–1912 time period. Figure 6.1 shows the total number of water-related cases found in each county during the time period of the study. Using descriptive statistics, we can answer a range of key questions to better understand water management and environmental knowledge in historical context.

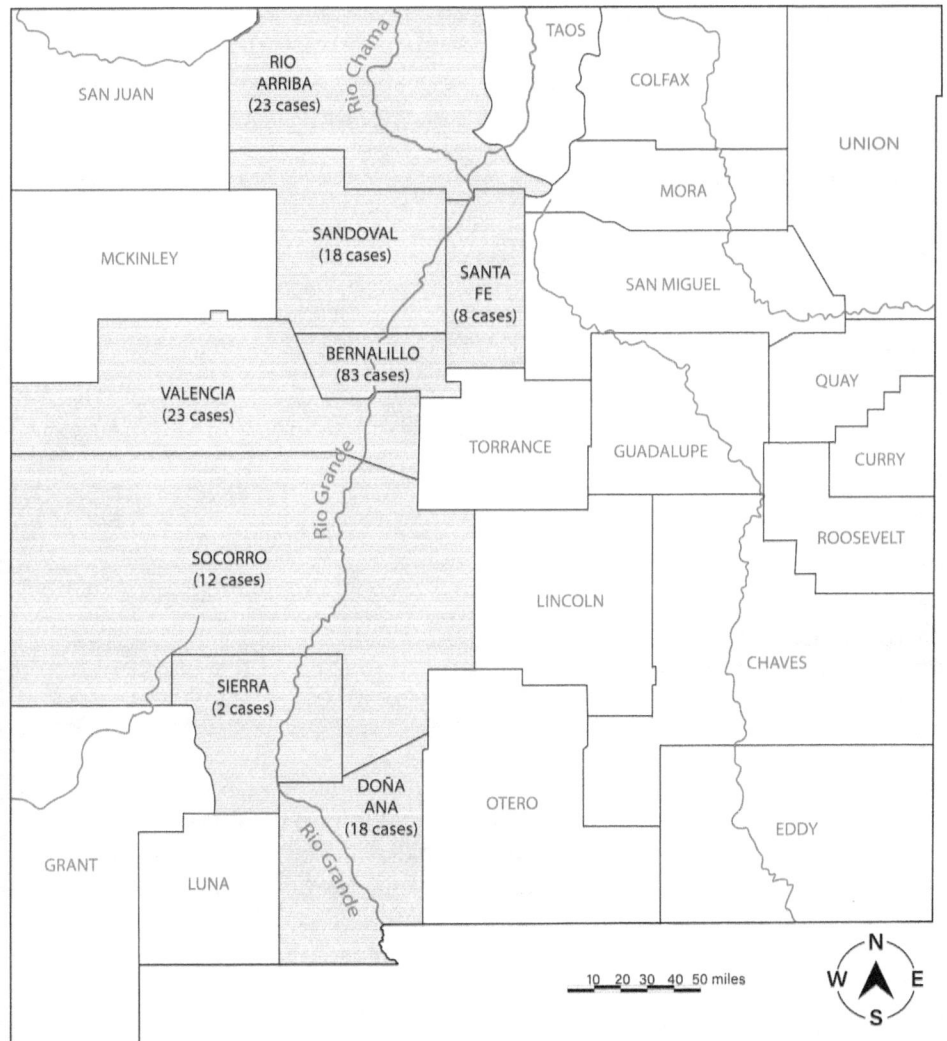

FIGURE 6.1 Water disputes in the Chama–Rio Grande valley, 1900–1912
Map by Maria Lane. County boundaries as of 1910

WHO PARTICIPATED IN LAWSUITS OVER WATER?

As shown in table 6.3, Nuevomexicanas/os made up the bulk of litigants across the study area, representing about half of the total plaintiffs and three-quarters of all defendants. This preponderance reflects the simple fact that Nuevomexicanas/os still outnumbered all other ethnicities in New Mexico at the turn of the century. Witnesses are known to have been

TABLE 6.3 Breakdown of court participants, New Mexico district court records, Chama–Rio Grande study area, 1900–1912

Total cases n = 187	Plaintiff*	Defendant*	Witnesses (present in 12.3% of cases)†	Attorney (present in 62.6% of cases)†	Judge (named in 77.5% of cases)†	Other (present in 11.2% cases)†
Nuevomex. individual(s)	103 (55.1%)	139 (74.3%)	19 (51.4%)	16 (11.0%)	0 (0%)	12 (54.5%)
Indigenous individual(s)	7 (3.7%)	8 (4.3%)	0 (0%)	0 (0%)	0 (0%)	0 (0%)
Anglo individual(s)	82 (43.9%)	39 (20.9%)	18 (48.6%)	129 (89.0%)	145 (100%)	10 (45.5%)
Corporation or business	35 (18.7%)	16 (8.6%)	n/a	n/a	n/a	n/a
Government entity	6 (3.2%)	2 (1.1%)	n/a	n/a	n/a	n/a

* Total percentages in this column exceed 100% because numerous cases included multiple litigants from different ethnicities. In those cases, plaintiffs or defendants are counted in multiple ethnicity categories.
† Attorneys, witnesses, judges, and other court personnel were not always named in the case record or were not present in the case at all. Percentages shown are based on only those cases in which they were named/present.

present in only about an eighth of cases and were split fairly evenly between Nuevomexicanas/os and Anglos, reflecting their growing parity as landowners and water-rights holders. Legal officials, however, were almost entirely Anglo, reflecting the increasing institutional control of Anglo settlers. About two-thirds of cases recorded one or more attorneys, nearly all of them Anglo. A handful of attorneys were Nuevomexicana/o, and none were Indigenous, as far as I can tell. In the 77.5 percent of cases where a judge's name was recorded, every single judge was an Anglo. Other court personnel named in the records were split between Anglos and Nuevomexicanas/os, including the occasional justice of the peace (usually Nuevomexicano), probate judge (usually Nuevomexicano), or law enforcement officer asked to serve a summons (usually Anglo). These numbers reflect the way the court system had begun to change after a half century of Anglo settlement, as described above.

Table 6.4 shows the breakdown of these statistics by county, revealing spatial variations that reflect both the historical cultural landscape of New Mexico and the emerging settlement geography across the study area at the end of the territorial period. For example, in the core Spanish

TABLE 6.4 Breakdown of court participants (by county), New Mexico district court records, Chama–Rio Grande study area, 1900–1912

County/ ethnicity	Plaintiff*	Defendant*	Witnesses†	Attorneys†	Judge†	Other
Rio Arriba						
n = 23 cases			n = 5	n = 21	n = 18	n = 11
Nuevomex.	20 (87%)	22 (95.7%)	4 (80%)	0 (0%)	0 (0%)	7 (63.6%)
Indigenous	3 (13%)	1 (4.3%)	0 (0%)	0 (0%)	0 (0%)	0 (0%)
Anglo	2 (8.7%)	1 (4.3%)	1 (20%)	21 (100%)	18 (100%)	4 (36.4%)
Corporation	0 (0%)	0 (0%)	n/a	n/a	n/a	n/a
Government	0 (0%)	0 (0%)	n/a	n/a	n/a	n/a
Santa Fe						
n = 8 cases			n = 7	n = 6	n = 7	n = 2
Nuevomex.	2 (25%)	6 (75%)	3 (42.9%)	0 (0%)	0 (0%)	0 (0%)
Indigenous	0 (0%)	2 (25%)	0 (0%)	0 (0%)	0 (0%)	0 (0%)
Anglo	6 (75%)	1 (12.5%)	4 (57.1%)	6 (100%)	7 (100%)	2 (100%)
Corporation	0 (0%)	0 (0%)	n/a	n/a	n/a	n/a
Government	0 (0%)	0 (0%)	n/a	n/a	n/a	n/a
Sandoval						
n = 18 cases			n = 6	n = 13	n = 10	n = 0
Nuevomex.	16 (88.9%)	13 (72.2%)	3 (50%)	0 (0%)	0 (0%)	n/a
Indigenous	1 (5.6%)	0 (0.0%)	0 (0%)	0 (0%)	0 (0%)	n/a
Anglo	1 (5.6%)	2 (11.1%)	3 (50%)	13 (100%)	10 (100%)	n/a
Corporation	1 (5.6%)	3 (16.7%)	n/a	n/a	n/a	n/a
Government	0 (0%)	0 (0%)	n/a	n/a	n/a	n/a
Bernalillo						
n = 83 cases			n = 11	n = 53	n = 73	n = 5
Nuevomex.	31 (37.3%)	57 (68.7%)	5 (45.5%)	9 (17%)	0 (0%)	2 (40%)
Indigenous	1 (1.2%)	4 (4.8%)	0 (0%)	0 (0%)	0 (0%)	0 (0%)
Anglo	48 (57.8%)	20 (24.1%)	6 (54.5%)	44 (83%)	73 (100%)	3 (60%)
Corporation	33 (39.8%)	5 (6.0%)	n/a	n/a	n/a	n/a
Government	6 (7.2%)	2 (2.4%)	n/a	n/a	n/a	n/a
Valencia						
n = 23 cases			n = 1	n = 23	n = 10	n = 2
Nuevomex.	14 (60.9%)	18 (78.3%)	1 (100%)	7 (30.4%)	0 (0%)	2 (100%)
Indigenous	2 (8.7%)	1 (4.3%)	0 (0%)	0 (0%)	0 (0%)	0 (0%)
Anglo	7 (30.4%)	3 (13%)	0 (0%)	16 (69.9%)	10 (100%)	0 (0%)
Corporation	1 (4.3%)	4 (17.4%)	n/a	n/a	n/a	n/a
Government	0 (0%)	0 (0%)	n/a	n/a	n/a	n/a

(*continued*)

TABLE 6.4 (continued)

County/ethnicity	Plaintiff*	Defendant*	Witnesses†	Attorneys†	Judge†	Other
Socorro						
n = 12 cases			n = 1	n = 10	n = 10	n = 1
Nuevomex.	8 (67.7%)	6 (50.0%)	0 (0%)	0 (0%)	0 (0%)	1 (100%)
Indigenous	0 (0%)	0 (0%)	0 (0%)	0 (0%)	0 (0%)	0 (0%)
Anglo	6 (50.0%)	6 (33.3%)	1 (100%)	10 (100%)	10 (100%)	0 (0%)
Corporation	0 (0%)	6 (33.3%)	n/a	n/a	n/a	n/a
Government	0 (0%)	0 (0%)	n/a	n/a	n/a	n/a
Sierra						
n = 2 cases			n = 2	n = 2	n = 2	n = 0
Nuevomex.	0 (0%)	2 (100%)	1 (50%)	0 (0%)	0 (0%)	n/a
Indigenous	0 (0%)	0 (0%)	0 (0%)	0 (0%)	0 (0%)	n/a
Anglo	2 (100%)	0 (0%)	1 (50%)	2 (100%)	2 (100%)	n/a
Corporation	0 (0%)	0 (0%)	n/a	n/a	n/a	n/a
Government	0 (0%)	0 (0%)	n/a	n/a	n/a	n/a
Doña Ana						
n = 18 cases			n = 4	n = 17	n = 15	n = 1
Nuevomex.	12 (66.7%)	15 (83.3%)	2 (50%)	0 (0%)	0 (0%)	0 (0%)
Indigenous	0 (0%)	0 (0%)	0 (0%)	0 (0%)	0 (0%)	0 (0%)
Anglo	10 (55.6%)	8 (44.4%)	2 (50%)	17 (100%)	15 (100%)	1 (100%)
Corporation	0 (0%)	0 (0%)	n/a	n/a	n/a	n/a
Government	0 (0%)	0 (0%)	n/a	n/a	n/a	n/a

* Total percentages in this column exceed 100% because numerous cases included multiple litigants from different ethnicities. In those cases, plaintiffs or defendants are counted in multiple ethnicity categories.
† Attorneys, witnesses, judges, and other court personnel were not always named in the case record or were not present in the case at all. Percentages shown are based on only those cases in which they were named/present.

colonial areas of northern New Mexico and the lower Rio Grande valley, Nuevomexicano litigants and witnesses were much more common than in other areas. They dominated most legal participation in Rio Arriba County. Anglo participants show up in greater numbers in courts spanning the settlement zone of the middle Rio Grande valley, particularly in Bernalillo County. Corporations show up as court participants only in these central counties, with especially high representation in Bernalillo County, where the Albuquerque Land and Irrigation Company brought several dozen condemnation cases in 1900 in support of a major canal project.

Looking specifically at who brought these suits to court, we see that

Nuevomexicanas/os were most active in initiating water-related litigation. (Table 6.5 provides an overview; table 6.6 provides a detailed breakdown.) Nuevomexicanas/os brought just over half of all cases (see table 6.5), and 85 percent of all cases brought by Nuevomexicano plaintiffs named Nuevomexicano defendants (see table 6.6, first row). Indigenous-initiated cases were the least common (less than 4 percent of all cases) and always involved contestation against at least one Nuevomexicano defendant, with a single case also including an Anglo defendant. Court records show no cases in which an Indigenous plaintiff sued an Indigenous defendant in this time period in any of these counties. Anglo plaintiffs initiated just under half of all cases, targeting about two-thirds of their cases against Nuevomexicanas/os, about one-third against other Anglos, and a small handful against Indigenous defendants (see table 6.6, far-right column). Corporations and businesses, similarly, brought most of their lawsuits against Nuevomexicanas/os (77 percent), with Indigenous and Anglo defendants targeted much less frequently.

On the receiving end of these suits, Nuevomexicanas/os were by far the most likely to be sued over water-related disputes during the study period (see table 6.5). Three-quarters of all cases named Nuevomexicanas/os as defendants, compared to only 4 percent of cases brought against Indigenous defendants and 21 percent against Anglo defendants. As shown in table 6.6, nearly two-thirds of all cases brought against Nuevomexicanas/os were brought by other Nuevomexicanas/os, with one-third brought by Anglos. Indigenous defendants were sued about equally often by Nuevomexicanas/os and Anglos, with no suits brought against them by other Indigenous plaintiffs. Cases involving Anglo defendants were most likely to be brought by other Anglos (64 percent of these cases) or Nuevomexicanas/os (39 percent). Numerous cases had mixed-ethnicity plaintiffs or defendants

TABLE 6.5 Overview of litigants, New Mexico district court records, Chama–Rio Grande study area, 1900–1912

Litigants n = 187	Appearing as plaintiffs No. of cases (percent of total)	Appearing as defendants No. of cases (percent of total)
Nuevomexicano/a individual(s)	103 (55.1%)	139 (74.3%)
Indigenous individual(s)	7 (3.7%)	8 (4.3%)
Anglo individual(s)	82 (43.9%)	39 (20.9%)
Corporation or business	35 (18.7%)	16 (8.6%)
Government entity	6 (3.2%)	2 (1.1%)

Note: Total percentages exceed 100% in both columns because numerous cases included multiple litigants from different ethnicities.

TABLE 6.6 Breakdown of litigants, New Mexico district court records, Chama–Rio Grande study area, 1900–1912

Litigant ethnicity or status	No. of cases	% of all cases n = 187	% of all cases against defendants of this ethnicity	% of all cases brought by plaintiffs in this group
Nuevomexicana/o plaintiff (n = 103) against:				
Nuevomex. def.	88	47.1%	63.3%	85.4%
Indigenous def.	4	2.1%	50.0%	3.9%
Anglo def.	15	8.0%	38.5%	14.6%
Indigenous plaintiff (n = 7) against:				
Nuevomex. def.	7	3.7%	5.0%	100.0%
Indigenous def.	0	0.0%	0.0%	0.0%
Anglo def.	1	0.5%	2.6%	14.3%
Anglo plaintiff (n = 82) against:				
Nuevomex. def.	50	26.7%	36.0%	61.0%
Indigenous def.	3	1.6%	37.5%	3.7%
Anglo def.	25	13.4%	64.1%	30.5%
Corporation/business plaintiff (n = 35) against:				
Nuevomex. def.	27	14.4%	19.4%	77.1%
Indigenous def.	4	2.1%	50.0%	11.4%
Anglo def.	4	2.1%	10.3%	11.4%
Government plaintiff (n = 6) against:				
Nuevomex. def.	2	1.1%	1.4%	33.3%
Indigenous def.	0	0.0%	0.0%	0.0%
Anglo def.	4	2.1%	10.3%	66.7%

Note: Percentages exceed 100% because (1) numerous cases included multiple litigants from different ethnicities, and (2) corporate/business and government *defendants* are excluded from this breakdown.

throughout the study area, which will be discussed in more detail in the next chapter, where I explore a subset of individual cases.

This detailed analysis of dispute participants reflects a few key aspects of settler colonialism in the Rio Grande valley. First, Nuevomexicanas/os remained dominant in the upper part of the valley, where they had for some time controlled legal systems and government administration, long after Anglo settlers began arriving. Nuevomexicanas/os appeared across all counties as active disputants and witnesses, but rarely as court personnel. Anglo influence was concentrated in the central valley, where they initiated numerous lawsuits, but their influence was not limited to that area. Anglos showed up as robust disputants throughout the study area, always more likely to sue than be sued. Indigenous people have a vanishingly small presence in the court record, appearing very occasionally as plaintiffs or defendants and never as witnesses, attorneys, or judges. And Anglos overwhelmingly dominated court administration. Together these statistics paint a picture of increasing Anglo control over territorial institutions, with Nuevomexicanas/os maintaining strength through strategic adaption to and manipulation of institutions they were less and less likely to control directly.

WHAT WERE THE DISPUTES ABOUT?

After establishing ethnic groups' differential participation, I analyzed the topics most likely to cause water-related lawsuits in different counties. Table 6.7 breaks down dispute topics, using the six aggregate categories

TABLE 6.7 Breakdown of dispute topics, New Mexico district court records, Chama–Rio Grande study area, 1900–1912

County	Water governance	Water damage	Land ownership	Water delivery	Physical changes	Water rights
	Shown: number of cases and percentage of total cases in county for all topics.					
Rio Arriba n = 23	8 (34.8%)	6 (26.1%)	5 (21.7%)	10 (43.5%)	4 (17.4%)	5 (21.7%)
Santa Fe n = 8	0 (0.0%)	3 (37.5%)	5 (62.5%)	3 (37.5%)	2 (25.0%)	3 (37.5%)
Sandoval n = 18	13 (72.2%)	3 (16.7%)	1 (5.6%)	0 (0.0%)	4 (22.2%)	2 (11.1%)
Bernalillo n = 83	25 (30.1%)	19 (22.9%)	32 (38.6%)	9 (10.8%)	5 (6.0%)	3 (3.6%)
Valencia n = 23	4 (17.4%)	10 (43.5%)	5 (21.7%)	9 (39.1%)	3 (13.0%)	8 (34.8%)
Socorro n = 12	4 (33.3%)	8 (66.7%)	1 (8.3%)	2 (16.7%)	2 (16.7%)	3 (25.0%)
Sierra n = 2	1 (50.0%)	1 (50.0%)	0 (0.0%)	2 (100.0%)	1 (50.0%)	1 (50.0%)
Doña Ana n = 18	11 (61.1%)	13 (72.2%)	4 (22.2%)	6 (33.3%)	10 (55.6%)	2 (11.1%)
Total n = 187	**67 (35.8%)**	**66 (35.5%)**	**61 (32.6%)**	**42 (22.5%)**	**36 (19.3%)**	**32 (17.1%)**

Note: Total percentages exceed 100% for each row because most cases included multiple points of dispute.

listed in table 6.1. Across all counties, the most common disputes focused on damage to property and crops (part of the "water-related damage" category), election results for acequia administration (within "water governance"), and the delivery of water (in its own category). In some counties other topics were far more likely, such as condemnation of land to create rights-of-way for irrigation infrastructure in Bernalillo and Santa Fe Counties (in the "land ownership impacts" category), acequia maintenance in Sandoval County (aggregated under "water governance"), or changes to canal and river channels in Sierra and Doña Ana Counties (part of "physical changes"). Topical variations throughout the study area indicate differences in settler colonialism's mechanisms and impacts.

Overall, the largest number of disputes in the 1900–1912 district court records fell into the water-governance category. This aggregate category includes a range of dispute topics associated with the administration of acequias or shared community ditches: elections for leadership officials (mayordomos and commissioners), allocation of water to acequia members, required contributions of labor or money to maintain ditches and other shared infrastructure, and management of public funds. Across all counties except Santa Fe, governance disputes constituted a significant portion of total cases. Sandoval County was an outlier, with nearly two-thirds of its cases in this category because of repeated litigation over elections and administration for a single acequia, and Santa Fe County was an outlier as well, with no cases related to governance in this time period. In the first year of the twentieth century, acequias and community ditches were still the dominant form of water management throughout New Mexico. As shown in chapter 7's detailed case reviews, however, traditional systems were under increasing pressure from settlers who brought new politics and private-property norms that challenged long-standing custom.

Second most common: disputes over "water-related damage," including damage to crops, property, and infrastructure. Across all counties, this category accounts for around a third of all court cases. Socorro and Doña Ana counties recorded especially high numbers in this category, with two-thirds or more of all cases revolving around damage topics. Typically, these cases hinged not on questions about the *nature* of damage to fields, ditches, headgates, pastures, and riverbanks, but rather on the *causes* of such damage. As we will see in the detailed case briefs, defendants accused of causing crop or infrastructure damage often turned to an environmental defense, arguing that the damage was in fact due to natural environmental processes and not to any action of their own.

Across the study area, the third highest number of disputes fell into the aggregate category of "land ownership impacts," which includes two significant but different types of court cases: trespassing and condemnation. Trespassing is an individual action of entering another person's property, often (in these cases) to get to a water source or to maintain infrastructure for water diversion and irrigation. Condemnation cases, on the other hand, request that the government itself seize an individual's property and make it available for another's use. In these cases, condemnation efforts typically focused on seizing land for use as a right-of-way for transportation or irrigation infrastructure. The overall prominence of this dispute type in the study area is substantially inflated by the numbers in Bernalillo County, where a single company brought condemnation cases against thirty-two different landowners to establish rights-of-way for a major canal project. This single condemnation issue in one county thus produced more cases than the *total* caseload in any other county, skewing overall percentages and making this dispute type appear more prominent than it is. But condemnation cases were not unimportant elsewhere. In Santa Fe County, condemnation was the most common dispute type during the study period, with five distinct condemnation requests in the court record (out of eight total cases). Valencia and Doña Ana counties each recorded a fifth of their total caseload in the condemnation subcategory. In Rio Arriba County, by contrast, all of the cases in the "land ownership impacts" category focused on trespassing disputes.

Disputes over water delivery also took place frequently during the study period, usually focusing on the quantity, timing, or location of water flows as they arrived at individual fields. Because most irrigators in New Mexico participated during that time in shared water systems—either directly as members of acequias and community ditches, or indirectly as private appropriators who irrigated alongside others using the same water source—disputes often erupted when someone either didn't get enough water or didn't get it at the right time and place to keep crops alive. In Rio Arriba, Santa Fe, Valencia, and Doña Ana Counties, water-delivery disputes accounted for at least a third of all cases. And in Sierra County, which had only two cases in the study period, both dealt with water delivery. As we will see in more detailed discussion of individual cases, water-delivery disputes frequently correlated with disputes over crop damage and loss.

A fifth dispute category—"physical changes to water systems"—includes disagreements over ditch construction, changes to river and canal channels, and modifications or additions to existing irrigation infrastructure. This was not an especially prominent type of dispute, but it accounted for a fifth of all court cases in the study period, and every county had at least one case dealing with this issue (including Sierra County, which again had only two cases in total). Typically, cases in this category focused on intentional modifications to natural or man-made waterways. Disputes could flare up quickly when one party's project—to widen a ditch, create an embankment, or create a cutoff canal, say—impacted another party's water delivery. As discussed in a few detailed examples in chapter 7, courts were quick to issue injunctions that temporarily stopped construction or modification projects until the dispute at hand could be resolved. But judges rarely put a stop to water development projects altogether; instead, they looked for resolutions that allowed irrigation development and expansion to go forward.

Finally, a small set of cases dealt with water rights, where the court ruled on either the existence or the seniority of irrigators' rights. Water rights rarely surfaced in litigation in areas dominated by Indigenous and Nuevomexicano irrigation systems with well-known and long-settled water rights. But in areas with shorter agricultural histories, the Office of the Territorial Engineer served as a primary arbiter of water rights. In those areas the courts might call on the engineer to help resolve disputes, or the court itself might rule on appeals that protested a decision made by the engineer. Often water-rights cases revolved around questions of whether water use had been "continuous" and "beneficial," the two bases for holding a water right under the doctrine of prior appropriation. Several of the cases profiled in chapter 7 illustrate the different ways courts addressed questions over water rights that had been settled before Anglo settlement versus questions about the engineer's more recent issuance of water permits to speculative settlers.

IN WHAT WAYS DID DISPUTANTS MAKE THEIR ARGUMENTS?

Table 6.8 shows that litigants in water-related disputes engaged in a variety of argumentation strategies to make their case to the court, which I have aggregated into the categories of "simple assertion," "appeals to authority," "direct evidence," and "witness testimony." Some court records were too incomplete for me to determine how arguments were made, but the vast majority contained sufficient information for at least partial reconstruction of the strategies used by one or both sides. A plaintiff's complaint typically includes simple assertions about the facts of the case and occasionally refers to witness affidavits or evidentiary materials. The same is true of a defendant's answer and a plaintiff's reply, all of which become part of the pretrial court record. If a case includes courtroom hearings, in which the two sides present arguments to a judge or referee, sometimes with a jury, such hearings were documented in transcripts. Extant tran-

TABLE 6.8 Argumentation strategies used in water-related cases, New Mexico district court records, Chama–Rio Grande study area, 1900–1912

Strategies used by at least one side	For all cases n = 187	Cases with environmental issues n = 79*
Simple assertion	127 (67.9%)	63 (79.7%)
Direct evidence	84 (44.9%)	42 (53.2%)
Sketch map or illustration	12 (6.4%)	12 (15.2%)
Scientific survey or map	10 (5.3%)	9 (11.4%)
Hydrologic Data	3 (1.6%)	3 (3.8%)
Legal document	71 (38.0%)	29 (36.7%)
Photograph	1 (0.5%)	1 (1.3%)
Appeal to authority	59 (31.6%)	26 (32.9%)
Witness testimony	32 (17.1%)	22 (27.8%)
Eyewitness	30 (16.0%)	21 (26.6%)
Expert	4 (2.1%)	2 (2.5%)
Unknown	8 (4.3%)	1 (4.3%)

Note: Total percentages exceed 100% for each row because all strategies used by both sides are included for each case.
* See table 6.9 for breakdown of environmental issues.

scripts provide considerable information about the use of witnesses and the submission of evidence. Even if no transcript survives, however, we can occasionally determine from the presence of summonses or related evidence whether witnesses were involved. In terms of direct evidence, a few cases either referred to or included maps, surveys, photographs, or legal contracts. Simple reference to this type of material, even if a specific document or piece of evidence was not itself present in the files, was sufficient for me to include it in the count for that case.

Overall, table 6.8 shows that simple assertion was by far the most common method of argumentation, since this is the standard way of initiating a lawsuit. Next most common: litigants submitted direct evidence in almost half of all cases, with a slightly higher proportion for cases that included at least one environmental issue, as defined above. Among the different forms of direct evidence, legal documents such as contracts or ownership titles were most common, with maps and surveys also appearing occasionally to support arguments on multiple sides. Most often the maps were hand-drawn to illustrate water flows or locations within a water system. When scientific survey or professional cartography was brought to court, it was typically on the side of a corporation or individual speculator. And if one side submitted a map or sketch as part of its case, the other side would invariably respond with commentary on the accuracy of the map or sketch and often would offer its own to give an alternative view.

After evidence, the next most common strategy—appeal to authority—was used in about a third of cases, with nearly identical proportions for the study as a whole and for the subset of cases in which environmental issues appeared. This type of argumentation referenced the authority of specific legislation or specific political leaders or governments to support claims. For example, individual irrigators sometimes appealed to the authority of the Homestead Act to support their claims regarding the validity of water appropriations. Longtime Nuevomexicano residents sometimes appealed to the authority of the Spanish Crown as the basis for historical land and water rights.

Finally, many of these cases included witness testimony to support various claims and arguments. As the statistics show, it was noticeably more common for litigants in environment-related disputes to bring witness testimony than is shown in the overall rate for all cases. Eyewitnesses were far more common than expert witnesses, although we should note that court-appointed expert observers are not included in this count, as they were counted instead as court personnel. Witnesses testified—both by written affidavit and in person—to a variety of facts, confirming landownership claims, providing detailed chronologies of water appropriation, reporting on irrigation agreements, vouching for litigants' personal character, and testifying to the changing conditions of flowing water, natural geomorphology, infrastructure, and crops. Occasionally witnesses rendered judgments about how much water an individual irrigator actually needed to maintain crops or expand cultivation.

Strategies of argumentation did not vary significantly by county, with a couple of exceptions. Cases in Valencia County never relied on witness testimony during the time period of the study, and Sandoval County cases showed low rates of evidence use compared to the overall average. I draw no significant findings from these outliers or from other variations among county statistics. Most surprisingly, the cases included in this study showed very little change in the nature of argumentation from the beginning to the end of the study period, despite fundamental changes to water management in the first decade of the twentieth century. Although the records show a break between disputants' use of local irrigators as eyewitnesses and the use of expert witnesses or observers, this does not appear to be a chronological transition. Rather, it aligns with the status and ethnicity of those involved in the dispute. Anglo and Nuevomexicano elites (and corporations they led) were more likely than nonelite Nuevomexicano or Indigenous litigants to rely on expert witnesses. This reflects the fact that Anglo settler colonialism was predicated largely on a racialized redefinition of expertise that elevated the knowledge of those who claimed whiteness and minimized the knowledge of nonwhites.

HOW DO THESE CASES ADDRESS ENVIRONMENTAL KNOWLEDGE?

Across all of the topical areas listed above, litigants often prompted the court to consider an explicitly environmental argument or question. As the statistics in table 6.9 show, surface-water hydrology was at issue in three-quarters of the cases that contained an environmental question (or

TABLE 6.9 Breakdown of environmental issues, New Mexico district court records, Chama–Rio Grande study area, 1900–1912

County	Total cases with environmental issues	Surface hydrology	Channel geometry	Environmental events	Groundwater hydrology	Other*
		Percentages based on total cases with environmental issue(s).				
Rio Arriba (n = 23)	11 (47.8%)	9 (82%)	4 (36%)	4 (36%)	1 (9%)	n/a
Santa Fe (n = 8)	3 (37.5%)	2 (66.7%)	2 (66.7%)	1 (33.3%)	0 (0.0%)	2 (66.7%)
Sandoval (n = 18)	5 (27.8%)	5 (100%)	3 (60%)	3 (60%)	1 (20.0%)	1 (20%)
Bernalillo (n = 83)	26 (31.3%)	22 (84.6%)	8 (30.8%)	8 (30.8%)	1 (3.8%)	n/a
Valencia (n = 23)	13 (56.5%)	9 (69.2%)	5 (38.5%)	1 (7.7%)	2 (15.4%)	1 (7.7%)
Socorro (n = 12)	7 (58.3%)	4 (57.1%)	2 (28.6%)	2 (28.6%)	1 (12.5%)	2 (28.6%)
Sierra (n = 2)	2 (100%)	1 (50%)	2 (100.0%)	0 (0.0%)	0 (0.0%)	n/a
Doña Ana (n = 18)	12 (66.7%)	8 (66.7%)	4 (33.3%)	9 (75.0%)	1 (8.3%)	n/a
Total (n = 187)	**79 (42.2%)**	**60 (75.9%)**	**30 (38%)**	**28 (35.4%)**	**7 (8.9%)**	**6 (7.6%)**

Note: Total percentages exceed 100% for each row because most cases included multiple environmental issues.

* Includes agronomy, arability, water quality, etc.

one-third of all cases in the study). Courts addressed intersecting questions about rivers, streams, and canals: how much water was flowing, when it flowed, where it flowed, and how channel flow was impacted by irrigation activities or seasonal change. About one-third of the cases that addressed environmental questions focused on the shape or configuration of surface-water channels. Another third included questions about environmental events such as floods, droughts, or erosion. In most of these categories, disputes tended to revolve around either specific characteristics of a physical system or the causes of changes to physical systems. As noted above, individuals accused of causing damage to property, crops, or infrastructure often pointed the finger in turn at natural causes and conditions. To evaluate these claims, the court sometimes had to make determinations about the nature of environmental events and their causality. By raising questions about natural versus human impacts on the banks, beds, and bends of rivers, however, attorneys often managed to confound judges' attempts to resolve disputes with finality. Disputants made physical claims about environmental systems in different ways, as we will see, and the courts ruled on fundamental environmental questions in only a small number of cases.

These statistics provide little information about exactly how environmental questions influenced disputes and dispute resolution in the district court system. Yet it is clear from these data that many environmental topics *were* disputed in district court. Knowledge, then, was a critical variable in water management, and courts helped determine how to resolve disputes over environmental characteristics, realities, and causalities. Chapter 7 moves past these global statistics and takes a closer look at how individual court cases reveal the changing role of science and expertise in the courtroom, the mediation of environmental knowledge in the legal arena, and the upheaval of ethnic relations in response to increased Anglo settlement.

❋ 7 ❋
Displacement

GEOGRAPHIES OF POWER IN AN
IRRIGATED LANDSCAPE

Now, finally: stories.

In this chapter I dive into individual court cases. By viewing disputes as stories rather than as statistics, I offer a more complex view of water management during the last decade of New Mexico's territorial period. The foregoing chapters show that the Anglo settler project relied on notions of modernist science and expertise to legitimize and institutionalize their own attempts at domination. Through the narrative analysis of this chapter, I offer a final review of whether, where, and how exactly this knowledge project worked. The legal arena is a place of "encounter" where assumptions about authority, worldview, and power are laid bare.[1] The disputes argued in New Mexico's late territorial courts reveal multiple personalities, places, institutions, and infrastructures behind specific water-management arrangements. They show that the contestation and negotiation of knowledge in water disputes are linked to specific sociopolitical arrangements in specific places. And they reveal that Anglo power—and the knowledge claims on which it relied—varied in both time and space. These stories show that truth, expertise, and knowledge change from place to place. Modernist science is not placeless.

Methodologically, this chapter focuses on a subset of water-related disputes between 1900 and 1912. For each county in the Chama–Rio Grande corridor, I chose one to three district court cases to illustrate key themes and trends in that area, with a bias toward cases with fairly complete documentary records. (See fig. 7.1 for approximate locations of selected cases.) As a whole, these fourteen exemplars highlight spatial variations in water management and legal administration across different parts of the New Mexico territory. By delving into procedural issues, structures of argumentation, assemblages of evidence, and individual personalities, these stories bring to life deep understandings of the relationships among hydrologic knowledge, water management, displacement, and dispossession.

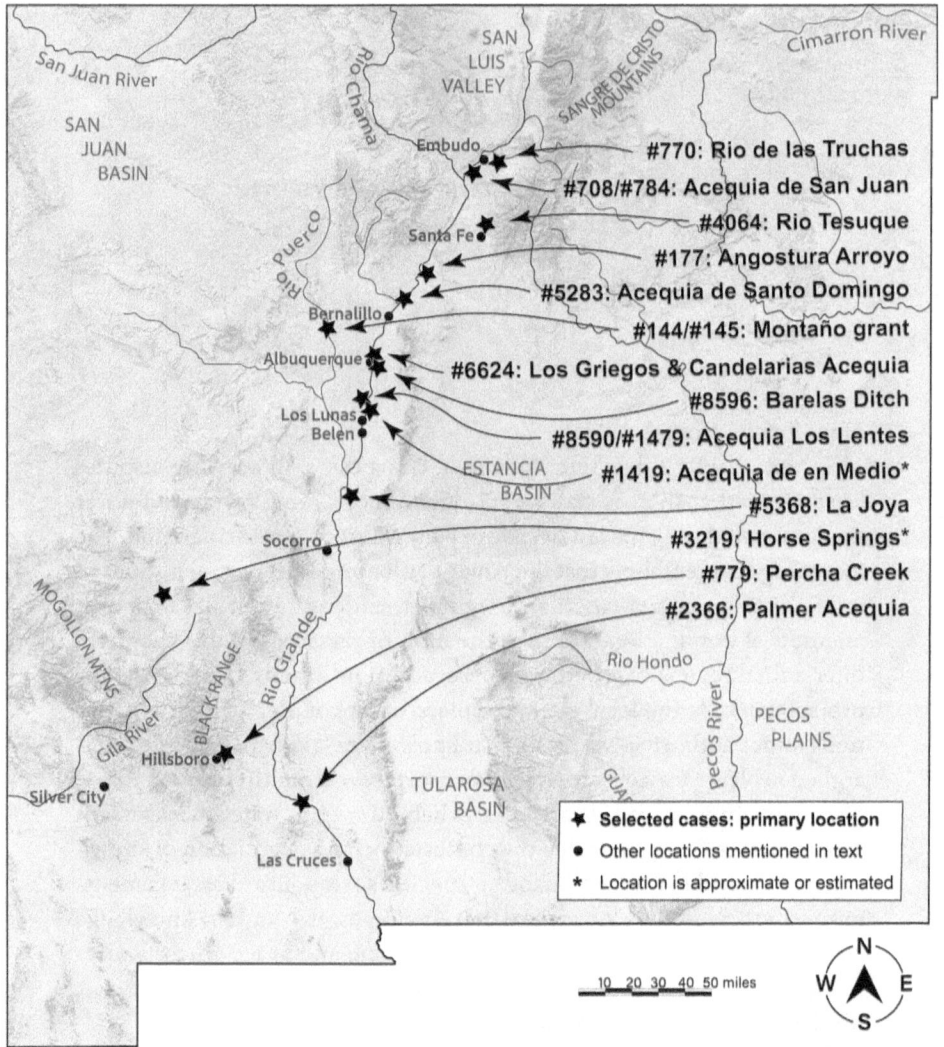

FIGURE 7.1 Location of water disputes discussed in narratives
Map by Maria Lane. Shaded relief: Resource Geographic Information System (RGIS)

The chapter is broken into subsections by county. Each subsection opens with a short discussion of the county's cultural and economic context and a description of its overall district court caseload from 1900 to 1912. The remainder of each subsection provides one or more detailed case summaries that illustrate broader trends in the county. The cases unfold in a narrative format that outlines the dispute, describes its court procedures and filings, and interprets key issues regarding how the dispute was argued, executed, and resolved. Although some of these cases continued beyond the district court through an appeals process, the summaries below do not analyze any materials beyond the district court record. As a group, the cases illuminate the role of knowledge, both in the imposition of Anglo settler colonialism, and in the resistance to it.

Before embarking on the remainder of this chapter, I advise the reader to pour a refreshing beverage and prepare a snack. Each dispute includes numerous details, and the cases follow many twists and turns as they trace a winding path through the Rio Chama and Rio Grande valleys. I highlight key insights along the way, but it's still a lot to digest. Give yourself some time.

In working through these stories, you will see that modernist science played an important role in court-mediated water disputes. Judges prioritized scientific data and expert testimony as evidence, and they tried repeatedly to implement technology-driven solutions. But even modernist science *never* trumped the economic-development goals of Anglo settlers. Scientific cartography could be sidestepped in order to protect a railroad right-of-way. Strict quantification of water flow was ignored if it would impede Anglos' speculative development goals. Judges made environmental determinations from the bench on the basis of limited or no credible environmental evidence, sometimes contrary to federal agencies' detailed environmental claims. And in cases involving no Anglos at all—where Nuevomexicano communities came into conflict with one another or with Indigenous neighbors—judges put less effort into the enforcement of modernist scientific standards or perspectives. Modernist science was simply a tool of settler colonialism.

These stories also narrate the disruption, displacement, and dispossession that attended Anglo settlement in New Mexico. In county after county, Anglo settlers pushed Nuevomexicano and Indigenous peoples and institutions into new and uncomfortable situations. Water disputes provide a rich vein for exploring the terrain of ethnic relations as they evolved in response to land encroachment, environmental change, and infrastructure installation.

One final note: court records for these cases typically do not include any diacritical marks for participants' names or for place-names. This is true for both handwritten and typed documents. Because Nuevomexicanas'/os' use of diacritics in names became increasingly variable during the territorial period, I have reproduced names exactly as they are shown in the court record, unless I was able to confirm via signature or other evidence that the correct spelling includes diacritics.

Rio Arriba: Disputed Technology in the Nuevomexicano Homeland

Rio Arriba County contains the original seat of European colonization in New Mexico. Spanish colonists established their first settlement in 1598 near the junction of the Rio Chama and the Rio Grande, where the city of Española now sits.[2] The modern county boundary follows the Chama from the Colorado state line to its Rio Grande confluence and a short way down the Rio Grande main stem. Area terrain is extremely mountainous, with numerous small valleys dividing the landscape into pockets of settlement and agriculture. During the early Spanish colonial period, ranchos and haciendas produced subsistence crops, and inhabitants tended sheep throughout the many valley fingers. After the coordinated Pueblo Revolt expelled all colonists in 1680, Spanish settlers reentered Rio Arriba's valleys in 1693 with a less dispersed approach. Over the next three centuries, Rio Arriba's Nuevomexicano communities focused on a combination of acequia-irrigated agriculture and vertical transhumance within a mixed Indigenous-Nuevomexicano cultural landscape. Anglo settlers never penetrated this area significantly, aside from a few fruit-growing operations and a timber-extraction program managed by the federal government. Instead, Rio Arriba became New Mexico's primary Nuevomexicano homeland, where unique cultural and political traditions persisted, and acequia governance endured as the mainstay of political life.[3] After 1848 the Anglo-dominated territorial legal system took on the task of settling water disputes for this county as for all others. District court records for Rio Arriba County reveal that communities long accustomed to Spanish legal norms struggled with the abrupt legal transition to Anglo customs.

From 1900 to 1912 the Rio Arriba district court handled twenty-three cases that concerned water. Almost half involved disputes over water delivery (44 percent), with many others also focusing on the governance and maintenance of shared acequia systems (35 percent) and damage to infrastructure or crops (26 percent). Overall, about half of Rio Arriba's disputes involved some kind of environmental question—typically related to the nature or quantity of channel and tributary flows—and disputants usually addressed these questions in court through simple assertion or appeals to authority, using both sketch maps and scientific cartography as evidence. The vast majority of all plaintiffs in Rio Arriba's cases were Nuevomexicana/o (87 percent), although some Indigenous plaintiffs brought cases as well (13 percent), and Nuevomexicanas/os were essentially always listed as defendants (96 percent). In contrast, Anglos dominated the court personnel, constituting 100 percent of all judges and attorneys, although 64 percent of cases included a Nuevomexicano official in the role of probate judge, appraiser, justice of the peace, or sheriff. No Indigenous personnel appear as court officials in any of these case records.

The two cases summarized below illustrate the difficulty of imposing new norms—both scientifically and legally—in places with culturally important customs for water sharing through the institution of the acequia.[4] As described in chapter 2, an acequia comprises much more than a physical assemblage of diversion dams, conveyance ditches, laterals, and headgates. It constitutes an institution of water governance grounded in assumptions about a community's shared right to water. The first case below centers on a disagreement between Indigenous and Nuevomexicano communities over water delivery in two related acequias. At its heart, the case turns on an underlying question of whether the disputants' ancestors had worked together to create the ditches in question, thereby creating shared water rights. The second dispute, between two Nuevomexicano acequia communities on opposite banks of a small Rio Grande tributary, highlights the difficulty territorial courts faced in addressing both political and technological questions.

GEORGE ANTON ET AL. V. JUAN BAUTISTA TALACHE AND PUEBLO OF SAN JUAN V. ACEQUIA NUEVA

From 1903 to 1905 two acequia communities at the confluence of the Rio Grande and Rio Chama struggled through an entrenched dispute over the connection between their acequias. At issue was a small wooden structure that diverted water from San Juan Pueblo's Acequia Madre into the Acequia Nueva, a fairly new downstream ditch.

The Acequia Madre de San Juan Pueblo was an old acequia.[5] It drew waters from the Rio Grande at a diversion point well upstream of San Juan, then snaked along a gravity-driven path toward San Juan. Along the way the Acequia Madre fed the upstream Nuevomexicano communities of La Joya and Plaza Alcalde, where farmers turned its water toward hearty subsistence crops. About a decade before the 1903 court case (George Anton et al. v. Juan Bautista Talache) began, a group of Nuevomexicano irrigators left this upstream area and moved to Ranchitos, a new settlement downstream of San Juan. Settlers in Ranchitos successfully petitioned the main ditch for permission to divert surplus water from the Acequia Madre's *desagüe* (outflow channel) at a point downstream of the pueblo.[6] Based on the agreement, the resettled irrigators dug a ditch branching off the desagüe toward their fields, and they installed a wooden control structure to control water flow at the diversion point.

The wooden box, or spillway, operated in the usual way, with a set of removable boards that could be installed to block the desagüe's flow at different heights. With all of the boards in place, the structure completely blocked the desagüe and diverted its entire flow into the Acequia Nueva. With all the boards removed, water bypassed the Acequia Nueva intake and continued on its outflow path back toward the Rio Grande. By using a few of the boards, a water manager could divide the water flow between both ditches.

In 1903 the Nuevomexicano irrigators using the Acequia Nueva sued irrigators from San Juan and charged them with destroying the wooden spillway structure and physically preventing its repair by "threatening personal violence and using force."[7] Without a functioning control structure, the Acequia Nueva community could not divert water into its ditch and therefore could not irrigate its fields. As plaintiffs, they asked the judge to order San Juan to replace the control structure and leave it alone.

San Juan Pueblo responded forcefully. Pueblo irrigators admitted they had cut off the Acequia Nueva intake, but they justified their actions as necessary to prevent flooding. It turned out that the Acequia Nueva ditch was not as deep as the Acequia Madre, which meant water would not flow into the new ditch until a significant pool developed behind the spillway structure. During storm season, the Pueblo defendants claimed, heavy precipitation sent water rushing into the Acequia Madre and caused the pool to extend well up the acequia channel, inundating land and crops on both sides. The Pueblo's attorneys blamed the wooden spillway for this damage, and they also pressed a devastating counterclaim. According to the defense, Acequia Nueva's permission to use surplus waters from the Acequia Madre existed only as a courtesy or "matter of grace."[8] San Juan Pueblo argued that it had no obligation to provide water to the fields and irrigators of Acequia Nueva because the new ditch did not hold any true water rights.

The Acequia Nueva irrigators disagreed, insisting they enjoyed shared rights to the ditch because their ancestors had jointly built the Acequia Madre de San Juan with the Pueblo peoples. As the Nuevomexicano plaintiffs stated in a court filing: "[the] Acequia Madre is not owned exclusively by the Indians of the village of San Juan, but it is owned by the plaintiffs in this case, the defendants, and other parties who live outside from the said Indian village and are not members thereof, but are Mexican people and it has always been owned by all of the said parties in common."[9] Acequia Nueva irrigators also disputed the Pueblo's analysis of the upstream flooding problem, rejecting the idea that it was caused by the depth of their ditch. They pointed the finger instead at an upstream arroyo that delivered particularly forceful freshets into the Acequia Madre during storm events.[10]

To settle the dispute, Judge John R. McFie ordered the Pueblo defendants to maintain and control a spillway structure at the point of Acequia Nueva's intake. He included specific height specifications and noted that the spillway box must have an ability "to operate automatically" in times of rising water. McFie assigned to the Pueblo responsibility for maintaining this spillway "forever" and for reinforcing the ditch channel to prevent flooding. He did not address the underlying dispute over water rights.

McFie's seemingly straightforward technological solution did not, however, resolve the dispute. Since a wooden spillway was already in place at the time of the court's ruling (and was in fact the reason for the case in the first place), the Pueblo did not see fit to rebuild it to meet the court's specifications. Most notably, the spillway did not operate in an "automatic" way, as the judge prescribed. It relied on removable planks that required manual insertion to divert water into the Acequia Nueva and manual removal to allow faster flow-through in the Acequia Madre. The plaintiffs complained about the spillway in follow-up petitions. They reported that the wooden planks "constantly fall off [as] the water rises behind them," and "it is utterly impossible, without sitting at the spill-way and holding these boards down firmly and in place, to divert any water into the Acequia Nueva."[11]

The wooden spillway's manual operation requirements not only undermined the judge's vision for an automatic system but also perpetuated a significant problem: people from both sides of the dispute were continually drawn into contact at the spillway site. The court gave the Pueblo responsibility for maintaining the spillway, yet Acequia Nueva had the biggest stake in its proper functioning. It was a recipe for further conflict.

The Pueblo delegated responsibility for monitoring and maintaining the wooden planks to Alejandrino Garcia, an individual who lived nearby. Garcia reportedly kept the top two boards in his possession and claimed publicly "that he alone was authorized to touch the boards." If waters rose behind the spillway while Garcia was absent, the planks inevitably fell down, leaving Acequia Nueva irrigators unable to fix the spillway without violating the judge's orders.[12] In other words, McFie's prescribed technological solution for the Acequia Nueva intake had defaulted instead to a mode of ditch maintenance common to every acequia system in New Mexico, where an individual person was vested with final authority for controlling the flow of water. In response to a follow-up petition, McFie agreed that this was problematic and modified his ruling. Seeking to remove individual decision-making from the spillway's operation, McFie ruled that the wooden planks had to be secured in place and could not be touched for any reason "except that when there shall be imminent a storm or flood which may cast a heavy burden of water into the said Acequia

Madre." At that point, and only at that point, Garcia could remove the boards. And they had to be replaced as soon as "such storm or flood has spent its force."[13]

Although McFie's second ruling provided for a more automatic and less political resolution, the dispute was back in court within a year. In Pueblo of San Juan v. Acequia Nueva and Taofilo Archuleta, mayordomo (1905), the Pueblo sued for permission to remove the flashboards, claiming that their permanent installation had turned the spillway into a dam.[14] They charged that silt and sediments had filled in behind the wooden structure, significantly compromising its original function as an outlet for floodwater. The Pueblo requested permission to remove the boards for the purposes of cleaning out accumulated silt and returning the channel of the Acequia Madre to its original depth. Additionally, the Pueblo asked that Acequia Nueva irrigators be required to deepen the intake of their ditch, essentially reasserting their original point that the Acequia Nueva intake was too high and caused upstream flooding. This second suit petitioned the judge for relief from the technological solution he himself had imposed, arguing that Acequia Nueva irrigators must be denied water until their ditch was deepened.[15]

In the second suit the judge relented, implicitly acknowledging that his technological solution had failed. He ruled that San Juan Pueblo could remove the flashboards to clean the Acequia Madre and that the Acequia Nueva must clean and deepen their ditch.[16] After attempting twice to fix the conflict by mandating water-control technology, he finally made a ruling that dealt with the underlying water-rights issue. In decreeing that irrigators dependent on the Acequia Nueva would not get any water unless they deepened their intake channel, Judge McFie confirmed that the newer community's right to water in the main ditch was contingent on its participation in a water- and infrastructure-sharing scheme that fully accounted for the rights of other water users. McFie had seemed unwilling to rule on this issue in earlier petitions, but the failure of his technological workaround forced him to revert to an older norm for dispute resolution. This dispute shows that technological solutions did not always live up to their billing, frustrating attempts to deploy modernist science as a cure for local cultural conflict.

ACEQUIA DE LOS GARCIAS V. ACEQUIA DEL MEDIO

In a second case from Rio Arriba County, flood diversion technology again caused a dispute between neighboring acequia communities. In a narrow valley downstream from the old USGS Embudo training camp, two

Nuevomexicano settlements sat pinned to the Rio Grande's east bank by Sangre de Cristo mountain slopes. Nestled next to the big river, the two communities looked at one another across the Rio de las Truchas, a minor tributary. Although the Truchas channel often sat dry, it ran heartily in spring with mountain snowmelt and in summer with monsoon-driven precipitation. To protect low-lying agricultural lands, users of the Acequia de los Garcias (on the Truchas left bank) and Acequia del Medio (on its right bank) had long built "breakwaters" of brush, stone, and logs to prevent Truchas waters from entering their fields.[17] Each community installed and maintained its own protective structures, often rebuilding them after seasonal floodwaters inflicted heavy damage.

In 1905 the Acequia de los Garcias sued the Acequia del Medio for building a new breakwater. The Garcias irrigators' lawsuit claimed that the new structure cut a near-perpendicular angle across the Truchas channel, rerouting water toward the opposite community and glutting the Acequia de los Garcias with mud. The plaintiffs provided a map in support of their complaint. It showed both rivers, both acequias, both breakwaters, and all of the plaintiffs' cultivated fields (fig. 7.2). The map was meant simply to illustrate the legal complaint, but its cartographic veracity quickly emerged as a target in the dispute. When the defendants from Acequia del Medio replied to the initial charge, they argued that the plaintiffs' map misrepresented the Truchas as flowing through a "northwesterly" channel instead of flowing "from east to west" where it entered the Rio Grande.[18] This distinction mattered deeply to both sides, with each party arguing that its own breakwater ran *parallel* to the river, while the other community's breakwater *crossed* the channel and diverted the river's natural flow.

The Medio defendants asked the judge "not to consider the [map] as reliable" because "there is nothing to show when and by whom it was made, nor that [it] was made by a competent civil engineer, or surveyor."[19] After contesting the plaintiffs' cartographic expertise, the defendants submitted their own map as "a more reliable guide for the court to follow," noting that it had been prepared by an engineer who had signed both the map and a legal affidavit to verify its truthfulness.[20] On the defendants' map (fig. 7.3), the Rio de las Truchas indeed runs east to west. The map shows a north-bank breakwater that runs parallel to the natural course of the river, causing no diversion of water flow. In the defendants' cartographic reinscription, in fact, it is the plaintiffs' "breakwater" on the south side of the Truchas that juts into the river and diverts floodwater across the north-bank fields, rather than the opposite scenario.

The second map completely rewrote the geography of the dispute. It called into question both the natural channel of the tributary and the

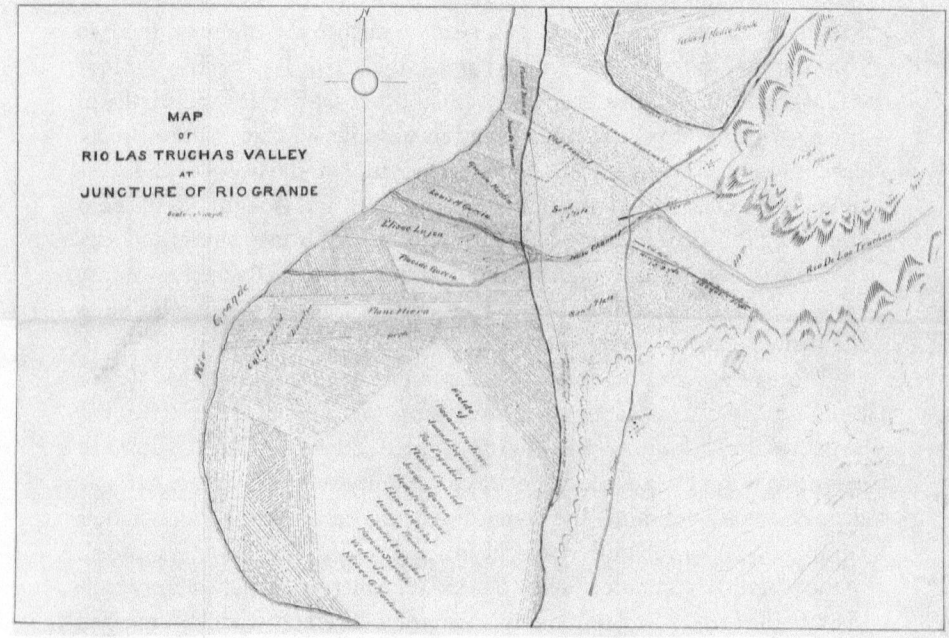

FIGURE 7.2 Map of Rio Las Truchas valley at the juncture of the Rio Grande
Map filed with Complaint in Civil case no. 770: *La Acequia de Los Garcias, et al. v. La Acequia del Medio, et al.*, 1905; Collection 1973-017; Records of the United States Territorial and New Mexico District Courts for Rio Arriba County, Box no. 12, Serial no. 13515. New Mexico State Records Center and Archives, Santa Fe, NM

human-made flood-control structures. Both sides drew a distinction in court documents between a "breakwater" running parallel to the river channel, like a berm or levee, and a "dam" or "wing-dam" crossing the river course and diverting waters away from the natural channel. In the original complaint, Acequia de las Garcias irrigators referred to their own structure as a breakwater and characterized the defendants' structure as a dam. The defendants from Acequia del Medio claimed the exact opposite. The defendants grabbed the advantage by submitting a map created by an engineer who signed an affidavit stating that his map was "a true exemplification" of field measurements and observations.[21] In addition, defendants claimed that two independent observers had already visited the site and recommended removal of the plaintiffs' south-side breakwater/dam. Acequia del Medio asked the judge to accept their second map as the true geographic representation, based on the opinions of independent observers and a "public competent surveyor."[22]

Judge McFie was on the bench again for this case. He brokered an agree-

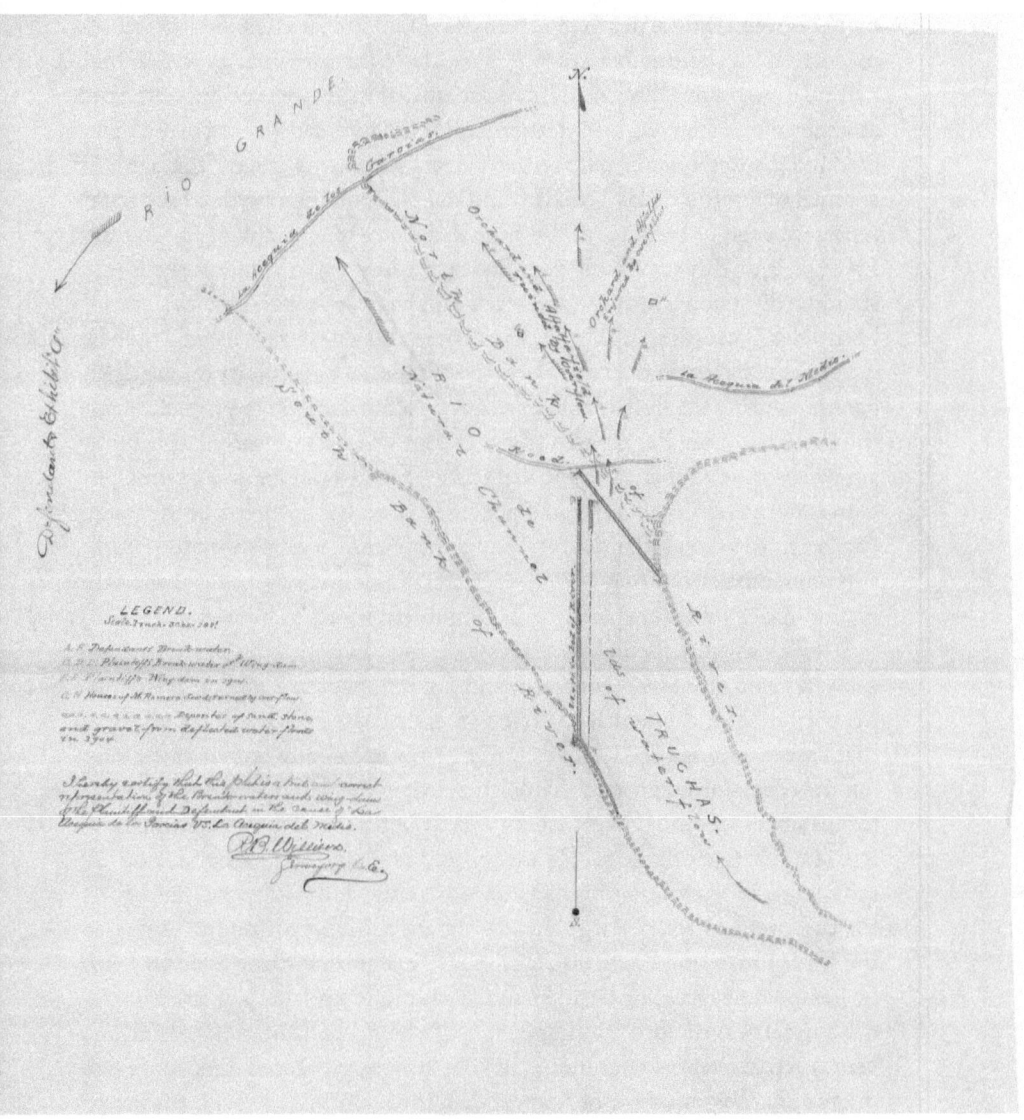

FIGURE 7.3 Map depicting breakwaters and wing-dam
Defendant's Exhibit A filed with Defendant's Answer to Show Cause in Civil case no. 770: *La Acequia de Los Garcias, et al. v. La Acequia del Medio, et al.*, 1905; Collection 1973-017; Records of the United States Territorial and New Mexico District Courts for Rio Arriba County, Box no. 12, Serial no. 13515. New Mexico State Records Center and Archives, Santa Fe, NM

ment between the parties that he himself would "make a personal view and inspection" of the site to assess the position of the breakwaters within the natural topography.[23] McFie visited the site in April 1905, accompanied by attorneys for each side, and determined that *both* maps were correct. He credited the defendants' map with a correct representation of "the natural channel of the Rio de las Truchas" and the plaintiffs' map with an accurate representation of the site "at the time this suit was brought."[24] Judge McFie explained this seemingly paradoxical finding as the result of the longstanding diversion and containment of Truchas waters with breakwaters on both sides. According to McFie, the Garcias breakwater diverted Truchas water out of its "natural" channel toward the Medio community on the right bank, requiring the defendants to maintain a breakwater for protection, as shown in the defendants' map (fig. 7.3). But when those defendants built a new breakwater that rerouted water back toward the natural channel, it damaged the left-bank fields and acequia, as shown in the plaintiffs' map (fig. 7.2). To resolve the dispute, Judge McFie decreed simply that both sides must maintain their own breakwaters in perpetuity, given that both communities were constantly under imminent threat of flooding.

McFie's suggestion that better engineering (on both sides) was the fairest and most obvious means of resolving the dispute appears similar to his reasoning in the first Rio Arriba case, discussed above. But unlike in that case, the judge seemed hesitant to embrace a fully technocratic ruling. His decision to go into the field and view the geography for himself, for instance, was most likely calculated to settle the dispute in a way that felt familiar to both sides. He essentially repeated the earlier action of independent observers who had viewed the site and made a ruling before the case went to court. By going into the field, McFie refused to embrace the surveyor's signed map outright, treating it as something to be verified by personal observation. And he made a point in his ruling of referring to the correctness of both maps, focusing on their representations of natural versus actual channel alignment. The defendants presented their surveyed map as unambiguously more expert than the plaintiffs' less scientific map, yet McFie refrained from giving the survey higher authority than personal observation at the site of the conflict. His actions indicate that he thought strategically about how to derive a culturally relevant resolution that would head off repeated lawsuits.

Santa Fe: New Irrigators in a Settled Landscape

As we move downriver past the Chama confluence, the Rio Grande flows through Santa Fe County, which is "probably the oldest political sub-division in the United States," having hosted New Mexico's capital from early Spanish colonial times through the Mexican and American periods.[25] The county is mountainous in its northern sections and opens into broad and rolling plains to the south. Historically, the Rio Grande and its numerous small tributaries have supported subsistence farms alongside pasturage throughout the area. When Spanish colonists arrived around 1600, they established acequia irrigation alongside the ditch systems of their Indigenous neighbors, sometimes sharing infrastructure and management responsibilities. By the time of American annexation in 1848, small Nuevomexicano, Indigenous, and mixed-ethnicity communities had long been established through Santa Fe County, including the government seat of Santa Fe itself.

Santa Fe did not emerge as a major economic or population center in territorial-era New Mexico, despite its dominant importance as a Spanish and then Mexican center of administration. The town anchored the Camino Real during Spanish colonial times and provided an essential connection node on the Santa Fe Trail during the Mexican period. But without a terminal on New Mexico's primary AT&SF railroad, the capital struggled to achieve economic importance in the American era. During a time of major population growth for the territory overall—1900 to 1910—Santa Fe County's population changed barely at all, holding steady at just under fifteen thousand people. Anglos who arrived in the area typically focused on timbering in the northern mountains, ranching in the county's southern plains, or fruit cultivation in Rio Grande tributary valleys. Aspiring fruit growers found it difficult, however, to establish cash-crop production in settled valleys already dominated by subsistence-oriented acequia systems. As the sample case below shows, some Anglos pieced together large tracts of suitable land and worked outside community ditch systems altogether. It was a difficult path.

From 1900 to 1912 the Santa Fe district court handled only eight cases that concerned water, and half of them involved condemnation of Nuevomexicano lands for Anglo irrigation projects. Overall, three-quarters of the cases were brought by Anglo plaintiffs, with Nuevomexicano defendants on the receiving end in all but one of these cases. Given such a small number of cases, it is difficult to make broad generalizations. The dispute summarized below may seem an odd choice for an exemplar; it is the single Santa Fe case in which both plaintiff and defendant are Anglo, and the only Santa Fe case where arguments hinged on an environmental question. I chose this case for detailed discussion because it addresses irrigation techniques, crop types, environmental conditions, and ethnic relations among Anglo and non-Anglo irrigators. It also centers on a conspiracy accusation that eventually embroiled nearly everyone in the village and took more than a year to investigate.

The robust case record for Edward Miller v. Alphonso Dockwiller and Henry Pullman (1899) offers a clear view of Anglo settlement's complex impacts on New Mexico's cultural and physical landscapes. Ethnic relations and bias played a key role in this case, reflecting the fraught territorial-era history of Anglo irrigators encroaching on Nuevomexicano irrigators' lands in northern New Mexico. In the process of encroachment, Anglos disrupted cultural norms for water management, primarily by turning to private ditches instead of shared infrastructure such as the acequia.

EDWARD MILLER V. ALPHONSO DOCKWILLER AND HENRY PULLMAN

In 1899 three Anglo farmers found themselves locked in a dispute over water rights along the Rio de Tesuque. Edward Miller sued two of his neighbors, accusing them of a dirty conspiracy to deprive him of water for cultivating fruits, vegetables, grains, and fishponds. Along this stretch of the Tesuque most farms were located on the east side of the river and primarily drew irrigation water from two public acequias—Acequia Madre and Acequia en Media. Those few farmers who owned properties directly on the riverbank also used private ditches to move river water straight to their fields. No acequia served the sparsely settled west bank of the Rio; west-bank farms relied entirely on private ditches. These private ditches on both banks held junior water rights compared to the older public acequias, but they usually enjoyed good water flow. Downstream of the diversion points for the public acequias, several riverbed springs added to the Tesuque's flow and ensured at least a moderate water supply would reach the downstream intakes of the private ditches.

Miller, the plaintiff, owned a large property on the east bank of the Tesuque, where he irrigated numerous fields from two private ditches and two public acequias. He had purchased the land from a Nuevomexicano farmer in the 1860s and had been running a profitable agricultural operation for thirty years, cultivating fruit trees, vegetables, grapevines, and fishponds from the four ditches. Miller's neighbor, Henry Pollmann, had a similar story. (Pollmann's surname was misspelled as "Pullman" when the case was filed and is therefore incorrect in the official name of the case.[26]) Pollmann had also bought his property from a Nuevomexicano owner in the 1860s, and he too had been cultivating fruits, vegetables, and alfalfa for about thirty years before the suit began. Pollmann was on the west side of the river, where he had no access to a public acequia, and his operation relied entirely on a private ditch. His property sat slightly upstream and across the river from Miller's, and Pollmann's private water right was more senior than either of Miller's two private ditches. The third party to the suit was a relative newcomer. In the 1880s Alphonso Dockwiller bought land upstream from and adjacent to Miller's on the east bank.[27] He bought it from an Anglo who had himself purchased it from a Nuevomexicano owner, and Dockwiller did not hold any water right for a private ditch. Instead, Dockwiller relied on the public Acequia en Medio to irrigate fruit trees and vegetables.

But sometime in the mid-1890s Pollmann offered Dockwiller an interesting opportunity. Pollmann allowed his fellow Dutchman to install an iron water pipe that connected their two properties on the opposite sides of the Rio de Tesuque. The pipeline collected surplus domestic water from the Pollmann property on the west bank and transported it under the riverbed to the east side; Dockwiller then conveyed the water to his crops with a pump, hydrant, and hose. Miller cried foul and sued both neighbors, arguing that Dockwiller had no right to river water and charging Pollmann with taking excess water to create an unwarranted "surplus" for Dockwiller's use. By means of this conspiracy, Miller claimed, the two defendants had reduced the amount of water flowing to his own downstream ditches, thus subjecting his crops to the threat of "utter destruction and ruin."[28] To punctuate the gravity of his charges, Miller submitted a follow-up affidavit claiming that his spring strawberry crop had perished entirely because of a lack of water.[29]

The two defendants responded with lengthy rebuttals. Pollmann defended his right to draw river water for domestic use and explained that any surplus flowed "into uncultivated lands and dry, sandy arroyos, where it would be utterly worthless and useless to any other person," meaning that his pipeline arrangement with Dockwiller was a smart way of preventing water waste.[30] Dockwiller went on the attack, rejecting nearly all of Miller's environmental and hydrologic claims. He submitted a detailed, hand-sketched map of Miller's property and ditches showing that Miller's suffering strawberry plants and many of his trees were dependent on the public acequia, not on the private ditches, and could not be impacted in any way by the new pipeline.[31] Dockwiller's map showed that riverbed springs in the Rio de Tesuque ensured a robust and permanent flow to Miller's two private ditches. His affidavit went even further, accusing Miller of overwatering (and thereby damaging) a number of fruit trees with the excess flow from his private ditches. According to Dockwiller, the only water problems on Miller's property were located in the areas served by the public acequias, which had run nearly dry in 1899, causing crop failures throughout the community. Dockwiller suggested to the judge that Miller had fabricated the lawsuit as a way of gaining access to the Pollmann-Dockwiller pipeline.[32]

Dockwiller's sketched map animated many claims and counterclaims about environmental conditions in the dispute area. Pollmann endorsed Dockwiller's map as "substantially correct" and agreed that Miller had been overwatering fruit trees, needlessly filling fishponds, and even running water onto dry land simply to deprive others of water.[33] Miller disagreed, charging that Dockwiller's map was "made by a party unaccauinted [sic] with the land in Rio de Tesuque" and denying "each and every allegation" against him.[34] Property owners from the surrounding community also found themselves drawn into the suit. Attorneys for the defendants produced statements from fellow fruit growers, who endorsed the map and agreed that Miller's private, spring-fed ditches were full of water.[35] One grower claimed to have heard Miller admit he was wasting water (by running it onto dry land) simply "to annoy and get even with 'those dam Dutchmen.'"[36] Miller's attorney submitted contrasting statements from previous and current landowners and from the mayordomos of the two public acequias. Claiming detailed knowledge of the land and water rights in question, these statements revealed a decades-long arrangement in which the owner of the Pollmann property had typically returned surplus water to the river at a point where it would flow past both of Miller's downstream ditches. They implied that Pollmann had changed the arrangement maliciously, to harm Miller, when he permitted Dockwiller to collect the surplus with his pipeline.

In one audacious twist, Dockwiller and Pollmann submitted a statement of support signed by twenty-seven neighboring Nuevomexicano irrigators, only for some of them to recant their support just days later. Dockwiller had walked around the area fields, asking farmers to sign a document attesting to the harmlessness of his pipeline and the unlawfulness of Miller's claim.[37] But no one could read or explain the document because it was written in English, and Dockwiller could not translate it into Spanish. Some believed the statement asserted or protected their own water rights, and others apparently signed it on the advice of people who vouched for Dockwiller. But a few days later Miller's attorney submitted sworn statements from a subset of the original twenty-seven signatories claiming that they had been tricked into signing the document. These individuals' follow-up affidavits clarified they had no knowledge of nor any interest in the dispute. One affiant claimed, "The whole transaction is a fraud and an imposition upon us who cannot read nor write the English language."[38] The local justice of the peace who certified the original document also claimed he had been tricked, explaining that Dockwiller was unable to translate the document into Spanish and instead provided assurances that a certifying signature would indicate simply that he personally knew those who had already signed the document.[39]

In response to all these filings, the judge appointed a referee to investigate the case. William H. Whiteman apparently took months of sworn witness statements, which required weeks of transcription and resulted in 652 pages of oral testimony. Whiteman also collected a number of sketch maps to ascertain the location of relevant ditches, springs, and irrigated fields.[40] He presented his findings to Judge John McFie more than a year after the case began, concluding that Pollmann had indeed engaged in a conspiratorial ruse to accumulate a false surplus of domestic water that could then be diverted into Dockwiller's pipe. More broadly, Whiteman's report characterized the Rio de Tesuque's origin and flow, described the position and size of the many ditches in question, detailed the crops grown on irrigated fields, outlined the historical ownership and water rights for each property, and chronicled the suffering of fruit orchards and other crops on Miller's land.[41]

Although Whiteman focused mainly on Anglo and Nuevomexicano landowners and farmers, he raised two issues related to Indigenous water rights. First, he noted that Miller had originally shared one of his private ditches with Indigenous irrigators on an adjoining ranch. According to the referee's findings, Miller only became the sole rights holder in the ditch when the Indigenous irrigators abandoned their water rights. Second, Whiteman cautioned that the Pueblo of Tesuque, situated downstream of the dispute area, held senior water rights along the entire contested stretch of the river and could theoretically take water at any time before anyone else involved in the suit. Dockwiller and Pollmann disputed Whiteman's findings in a response longer than the referee's own report, including his assertion that Miller's Indigenous neighbors had abandoned their water right in the shared ditch. The defendants' rebuttal argued instead that Miller himself had prevented Indigenous irrigators from using the shared ditch.[42] But Judge McFie had heard enough. He moved quickly to a final ruling that accepted some parts of Whiteman's report and modified others. He ordered Dockwiller to cease pumping Pollmann's domestic water and provided a detailed listing of the priority order for all water rights downstream of the public acequia intakes.[43]

This case seems fairly standard for the early years of the study's time frame. The judge deferred to a local referee who in turn relied on eyewitness testimony to understand conditions, claims, and damages. The court never invoked or requested expert personnel but accepted eyewitness accounts as credible and reliable. Judge McFie based his ruling on a clear statement of water-rights priority order rather than venturing into cartographic, scientific, or technological reasoning. He left disputes over the location of fields and the flow of ditches unaddressed, and he made no mention of the conflicting sketch maps. He nominally held Indigenous water rights superior by recognizing downstream Tesuque Pueblo as the senior rights holder. Yet he also ignored Indigenous irrigators in legal proceedings by dismissing the claim that the Indigenous co-users of Miller's ditch had been wrongfully stripped of their rights.

Overall, ethnic relations played a major role in this case. Miller was reportedly biased against the defendants on account of their Dutch national origin, and his supporting witnesses were almost uniformly Nuevomexicano, indicating that political alliances crossed ethnic lines in this area at the turn of the century. The case also makes clear, however, the extent to which Anglo irrigators had expanded their landholdings and cultivation areas at the expense of non-Anglo neighbors. Sometimes this happened through land purchase, and other times through trickery, as in Pollmann's and Dockwiller's exploitation of Nuevomexicano farmers' lack of English literacy in a bid to gain additional water rights. All three of the Anglo settlers involved in the dispute preferentially appropriated water from private ditches rather than relying on public acequias in areas where most of the Nuevomexicano farmers lived. In all of these ways, Anglo settlement disrupted the cultural and political landscape of New Mexico and destabilized water-management norms previously cultivated by Indigenous and Nuevomexicano irrigators.

Sandoval County: Speculators Enter the Valley

Proceeding downstream, we come to Sandoval County, which became a new administrative division in 1903 when it was split from the northwestern part of Bernalillo County. Just east of the volcanic Jemez Mountains complex, the Rio Grande flows through broad, sloping bottomlands that at the time of Spanish contact hosted numerous Indigenous pueblos. Through repeated conflicts with Spanish settlers and soldiers, many Pueblos suffered destruction, abandonment, or impoverishment before the nineteenth century. When Mexico ceded its northern territory to the United States, this area contained a number of small Spanish villages (Corrales, Bernalillo, Algodones, Peña Blanca, and San Ysidro) interspersed with Indigenous villages concentrated into remnant lands (Santa Ana, San Felipe, Santo Domingo, Cochiti, Zia, and Jemez). In all of these communities farmers drew irrigation water from the Rio Grande and its tributaries, including the Rio Puerco. As was true in Santa Fe County to the north, acequia irrigation dominated, with small groups of irrigators working together to build, maintain, and repair ditch systems that supported small but fertile plots of farmland.

Outside the immediate floodplains of the Rio Grande and Rio Puerco favored by Nuevomexicano and Indigenous communities, Sandoval County contained extensive stretches of arable land situated farther upslope in the broader valleys. Soon after New Mexico became a territory, the U.S. Congress opened its lands to homesteading, and the AT&SF railroad extended tracks through the central Rio Grande valley. After 1880, railroad access spurred increased Anglo settlement and corporate investment in irrigation infrastructure on a new and larger scale. Just north of Albuquerque the Nuevomexicano town of Bernalillo rose to sufficient prominence as a center of agriculture and ranching that it became the seat of the newly established Sandoval County in 1903. In the 1910 census this new county had more than eight thousand people, already more than half the population of its northern neighbor, Santa Fe County.[44]

Between 1903 and 1912 the Sandoval district court handled eighteen cases that concerned water. More than two-thirds of these were disputes over acequia maintenance or elections in the Peña Blanca community (72 percent). Although this single acequia dominates the court records for this time period, other disputes centered on changes to river and canal channels (22 percent) and on damage to crops and property (17 percent). Nuevomexicanas/os were by far the most common litigants, involved in 89 percent of the cases as plaintiff and in 72 percent of cases as defendant. Corporations also emerged in this county as legal players, participating as both plaintiffs and defendants. In cases dealing with environmental issues—typically related to channel flows—disputants based their arguments on simple assertion or on eyewitness accounts, with Anglo and Nuevomexicano witnesses appearing in the court record equally often. In terms of courtroom personnel, however, we see again complete dominance by Anglos, who made up 100 percent of the judges and attorneys.

The two disputes summarized below focus on conflicts between corporations and individual landowners. In the first, a Nuevomexicano landowner sued a railroad corporation for causing flooding and property damage through its construction activities. In the second, an irrigation company sued an Anglo landowner, who then countersued the irrigation company, over a water-permit application. These three cases reveal the impact of speculative irrigation development in the late territorial period as New Mexico's government and legal system navigated the need to protect new settlers' investments alongside existing communities' rights to engage in irrigated agriculture.

JUSTINIANO CASTILLO V. THE ATCHISON, TOPEKA AND SANTA FE RAILWAY

Between the Spanish towns of Bernalillo and Algodones, the Rio Grande flows through a narrow pass (*angostura*) and crosses the traditional territory of Tamaya (Santa Ana Pueblo). Near the pass, a small arroyo connects with the river after cutting across a relatively flat section of the eastern floodplain. In the early 1900s farmers cultivated small fields scattered around this Angostura Arroyo, where they could take advantage of the floodplain's gentle slope and fertile soils. Proximity to the arroyo proved to be both blessing and curse. Arroyos channelize and concentrate ephemeral moisture in a dry landscape, but summer storms can drive torrential flows that overflow their sandy banks. Then as now, farmers carefully calculated their distance from the arroyo before planting to avoid the risk of seasonal flooding.

In the summer of 1909 floodwaters from a summer downpour inundated Justiniano Castillo's fields along the Angostura Arroyo. When his alfalfa crop was destroyed, Castillo sued the Atchison, Topeka, and Santa Fe Railway for damages. The railroad had recently built an embankment partway across the arroyo to support train tracks, and Castillo claimed the embankment disturbed the arroyo's "natural flow" and diverted waters that otherwise would have passed through the arroyo. The railroad admitted building the embankment but denied that its construction caused any flooding. According to the AT&SF attorneys, the arroyo did not naturally carry water and should not even be considered a waterway. Instead, they argued, a summer downpour caused a natural flood for which the railroad could not be held accountable. The trial thus revolved around a simple environmental question—whether the Angostura Arroyo was in fact a natural waterway.

Little of the original case file remains, and we do not know the name of the judge in this case. His instructions to the jury, however, provide critical information about how the two sides presented their cases. The judge instructed jurors first to determine whether the Angostura Arroyo was "a natural water course" at the time of the flood and at the location of the railroad embankment and crossing. To assist jurors in this task, the judge gave explicit instructions: "there must be a channel, a bed to the stream, not merely low land or depression in the prairie over which the water flows. It matters not what the width or depth may be. A water course implies a distinct channel, a way cut and kept open by running water."[45] He also clarified that a natural watercourse "must have running in it *living* water as distinguished from *surface* water coming from rain or snow which has not entered into the earth and come out again in the form of springs" and instructed the jury to focus on "the course and channel of living water" when determining flood causation.[46]

The jury may have found these instructions confusing, for two reasons. First, the judge made a curious distinction between "living water" (from underground springs) and "surface water" (from precipitation) that is exactly backward in terms of flood causality in a desert hydrologic system. Farmers throughout the Rio Grande valley had long made decisions about where to plant by examining and avoiding arroyo beds, knowing that arroyos channel storm freshets and snowmelt floodwaters in different seasons. In an arid environment, surface waters are much more likely to cause flooding than perennial springflows. But the judge discounted surface water as part of a natural waterway and excluded arroyo-channeled surface flows from blame after a flood. In essence, his instructions indicated that the most torrential water flows in the area could be diverted with no legal consequences.

A second matter of confusion would have been the method of determination. How should the jury decide whether the Angostura Arroyo was "a natural water course" with "living water" in it? The case file includes a set of seven photographs with indications that attorneys enlarged and presented them in the courtroom. Each photograph provides a landscape view of the Angostura Arroyo and includes one or two men somewhere in the image, presumably for scale. Some photos also show the railroad bridge and embankment in relation to the surrounding landscape. We don't know whether any other evidence was presented in the trial, since the case file contains no court transcripts, maps, or witness testimony (or even a final ruling). The simple photo captions do not include argumentation, but we can safely assume that the defendant, the AT&SF, submitted them to depict the Angostura as a non-waterway. Each photograph shows a dry landscape in which the railroad's dirt embankment is no taller than a person while the railroad bridge is much taller. Visually, the photographs imply that the railroad's infrastructure left plenty of room for water to flow through the arroyo.

The preservation of these photographs in the case record indicates that visual evidence helped establish environmental knowledge in this particular case. Once the judge declared that only spring waters could be considered part of a natural watercourse, and that torrential floodwaters should be excluded from consideration, disputants' arguments were constrained by his ruling. The railroad was able to muster photographs as an appropriate form of evidence to support their claim. The judge's introduction of an environmental-knowledge constraint worked to the disadvantage of an individual farmer and for the benefit of the railroad corporation.

RIO PUERCO IRRIGATION COMPANY V. H. A. JASTRO AND H. A. JASTRO V. RIO PUERCO IRRIGATION COMPANY

In 1911 an irrigation company financed by New York investors sued a California resident who had purchased a land-grant property in Sandoval County. Both parties planned to irrigate the property, and the two court cases centered on their competing water permits. The Rio Puerco Irrigation Company (RPIC) filed its 1911 suit against H. A. Jastro in hopes of blocking him from constructing irrigation infrastructure on the Bernabe M. Montaño land grant, which Jastro had purchased after the RPIC filed a water-permit application.[47] Jastro returned the favor with a countersuit in 1912 asking the court to nullify the RPIC's permit application and approve his own. This is a complicated dispute. It involves environmental degradation, land-grant dispossession, faulty engineering, federal meddling in territorial affairs, and incredible sums of money from outside New Mexico, most of it wasted. Also beavers.

The Spanish government established the Montaño grant in the 1750s on lands that now span Bernalillo and Sandoval Counties in the valley of the Rio Puerco. Over the grant's first century, four small communities installed irrigation infrastructure across grant lands, drawing water from the Rio Puerco to support subsistence agriculture and grazing. In the decades before and after the 1848 Mexican cession, many more Nuevomexicanas/os moved into the Puerco valley, sharing its seasonal flow. Once Anglo commercial operators also began encroaching into the grasslands, however, the increased grazing pressure and concentration became unsustainable. Denuded grasslands eroded quickly in the face of torrential seasonal flooding, leaving irrigation ditches and laterals vulnerable to damage and destruction.[48] Such rapid environmental change cut deeply into the Puerco communities. Many residents and heirs of the Montaño land grant began to move away.

The exodus from the Puerco valley accelerated even though the Montaño grant heirs' legal claim to the land held unexpectedly firm. Unlike most Spanish and Mexican land grants, the Montaño achieved affirmation under U.S. law without much difficulty. New Mexico's Office of the Surveyor-General confirmed that land-grant heirs legitimately owned its lands, and New Mexico's General Land Office reported the grant's validity to the U.S. Department of the Interior in 1887, with the U.S. Court of Private Land Claims (CPLC) confirming it again in 1892.[49] Unfortunately for generational residents, these legal confirmations could not protect Montaño communities in the face of accelerating environmental degradation. With every new flood that destroyed more irrigation infrastructure, additional residents streamed off the grant to seek opportunity elsewhere.

During the exodus, the Anglo speculator Charles Lewis, of New York, mounted an aggressive bid to take control of the Montaño grant. In 1892 he petitioned the CPLC for title even though New Mexico authorities had already confirmed the grant's legal legitimacy. The CPLC reviewed the grant's derivation from the Spanish government (again), confirmed its valid ownership by surviving heirs of the original grantees (again), and accordingly denied Lewis's petition. Undeterred, Lewis changed tack. In 1893 he filed a lawsuit to partition the grant into individual properties that would then be available for private purchase. Before the partition case was decided, though, Lewis went ahead and "purchased" a part of the grant from an heir who did not actually have title to any piece of the grant. Lewis took possession and soon incorporated the Rio Puerco Irrigation Company to raise funds for building ditches and canals. In 1895 he began constructing irrigation infrastructure on the grant and adjacent lands, apparently certain that he would eventually acquire title to a meaningful amount of irrigable land. This was a common maneuver in territorial-era New Mexico: Anglo speculators made shady deals with individual land-grant heirs (who knew their lands were in decline) and then quickly installed irrigation infrastructure before legal proceedings could be completed, throwing questions of ownership into disarray. In Lewis's case, the protracted legal process ended when the court determined in early 1908 that the Montaño grant could *not* be partitioned "consistently with the interests of the estate."[50] But thanks to the continued outflow of residents and the decimation of the grant's agricultural productivity, the court ordered that the entire unpartitioned grant be put up for sale at auction a month later. End result: dispossession, either way.

According to the many exhibits entered into the court record in 1911 and 1912, an Anglo California resident, H. A. Jastro, purchased the entire Bernabe M. Montaño grant at the March 1908 auction and took fee-simple ownership. As Jastro claimed in a later water-permit application, he planned to build reservoirs, canals, and ditches that would allow the original four communities to resume their interrupted irrigation using the Montaño land grant's original water rights. But Jastro didn't have a clear path to implement his plan. Charles Lewis's RPIC had applied months earlier for a permit to irrigate 24,000 acres in central New Mexico, 6,000 of which overlapped the Montaño grant. Jastro could not proceed until the RPIC permit application was resolved.

By that point, Lewis had spent more than a decade assembling investors in New York and securing capital for the RPIC to begin construction.[51] The company contracted an unnamed Chicago engineer to design a dam and reservoir project in the early 1890s, and workers began construction in 1894. A massive earthen dam was near completion in 1895 when a storm-triggered "severe freshet" wiped it out almost entirely, also obliterating other under-construction infrastructure. Concerned but still undeterred, Lewis turned to a local engineer, Philip Harroun, of Santa Fe, for help. In 1896 Harroun declared the original plans woefully inadequate to stave off potential erosion. He offered new plans and specs for infrastructure sufficient to withstand New Mexico's torrential seasonal floods, but Harroun's design came with a price tag many times larger than the original. For the first time Lewis's aggression and ambition lagged. The RPIC proceeded with as much work as it could afford, but the operation ground to a halt in 1897 after exhausting the company's funds. Ten years later, in 1907, just as the Office of the Territorial Engineer became operational, the RPIC entered a formal application for a water permit. According to witness testimony, the permit application was a desperate, last-ditch effort to leverage additional capital and proceed with Harroun's plan. New Mexico's territorial engineer approved the permit in July 1908, just a few months after Jastro had purchased the Montaño grant at auction. Following a detailed review, the still-new Office of the Territorial Engineer approved Lewis's permit application in summer 1908.

And this is where the 1911 and 1912 court cases begin. Despite winning a water permit in 1908, the RPIC simply could not raise enough money to finish construction on Harroun's infrastructure design. In early 1909 the company still hadn't started the planned work and was in danger of violating the permit's requirements that work begin by March 1909, and that it be 20 percent complete by January 1910.[52] While Lewis dashed around New York begging for investment funds, Jastro waited patiently in the wings to submit his own water-permit application. When the RPIC applied to the territorial engineer for a construction extension in February 1909, Jastro opposed it. And when the territorial engineer extended the RPIC's construction deadline to August 1909, Jastro used the extra six months to finalize his infrastructure design and prepare his permit paperwork. When August came the RPIC still had not started any construction, and its permit lapsed. Jastro submitted his permit application immediately; at the same time, the RPIC requested a second extension.

Much to Jastro's surprise, the territorial engineer denied his permit, providing two justifications. First, the engineer refused to approve a competing application while still considering the RPIC's latest extension request. Jastro apparently accepted this explanation and was prepared to continue waiting for the cash-poor RPIC to exhaust its options. But he objected strenuously to the engineer's second justification, which cited a request by the U.S. Reclamation Service for the New Mexico territorial engineer to halt all new dams and diversions on the middle and upper Rio Grande, including the Rio Puerco tributary. Reclamation officials expressed concern that upstream water diversions would negatively impact a major federal project—the Elephant Butte Dam and Reservoir—by reducing overall water flow to the lower Rio Grande valley.[53] Jastro's appeal of this justification sent the issue to the Board of Water Commissioners for review. The Board overturned the engineer in 1911 and directed him to reject the RPIC's extension request and issue a permit to Jastro instead. The RPIC then sued Jastro in 1911 to block the Board's reversal of the engineer and to gain an extension for their own lapsed permit. Jastro then countersued the RPIC in 1912, asking the court to nullify the extension and confirm the Board of Water Commissioners' decision to grant him a permit.

In the end, Judge Raynolds sided with Jastro, upholding the Board's decision to overturn the engineer. The judge agreed with the water commissioners that the RPIC had not fulfilled the expectations of its 1907 permit, forfeiting any right to water through its failure to construct any irrigation works despite holding the permit for more than a year. Raynolds also agreed with the Board that new irrigation works on the Montaño grant would not impede downstream water flows to the Elephant Butte project area. He endorsed the Board's finding that land-grant communities held preexisting water rights that should already have been included in federal calculations of available water at Elephant Butte. He also apparently accepted Jastro's argument that those long-standing water rights were never "abandoned" despite irrigation lapses, which he attributed to the disruption of ongoing administrative and legal proceedings.

Beyond these administrative judgments, Judge Raynolds's decision engaged a key environmental question about watershed hydrology. Raynolds accepted the Board's argument that upriver diversions promote healthy downstream flows, which went directly against Reclamation Service claims to the contrary. As evidence, the Board had identified several systems where return water from upstream irrigation fed into downstream canals and supported an expansion in the total number of irrigated acres. More provocatively, they argued that Jastro's project on the Rio Puerco would *benefit* the Elephant Butte project by restoring natural upstream storage that was previously provided by beavers. To support this claim, the Board's report pointed out that the removal of beaver dams had been cataclysmic for Western landscapes: "since the destruction of the beavers ... the waters come down in torrential floods causing great and constantly increasing damage by erosion of the soil."[54] Water commissioners suggested that man-made reservoirs like the one Jastro proposed would return proper balance to natural systems by mimicking beaver lodges: "when the waters of the many tributaries forming our rivers were impounded and retarded by countless beaver dams, ... the flow of the streams was much more constant, the water carried comparatively little silt and there was little damage done by floods."[55] The Board directed the territorial engineer to "encourage and promote in every possible manner" the impoundment of waters that had been set loose by the elimination of beavers "in the upper valleys and tributaries of the large streams and in the lakes and natural depressions on the prairies."[56]

Although Judge Raynolds did not elaborate on the Board of Water Commissioners' environmental findings, his final judgment hinged on the problematic nature of land and water speculation conducted in environmental ignorance of arid landscapes. Across New Mexico, Anglo settlers' commercial exploits—from lumbering to mining to large-scale irrigated agriculture—often caused land degradation that destabilized existing communities through environmental degradation, which massive amounts of capital could not fix. An RPIC investor and witness named McChesney illustrated the way this played out when he explained at trial how the company lost its primary dam: "This thing was started in a hurry and a lot of things were done on assumption.... We spent some thirty odd thousand dollars, and it was washed out. That was done by a man ... who had no experience in this western country as to the force of the waters of the streams."[57] Even after RPIC hired a new engineer "who understood the country and understood the force of the streams"[58] (Philip Harroun), the company could not succeed because of the prohibitive cost of building Harroun's prescribed infrastructure.[59]

The judge agreed with the Board of Water Commissioners that ignorance-based failures did not justify an extension of the RPIC permit, but he never rejected the notion of building speculative irrigation infrastructure. In fact, he endorsed the Board's enthusiasm for speculative irrigation projects that might replace the long-gone beaver dams, stem regionwide erosion, improve water flows, reduce silting, and expand the irrigation potential for downstream basins. On this basis Jastro's appeal succeeded, and he obtained a water permit to build infrastructure and restore irrigation services to the communities of the Montaño land grant.[60] Disagreements over environmental knowledge took a back seat to the judge's desire to support continued irrigation development through speculation.

Bernalillo County: Managing the Strains of Settlement

Making our way further downriver, we arrive at New Mexico's economic hub and population center: Bernalillo County. Its main city of Albuquerque, important since Spanish times as a military post in the middle Rio Grande valley and as a transportation node along the Camino Real de Tierra Adentro, was renewed in the nineteenth century as a critical transportation junction.[61] When the Atchison, Topeka & Santa Fe railroad entered central New Mexico and reached Albuquerque in 1880, the railroad established a station about a mile from the old Spanish *plaza*, at the eastern edge of the Rio Grande's floodplain. The railroad's subsidiary corporation, New Mexico Town Company, laid out a new town that became the anchor for an Anglo-dominated settlement that grew quickly along the edge of the Spanish villa. In 1900 Bernalillo County boasted a population of 28,000, nearly twice that of Santa Fe County. The creation of Sandoval County in 1903 from a northwest portion of Bernalillo's territory removed a third of Bernalillo's population, but it still ended the decade with more than 23,000 residents, retaining its status as New Mexico's most populous county.

In addition to drawing Anglo settlers, the new railroad town at Albuquerque also served as a connection point for the Nuevomexicano-dominated agricultural villas and ranchos quilting the Rio Grande bottomlands between the Indigenous pueblos of Sandia and Isleta at the county's eventual northern and southern boundaries, respectively. Within this broad and fertile valley, community acequia systems had long provided the primary irrigation infrastructure. Communities invested themselves in regular repairs and maintenance, abiding the seasonal flooding of New Mexico's biggest river with communal labor and social coherence. The arrival of numerous Anglo residents and the growth of the Albuquerque town site did not change the structure of water management immediately, although the politics of acequia governance began to shift as Anglo settlers purchased farmland acreage and joined acequias alongside Nuevomexicanas/os whose families had already farmed the area for long generations. Rapid population growth and urbanization in this central city eventually led to the development of new drainage canals on either side of the Rio Grande and to the consolidation of individual acequia systems into irrigation districts, but during the first decade of the century acequia systems and communities found ways to absorb the strain of settlement influx with little structural change.

From 1900 to 1912 the Bernalillo District Court handled eighty-three cases that concerned water. More than a third of these (39 percent) were condemnation cases filed by the Albuquerque Land & Irrigation Company to establish rights-of-way for new irrigation infrastructure in the northern villa of Algodones.[62] Outside this major condemnation effort, a similar number of cases concerned acequia governance or elections (30 percent) in Bernalillo County proper. Damage to crops and property constituted another major area of dispute, with 23 percent of cases falling into this category. Overall, about a third of the disputes involved some kind of environmental question—typically related to the nature or quantity of channel flows—and disputants addressed these environmental questions in court most often by appealing to authority, using both sketch maps and scientific cartography. About half of all plaintiffs included at least one Anglo complainant (58 percent), but Nuevomexicanas/os were also common as plaintiffs (37 percent of cases), as was the Albuquerque Land & Irrigation Company (39 percent). Nuevomexicanas/os were by far the most likely target of lawsuits, representing 69 percent of defendants versus 24 percent for Anglos. Indigenous plaintiffs brought only one single water-related case during this time period but found themselves on the receiving end four times. In terms of court personnel, Anglos were significantly overrepresented. For the 52 percent of cases in which attorney names were listed in the case records, 83 percent of those attorneys were Anglo versus 17 percent Nuevomexicano and 0 percent Indigenous. One hundred percent of the cases with judge names listed were handled by an Anglo judge.

The three cases summarized below give a sense for the range of issues taken up in this time period by the Bernalillo County district court in an area of considerable settlement influx. The first involves an Indigenous plaintiff suing a community of Nuevomexicano irrigators over water rights in the northern reaches of the middle Rio Grande valley, in what eventually became part of Sandoval County. The second dispute concerns water distribution between two community acequias in the Albuquerque area. The third case—a long-running nuisance dispute between the City of Albuquerque and individual irrigators along a ditch system—provides a fascinating view of various tensions in the middle of a growing city. Together these cases show that district court judges put considerable energy toward supporting irrigation development and resolving disputes that involved Anglos. Other groups, not so much.

PUEBLO OF SANTO DOMINGO V. DE BACA ET AL.

In the spring of 1899 the Pueblo of Santo Domingo sued a group of upstream irrigators for "willfully and wrongfully" taking water from the Acequia de Santo Domingo, a ditch arcing from the river to a cluster of fields in the eastern floodplain of the Rio Grande.[63] All of the plaintiffs and defendants lived near the north end of the Rio Grande's middle valley, where the river enters flatter terrain after descending from northern canyonlands. The defendants lived in the Nuevomexicano village of Peña Blanca, where they enjoyed an upstream location relative to the plaintiffs from the Pueblo of Santo Domingo.[64] Both communities relied on ditches to draw irrigation water from the river, and they were situated fairly close to each other. The contested ditch that became an issue in 1899—the Acequia de Santo Domingo—originated just upstream of Peña Blanca and crossed through its lands on a winding path to the Pueblo's downstream fields.

In its complaint to the judge, the Pueblo claimed it had been irrigating from the Acequia de Santo Domingo for fifty years before New Mexico entered the United States of America (or one hundred years before the date of the case). The Pueblo pointed out that the community of Peña Blanca maintained its own acequia and had no need or right to use Santo Domingo's ditch. Santo Domingo appealed to the judge for relief, asking him to grant an immediate injunction to stop Peña Blanca farmers from taking Pueblo water. According to the Pueblo, Santo Domingo irrigators needed every drop of their acequia's water, and the unauthorized water withdrawals had significantly damaged Pueblo crops over several years. On 2 April 1899, as the Rio Grande ran high with snowmelt and the irrigation season's first waters began flowing into ditches throughout the middle valley, the judge granted Santo Domingo's request. He issued a temporary injunction ordering Peña Blanca's irrigators to stop taking water from the Acequia de Santo Domingo until the case could be heard.

The defendants quickly submitted a vigorous response, rejecting the Pueblo's timeline as well as its geographic claims. According to the Peña Blanca defendants, the old Acequia de Santo Domingo was no longer in use, since it had been "several times washed away by . . . floods" in the years after the Mexican cession.[65] Defendants asserted that the Pueblo built a new ditch barely three decades prior to the case, and the new ditch's water had always been shared with the Peña Blanca residents whose land it crossed. At the time of ditch construction in 1870, a Peña Blanca landowner had apparently granted permission for the Pueblo's ditch to cross his lands only in exchange for a written agreement giving him rights to the new acequia's water. Thus, the defendants claimed that Peña Blanca residents held a legitimate water right in common with the Pueblo. In their spirited response, they also rejected the Pueblo's argument that they should be using water from the main Peña Blanca Acequia, claiming that would be impossible given the location of the lands in question. Arguing that Peña Blanca farmers had been irrigating lands from the new Santo Domingo ditch continuously since 1870, the defendants asked urgently that the court lift the temporary injunction. They worried their crops for the year would fail—an alleged loss of more than $1500—if no irrigation water was made available to them by 10 May.

The judge acceded to this request, dissolving the temporary injunction while the case continued. But the Peña Blanca defendants soon returned to court with another complaint: the Pueblo plaintiffs had apparently built a diversion on the acequia upstream from Peña Blanca, removing water from the ditch and preventing any flow from reaching the defendants' lands. The case file does not include any record about how or whether the judge responded to this specific complaint, but we know the case proceeded quickly because a trial hearing took place—complete with extensive witness testimony—sufficient for the judge to make a decision by the third week of May. The Anglo judge found in favor of the Pueblo, concluding that the Indigenous community held a sole and complete right to the water in the Acequia de Santo Domingo. He rejected all of the Nuevomexicano defendants' claims to the ditch and to its water.

The case file is missing both the trial record and witness testimony, but the defendants filed a motion for retrial that illuminates several key elements of the trial proceedings. First, it shows that the judge accepted evidence and testimony on the "custom and regulations of the plaintiff Pueblo Indians in managing and conducting the ditch," despite the defendants' objection.[66] In its original complaint, the Pueblo had claimed a "power and privilege of governing and managing itself and its interior affairs and properties, including that of its irrigating ditches or acequias" according to its own customs.[67] The defendants objected at trial that water management could be "regulated and controlled by statute" alone, not by any separate system of Pueblo governance.[68] Yet the judge rejected this objection and apparently accepted evidence about Pueblo governance and custom at the trial. The motion for retrial also reveals that Pueblo witnesses testified in their own language (Keres), using an interpreter. Peña Blanca defendants objected to this, arguing that witnesses from Santo Domingo could have spoken in Spanish. By using an interpreter, however, they left the defendants with no one "who could understand the conversation had by the Indian witnesses and the Indian interpreter."[69] Finally, the motion for retrial indicates that the judge accepted the Pueblo's environmental claims about the age and location of the ditch in question, despite defendants' evidence to the contrary. In the end, the court allowed Peña Blanca farmers to take water from the acequia only for domestic purposes, leaving them with no remedy for the imminent failure of their crops as planting season came to an end. The case file contains no indication that the request for retrial led to further litigation in this dispute.

This case is consistent with the way New Mexico's courts addressed water disputes before the 1905 water law was passed. The court focused not on quantification or scientific survey, as became the norm later, but on history, custom, and traditional forms of governance. The Anglo and Nuevomexicano attorneys (for the plaintiffs and defendants, respectively) called local irrigators and other direct observers as witnesses. The Anglo judge entered a definitive finding, but he did not necessarily quash the conflict because he determined that an entire group of farmers should go without water. This case also illustrates that Anglo administrators were less concerned about the applications of modernist science in matters where Anglo settlers were not involved. This case is similar to the Rio Arriba cases, which centered on disputes among Nuevomexicano communities. Judges didn't worry too much about implementing rational management ideals when irrigation disputes focused primarily on subsistence uses.

TERRITORY OF NEW MEXICO EX REL J. E. MATTHEWS ET AL. V. GREGORIO GARCÍA, MACEDONIO HERRERA, AND GUADALUPE NUANES

In the Rio Grande's central valley, a complex acequia system experienced a destabilizing influx of new residents and irrigators as the city of Albuquerque began to grown as an urban center. The Los Griegos and Los Candelarias acequia system consisted of two connected ditches. The Los Griegos acequia comprised the upper portion, which flowed into the lower Los Candelarias section. The two ditches worked cooperatively as if they were a single acequia, but each section elected its own mayordomo. A single three-person board of commissioners provided oversight for the entire system.

In August 1904 twenty-five members of the Los Griegos and Los Candelarias Acequia sued the Los Candelarias mayordomo and two of the acequia commissioners. The lawsuit alleged that the Candelarias mayordomo, Guadalupe Nuanes, had distributed water inequitably throughout the summer irrigation season, and that the two defendant commissioners (Gregorio García and Macedonia Herrera) had refused to intervene when petitioned.[70] The group of plaintiffs, including seventeen Anglo and eight Nuevomexicano acequia members, asked the court to force the mayordomo and two commissioners (all Nuevomexicano) to provide the plaintiffs with a fair share of water.

The judge issued writs of mandamus (legal directives) to all three defendants, requiring immediate response to the petition's claimed facts. The writ addressed to the mayordomo commanded that he provide water to everyone who had been denied and refrain from giving more than their share to all others who had been favored. The writ addressed to the commissioners obligated them to compel the mayordomo (or anyone appointed in his stead) to take action to distribute water equitably.

The mayordomo and commissioners responded within days. García and Herrera met with their fellow commissioner, Manuel Springer, at his Albuquerque office to hold a formal commission meeting, in which they signed a statement ordering Nuanes to carry out his full duties as mayordomo and to deliver water without favoritism. They sent a written reply to the judge confirming they had done everything in their power to ensure equitable water distribution. But they also defended Nuanes in their response, blaming environmental conditions and an intractable governance issue as the source of acequia members' complaints about water delivery. Environmentally, they argued that the mayordomo's hands were tied by the meager amount of water available in the river: "because of the great scarcity of water in the river, there has [sic] been many complaints made to the Board by owners of water rights along the ditch [and] the conditions could not have been fore seen nor remedied."[71] In terms of governance, the two commissioners suggested that a "great deal of the cause of the trouble is because of the fact that there are two Mayordomos on said ditch, one Anastacio Tapia having charge from the headgates to Los Griegos, and the other Guadalupe Nuanes having charge of the remainder."[72] They suggested that Nuanes, as the downstream mayordomo, had very little control over how much water reached the Candelarias potion of the system compared to Tapia. Finally, they acknowledged that frustrated water users had asked the commission to appoint a new mayordomo for the lower part of the ditch. They explained that they refused this request because they believed Nuanes was competent and saw no reason to subvert the decision of those owners who had duly elected him.

In his own response, Nuanes argued that he delivered water to the best of his abilities and denied the charge of favoritism. He echoed the environmental argument of the commissioners, explaining to the judge "that during the present season the river has many times been entirely dry ... Such a course oftimes [sic] caused great complaint for the reason that owners refused to understand why they could not have the water just when they wanted it."[73] He also echoed the commissioners in noting that he was sometimes "powerless to supply the water when it was demanded of him" because he did not control the upper portion of the acequia, which received water before the lower portion.[74] Nuanes lamented his powerlessness and admitted that irrigators in the Los Candelarias section had pressed him to demand water from the Los Griegos mayordomo, Antonio Tapia, but he confessed he had no idea how to force Tapia's hand. The case file does not contain any further complaints and no subsequent cases were filed on this issue, but it is not clear whether the original complainants were satisfied with the mayordomo's response or whether the commissioners eventually acted to replace him.

This case *does* make clear that water-governance issues and environmental claims became linked in complex ways. Was Mayordomo Nuanes making excuses for favoritism in water allocations by claiming that the river was running low? Or was the mayordomo of the upper acequia exaggerating the decreases in water flow as an excuse to politically undermine his downstream counterpart? Or perhaps the Rio Grande really was running exceptionally low that year, and the two mayordomos got caught in a struggle to meet water-delivery expectations under very difficult circumstances that provoked understandable frustrations among their constituents? Regardless of the true answers to these questions, ethnic friction clearly exacerbated the conflict over water delivery in the Los Griegos and Los Candelarias Acequia system. Anglo plaintiffs led the complaint (the first ten names listed in the complaint were Anglo), and their court filing named every Nuevomexicano officer of the acequia without naming the sole Anglo officer. The Anglo judge acted quickly on the complaint, assuming that all of its charges were true. The Nuevomexicano defendants' responses revealed considerable preexisting and ongoing discord: Anglo irrigators had repeatedly complained to the commission throughout the irrigation season and tried to unseat an elected Nuevomexicano officer. In their effort, they enjoyed support from the one Anglo commissioner, who worked against the wishes of the two Nuevomexicano commissioners. The case record does not indicate whom the plaintiffs wanted appointed in place of Nuanes or the ethnicity of that person. But the Nuevomexicano defendants appear to have avoided significant governance claims by focusing their response on environmental conditions as the cause of irregular water delivery.

CITY OF ALBUQUERQUE V. ANTONIO GARCIA ET AL.

In 1880 the AT&SF railroad built a depot at the edge of the Rio Grande floodplain, about a mile east of the original Spanish plaza of Albuquerque. Over two short decades the depot spurred significant commercial development and attracted a steady flow of new Anglo settlers. As the new urban core expanded westward toward a concentration of Spanish, Mexican, and Anglo farms in the Rio Grande bottomlands, irrigation ditches and urban infrastructure crossed paths in problematic ways.

At the same time the AT&SF built its Albuquerque railroad and depot, it also dug the Barelas Ditch to drain swampy areas of the eastern Rio Grande floodplain. On the ditch's path from the rail yards to the Rio Grande, it flowed under a meat market and a livery stable, past numerous businesses, and through residential neighborhoods that became increasingly dense as Anglo settlement accelerated. The Barelas Ditch frequently filled with effluent, waste, sand, and debris, making it a major nuisance and landing it in court again and again. Soon after the City of Albuquerque took over management of the ditch in 1891, residents sued the city for allowing "stench and malarial fumes" to threaten residents' health.[75] But City attempts to clean the ditch often only made things worse, so several landowners blocked city agents from accessing their lands along the ditch.[76] In 1905 the city sued Los Griegos and Los Candelarias Acequia (discussed above) for directing its own waste and surplus outflow into Barelas Ditch,[77] and then in 1906 several landowners sued the city for repeatedly trespassing on their lands for maintenance purposes.[78] By 1911 the city had grown substantially, and it contracted municipal water delivery to the Albuquerque Water Supply Company. It didn't take long until the utility company found itself involved in multiple lawsuits on account of delivering contaminated water drawn from the Barelas Ditch.[79]

The Barelas Ditch was not solely a drainage ditch; it also intersected with irrigation networks in the mixed urban-agricultural parts of the valley. In February 1911 the City of Albuquerque sued the users and elected leaders of a *contra* acequia (lateral irrigation ditch) that branched off the Barelas Ditch just north of the Albuquerque Foundry and Machine Shop. The City contended that the twelve-foot-wide contra acequia, which crossed the AT&SF railyard and ran through numerous neighborhoods as it made its way down the Rio Grande floodplain, had become a major nuisance. Because the ditch crossed some city thoroughfares (including South First, Second, and Third Streets) or ran down the middle of others (South Fourth and Fifth Streets, Hazeldine Avenue, and an unnamed alley), its poor condition prevented city workers from repairing streets or improving their condition and safety. The City charged thirteen defendants with failing to maintain the contra acequia and allowing its waters "to overflow the banks and spread upon the property of the adjacent property owners and upon the streets of the City of Albuquerque, rendering the streets muddy, and at times, almost impassable."[80]

The City told the court it had ordered the members and officers of the contra acequia to maintain the ditch, but to no avail. For a "large portion" of the year, the City claimed, the contra acequia was filled with "rubbish, dead animals, chickens, old clothing, boots and shoes, and various other refuse and garbage." In this "unwholesome and unhealthy condition," the City attorney asserted, the lateral ditch "greatly endangers the life, health, and convenience" of the city's residents. The City also reported it had offered to purchase the land from the defendants, but no price could be agreed upon.[81] The lawsuit requested that the court initiate a condemnation process, in which the judge would appoint three independent appraisers to set a price for damages and compel the owners to sell their lands and rights at that price. The City's end goal was to close the contra acequia and eliminate the nuisance of "putrid, stagnant, and unhealthy water."[82]

Although the contra acequia was theoretically an irrigation ditch, the City's lawsuit asserted that "only a very small amount of land" was actually irrigated from its water, and thus its "abandonment and discontinuance" would "greatly" serve the public interest while causing minimal damage to defendants. The most complicated aspect of the City's request, however, involved determining the "individual and separate damage of each defendant" owing to condemnation, since the ditch was owned and operated in common as a community ditch. The list of defendants apparently included a combination of water users who didn't own their land and landowners who didn't use any water, including owners with and without ditch easements on their land. And some water users were left out of the lawsuit entirely, without explanation. Several defendants immediately protested that the City had not presented sufficient information to proceed with a condemnation process. Especially problematic was that the city had not made clear what exactly was to be condemned—land, water from the ditch, the ditch itself, individual property, or something else. If the City intended primarily to close the ditch (rather than to take possession of individual properties), some defendants argued, it would essentially need to remove individuals' water rights, which was outside City authority. Seven of the thirteen defendants filed demurrers raising these and other objections to the condemnation's validity. Some of these court filings simultaneously presented preemptive evidence about the value of individual properties, based on decades of irrigation from the contra acequia. Two landowners—Wiliam Bietz (or Dietz, as his surname is spelled in other documents) and Nick Metz—claimed that their properties would lose all value without rights to the water in the ditch. They each asserted specific values for the fruit trees, vines, alfalfa and vegetable fields, residences, and outbuildings on their land (including Bietz's "chickenpark"), which they claimed would become useless if the contra acequia were closed. By condemning the contra acequia, these defendants suggested, the City would also be condemning their lands and would incur an obligation to reimburse the owners for their full value.

Over the defendants' objections, Judge Abbott proceeded to appoint three appraisers and asked them to investigate the properties and individuals that would be impacted by the City's intended closure of the contra acequia. The court asked the appraisers to submit a report enumerating specific damages to each defendant, gave them the power to compel witness testimony under oath, and required that they submit a report within twenty days. The three (Anglo) appraisers, Manuel Springer, Herman Blueher, and W. P. Metcalf, reported back to the court in mid-June 1911, listing the properties they had investigated and prescribing a dollar amount of damages for each defendant. Their report also listed eight defendants who had already reached financial settlements with the City and whose lands the appraisers therefore did not review. Two landowners—Tomás Apodaca and Nick Metz—objected to the appraisers' report on the basis of both improper process and insufficient valuation of projected damages. Apodaca argued that the City didn't have the authority to condemn water rights and objected to the low valuation of his projected damages, charging that the appraisers' "examination of the lands was cursory, hurried, and with little regard to the requirements of the law in such cases."[83] Metz agreed with Apodaca that the City had no condemnation authority and claimed that his property had been significantly undervalued through an appraisal that was "socialist, arbitrary, without hearing, inadequate, not based on the law and contrary to the statute."[84]

Over these objections, the judge declared the appraisers' report to be valid and accepted their valuation. He entered a judgment in favor of the defendants and assessed the reported appraisal amounts against the City. Upon confirming that the court had received payment from the City sufficient to compensate the defendants, the judge confirmed that the City had gained "the right to enter into possession of the ditch."[85] Metz appealed this decision and was successful in New Mexico's high court, which found in his favor and ordered the case reversed in the district court, with Metz's legal costs to be paid by the City of Albuquerque. It is unclear whether this dismissal invalidated the condemnation entirely or resulted solely in

Metz's retaining his individual access to water from the contra acequia. It is possible that the ditch had been removed by that time, since most other landowners had settled with the City two years prior, but the case record contains no further information beyond a statement of dismissal and a return of $1,000 to the City of Albuquerque that the court had been holding to pay condemnation-related damages to Nick Metz.

What becomes evident from this case—and in the series of nuisance cases related to the Barelas Ditch—is simply that New Mexico's increase in Anglo population and urbanization produced new complications for water-rights disputes. In the case of *City of Albuquerque v. Garcia et al.*, municipal needs came into conflict with irrigation claims in legally unprecedented ways. The City as plaintiff didn't know whom to sue, and defendants didn't know what they were being asked to give up in the condemnation of Barelas Ditch. Legal questions of standing, authority, and condemnation procedures went all the way to the New Mexico Supreme Court, but a high court ruling produced little clarity. This case also confirms that Bernalillo County's acequia communities were more ethnically mixed than elsewhere in New Mexico. Along the Barelas Ditch, both Anglo and Nuevomexicano water users participated in acequia leadership and ownership, and they were jointly represented by attorneys of both ethnicities. As elsewhere, however, the judges were 100 percent Anglo, and Anglo disputants entered the most aggressive legal claims. In this case, Nuevomexicano defendants constituted the great majority of those who proceeded quickly to settlement, while Anglos were more likely to persist in submitting demurrers, exceptions, and appeals. Thus, even in New Mexico's emerging urban center, where mixed-ethnicity water communities had become the norm by the turn of the century, Anglos found more success than Nuevomexicanas/os in the legal system.

Valencia County: Non-Anglo Communities in Crisis

During Spanish colonial times, Bernalillo County and the rest of New Mexico's territory to the south functioned as a single administrative unit—the *partido* of Valencia—that stretched from Texas in the east to Arizona's Colorado River in the west.[86] Throughout this extensive area, early Spanish explorers had encountered thriving Indigenous pueblos, most of them producing irrigated cotton and grain crops in valleys, near springs, along floodplains, and on the alluvial fans and *bajadas* sloping from canyon mouths into the lower basins. In the central valley of the Rio Grande, Spanish settlers established numerous haciendas along the floodplain, taking advantage of the rich alluvium and using ditch systems to route and control the river water for irrigation. When the Pueblo Revolt drove the Spanish out of New Mexico in 1680, they abandoned these haciendas; the return of the Spanish in 1692 prompted a considerably more defensive posture that favored concentrated plaza settlements over spread-out haciendas. South of Isleta Pueblo, the Spanish resettled the villas of Belen and Los Lunas in the mid-eighteenth century, primarily to serve as buffers against Apache contact from the east, west, and south. By the time American territorial rule began in 1848, all of the original Indigenous pueblos across the old partido of Valencia (excepting Isleta, in southern Bernalillo County) were gone. The American territorial government acted quickly to drive out nomadic Apaches as well.

New Mexico's territorial government broke Valencia into several administrative pieces, removing its southern extent and leaving the old Nuevomexicano buffer towns as the primary population center. By the turn of the nineteenth century, the central-valley towns in the western shadows of the Manzano Mountains had emerged as important sites of agricultural production. As elsewhere in New Mexico, irrigators typically worked together to share and maintain community acequias, repairing ditches and flow-control infrastructure when river- and storm-driven floods caused inevitable damage. Most farms were small, but they produced copious alfalfa and cereal harvests. The surrounding grasslands enjoyed a strong reputation as some of the best stock land in the territory, thanks to an ideal combination of mild winters and cool summers that could not be found to the north or south. Throughout the nineteenth century, Valencia County was an important power center in territorial politics based on its economic prominence. Even its smallest valley towns participated actively in trade along the Santa Fe Trail, and the first east–west railroad in New Mexico established its junction with the AT&SF in Belen rather than Albuquerque, confirming its importance. Between 1900 and 1910 Valencia County continued to grow, but it lost some of its population in 1903 when the creation of Torrance County removed the Manzano Mountains and its eastern towns from Valencia's population rolls.

From 1900 to 1912 the Valencia County District Court handled twenty-three cases concerning water. Most dealt with either property and crop damage (44 percent) or water-delivery disputes (39 percent). Other prominent topics included disputes over acequia labor and maintenance (17 percent) and trespassing (22 percent). Overall, just over half of the disputes involved some kind of environmental question—typically related to the nature or quantity of channel flows—and disputants addressed environmental questions in court most often through simple assertion and appeals to authority. Nuevomexicano disputants were most commonly involved in Valencia County cases, making up a large majority of both plaintiffs (61 percent) and defendants (78 percent). Anglos were also commonly participants in Valencia's water-related cases, making up a third of plaintiffs (30 percent) but only a small number of defendants (13 percent). Corporations appear as plaintiffs in only 4 percent of cases but were on the receiving end of lawsuits 17 percent of the time. Indigenous people show up in only three cases, twice as plaintiff and once as defendant. In terms of court personnel, Anglo attorneys represented clients in 70 percent of all cases that listed attorneys, but Nuevomexicano attorneys had a significant presence (in 30 percent of cases) that is quite striking in comparison to other New Mexico district courts, where attorneys were almost uniformly Anglo. As elsewhere, however, 100 percent of all judges were Anglo.

The following briefs revolve around water rights and ditch modifications in response to changing environmental and political conditions. In the first dispute, a landowner and irrigator sued his own mayordomo and a group of neighboring irrigators who had requested water rights in a new ditch after their own ditch became unusable. In the second case, the Pueblo of Isleta sued two downstream acequia systems for conspiring to take the Pueblo's water and damage its ditch in an effort to consolidate water management for their two Nuevomexicano communities. In both cases we see small irrigators struggling to maintain economic viability in a changing floodplain landscape.

JESUS H. SANCHEZ V. ROMULO ARAGON ET AL.

Among the many small acequias blanketing the Rio Grande floodplain in Valencia County, the Acequia de en Medio was typical and unremarkable.[87] Its small membership of Nuevomexicano parciantes relied on acequia water to grow a wide variety of vegetable crops while struggling with both environmental change and political disagreement. In 1885 a flood rampaged through the Rio Grande valley, damaging many ditches, including the Acequia de en Medio. When community members came together to reconstruct the ditch after the flood, a group of seven siblings from the Aragon family decided not to participate. Instead, they helped construct a parallel ditch, the Acequia de Picurie, which was closer to their lands.[88] In cooperation with a separate group of parciantes, the Aragons used the Picurie exclusively to meet their irrigation needs after the 1885 flood. Until they changed their minds.

Fifteen years later, in 1899, the Aragons asked to return to the Acequia de en Medio. They petitioned Mayordomo Jesus Sanchez y Alarid to reinstate their rights to the ditch, and he approved. But as soon as the Aragons started taking water that spring, the parciante Jesus Sanchez sued them, along with the mayordomo; note that the plaintiff Jesus Sanchez is not the same person as the defendant Jesus Sanchez y Alarid.[89] Sanchez claimed to have purchased all surplus water in the Acequia de en Medio five years prior, which would preclude the granting of any additional rights to water. The Aragon siblings claimed they had an old right to water in the ditch, since their father had been an original member of the Acequia de en Medio and had passed his rights to them as inheritance. Despite having used the Acequia de Picurie exclusively since 1885, the Aragons claimed never to have abandoned their rights in the Acequia de en Medio. They swore in a court filing that it had become "wholly impracticable" to use the Acequia de Picurie in recent years, which prompted them to seek reinstatement in the Acequia de en Medio.

Sanchez rejected these claims, arguing that the Aragons had definitively abandoned their right when they "openly refused . . . to perform or furnish any labor or money" to repair the ditch in 1885.[90] Furthermore, Sanchez noted, the Picurie ditch was in fine condition with ample water flow. He suggested the defendants were deceptive in claiming it was "impracticable" for them to use the Picurie. (The defendants never explained why they could no longer use the Picurie ditch, so if it indeed had plenty of water, as Sanchez asserted, it was likely a political disagreement that led the Aragons to return to the Acequia de en Medio.)

Sanchez's most strenuous objection to the Aragons' return concerned his own water rights. To adequately irrigate his properties, cultivated with corn, wheat, alfalfa, beans, and other cereal crops, Sanchez claimed, he needed water every few days. He had purchased the ditch's surplus water to support this watering schedule, and he objected to the Aragon siblings' water use because it reduced the surplus flow available to him as the last user on the ditch. Sanchez also complained that the Aragons had trespassed on his land to create a diversion intake upstream from his own diversion. The Aragon defendants contested this claim, countering that their lands sat well downstream of Sanchez's properties on the ditch. They told the court their water use had caused Sanchez no harm since they drew water "entirely below all lands of the plaintiff at a place where it was and is purely waste water on its way back to the Rio Grande."[91] The Aragons also scoffed at Sanchez's claim to need water every few days. They asked the court to acknowledge "that to irrigate . . . every three or four weeks is amply sufficient and is the customary frequency of irrigation" across New Mexico.[92]

Both sides addressed these environmental questions—about ditch geometry and agronomy—via simple assertion. The case record contains no maps or surveys nor any reference to them in document filings. All of the evidence produced in the plaintiff's complaint and defendant's response focused instead on the validity of various agreements between irrigators. The Aragons, for example, charged that Sanchez's contract to purchase surplus water was illegitimate, since it did not include signatures or signature lines for all members of the acequia. For a water sale to hold legal validity, they claimed, "no number less than the whole of the owners and proprietors of any community ditch have any right to sell outright any portion of said ditch or its waters."[93] Sanchez argued in reply that the mayordomo's decision to grant a water right to the Aragons was unlawful, since only the commissioners have the authority to do this, and two of the commissioners had specifically ordered the mayordomo not to approve their request. Sanchez y Alarid reportedly acted on his own by taking the justice of the peace to each acequia member's home to seek consent or objection before making his decision.[94]

The case file contains no final ruling from the judge, so we are left to wonder how these legal principles played out. But even without knowing the outcome, this case illuminates shifting environmental and political conditions in the turn-of-the-century middle Rio Grande valley. Disputants addressed environmental concerns through simple assertion and focused most of their energy on the need to address political issues. Disputes over acequia membership and water rights dominated the court record through documentary and testimonial evidence about the nature, origins, and force of various customs and agreements.

FREDERICK TONDRE ET AL. V. PUEBLO OF ISLETA AND PUEBLO DE ISLETA V. J. A. PICHARD ET AL.

A dozen years later a multiparty dispute unfolded on the boundary between Valencia and Bernalillo Counties. The conflict stemmed from environmental changes in the Rio Grande floodplain that provoked a reorganization of political alliances and infrastructure connections among acequia communities. The disagreement quickly ensnared disputants of numerous ethnicities across two different court districts, and court-ordered resolutions did little to quell the animosity. The losing party filed multiple appeals, engaged in infrastructure sabotage, and even threatened bodily harm against adversaries. Just another typical conflict.

In early 1911 five irrigators from the Los Lentes community in northern Valencia County sued the Pueblo of Isleta, an Indigenous pueblo at the southern edge of Bernalillo County. The Los Lentes irrigators wanted to enlarge a shared ditch—referred to by Isleta Pueblo as "Acequia los Charcos" and by Los Lentes as "Acequia los Lentes"—but the Pueblo refused. Farmers in both communities had long shared the ditch, but they held different understandings of its ownership and water rights. Isleta's leaders believed the Pueblo alone owned all water rights in the Acequia los Charcos and had simply granted Los Lentes "courtesy" access to surplus water that flowed downstream. The Los Lentes acequia commissioners, on the other hand, claimed a legal right to the ditch and to the Rio Grande water flowing through it.

The Los Lentes plaintiffs went to court seeking to condemn a strip of Isleta's land. They asked the judge to create a legal right-of-way wide enough to allow access for construction, maintenance, and operation of the acequia from its head in Bernalillo County to the south boundary of the Antonio Gutierrez land grant in Valencia County. To initiate the condemnation, the plaintiffs requested that the court appoint three disinterested referees to assess monetary damages so that Los Lentes could compensate the Pueblo and move ahead with the acequia enlargement project.[95]

The Pueblo had no interest in a financial settlement and rejected the premise of the condemnation. It insisted on its sole ownership and denied that Los Lentes irrigators had any right to enlarge the acequia or even to bring the case.[96] In response, the Los Lentes plaintiffs explained that they needed to expand the acequia so that it could serve both Los Lentes and its neighbor, Belen, a large farming community to the south. In Belen irrigators had long relied on the Acequia Nuestra Señora de Belen de la Ladera (hereinafter Acequia de Belen), but the Rio Grande changed its main channel in 1899 and cut off the Acequia de Belen's intake. For twelve years prior to the lawsuit, Belen had been receiving its water through an agreement with a private landowner, Louis Huning, who connected his private ditch with the Acequia de Belen and passed Belen's share of the Rio Grande through his ditch. But this fragile arrangement collapsed when Huning sold the property and the new owner did not want to negotiate with the Acequia de Belen commissioners.[97] To protect their farms, Belen instead proposed a merger with the Los Lentes acequia "so that the two should become one single, continuous public acequia for the benefit of both communities."[98] The two Valencia communities both saw the merger as a win-win: Belen irrigators would gain access to critical irrigation infrastructure, and Los Lentes would gain support from a larger community to help handle the burdens of acequia maintenance.

The Los Lentes commissioners tried to convince Bernalillo District Court Judge Abbott that their project would cause no harm to the Pueblo of Isleta beyond the inconvenience of allowing access to the ditch where it crossed Isleta land. Los Lentes claimed the ditch enlargement would simply convey river water more efficiently to cultivated lands without affecting any existing water rights held by Isleta, Los Lentes, or Belen. They painted the Pueblo defendants as irrational and obstinate in their refusal to cooperate on a necessary infrastructure improvement project.

Judge Abbott agreed with the Los Lentes plaintiffs. He appointed three referees to work with a civil engineer to assess damages to the Pueblo and used their report to set a price for the condemnation. The Los Lentes commissioners paid the damages immediately and quickly sent crews out to work on the ditch. To their surprise, however, Pueblo representatives (including the governor of the Pueblo of Isleta) met them in the field and obstructed their access to the ditch. When construction crews persisted in their efforts, Pueblo representatives changed their strategy from obstruction to sabotage; they opened the acequia headgate and allowed water to rush from the Rio Grande into the construction area. Los Lentes returned to court and asked Judge Abbott to order Isleta to stand down. According to their petition, the work crews believed that any attempt to reach the headgate and stop the flow "would result in violent, physical colision [sic] with some of said Indians and might result in bloodshed, and possibly, loss of life."[99] The judge must have ordered the Pueblo to stop its obstruction and respect the condemnation decision, because the final document in the case file is a signed agreement in which both sides' attorneys acknowledged that the Pueblo would cease its interference and that the Pueblo held exclusive ownership and use of its old acequia from the point where the new ditch diverged.

But the Pueblo of Isleta did not consider the case closed. Soon after losing in Bernalillo District Court, the Pueblo appealed the case to the New Mexico Supreme Court and simultaneously sued the commissioners of Acequia de Belen in Valencia County District Court. In the second suit, Isleta charged its downstream neighbors with (1) unlawful entry onto Pueblo land, (2) unlawful use and modification of the Pueblo's acequia, and (3) building "faulty and defective construction" that caused water in the new ditch to overflow onto Pueblo land. According to Isleta's complaint, the Los Lentes and Belen construction crews had done such shoddy work on the new ditch that its waters had begun "submerging ... and ruining growing crops, and causing ... a deposit of alkali, all of which has caused irreparable damage."[100] The Pueblo asked that the defendants be restrained from entering its land or using its water, and it asked for $1,000 in damages for lost crops. This argument did not go anywhere. The defense argued successfully that the trespassing issue had already been settled in Bernalillo County case and could not be litigated again. Valencia

District Judge Merritt Mechem dismissed the case based on attorney's arguments, defense affidavits, and a survey blueprint showing the routes of the old and new acequias. Rather than amend its complaint, the Pueblo indicated its intention to appeal the second case to the New Mexico Supreme Court instead, as it had done with the Bernalillo case.

It is not necessary to follow these cases to the supreme court to grasp the ways in which Anglo settlement in central New Mexico began to pressure existing agricultural communities. At the time of these cases, the Los Lentes community included a mix of Nuevomexicano and Anglo (mostly German) irrigators, and it was losing population at a rate that made it hard to keep up with acequia maintenance. The much larger and more prosperous Nuevomexicano community in Belen, however, also found itself at risk because of its dependence on an Anglo landowner for water access after the river shifted the course of its channel. A simple turnover in ownership for that property—a hallmark of Anglo speculation in the middle valley—revealed Belen's own vulnerability and created the urgent situation in which Los Lentes and Belen sought to merge their irrigation systems. Other than the Pueblo itself, everyone involved in this case was non-Indigenous. Of the three referees and one civil engineer who assessed the situation for the judge, three were Anglo and one was Nuevomexicano. All the attorneys were Anglo, as was the judge. It is perhaps no surprise, then, that the court's support for an arrangement preserving agricultural production in Los Lentes and Belen came at the expense of Indigenous sovereignty over the Isleta irrigation system. Finding little recourse in the legal system, Pueblo members perceived few options beyond the physical obstruction of irrigation work in the field.

Socorro County: Protecting Settler Investments

When New Mexico attained statehood in 1912, Socorro County was by far its largest county, extending from the Rio Grande valley westward to the Arizona border. Its expansive territory included mountainous uplands as well as grassy lowlands and fertile valleys. In the decades after U.S. annexation, mining, ranching, and agriculture all emerged as potential economic foundations. U.S. military campaigns targeted Apache groups, which had long prevented any permanent Spanish and Mexican settlements south of Socorro, thus opening space for Anglo settlement. Soon afterward the railroad made its way south along the Rio Grande in the 1880s, spurring concentrated settlement and economic development alongside the river.[101] Between 1900 and 1910 Socorro County's census count increased by 21 percent, rising to nearly fifteen thousand total residents by the end of the decade.

Ranching was more widespread than farming across Socorro County as a whole, but irrigated agriculture dominated the Rio Grande bottomlands. With crops ranging from alfalfa to grapes, and including everything in between, new settlers began farming a wide variety of cash crops that could be moved easily by rail to market. New Anglo settlers purchased lands in existing Nuevomexicano villages and land grants in the northern part of Socorro County and patented homestead or ranching claims in southern areas that had not previously been settled or had been parceled out in land grants. In northern areas, as elsewhere in the Spanish colonial realm, acequia irrigation served as the dominant form of both agriculture and community governance. Similar to the acequia communities of Bernalillo and Valencia counties to the north, Socorro's water users not only shared common water supplies but also took joint responsibility for maintaining ditch infrastructure, which suffered according to the vagaries of the Rio Grande in its active floodplain. In unpatented lands outside the river valley, Anglo settlers found themselves obligated to invest heavily in private infrastructure such as diversion dams, ditches, and tanks before they could secure rights to water from springs, creeks, and arroyos. Typically, water sources outside the Rio Grande floodplain ran in mere trickles for most of the year but transformed during storms into dangerous, torrential freshet flows.

From 1900 to 1912 the Socorro County district court handled twelve cases concerning water. Two-thirds of the cases dealt with damage to crops or infrastructure, while one-third addressed acequia governance. Overall, more than half of the cases (58 percent) involved some kind of environmental question—related either to water flow or channel form— and disputants addressed environmental questions most often through simple assertion or by presenting eyewitnesses. Nuevomexicano (67 percent) and Anglo (50 percent) plaintiffs brought most cases to court, often jointly. Nuevomexicanas/os showed up as defendants in half of all cases, while Anglo accounted for one-third of defendants, as did corporations. (In Socorro, mixed-ethnicity defendants were common and prominent.) As was true across the territory of New Mexico, Anglos dominated the court personnel, representing 100 percent of all attorney and judges in Socorro County district court.

The two cases discussed below span the geographical range of Socorro County. The first is an early dispute between Anglo homesteaders over water rights to a spring in western rangelands experiencing increasing settlement. In the second case, Nuevomexicano trustees of a land grant in the middle Rio Grande valley sued the AT&SF railroad for manipulating the riverbank and changing channel flows, to the detriment of a downstream farming area. In both cases the court supported resolutions calculated to promote and maximize development activities, regardless of whether they made scientific arguments in court.

GEORGE BELCHER V. MONTAGUE STEVENS AND AUGUST HELEN GORDON STEVENS

In 1899 Anglo homesteaders faced off over a small amount of water flowing from Horse Springs, in the upper Gila River watershed in what is today Catron County.[102] In February 1899 an Anglo settler named George Belcher moved onto a land parcel that the United States had designated as available for homesteading. He built a dwelling and began preparing the property for crop cultivation. On 20 April Belcher entered a homestead claim and built a diversion to appropriate the water from a stream that flowed across the property. Belcher directed the water first into a small earthen tank and then into a large reservoir, where he could use it for watering livestock, irrigation, and domestic needs. Around the same time, a husband and wife, Montague and Helen Stevens, purchased and took possession of a neighboring property that included Horse Springs, the source of the stream that flowed across Belcher's homestead claim. In July 1899 the Stevenses built a dam just downstream from the springs and diverted all of the spring's water for their own purposes, leaving nothing to flow to Belcher's property "except for a few short intervals" when the Stevenses' dam was washed out by floods.[103] Belcher complained to the court in November that the Stevenses' unlawful diversion of water caused him to lose all his crops for that season. He also accused the Stevenses of dumping "large quantities of poisonous and deleterious materials" into the stream next to their sheep corral. According to Belcher, the Stevenses' sheep-dip operation made the stream "foul and unwholesome and unfit for plaintiff's use" even on those few occasions when water was allowed to run past the dam and down to Belcher's property.

The Stevenses defended themselves by claiming they bought the land from owners who had used Horse Springs for many years to support irrigation, household needs, and "vast herds of sheep and cattle." Although the spring had fallen into disrepair by the time the Stevenses took possession of the land in April, they argued to the judge that their water right was based on a long-standing appropriation. Their new dam was merely a replacement for "other and similar dams, which had been constructed from time to time by defendants' predecessors in title."[104] They also argued that very little water ever flowed all the way to Belcher's land, "owing to the great distance it had to travel and the peculiar condition of the soil through which the channel is laid."[105] In fact, the Stevenses claimed, their own work in "cleaning out and walling up" three connected springs in July had significantly increased the spring flow. Belcher rejected all of these claims, denying that past owners had engaged in any appreciable level of irrigation, denying that dams had existed on the Stevenses' land prior to their arrival, denying they had done anything to increase the flow of the springs, and denying that the natural streamflow was insufficient to reach his land.

Judge Leland held a three-day hearing on this case and in the end agreed that the Stevenses had unlawfully diverted the entire flow of Horse Springs when they built their dam in July. Although Leland agreed that the Stevenses' predecessors had long used the springs for watering livestock, he determined that the historical appropriation was only half of the spring's total water flow. Belcher's February diversion of surplus water in the stream thus constituted a lawful appropriation of available water. In order to equitably divide and apportion the springwater, the judge set a schedule for the two parties to follow, allowing the Stevenses to use the entire spring flow for half of each week and Belcher to use the entire flow for the other half. He also ordered the Stevenses to cease "causing or permitting any filth or poisonous, or deleterious material" from entering the stream due to their sheep-dip activities.[106]

It is not clear how the judge arrived at his decision to split the spring water evenly in half between Belcher and the Stevenses. Surviving court documents indicate that both sides made all of their environmental claims through simple assertion, and the case file includes no scientific or quantitative evidence about the springs' flow, soil conditions, pollutant levels, or any other environmental question. As was common in other cases from the turn of the century, the judge focused not on defining environmental conditions and calculating exact water flows, but on brokering a resolution that both sides could live with. Judge Leland's simple schedule simultaneously supported two Anglo initiatives—sheep ranching and crop irrigation—in an area with minimal prior Anglo settlement or development.

SILVESTRE ESQUIBEL ET AL. V. THE ATCHISON, TOPEKA, AND SANTA FE RAILWAY COMPANY

Back in the Rio Grande valley, numerous Nuevomexicano and Anglo farmers cultivated varied crops on the large Cebilleta de La Joya land grant, which spanned both sides of the river between Belen and San Marcial. The small agricultural community of La Joya was concentrated on the east bank, where farmers could take advantage of rich bottomland soils. In late 1909, however, land-grant trustees focused obsessively on the west bank.

On the other side of the river, the Atchison, Topeka and Santa Fe railroad had begun developing a narrow right-of-way corridor that crossed the Cebilleta de La Joya land grant from north to south. In some places the railroad ran very near the bank of the Rio Grande, including a stretch directly across the river from La Joya. By early 1909 AT&SF had established a small depot (named "La Joya") on the west bank and had begun running tracks southward along the bank. In order to protect the roadbed and tracks from riparian erosion, AT&SF brought in loads of rock to create a "riprap" structure along the riverbank. But when the railroad workers began extending the rock structure out into the riverbed, farmers in La Joya noticed that the riverbank on the *east* side began to wash away. In October the land-grant trustees sued AT&SF in district court to stop the railroad from dumping rock into the river channel. The plaintiffs alerted the district court that the annual spring rise of the river would begin any day, placing productive farmland and the town of La Joya itself in imminent jeopardy.

La Joya's attorneys argued that AT&SF had no right to build stabilization structures outside the railroad's right-of-way, and they submitted a detailed map to explain the problem. The map (fig. 7.4) showed the locations of riverbanks, sandbars, bottomlands, rights-of-way, construction work, and river currents both at low stage and at medium or high stages. The unknown cartographer titled the map a "survey" and used pencil to emphasize that it had been prepared in the field, based on direct observations. The mapmaker also included bank height measurements and two layers of directional arrows to show current directions at low flow and at medium/high stages. A small label—"recently washed away"—next to the riverbank nearest La Joya carried the plaintiff's primary argument. In the written brief, attorneys accused the railroad of deflecting the Rio Grande's flow with their rock work, causing it to erode the opposite bank. They claimed that "the town of La Joya with the lands below it . . . will surely be destroyed" during spring floods.[107] Given the "imminent" destruction and "emergency" of the situation, grant trustees asked the court to grant an injunction stopping any further construction or maintenance on this project. The court issued a temporary injunction against further work until the case could be heard.

In response, the railroad's attorneys filed a brief rejecting all of the charges against them and accusing the plaintiffs of needless hysteria and

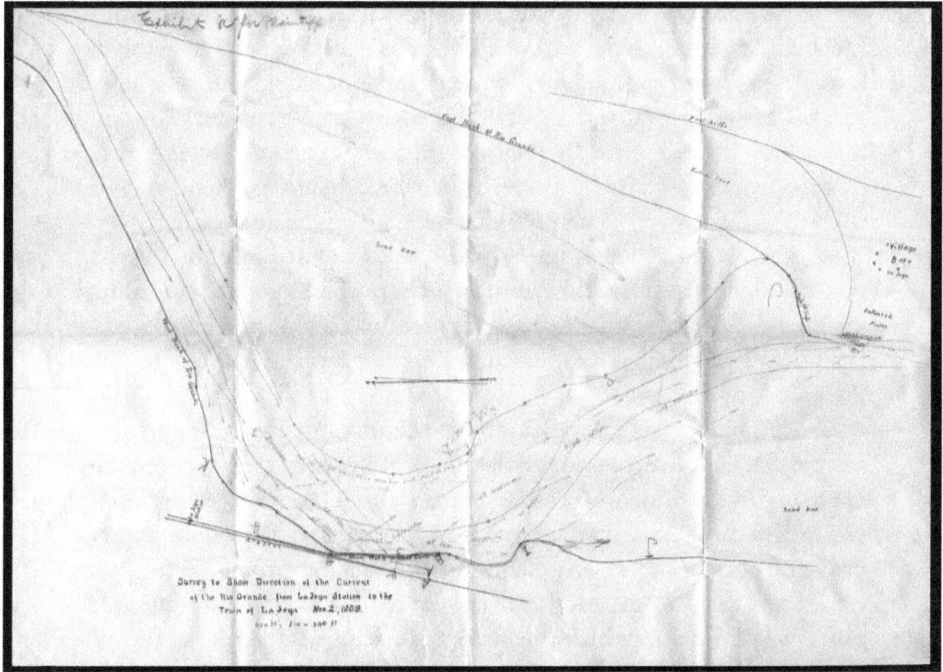

FIGURE 7.4 Survey to show the direction of the current of the Rio Grande from La Joya station to the town of La Joya, 2 November 1909
Map filed with Complaint in Civil case no. 5368: *Silvestre Esquibel et al. v. the Atchison, Topeka, and Santa Fe Railway Company*, 1909; Collection 1976-031; Records of the United States Territorial and New Mexico District Courts for Socorro County, Box no. 18068. New Mexico State Records Center and Archives, Santa Fe, NM. (Original is in full color)

false predictions about imminent flooding and erosion. The defendants admitted to "placing rock" along the railroad right-of-way and the west riverbank, claiming it was critical to contain the "Rio Grande in its present course and channel" to protect the railroad tracks. They denied that their project deflected any flow onto La Joya and scoffed at the idea of an imminent rise in the river. But the defendants also took care to note that *if* the river did rise, and *if* floodwaters entered La Joya, any destruction of loss of fields could not be attributed to "any act of this defendant."[108]

After hearing arguments in December 1909, Judge Merritt Mechem went to the riverbank himself to conduct a "personal inspection" of the riprap location at the request and in the presence of both sides' attorneys. Mechem confirmed that the AT&SF was placing rock (or "rip-rapping") south of the station and extending two hundred yards into the river. Although the project clearly violated the railroad's right-of-way boundaries, Mechem determined that the rock work was necessary, and therefore allowable, to protect the railroad's property. Judge Mechem also determined that the existing riprap did not deflect the Rio Grande current and would not channel waters onto La Joya should the river rise. Mechem noted that any extension of riprap along the bank "might possibly tend to divert the waters," however, so he provided detailed guidance on where rocks should be placed along a southerly line that extended into the riverbed instead. Mechem's final ruling authorized the AT&SF to continue filling, rip-rapping, and constructing rock barriers both within and outside of its right-of-way, so long as it followed his instructions about where to place the rock.

This is one of a few cases that revolved almost entirely around environmental claims. What I see in this case is an example of the judge deciding *not* to enforce a rational-scientific standard for determining environmental truth because it would undermine an Anglo commercial development project. The Nuevomexicano plaintiffs knew that they would need a scientific survey to be taken seriously in the courtroom, and their cartographic portrayal of the river's hydrology painted a damning picture of the railroad's rip-rapping project as jeopardizing the land-grant community. But the Anglo attorneys and judge found a convenient way to sidestep the environmental claims in the map. By inviting the judge to view the site and conduct a personal observation, the attorneys opened the door for the judge to make his own determination, which ended up contradicting the surveyed map. Mechem's final decree in this case gave priority to the railroad's interests, providing considerable latitude for the railroad to go beyond its right-of-way in order to protect railway infrastructure within the floodplain. This despite the evidence of the map.

Sierra County: An Imbalance of Power

Flowing downriver into Sierra County, the Rio Grande enters a broken landscape in which long canyons connect mesas and valleys in a geologic complex generally considered unsuitable for agriculture. At the time the Spanish entered, explorers found no sedentary Indigenous communities in this area, and Spanish colonial authorities did not themselves target the area for farming. At the western edge of the Rio Grande valley, however, the Spanish found a wealth of mineral resources in mountainous uplands, where they established a mining extraction complex separate from the upper Rio Grande settlements. During the American territorial period, mining opportunities similarly drew Anglo attention, and many new arrivals headed to the easternmost mountain range in the Gila headwaters area: the Black Range, or Sierra Diablo.[109] Sierra County was created in 1884 to center the Black Range and the mining town of Hillsborough (now Hillsboro), which became its first county seat.

Despite Sierra County's primary focus on precious metals, it included a considerable swath of Rio Grande floodplain within its boundary. With the advent of water management's high-modernist era, New Mexico's boosters and speculators changed their perspective on the canyon-riddled badlands of central Sierra County. Instead of seeing narrow canyons as impenetrable obstacles, water authorities began to consider them anew as potential reservoir sites: where river water might be harnessed behind high-tech dams to generate power, prevent flooding, and increase irrigated agriculture. It was in Sierra County, in fact, that the fledgling U.S. Reclamation Service undertook its first major project, Elephant Butte Dam, which was then the biggest irrigation project in the world. Authorized in 1905 and completed in 1916, Elephant Butte was intended to store water for downstream delivery to Mexico and Texas while also providing irrigation water to farmers in Doña Ana County's Mesilla and Rincon Valleys. The massive scale of the Rio Grande Project, however, spurred interest in Sierra County's own agricultural prospects. Around the turn of the century, increasing numbers of Anglo and Nuevomexicano settlers developed small farming operations throughout the county. Some relied on scarce surface waters, while others prospected for groundwater. Despite some limited success in these initiatives, Sierra County never developed into an agricultural powerhouse. From 1900 to 1910 it was a small but growing county, with a 12 percent population increase that saw it end the decade with just over 3,500 residents.

For the period 1900–1912, Sierra County's district court records contain only two water-related cases. In both, Anglo plaintiffs sued Nuevomexicano defendants in disputes over the waters of small creeks. This sample is too small to permit county-level generalizations, but the case summarized below gives a sense both of the fragility of area agriculture and of the easy dominance Anglo settlers achieved over their Nuevomexicano counterparts.

JOHN B. MCPHERSON V. GABRIEL CHAVEZ ET AL.

In early 1900 an Anglo landowner named John McPherson sued ten Nuevomexicano men for building a ditch to take water out of Percha Creek and cutting off the water supply to his own ditch in the town of Hillsborough. McPherson had to file the case in Silver City (in neighboring

Grant County) because the Sierra County judge, Frank Parker, was away and could not take cases. On behalf of his Sierra County colleague, a substitute judge, Charles Leland, granted a temporary injunction to prevent the defendants from using their newly dug ditch until the dispute could be resolved. In McPherson's complaint he reported having constructed a ditch in 1886 to bring water from Percha Creek through the Hillsborough townsite and down to a ranch where he cultivated fruit trees, alfalfa, and other crops. McPherson had the ditch surveyed in 1891 so he could enlarge it, and at that time he filed a formal ownership claim in probate court to the ditch and all of its waters. Since then, McPherson claimed, he had used the ditch continuously while also allowing others, including some of the defendants, to use water on a weekly schedule in return for their assistance in helping construct, enlarge, and annually maintain the ditch. McPherson's complaint accused the defendants of cutting his water flow drastically when they built a new ditch that diverted all water upstream on Percha Creek and returned only a small portion back to McPherson's private ditch. He explained to Judge Leland that the reduced water flow was not enough to keep his crops alive.

The defendants protested, arguing that *they* had built the ditch in 1881, well before McPherson bought his land in 1886. They claimed they dug a community ditch to bring water from Percha Creek to the Hillsborough Townsite "for the purpose of making adobes with which to construct their and other houses and buildings, and for the purpose of irrigating their gardens."[110] According to the defendants, the community ditch owners had allowed McPherson to use their surplus water because he was situated downstream of the townsite, and he dug a second, two-hundred-yard-long ditch in 1886 in order to connect to the existing community ditch. Since that time, defendants agreed, the two ditches operated as one community ditch, with McPherson getting a right to water half the week, while those in town received their share on the other days. The defendants claimed that no one knew McPherson had ever filed a private ditch claim in 1891, and they formalized the community ditch in 1896 by electing a mayordomo and ditch commissioners. When the ditch sustained considerable flood damage a few years later, however, members of the ditch cooperative decided in February 1900 to build a new ditch at a higher elevation. Defendants claimed that McPherson was the only member of the community ditch who refused to participate in meetings or in the work required to dig the new ditch, which was "much better adapted to the use of the community generally" and did not decrease the overall water flow to McPherson or any other member.[111]

McPherson denied that the ditch had ever been managed as a community ditch, and he submitted three affidavits from supporting witnesses. Each witness said they had known McPherson for two decades and confirmed that he had constructed a ditch twelve or fourteen years prior to the suit. Each attested that McPherson had used his private ditch continuously "until recently, when certain Mexicans [diverted] the water that flowed through said McPherson's ditch."[112] All of these witnesses were Anglos.

Judge Parker was back by autumn, and he held hearings in late November on the case, with the attorneys brokering a settlement agreement in the first week of December. Essentially, the two sides agreed to return everything to the way it had been before the lawsuit. Defendants agreed to abandon their new ditch and return to the old ditch on an evenly split watering schedule between the in-town users and McPherson. Each side agreed to take a half share in the ditch, with the defendants free to operate their share as a community ditch, as before. Neither side could make any changes to the ditch without getting permission from the other, and maintenance would be split evenly between the two sides.[113] The judge accepted the settlement in toto, quoting it in his final decree, and there is no evidence that this dispute continued or returned to court over the next decade.

This case illustrates the relative power that Anglos wielded as settlers. Hillsborough was founded in 1877 as a mining camp, and it attracted settlers of multiple ethnicities in the decades before this case, with no one group establishing a monopoly on land or water claims. But McPherson easily outmaneuvered the Nuevomexicano defendants in this case. Although the defendants pursued a collective approach to water use, presumably based on Nuevomexicano norms in other New Mexico locales, McPherson acted from the beginning as if private ditch ownership were the norm. He treated the ditch as if everyone were working for him and receiving water as a transaction, while the Nuevomexicano defendants in the townsite assumed they were all working together to share the water and maintain the ditch. When it came time to deal with a major infrastructure issue—caused by repeated flooding and ditch damage—these differences became clear. McPherson did not support the idea of constructing a new ditch, so he simply refused to participate. When the new ditch didn't live up to expectations in terms of water flow, McPherson quickly brought suit in an Anglo-dominated legal system to force the defendants to return to the status quo. He was able to use the English-language legal system more effectively than Spanish-speaking Nuevomexicano defendants, and he enjoyed the confidence of knowing all of the court personnel were Anglo: both judges, the three attorneys representing the two sides, the probate clerk, the sheriff, and even the deputy who delivered the court summons. The settlement agreement stipulated that the Nuevomexicano defendants abandon the ditch they had just labored to build, while leaving their underlying concern—damage caused by flooding—unaddressed. By allowing McPherson to operate as a private half owner in the ditch while the defendants operated it as a community ditch, however, the court *did* address the underlying issue that drove McPherson to bring the suit: the need to clarify water rights to avoid conflict and protect investment.

Doña Ana: New Norms Maximize Private Agriculture

Before crossing into Texas and taking up its imposed duty as the international border between the United States and the Republic of Mexico, the Rio Grande passes through New Mexico's Doña Ana County. In this final stretch before entering the Big Bend canyonlands of Texas, the river flows through mountainous and sloping land, creating a wide valley. Despite the agricultural advantages of a broad valley, no Spanish colony emerged or persisted in this area. Apache bands had long controlled the northern Chihuahuan Desert, and they guarded against colonial incursions in what is today southern New Mexico. As a result, Spanish colonial authorities concentrated their presence at El Paso del Norte, using it as a launch point for hurried transit to the northern settlements.

After Mexico gained its independence from Spain in 1821, however, some mixed Anglo and Nuevomexicano communities began to expand northward into the fertile floodplain of the Mesilla valley. And when the United States took control of New Mexico as a territory in 1848, the U.S. government targeted Apaches for removal, launching military operations that drove them away from potential agricultural lands. This military action worked hand in hand with the offering of homestead patents that attracted numerous Anglo settlers and established the lower valley as a new economic and power center for New Mexico.

At the same time, the new international border divided the valley and prompted a social reorganization. Many Mexican citizens living in Las Cruces chose a short move across the river border—to the new Villa de Mesilla—in order to remain subject to Mexican sovereignty after 1848. But the 1853 Gadsden Purchase shifted the border again, pushing it significantly southward and once again marooning Mesilla's many Mexican residents in U.S. territory. Some of these accidental immigrants moved further south to cross the border a second time, but most stayed put in Mesilla. The border's first incarnation thus produced an enduring divide between Nuevomexicano dominance on the west side of the river and Anglo dominance on the east side.[114]

Despite these broad patterns, Nuevomexicano and Anglo agriculturalists owned land and worked side by side in many areas of Doña Ana County. And neither group had an advantage in facing off against the river itself. Subject to increasingly variable flows when its northern headwaters forests disappeared as timber, the southern stretches of the Rio Grande alternated between drought and flood. Sometimes the river failed to flow into the southern valleys, and other times it radically reshaped its channel in unpredictable and torrential floods. Irrigators found it difficult to keep ditches, canals, and other infrastructure in working order under these conditions, and many abandoned their lands relatively soon after settling them. Owing partly to considerable lobbying on the part of New Mexicans, Congress approved the federal Rio Grande Project in 1905 to build a dam and reservoir at Elephant Butte. The U.S. Reclamation Service announced a tripartite goal for the project: taming the river's notorious floods, providing consistent irrigation water to the Rincon and Mesilla Valleys, and ensuring water delivery to meet interstate and international agreements at New Mexico's southern border. With a promised end to the river's unpredictability on the horizon, settlement gained steam around the turn of the century, and speculators patented grants throughout the lower valley. Doña Ana's population grew by 27 percent from 1900 to 1910, ending the first decade of the twentieth century with nearly thirteen thousand residents, most of them living in Las Cruces, Mesilla, or the agricultural towns lining the valley.

From 1900 to 1912 the Doña Ana District Court handled nineteen cases dealing with water, and a large proportion of them addressed damage to property, crops, or infrastructure (72 percent), with water-governance conflicts (61 percent) and channel changes (56 percent) also at issue in a number of disputes. About two-thirds of these cases involved some kind of environmental question as part of the dispute—either flood causes, channel flows, or channel geometry—and disputants addressed these environmental questions in court most often with simple assertion or by using eyewitnesses. Nuevomexicanas/os (67 percent) and Anglos (56 percent) were about equally represented as plaintiffs in these cases, while Nuevomexicanas/os were twice as commonly named among defendants, compared to Anglos. (There were no cases in 1900–1912 that involved any Indigenous plaintiff or defendant.) Court records are fairly complete in terms of naming all court personnel, with attorneys named in 95 percent of the cases and judges named in 84 percent of cases. All of these named personnel were Anglo.

The case summarized below reveals the complex water politics surrounding settlement expansion. It revolves around a disputed connection between a private lateral ditch and a public acequia madre in an area where Anglo farmers and investors had begun to leverage increasing power in comparison to Nuevomexicanas/os. When an intractable conflict emerged over water access, Anglo landowners had the upper hand.

SARAH PALMER AND WILLIAM PALMER JR. V. FELIX OTERO

In 1893 an Anglo settler named William Palmer built a long private ditch near Garfield, New Mexico. Along its path from San Ysidro's Acequia Madre to Palmer's four-hundred-acre property, the ditch crossed a number of other farms and fields. At each property Palmer requested permission to cross the land and typically offered access to his ditch (the Palmer Acequia) to any residents willing to contribute labor annually to help with its cleaning and maintenance.[115] Most of the residents along the route agreed, since Palmer's ditch was convenient to those whose land it crossed, and it had substantial capacity with a top width of seven feet. When Palmer reached the property of the Nuevomexicano farmer Luciano Duran, however, he discovered that Duran was nearly done constructing his own ditch connection to a different lateral and thus had no need for water from the Palmer Acequia. So the two landowners agreed to coordinate their plans for the ditch intersection point: Palmer's ditch would go under, and Duran's ditch would go over. At the point where they crossed, on Duran's property, the two owners installed a wooden box to secure the junction.

The last decade of the 1800s saw considerable ownership turnover in Doña Ana County. Some settlers entered homestead claims and then sold the lands as soon as they were patented. Others purchased lands and then sold them again after only a year or two. Even more commonly, speculators purchased lands and installed irrigation infrastructure before turning them over to renters for cash-crop cultivation. Ownership and residence were constantly in flux, creating a complex scenario in which agreements such as those between Palmer and Duran could be interpreted, misinterpreted, or contested by later owners and tenants.

Duran worked his property from 1892 to 1894, then moved to Hatch and leased it out to three different renters over the next three years. Charles Wilson bought the property in 1897 but sold it a year later to Felix Otero, the defendant in this case. Although Duran had built his own ditch to bring irrigation water to the property from a nearby ditch (the Ponsiano Arrey lateral),[116] Duran's renters after 1895 had instead entered agreements with Palmer to draw directly from the Palmer Acequia, since the flow was better. The original Duran ditch remained in place, crossing over the Palmer Acequia via a junction box, but it went unused.

When Otero bought his land from Wilson in 1898, Wilson explained that the land came with water rights in the Palmer Acequia, which engendered a standard obligation to provide annual fatigue labor both to the Palmer Acequia and to the San Ysidro Acequia Madre. When Palmer went around to area farmers to request fatigue workers in 1898 and 1899 (one man for every twenty acres of land), Otero sent the required labor or worked himself with his sons on the Palmer Acequia. But in 1900 a group of farmers who used the Palmer Acequia—both tenants and owners of the lands it crossed—protested Palmer's system for calculating fatigue work requirements. The protesters requested a new method of computation, and Palmer agreed under two conditions: first, each ditch user would need to calculate the exact area of his irrigated property; second, ditch users would need to pay up front for their water each year. Palmer also required for the first time that everyone using the ditch sign a paper contract to confirm the agreement. Otero arrived late to a community meeting where Palmer explained the conditions, and he refused to sign the contract because he didn't understand the English document. When Palmer explained it to him, Otero again refused to sign because he claimed the water right was part of his ownership of the land. The two of them had a "difficult discussion" afterward in which Otero asserted total control over the portion of the ditch that crossed his property.[117] Even though Otero did not agree to Palmer's conditions, Palmer allowed him to use the ditch in 1900 anyway, since the irrigation season was already under way. In December, however, Palmer notified Otero that he would need to make new arrangements for the following year unless he decided to accept the contract everyone else had already signed.

Otero fumed about Palmer's threat. Unlike his neighbors, who had apparently determined that Palmer held all the cards and could force them into an agreement, Otero held firm in his refusal to enter a disadvantageous contract. In early 1901 he sent men to the Palmer Acequia cleanup as usual and notified the San Ysidro mayordomo, Agapito Torres, that he planned to continue receiving his water right from the Acequia Madre via the Palmer Acequia. Torres agreed that Otero had a right to water from the main ditch but told him he did not want to be drawn into any dispute with Palmer.[118]

When Palmer and a party of workers showed up to clean the ditch across Otero's land, Palmer noticed that Otero had installed a headgate for irrigation. Palmer confronted Otero and asked whether the headgate indicated Otero's intention to sign the contract and take water from the ditch for irrigation. Otero defiantly stated that he would irrigate whenever he wanted but would sign no contract. In reply, Palmer ordered Otero to remove the headgate. Otero refused. Palmer then destroyed the headgate himself, smashing it with an ax in front of Otero, his sons, and a crowd of witnesses. One of Otero's sons was so enraged by the provocation that he attacked Palmer with a club, and Palmer and Otero then got in a fistfight, which bystanders finally broke up. Soon afterward Palmer sued Otero to prevent him from using or modifying the Palmer ditch. Palmer told the court that "that the members of defendant's family both sons and sons-in-law are dangerous and violent persons" and claimed he "would have been assassinated and murdered" that day if not for the bystanders' intervention.[119] Palmer also argued that Otero's meddling in the ditch would cause Palmer to lose crops worth $4,000 on the two hundred acres he irrigated for alfalfa, wheat, oats, barley, corn, and beans.

Judge Parker asked a referee, H. B. Holt, to collect affidavits and hold a hearing on his behalf. The many affidavits and legal briefs filed in this case revealed that landowners and water managers in the area often relied on unstable and hard-to-prove oral agreements. Otero, for example, relied on oral claims from previous owners about water rights that were not legally binding. In fact, he didn't even properly understand who owned the land. It emerged in sworn affidavits that Luciano Duran *thought* he gained ownership of the land by taking possession in 1892, but he had never actually filed a homestead claim and was never legally recognized as the owner. Instead, Ponsiano Arrey, the neighboring landowner who had originally allowed Duran to build a connecting ditch from his own contra acequia, quietly filed a claim to the land in 1893 while Duran himself was working the land and installing irrigation systems in the belief that he was the landowner. After Arrey received his patent in 1896, he sold the land to Wilson (who sold to Otero a year later). Similarly, Palmer *thought* he had obtained right-of-way permissions for his own contra acequia from all of the landowners whose land it crossed, but he didn't realize that most of those who made agreements with him were tenants and not owners. When Palmer sued Otero over the ditch segment crossing Otero's land, two absentee owners of large tracts near the head of Palmer's ditch signed affidavits saying that Palmer had never made any ditch-crossing agreements with them, and that they would expect to receive compensation for any such agreement under New Mexico law.[120] The case revealed that most of the agreements governing irrigation in cash-crop production areas worked fine until they ended up in court. Most of the discussions and negotiations over water-sharing took place in fields, alongside ditches, on the road, or in private homes, always in the presence of others who could then serve as witnesses or provide testimony in the event of a dispute. But their legal foundations were exceptionally flimsy.

When Palmer decided in 1900 to require ditch users to sign written contracts and pay up front for access to the ditch, he challenged water-management norms in a way that reflected the impacts both of Anglo settlement and of expanded irrigation in the lower Rio Grande valley. Across the area, large landowners—both Anglo and Nuevomexicano—could not turn a profit on their homestead claims without investing in private ditches for irrigation. Many partnerships of convenience emerged between Nuevomexicano smallholders and tenant farmers (or both, in cases where a farmer maintained his own small plot and also farmed one or more fields for an absentee landowner), who needed access to water but didn't have the means to develop robust infrastructure on their own. In return for providing labor at the outset and on an annual basis, Nuevomexicano farmers could gain access to a private ditch that reduced their own infrastructure cost burden. At most, they would need to construct a small ditch to bring water to their own plot from the larger ditch to which they provided labor. Through these agreements, a series of private ditches could operate almost like a traditional acequia, in which members enjoyed shared access to water and water-delivery infrastructure, providing in return labor and funds to maintain and repair the ditches when needed.

A traditional acequia system, however, is governed by annually elected leaders. In a private ditch system like Palmer's, a single owner managed the ditch as he saw fit, with little recourse available to those who disagreed with him. In the dispute that produced *Palmer v. Otero*, ditch users asked Palmer to change the way he managed the system, and he instead forced them all to sign disadvantageous contracts. That came as a rude surprise to many who thought they had been working within a community ditch system. A number of witnesses testified in court that the Palmer Acequia was "a public ditch" that belonged to several parties. One witness referred to Palmer's hired ditch overseer as a "commissioner," thus equating him with an elected representative.[121] Several witnesses also claimed to be part owners in the ditch, and this belief provided the basis for Otero's entire defense: "I claim the right to irrigate from that contra acequia because that ditch crosses my land, first; and second, because I have been working on it when there is any work to be done on the contra acequia, and I have a right in the main ditch. . . . I had it the same as the other co-partners in the main ditch; they work on the main ditch and then work in their contra acequias, lateral ditches."[122] For his part, Palmer admitted at the hearing that he did not have the right to provide or sell water to anyone. He claimed instead that he had the right to sell *access* to water through private agreements concerning the ditch infrastructure.

Along the Palmer Acequia, small farmers who believed they were part of a democratically governed water-sharing collective suffered a shock when the court process revealed they were actually obligated to accede to the demands of a single large landowner. This fundamental shift took place across Doña Ana County and other places in New Mexico. It was affirmed through court cases like this one, but it stemmed originally from the territory's effort to expand large-scale irrigation as a means to economic development and Anglo settlement. In Palmer's neighborhood, all of the large properties (and some small properties) functioned as investment properties. As soon as the infrastructure was in place to produce cash crops, owners typically sold the land for a profit, rented out various parcels to tenant farmers, or moved away altogether, leaving overseers and tenants to do the work.

Otero was only one of the many Nuevomexicanas/os disadvantaged in this settlement-driven system. He worked about thirty-five acres but owned only five of them, spending most of his time and energy on a large plot owned by Ponsiano Arrey, his Nuevomexicano neighbor. Otero held water rights in the main San Ysidro Acequia for his own five-acre plot, but he was forced to pay Palmer to use the ditch that could most efficiently bring this water to his land. San Ysidro's mayordomo, Torres, found himself caught in the middle, knowing that Otero had a water right yet pressured by Palmer not to let him use it if Otero didn't sign Palmer's contract. Torres actually submitted affidavits on behalf of both the plaintiff and defendant, confirming for the defense that Otero had a water right in the Acequia Madre and confirming for the plaintiff that Torres had instructed Otero not to use water out of the ditch. Otero faced a choice: meet Palmer's demands for payment or spend his money instead to repair the old Duran ditch. The latter option would have simply subjected him to the whims of another powerful landowner, since Duran's ditch drew its water through the private lateral ditch owned by Arrey. In the end, Otero chose neither option. His diffidence landed him in court, where his relative poverty and lack of English-language skills posed yet further disadvantage.

As should be clear by now to readers, the territorial-era legal system in New Mexico put numerous obstacles in the path of Nuevomexicano and Indigenous disputants. The case of *Palmer v. Otero* illustrates the broader reality: the judge and referee were both Anglo, all of the attorneys were Anglo, all sworn statements and documents were filed in English, and all of the Spanish-language testimony at the hearing went through interpreters in order to create an English-language transcript.[123] At one point in the hearing, Otero found himself under cross-examination about discrepancies between the statement he had signed before the hearing (which was written in English) and his testimony in the courtroom (which he gave in Spanish). Upon hearing the discrepancy explained to him in Spanish and asking several clarifying questions, Otero admitted, "My attorney who ... wasn't with me at Silver City; he asked me to sign that and I didn't understand it all perhaps."[124]

Otero's reference to Silver City also illustrates the ways the district court system reinforced financial disadvantage among those of lesser means. Otero had to take time away from his paid work to appear in court, and he incurred significant expenses traveling to nonlocal courthouses. In this case, Otero was required to appear at different times in both Las Cruces and Silver City, neither of which was close to his land near Garfield in Loma Parda, to give a sworn affidavit and attend a hearing overseen by the case referee. Otero also had to cough up funds to pay for legal representation, and he couldn't afford the best. In fact, Otero's attorney withdrew on the day of the hearing, for reasons unremarked in the case file. Otero met his new legal team as they walked together into the hearing room. And although the court protected Otero's right to use irrigation water until the case was decided, the end result went against him and inflicted yet another financial wound. Not only did Otero have to pay to bring water to his land after the verdict, but he also had to pay Palmer's court costs. In the middle of his testimony at the 23 December hearing, Otero stopped in the middle of answering a question and asked for permission to make a statement. Once the referee agreed, he offered a statement (in Spanish) that went into the court record as follows: "I know that Mr Palmer has said that he is going to bother me with that ditch, that he has ten thousand dollars to make me an injury, that he would ruin me. It is a mere caprice."[125] Palmer used Otero's poverty to his advantage, even stating in his complaint that Otero was too poor to pay for any damage his actions might cause and using that as justification that the court should stop him from interfering with the Palmer Acequia.

After taking testimony, the referee reported his findings of fact and law to Judge Parker, determining that no one had gained any permanent right to use water from the Palmer Acequia by simply agreeing to allow it to cross their land. The referee determined that Otero never received a permanent water right in the ditch, and that his use of the Palmer Acequia was subject to the terms and conditions imposed by Palmer. Otero's attorneys disputed the referee's report, but they were unsuccessful. Judge Parker accepted Holt's report in toto and decided the case in favor of Palmer, which ended Otero's access to the Palmer Acequia.

This case highlights the ways that water-management norms changed in response to settlement expansion, and how they created persistent advantages for Anglo setters. Small tenant farmers were the most likely to lose water control and access in the settlement model New Mexico's territorial leaders hoped to foster in the southern Rio Grande valley and elsewhere. Those tenant farmers were overwhelmingly Nuevomexicanas/os. Even when Nuevomexicanas/os tried to take advantage of the new homestead laws to stake agricultural claims and irrigate cash crops, they were less likely to succeed than their Anglo counterparts, although in this case Arrey is a counterexample.[126] In *Palmer v. Otero*, several Anglo and Nuevomexicano farmers undertook similar actions to control land and water but ended up with very different results. Luciano Duran took possession of a piece of land and started irrigating it for cash crops and to generate rents, but he ended up losing the property to someone else's homestead claim. His wealthy neighbor, Ponsiano Arrey, took possession of that piece of land *without* even irrigating it (because Duran was doing so already) by effectively navigating the legal requirements to patent a homestead claim.[127] Similarly, Palmer built his ditch by claiming right-of-way across other farmers' lands without any real legal basis or procedure to back it up. In an environment where many of the farmers didn't own the land, Palmer's speculative offer of ditch access gave him enough power to broker agreements all along the route of the ditch. When Otero himself tried to gain control over a portion of the ditch through the same tactic of outright assertion, however, it landed him in court. He ended up financially damaged, dispossessed of irrigation infrastructure, and vulnerable to the unfavorable ditch-access terms set by Arrey or Palmer, the two owners who controlled major private ditches crossing the Loma Parda area. As this case shows, Palmer enjoyed the benefits of the San Ysidro community ditch system—in which a mayordomo conducted land measurements, oversaw irrigation schedules, and calculated water-delivery amounts—but was not forced to submit to its governance, since his private ditch was fully under his own control. When a ditch user objected to this control and took an assertive stand against it, the court backed the private ditch with an interpretation that moved away from community ditch customs and toward the privatization of water rights.

Conclusions

When environmental concerns emerged in New Mexico's water disputes between 1900 and 1912, district court judges from across the study area turned often to technology-driven modernist solutions. If scientific data and expert testimony were unavailable, judges found ways to render prescriptive findings or to prioritize large-scale economic and urban development over subsistence-oriented water uses. More often than not, this priority favored Anglo settlers and disadvantaged Indigenous and Nuevomexicano residents.

These cases also show that Anglos did not at first find easy success for their speculative attempts to establish large-scale irrigation during the late territorial period. Such operations required large tracts of land, robust infrastructures for water diversion and conveyance, and legal access to water resources, all of which were in short supply in areas already densely settled by Indigenous or Nuevomexicano communities. When conflict erupted over one or more of these issues, New Mexico's district courts navigated the need to protect new settlers' capital investments alongside existing communities' rights to engage in irrigated agriculture according to long-standing custom. By raising a range of new issues and conflicts, however, Anglo settlement brought complex and sometimes unprecedented legal questions into the courtroom. In the handful of cases reviewed in this chapter, individuals sued cities and corporations for both maintaining and not maintaining infrastructure, cities sued corporations and community ditches over new water-quality concerns, Anglo and Nuevomexicano irrigators creatively dispossessed neighboring Indigenous communities, Anglo settlers manipulated Nuevomexicano irrigators in their suits against one another, and Anglo settlers selectively sued Nuevomexicano members of community ditches. As the territorial era unfolded in New Mexico, subsistence-oriented, non-Anglo irrigation communities struggled to remain viable as the new arrivals exploited their political and legal vulnerabilities.

In a substantial departure from pre-U.S. legal traditions, judges looked not to compromise or community coherence as foundations for dispute resolution. They instead looked for definitive solutions that declared clear winners and losers in each dispute. To this end, technology and infrastructure appeared regularly in court prescriptions, as if they had the power to stabilize social relations or relegate political agitation to the background. When infrastructure or technology animated the main issues in a case, judges typically sought to define and clarify technological parameters so they could minimize complaints while allowing technology-dependent development and environmental modification to continue. Judges thus actively protected the property and investments of speculative irrigators and corporations, whose presence in New Mexico constituted a massive disruption of the territory's political and cultural geographies. In this way, the district court system itself served the goals of U.S. settler colonialism by enabling and confirming the displacement of non-Anglo individuals and communities.

✹ 8 ✹
Conclusion

SETTLER COLONIALISM AND ITS AFTERMATH

The pages, chapters, and stories in this book trace New Mexico's transition in the late territorial era from community-based water management to an expert-led structure controlled by engineers and bureaucrats. The transition was slow and halting, and it remains incomplete due to ongoing administrative, legal, and cultural contestation. By looking closely at the rise of modernist water management in New Mexico's territorial period, however, we see that expertise, engineering, and efficiency were absolutely critical to U.S. settler colonialism during the foundational phase of western expansion. We can also follow modernist commitments into the present, linking science-based policy and its claims of authority to an ongoing and dispossessive racial project.

Chapter 2 shows that water management has long been central to life in New Mexico. Indigenous nations developed robust modes of water management suitable for numerous microgeographic and seasonal variations, building social and political structures that persisted over millennia of environmental and cultural change. Spanish colonizers focused on water management as a means of wealth production and territorial control in the sixteenth and seventeenth centuries, generating new social formations over generations. When American officials took possession of New Mexico in the nineteenth century, they also focused on water management as a key to colonial efforts. Anglo-Americans introduced and prioritized commercial-scale irrigation that disrupted Indigenous and Nuevomexicano irrigators simultaneously. Commercial irrigation then opened the door to a flood of Anglo settlers, upsetting social and political dynamics with a new colonial order that pushed Nuevomexicanas/os into a new position as colonized subjects.

In chapter 3 I reviewed the political philosophy and policy foundation that changed virtually everything about water management in New

Mexico. Progressivism prioritized centralized control, market efficiency, and expert leadership for all forms of resource management. It precipitated drastic environmental change across the western United States and incentivized Anglo settlement at the expense of long-standing irrigators across New Mexico. In tracing this origin story, the chapter shows that one of the most powerful weapons in the modernist-management arsenal was expertise. Expertise is not an objective characteristic; it is derived from political, social, and cultural contexts. Once encoded, however, expertise becomes naturalized and almost impossible to contest. The Progressives' racist political philosophy constructed expertise as a white Anglo characteristic. Official policy then systematically discredited non-Anglo knowledge holders and held them responsible for the environmental damages caused by Progressive policy.

Chapter 4 shows that New Mexico's development of water laws in the late territorial period functioned as a form of cultural imperialism. Pressured by federal officials to encode Progressive principles into law, territorial representatives passed a series of statutes that enabled Anglo settlement, incentivized commercial agriculture, and facilitated financial investments from eastern speculators. The underlying goal—to make New Mexico "American" enough to prevail in the U.S. Congress's vote on statehood—was finally achieved after the passage of the 1907 water law. The new statute created a centralized, expert-led process for quantifying and controlling water management through hydrographic surveys, permit allocation, and adjudication of water rights. Each of these policy elements challenged the long-standing cultural bases for water management among non-Anglo irrigators, tipping the balance of power in favor of Anglo settlers.

In chapter 5 I show that New Mexico's first modernist water bureaucracy engaged in multiple forms of knowledge work to support the settler-colonial project. Anglo engineers working for the new agency perceived their mission as producing data, maximizing profits, and preventing waste, all in the service of increasing Anglo settlement. Although they found it impossible to conduct territory-wide hydrographic surveys or to calculate accurately the correct amount of water needed to irrigate a given crop efficiently in a given location, engineers claimed success in reports designed to make New Mexico seem more "American." Official engineering reports regularly commented on the role of irrigation engineering in bringing white settlers to New Mexico and continually requested more resources to implement this mission. Ironically, official reports also show that engineers worried constantly about Anglo settlers' hydrologic and agronomic ignorance, at the same time they dismissed the knowledge and technology of subsistence irrigators with centuries of experience across the New Mexico territory.

Chapter 6 explores another arena in which environmental knowledge was produced and contested: the courtroom. Anglo colonial institutions for dispute resolution took the place of Nuevomexicano courts based on Spanish and Mexican law, while also relegating Indigenous forms of tribal dispute resolution to the margins. In the final years of the territorial period, many water disputes ended up in federal district courts, and *Fluid Geographies* takes a careful look at all cases recorded for the counties along the Rio Chama–Rio Grande corridor in the twelve years before statehood. The chapter shows that Anglos dominated the district courts, and that water-related court cases frequently took up questions of environmental knowledge dealing with hydrology, fluvial geomorphology, and weather-related events. Using a statistical analysis, the chapter confirms that district courts engaged regularly with disputes over environmental characteristics, realities, and causalities.

Chapter 7 dives into narrative analysis for a subset of the cases discussed in chapter 6, tracing a north-to-south path along the Rio Chama and Rio Grande valleys. Along the way, individual water disputes reflect the unfolding of settler-colonial science and environmental knowledge across the New Mexico territory. By examining each conflict in detail, I illuminate the fluid geographies of displacement, disruption, and resistance that attended the settler-colonial project. In these stories judges bend over backward to protect speculative investments and corporate property claims, but they also defer at certain times and places to cultural realities that resist the imposition of modernist science. The district court system served the goals of U.S. settler colonialism by enabling Anglo settlement, but it also struggled to enact and justify new forms of environmental knowledge.

Overall, *Fluid Geographies* argues that Anglo settlers' norms for producing environmental knowledge and developing water-management policy played a crucial role in making New Mexico "American" by displacing and disadvantaging Indigenous and Nuevomexicano peoples and communities. It contributes to the literature of historical geography and to settler-colonial studies by showing that water science, policy, and management helped stabilize broad structures of colonial dispossession. Critically, it shows that modernist water management constructed expertise as an exclusively Anglo characteristic, dismissing and delegitimizing non-Anglo irrigators despite their expansive environmental knowledge.

In addition, this research contributes to the literature in settler-colonial studies by prompting us to look more carefully at the groups impacted by modernist water management. New Mexico's territorial engineering agency marginalized Indigenous nations, yes, but Anglo-American colonialism also impacted a wide range of diverse peoples claiming Spanish, mestizo, genízaro, and other identities. The Progressives' political project remade environments and social relations simultaneously, collapsing cultural complexity into a simplistic "non-Anglo" category slated for marginalization, dispossession, and genocide. *Fluid Geographies* attempts to rescue some of this complexity, showing how claims to hydrologic, geographic, and other environmental knowledge forms shifted from place to place and from group to group. It contributes to the literature on the geography of science by foregrounding the spatiality of knowledge claims in different areas of New Mexico where Anglo settlers had varying levels of success in their colonial mission.

Historical Geographies of the Present

This book is historical, but none of these issues are relegated to the past. New Mexico's current approach to water management is founded in a settler-colonial structure that has never gone away. Environmental laws and policies originally created to enable Anglo settlement in the territorial period are still at work displacing people today, no matter how invisible or unchangeable they seem.[1]

The fact of this ongoing displacement is perhaps more visible in the Rio Grande watershed than in any other part of what is now the U.S. Southwest. In New Mexico, Indigenous cultures claim long histories in the valleys and plateaus connected to the Rio Grande, while Nuevomexicanas/os maintain strong cultural coherence in those same valleys and adjoining tributaries. The strength, resistance, and resurgence of these groups—notwithstanding their complicated formations, shifting alliances, and conflicting dynamics—throws the Anglo colonial presence into stark relief. Even the casual observer in New Mexico can perceive gross distinctions between commercial and subsistence activities, between land-based and property-based traditions, and between place-based and placeless lifeways. Through these distinctions, non-Anglo peoples provide fierce and vivid evidence in New Mexico and elsewhere that the settler project is destined to fail.[2]

What is the value, then, of studying settler colonialism? It is no longer enough to simply confirm its existence and identify its structure. What *is* useful is to deconstruct its origins, to show that contemporary vulnerabilities and patterns of inequality emerged from and are reproduced by specific policies and philosophies, and to denaturalize the white-supremacist project of accumulating wealth for white people through the dispossession of nonwhite people. Other scholars have written about the "environmental-racial order" that emerged when federal bureaucrats wrested control of New Mexico's forests from Indigenous and Nuevomexicano communities.[3] The goal of *Fluid Geographies* is to show that water management also participated in producing an environmental-racial order, and to identify the explicitly racist conceptions underlying policies, laws, agencies, and knowledge institutions that are still with us.

Looking up from the pages of this book to the ongoing management of water in New Mexico, we can see that it's a very short distance from the colonial past to the colonial present. As one example, consider the adjudication of water rights in the upper Rio Grande watershed. In 1907 New Mexico's territorial legislative body, the territorial assembly, asked its new engineering agency to identify all existing water uses, quantify them, and legally document their associated water rights. More than a century later, the Office of the State Engineer has still not finished the job. At the moment I am writing this sentence, and again at the moment you are reading it, someone in New Mexico is defending a lawsuit to prove the legitimacy of their water rights in court. Defendants range from small water users to large corporations, but the plaintiff is always the same: the State of New Mexico, supported by attorneys from the Office of the State Engineer.[4] The geographer Eric Perramond argues that New Mexico's "adjudication-industrial complex" creates jobs for expert engineers and attorneys while dispossessing smallholder irrigators without financial or legal resources to prove their water rights.[5] Perramond also shows that the adversarial and individualistic nature of the adjudication process threatens the social fabric of many communities. Today's primary work of the Office of the State Engineer—adjudication—thus perpetuates inequality and produces social discord as if by design.[6] It's a classic divide-and-conquer strategy, taken straight from the settler-colonial playbook.

Some have called for a new approach based on cooperative negotiation rather than disruptive litigation, since negotiation offers the potential for win-win solutions whereas litigation is always zero-sum.[7] I hope, however, that this book will lead readers to recognize that the underlying framework for adjudication is dispossessive at its very core. The legal mandate to define water rights through expert quantification and render them separable from land was a territorial tool meant to facilitate commercial speculation and Anglo settlement. That hasn't changed. Therefore, *any* process for quantifying water rights under the current statute will disadvantage subsistence-oriented, land-based, non-Anglo water users and communities, regardless of whether the parties frame it as confrontational or amicable in nature.[8] The same holds true for other environmental policies based entirely on scientific measurement, evaluation, and prescription: they can only produce negative consequences for already marginalized communities. That is what they were designed to do.

Over the years since it was created, the Office of the State Engineer has deepened and expanded its colonial mission through a radical commitment to expertise. Each time new conditions arise in the post-territorial era—for example, the discovery of hydrologic connections between groundwater and surface water, a shift in the federal reclamation mission, or extended drought—the Office of the State Engineer takes an aggressive stance to maintain its expert authority.[9] The OSE is now very powerful, with wide-ranging authority affirmed in court over the years on the basis of its engineering expertise. When a state legislator recently introduced a bill to widen eligibility for the state's top water post, New Mexico's water engineers and apologists cried foul, worried that the bill would devalue engineering expertise.[10] But truly, they needn't have worried. HB 83 would have opened the position requirements only minimally beyond licensed professional engineers, adding language to allow "a qualified or appropriately credentialed geohydrologist, hydrologist, geologist or attorney" to become the state engineer. The bill didn't even try to tackle the real problem—the science-based structure of settler colonialism—and in any case, it didn't pass.[11]

The 2022 dustup over exactly which experts are and are not qualified to serve as the state engineer for New Mexico was maddening yet predictable for those of us who would prefer to see the entire expertise-based framework dismantled. If it's so difficult to take even a small step, how will we ever take big ones? How long will New Mexicans have to wait, and how many more people will be dispossessed or displaced, before we find more equitable and just ways to live with each other and with our environments?

After the Aftermath

Fluid Geographies may seem pessimistic in its broad strokes, given its central task of describing the settler-colonial frameworks that created enduring and authoritative approaches to water management based in modernist science. But the details of this history also point toward the possibility for change. Everything that seems so certain about water management today actually emerged from complex and ambiguous interactions. The growing authority of New Mexico's territorial, and later state, engineer in the early twentieth century rested not on objective science, but on a complex conflation of scientific rhetoric and methods, national and state politics, local environmental knowledge, and existing legal norms for determining the proper relationship between Rio Grande communities and their limited water resources. Within these varied contexts, the Office of the State Engineer developed local and contingent forms of authority that must be understood as such today. The authoritative model of rational water management that dominates New Mexico's politics today is *not* a direct or necessary derivative of federal policy prescriptions from a century ago. It was produced in and by particular environmental and social contexts that were often contested during that early period of initial implementation.

In other words, there is nothing inevitable or natural about New Mexico's centralized water-management system. Settler colonialism can be challenged, even dismantled. Indigenous activists have long been demanding change in calls for #waterback and #landback, while activist Nuevomexicanas/os continue to push for policy that acknowledges and protects acequia institutions as a focus of cultural resurgence.[12] If we want our water management to supersede its settler-colonial foundations, the first step is to shift from an engineering-based approach to a relationship-based approach that has room for multiple knowledge forms and fosters social repair.[13] Indigenous scholars increasingly center water governance as a tool for self-determination and argue for moving policy toward "true pluralism," which would "protect the social and natural resource capital of marginalized communities."[14] Nuevomexicana/o scholars are leading a cultural-studies agenda that places lands and waters at the center of social relations and cultural formations.[15] The complexity of the cultural tapestry in New Mexico is just one reminder—in one place—that we must be careful with our theory-making and ask what and who it is for. Those of us who come from the dominant Anglo culture have a tremendous opportunity to learn from and amplify these voices as we go forward with our own work.

Debate will continue over whether the tools of the colonizer—science, cartography, and legal philosophy, among others—can be used to dismantle colonialism or only to perpetuate it. But it has become clear that territorial-era frameworks are under stress. The accelerating impacts of climate change in the U.S. Southwest threaten not only the very resources New Mexico law purports to manage, but also the scientific credibility on which centralized environmental management rests. For modernist science to maintain even a shred of dignity in the face of social disruptions triggered by warming, drought, wildfire, extinction, and other ecological disturbances, its practitioners must engage the idea of multiple knowledges and seek to detach from the settler-colonial framework. The anthropologist Sylvia Rodríguez, one of New Mexico's savviest interpreters of water histories, puts it best: "until researchers acknowledge the need to commit themselves actively to seek a radical alternative, they will continue to succumb to the machinery of class and regional ethnic-racial stratification.... their applied work will always remain fundamentally reactive, at best reformist, and however well intentioned, ultimately dependent upon and subservient to the prevailing system of inequality and exploitation."[16]

In researching this book, I learned that it wasn't only bad actors—swindlers and corrupt politicians—who participated in the displacement of Indigenous and Nuevomexicano people. "Good" actors played critical roles too. Everyone working to install a framework for rational-scientific water management was an agent of dispossession. Everyone working to lift commercial development above other uses of water was an agent of dispossession. Everyone who favored the testimony of civil engineers over the testimony of eyewitness observers in a legal dispute was an agent of dispossession. Everyone who circulated knowledge about New Mexico's waters to incoming settlers from the eastern regions was an agent of dispossession. And everyone who subsequently moved to New Mexico and settled on unceded Pueblo, Navajo, Ute, or Apache lands was an agent of dispossession. Including me.

* * *

I finished the first draft of *Fluid Geographies* between 2020 and 2022, during a complex and tumultuous national reckoning with racial injustice, social inequality, and climate crisis. In the summer of 2020, crowds gathered in central Albuquerque to protest a prominent statue of Juan de Oñate, the early Spanish colonial governor notorious for perpetrating gruesome abuses against Indigenous communities. As a right-wing militia of armed white men organized to defend the Oñate statue, Albuquerque police intentionally stayed out of sight, reportedly to avoid inflaming tensions after years of their own racially inequitable use-of-force abuses. In a violent swirl of cultural, political, and ethnic dislocations, an armed man who was defending the statue alongside the militia nonfatally shot a protester, and by morning the city had quietly removed the statue and carted it away on a flatbed truck.[17]

Many things about this incident drew my attention. I noticed that the most visible defenders of New Mexico's most violent settler colonialist were Anglo, even though Oñate himself was not. I noticed that Indigenous activists did most of the work to organize and launch the protest. I noticed that some in the multiracial group of protesters were Nuevomexicanas/os, perhaps using political speech to wrestle with the complicated legacies of their own Spanish heritage. And I also noticed that no one protested that day in front of the Office of the State Engineer. After researching this book for so long, it was this last fact that really struck me. We've taken down the statues, but we haven't taken down the broad structures of Anglo domination. While focusing our activism on symbols of historical, colonial, and racial abuse, we regularly turn a blind eye to colonialism's actual, ever-present, and ongoing deployments. We pay our water bills and file our property deeds, and no one grabs a bullhorn to protest against these mundane, pernicious colonial documents.

When an engineering project intercepts water bound for the Pacific Ocean, diverts it into the Rio Grande, and then pushes it up the arid slopes of a three-hundred-year-old city in a massive pipe system, the Water Authority knows that residents' first concern is whether the water will taste funny. The mailers that land in mailboxes across Albuquerque never say a thing about scientific uncertainty, engineering hubris, or technological vulnerability, much less about racial inequalities or environmental injustices. At least that was true in 2006, where I started my story. I am hopeful that the activism and scholarship of recent years will contribute to a growing consciousness of colonial forms and depths, and to the building of new relations and futures.

Notes

Chapter 1

1. Cole Harris, *Making Native Space: Colonialism, Resistance and Reserves in British Columbia* (Vancouver: University of British Columbia Press, 2002).

2. I discuss and cite the literature on irrigation histories in New Mexico (and the wider U.S. Southwest) in chap. 2.

3. Gregory Cajete, *Native Science: Natural Laws of Interdependence* (Santa Fe, NM: Clear Light, 2000); Leanne R. Simpson, "Anticolonial Strategies for the Recovery and Maintenance of Indigenous Knowledge," in "The Recovery of Indigenous Knowledge," special issue, *American Indian Quarterly* 28, nos. 3–4 (2004); Audra Simpson, "Settlement's Secret," *Cultural Anthropology* 26, no. 2 (2011); Linda Tuhiwai Smith, *Decolonizing Methodologies: Research and Indigenous Peoples* (London: Zed Books, 2012); Mishuana Goeman, "The Tools of a Cartographic Poet: Unmapping Settler Colonialism in Joy Harjo's Poetry," *Settler Colonial Studies* 2, no. 2 (2012); Corey Snelgrove, Rita Kaur Dhamoon, and Jeff Corntassel, "Unsettling Settler Colonialism: The Discourse and Politics of Settlers, and Solidarity with Indigenous Nations," *Decolonization: Indigeneity, Education & Society* 3, no. 2 (2014); Annette Watson and Orville Huntington, "Transgressions of the Man on the Moon: Climate Change, Indigenous Expertise, and the Posthumanist Ethics of Place and Space," *GeoJournal* 79, no. 6 (2014); J. Kēhaulani Kauanui, "'A Structure, Not an Event': Settler Colonialism and Enduring Indigeneity," *Lateral* 5, no. 1 (2016).

4. Daniel Clayton, "The Question of Making Native Space" [guest editorial], *BC Studies: The British Columbian Quarterly* 138–39 (Summer–Autumn 2003): 8.

5. Bruce Willems Braun, "Buried Epistemologies: The Politics of Nature in (Post)colonial British Columbia," *Annals of the Association of American Geographers* 87, no. 1 (1997); Leah M. Gibbs, "Just Add Water: Colonisation, Water Governance, and the Australian Inland," *Environment and Planning A* 41, no. 12 (2009); Timothy Neale and Stephen Turner, "Other People's Country: Law, Water, Entitlement," *Settler Colonial Studies* 5, no. 4 (2015); Paul Berne Burow, Samara Brock, and Michael R. Dove, "Unsettling the Land: Indigeneity, Ontology, and Hybridity in Settler Colonialism," *Environment and Society* 9, no. 1 (2018); Emma S. Norman, "Indigenous Space, Scalar Politics and Water Governance in the Salish Sea Basin," in *Negotiating Water Governance: Why the Politics of Scale Matter*, ed. Emma S. Norman, Christina Cook, and Alice Cohen (London and New York: Routledge, 2016); Leah Temper, "Blocking

Pipelines, Unsettling Environmental Justice: From Rights of Nature to Responsibility to Territory," *Local Environment* 24, no. 2 (2019).

6. Lorenzo Veracini, "Introducing *Settler Colonial Studies*," *Settler Colonial Studies* 1, no. 1 (2011); Sarah de Leeuw, Margo Greenwood, and Nicole Lindsay, "Troubling Good Intentions," *Settler Colonial Studies* 3, nos. 3–4 (2013); Matalena Tofa, "Incomplete Reconciliations: A History of Settling Grievances in Taranaki, New Zealand," *Journal of Historical Geography* 46 (October 2014); Sarah Maddison, Tom Clark, and Ravi de Costa, eds., *The Limits of Settler Colonial Reconciliation: Non-Indigenous People and the Responsibility to Engage* (Singapore: Springer Nature, 2016); Paulette Regan, *Unsettling the Settler Within: Indian Residential Schools, Truth Telling, and Reconciliation in Canada* (Vancouver: University of British Columbia Press, 2010).

7. Jodi A. Byrd, *The Transit of Empire: Indigenous Critiques of Colonialism* (Minneapolis: University of Minnesota Press, 2011).

8. Patrick Wolfe, *Settler Colonialism and the Transformation of Anthropology: The Politics and Poetics of an Ethnographic Event* (London: Cassell, 1999); Lorenzo Veracini, *Settler Colonialism: A Theoretical Overview* (Basingstoke and New York: Palgrave Macmillan, 2010); Veracini, "Introducing *Settler Colonial Studies*"; Adam J. Barker, "Locating Settler Colonialism," *Journal of Colonialism and Colonial History* 13, no. 3 (2012), Project MUSE database, doi:10.1353/cch.2012.0035.

9. Caroline Elkins and Susan Pederson, eds., *Settler Colonialism in the Twentieth Century: Projects, Practices, Legacies* (New York: Routledge, 2005), 2.

10. Richard Drinnon, *Facing West: The Metaphysics of Indian-Hating and Empire-Building* (Minneapolis: University of Minnesota Press, 1980); Neve Gordon and Moriel Ram, "Ethnic Cleansing and the Formation of Settler Colonial Geographies," *Political Geography* 53 (July 2016); Karl Jacoby, "The Broad Platform of Extermination," in *North American Borderlands: Rewriting Histories*, ed. Brian DeLay (New York: Routledge, 2013); Ben Kiernan, *Blood and Soil: A World History of Genocide and Extermination from Sparta to Darfur* (New Haven, CT: Yale University Press, 2007); Patrick Wolfe, "Settler Colonialism and the Elimination of the Native," *Journal of Genocide Research* 8, no. 4 (2006).

11. Robert A. Williams, Jr., *The American Indian in Western Legal Thought: The Discourses of Conquest* (Oxford and New York: Oxford University Press, 1990); Renisa Mawani, "Law, Settler Colonialism, and 'the Forgotten Space' of Maritime Worlds," *Annual Review of Law and Social Science* 12 (2016).

12. Richard White, *The Roots of Dependency: Subsistence, Environment, and Social Change among the Choctaws, Pawnees, and Navajos* (Lincoln: University of Nebraska Press, 1988); Eric V. Meeks, "The Tohono O'odham, Wage Labor, and Resistant Adaptation, 1900–1930," *Western Historical Quarterly* 34, no. 4 (2003); James Belich, *Replenishing the Earth: The Settler Revolution and the Rise of the Anglo-World, 1783–1939* (Oxford and New York: Oxford University Press, 2009); Anna Stanley, "Resilient Settler Colonialism: 'Responsible Resource Development,' 'Flow-Through' Financing, and the Risk Management of Indigenous Sovereignty in Canada," *Environment and Planning A* 48, no. 12 (2016).

13. Alyosha Goldstein and Alex Lubin, eds., "Settler Colonialism," special issue, *South Atlantic Quarterly* 107, no. 4 (2008); Fiona Bateman and Lionel Pilkington, *Studies in Settler Colonialism: Politics, Identity and Culture* (Basingstoke: Palgrave Macmillan, 2011).

14. Annie E. Coombs, ed., *Rethinking Settler Colonialism: History and Memory in*

Australia, Canada, Aotearoa New Zealand and South Africa (Manchester: Manchester University Press, 2006), xii.

15. Coombs, *Rethinking Settler Colonialism*, xii. See also Adam J. Barker, "The Contemporary Reality of Canadian Imperialism: Settler Colonialism and the Hybrid Colonial State," *American Indian Quarterly* 33, no. 3 (2009); Avril Bell, *Relating Indigenous and Settler Identities: Beyond Domination* (London and New York: Palgrave Macmillan, 2014); Penelope Edmonds, "Unpacking Settler Colonialism's Urban Strategies: Indigenous Peoples in Victoria, British Columbia, and the Transition to a Settler-Colonial City," *Urban History Review/Revue d'histoire urbaine* 38, no. 2 (2010).

16. Brian W. Dippie, *The Vanishing American: White Attitudes and U.S. Indian Policy* (Middletown, CT: Wesleyan University Press, 1982); Sarah de Leeuw, "Alice through the Looking Glass: Emotion, Personal Connection, and Reading Colonial Archives along the Grain," *Journal of Historical Geography* 38, no. 3 (2012); Susan M. Manning, "Contrasting Colonisations: (Re)Storying Newfoundland/Ktaqmkuk as Place," *Settler Colonial Studies* 8, no. 3 (2018); David Pearson, *The Politics of Ethnicity in Settler Societies: States of Unease* (Basingstoke and New York: Palgrave, 2001); Joshua Inwood and Anne Bonds, "Confronting White Supremacy and a Militaristic Pedagogy in the U.S. Settler Colonial State," *Annals of the American Association of Geographers* 106, no. 3 (2016).

17. Karen V. Hansen, Ken Chih-Yan Sun, and Debra Osnowitz, "Immigrants as Settler Colonists: Boundary Work between Dakota Indians and White Immigrant Settlers," *Ethnic and Racial Studies* 40, no. 11 (2017); Erich Steinman, "Settler Colonial Power and the American Indian Sovereignty Movement: Forms of Domination, Strategies of Transformation," *American Journal of Sociology* 117, no. 4 (2012); Glen S. Coulthard, "Subjects of Empire: Indigenous Peoples and the 'Politics of Recognition' in Canada," *Contemporary Political Theory* 6, no. 4 (2007); Thomas Biolsi, "Imagined Geographies: Sovereignty, Indigenous Space, and American Indian Struggle," *American Ethnologist* 32, no. 2 (2005); Hamish Dalley, "The Deaths of Settler Colonialism: Extinction as a Metaphor of Decolonization in Contemporary Settler Literature," *Settler Colonial Studies* 8, no. 1 (2018); Bruce Braun, "Colonialism's Afterlife: Vision and Visuality on the Northwest Coast," *Cultural Geographies* 9, no. 2 (2002); Kim TallBear, "Standing With and Speaking as Faith: A Feminist-Indigenous Approach to Inquiry," in "Giving Back in Field Research," special issue, *Journal of Research Practice* 10, no. 2 (2014), accessed 22 May 2023, http://jrp.icaap.org/index.php/jrp/article/view/405/371; Kimberly TallBear, *Native American DNA : Tribal Belonging and the False Promise of Genetic Science* (Minneapolis: University of Minnesota Press, 2013).

18. Byrd, *The Transit of Empire*; Regan, *Unsettling the Settler Within*.

19. Kauanui, "'A Structure, Not an Event.'"

20. Shaphan Cox et al., "Indigenous Persistence and Entitlement: Noongar Occupations in Central Perth, 1988–1989 and 2012," *Journal of Historical Geography* 54 (2016); Brian Egan and Jessica Place, "Minding the Gaps: Property, Geography, and Indigenous Peoples in Canada," *Geoforum* 44, no. 1 (2013); Burow, Brock, and Dove, "Unsettling the Land"; Bateman and Pilkington, *Studies in Settler Colonialism*; Dallas Hunt and Shaun A. Stevenson, "Decolonizing Geographies of Power: Indigenous Digital Counter-Mapping Practices on Turtle Island," *Settler Colonial Studies* 7, no. 3 (2017).

21. Matthew G. Hannah, "Space and Social Control in the Administration of the Oglala Lakota ('Sioux'), 1871–1879," *Journal of Historical Geography* 19, no. 4 (1993); Matthew G. Hannah, *Governmentality and the Mastery of Territory in Nineteenth-Century America* (Cambridge: Cambridge University Press, 2000); Harris, *Making Native Space*.

22. Hannah, *Governmentality and the Mastery of Territory*, 113.

23. Manu Vimalassery, Juliana Hu Pegues, and Alyosha Goldstein, "Introduction: On Colonial Unknowing," *Theory & Event* 19, no. 4 (2016); Jeremy J. Schmidt, "Bureaucratic Territory: First Nations, Private Property, and 'Turn-Key' Colonialism in Canada," *Annals of the American Association of Geographers* 108, no. 4 (2018); Kyle Whyte, "Settler Colonialism, Ecology, and Environmental Injustice," *Environment and Society* 9, no. 1 (2018).

24. Joshua F. J. Inwood and Anne Bonds, "Property and Whiteness: The Oregon Standoff and the Contradictions of the U.S. Settler State," *Space and Polity* 21, no. 3 (2017); Tracey Banivanua Mar and Penelope Edmonds, eds., *Making Settler Colonial Space: Perspectives on Race, Place and Identity* (Hampshire: Palgrave Macmillan, 2010); Traci Brynne Voyles, *The Settler Sea: California's Salton Sea and the Consequences of Colonialism* (Lincoln: University of Nebraska Press, 2022).

25. Most recently, for example, Myrriah Gómez, *Nuclear Nuevo México: Colonialism and the Effects of the Nuclear Industrial Complex on Nuevomexicanos* (Tucson: University of Arizona Press, 2022); Erin Murrah-Mandril, *In the Mean Time: Temporal Colonization and the Mexican American Literary Tradition* (Lincoln: University of Nebraska Press, 2020).

26. The Nuevomexicana scholar Myrriah Gómez argues that we have moved into a third period of colonialism in New Mexico, marked by nuclear exploitation and environmental racism that disproportionately and indiscriminately impacts nonwhite peoples, regardless of their specific ethnic or regional identity. Gómez, *Nuclear Nuevo México*.

27. Sheila Jasanoff, ed., *States of Knowledge: The Co-Production of Science and the Social Order* (London: Routledge, 2004), 2.

28. John Gascoigne, *Science and the State* (Cambridge: Cambridge University Press, 2019); Richard Harry Drayton, *Nature's Government: Science, Imperial Britain, and the "Improvement" of the World* (New Haven, CT: Yale University Press, 2000); James McClellan, *Colonialism and Science: Saint Domingue in the Old Regimes* (Chicago: University of Chicago Press, 2010); Morag Bell, Robin Butlin, and Michael Heffernan, *Geography and Imperialism, 1820–1940* (Manchester: Manchester University Press, 1995); Felix Driver, *Geography Militant: Cultures of Exploration and Empire* (Oxford: Blackwell, 2001); Matthew H. Edney, *Mapping an Empire: The Geographical Construction of British India, 1765–1843* (Chicago: University of Chicago Press, 1997); Anne Godlewska and Neil Smith, *Geography and Empire* (Oxford: Blackwell, 1994); Simon Ryan, *The Cartographic Eye: How Explorers Saw Australia* (Cambridge: Cambridge University Press, 1996); J. B. Harley, "Maps, Knowledge, and Power," in *The Iconography of Landscape: Essays on the Symbolic Representation, Design and Use of Past Environments*, ed. Denis Cosgrove and Stephen Daniels (Cambridge: Cambridge University Press, 1988).

29. Jasanoff, *States of Knowledge*.

30. Lorraine Daston, "The History of Science and the History of Knowledge," *KNOW: A Journal on the Formation of Knowledge* 1, no. 1 (2017).

31. Lukas M. Verburgt, "The History of Knowledge and the Future History of Ignorance," *KNOW: A Journal on the Formation of Knowledge* 4, no. 1 (2020): 4. See also John Dupré, "Metaphysical Disorder and Scientific Disunity," in *The Disunity of Science: Boundaries, Contexts, and Power*, ed. Peter Galison and David J. Stump (Stanford, CA: Stanford University Press, 1996); Peter Burke, *What Is the History of Knowledge?* (Cambridge: Polity Press, 2016); Cornel Zwierlein, *The Dark Side of Knowledge:*

Histories of Ignorance, 1400 to 1800 (Leiden: Brill, 2016); Giacomo Parrinello, Etienne S. Benson, and Wilko Graf von Hardenberg, "Estimated Truths: Water, Science, and the Politics of Approximation," *Journal of Historical Geography* 68 (April 2020).

32. Jasanoff, *States of Knowledge*.

33. Jürgen Renn, *The Evolution of Knowledge: Rethinking Science for the Anthropocene* (Princeton, NJ: Princeton University Press, 2020); James Delbourgo, "The Knowing World: A New Global History of Science," *History of Science* 57, no. 3 (2019); Johan Östling et al., "The History of Knowledge and the Circulation of Knowledge: An Introduction," in *Circulation of Knowledge: Explorations in the History of Knowledge*, ed. Johan Östling et al. (Lund: Nordic Academic Press, 2018); Sheila Jasanoff, *The Fifth Branch: Science Advisers as Policymakers* (Cambridge, MA: Harvard University Press, 1990).

34. David N. Livingstone, "The Spaces of Knowledge: Contributions towards a Historical Geography of Science," *Environment and Planning D: Society and Space* 13, no. 1 (1995); David N. Livingstone, "Putting Geography in Its Place," *Australian Geographical Studies* 38, no. 1 (2000).

35. Tanya O'Sullivan, *Geographies of City Science: Urban Life and Origin Debates in Late Victorian Dublin* (Pittsburgh, PA: University of Pittsburgh Press, 2019), 3. See also Steven Shapin, "Placing the View from Nowhere: Historical and Sociological Problems in the Location of Science," *Transactions of the Institute of British Geographers* 23, no. 1 (1998); Crosbie Smith and Jon Agar, *Making Space for Science: Territorial Themes in the Shaping of Knowledge* (New York: St. Martin's Press, 1998); Simon Naylor, "Introduction: Historical Geographies of science—Places, Contexts, Cartographies," in "Historical Geographies of Science," [special issue,] *British Journal for the History of Science* 38, no. 1 (2005); Simon Naylor, *Regionalizing Science: Placing Knowledges in Victorian England* (London: Pickering & Chatto, 2010); Diarmid A. Finnegan, "Finding a Scientific Voice: Performing Science, Space and Speech in the 19th Century," *Transactions of the Institute of British Geographers* 42, no. 2 (2017); David N. Livingstone, *Dealing with Darwin: Place, Politics, and Rhetoric in Religious Engagements with Evolution* (Baltimore, MD: Johns Hopkins University Press, 2014); Peter Meusburger, Derek Gregory, and Laura Suarsana, *Geographies of Knowledge and Power*, Knowledge and Space 7 (Heidelberg and New York: Springer, 2015).

36. Amy Donovan and Clive Oppenheimer, "At the Mercy of the Mountain? Field Stations and the Culture of Volcanology," *Environment and Planning A* 47, no. 1 (2015); Beth Greenhough, "Tales of an Island-Laboratory: Defining the Field in Geography and Science Studies," *Transactions of the Institute of British Geographers* 31, no. 2 (2006); Beth Greenhough, "Citizenship, Care and Companionship: Approaching Geographies of Health and Bioscience," *Progress in Human Geography* 35, no. 2 (2011); Gail Davies, "Mobilizing Experimental Life: Spaces of Becoming with Mutant Mice," *Theory, Culture & Society* 30, nos. 7–8 (2013).

37. Kean Birch and Fabian Muniesa, eds., *Assetization: Turning Things into Assets in Technoscientific Capitalism* (Cambridge, MA: MIT Press, 2020); David Tyfield et al., eds., *The Routledge Handbook of the Political Economy of Science* (Abingdon and New York: Routledge, 2017); Patrick S. Vitale, "Making Science Suburban: The Suburbanization of Industrial Research and the Invention of 'Research Man,'" *Environment and Planning A* 49, no. 12 (2017); Megan Raby, "'Slash-and-Burn Ecology': Field Science as Land Use," *History of Science* 57, no. 4 (2019); Mark Carey et al., "Glaciers, Gender, and Science: A Feminist Glaciology Framework for Global Environmental Change

Research," *Progress in Human Geography* 40, no. 6 (2016); Jessica Lehman, "Making an Anthropocene Ocean: Synoptic Geographies of the International Geophysical Year (1957–1958)," *Annals of the American Association of Geographers* 110, no. 3 (2020); Richard C. Powell, *Studying Arctic Fields: Cultures, Practices, and Environmental Sciences* (Montreal and Ithaca, NY: McGill-Queen's Press, 2017).

38. Bruno Latour, *Science in Action: How to Follow Scientists and Engineers through Society* (Milton Keynes: Open University Press, 1987).

39. Richard C. Powell, "Geographies of Science: Histories, Localities, Practices, Futures," *Progress in Human Geography* 31, no. 3 (2007): 319–20. See also Martin Mahony and Mike Hulme, "Epistemic Geographies of Climate Change: Science, Space and Politics," *Progress in Human Geography* 42, no. 3 (2018); Robert J. Mayhew and Charles W. J. Withers, *Geographies of Knowledge: Science, Scale, and Spatiality in the Nineteenth Century* (Baltimore, MD: Johns Hopkins University Press, 2020); Christopher R. Henke and Thomas F. Gieryn, "Sites of Scientific Practice: The Enduring Importance of Place," in *The Handbook of Science and Technology Studies*, ed. Edward J. Hackett et al. (Cambridge, MA: MIT Press, 2008).

40. Tom Griffiths and Libby Robin, eds., *Ecology and Empire: Environmental History of Settler Societies* (Edinburgh: Keele University Press, 1997).

41. Julia M. L. Laforge and Stéphane M. McLachlan, "Environmentality on the Canadian Prairies: Settler-Farmer Subjectivities and Agri-Environmental Objects," *Antipode* 50, no. 2 (2018); Miriam Wright, "Aboriginal Gillnet Fishers, Science, and the State: Salmon Fisheries Management on the Nass and Skeena Rivers, British Columbia, 1951–1961," *Journal of Canadian Studies* 44, no. 1 (2010); David A. Rossiter, "Lessons in Possession: Colonial Resource Geographies in Practice on Vancouver Island, 1859–1865," *Journal of Historical Geography* 33, no. 4 (2007).

42. D. Ezra Miller, "'But It Is Nothing except Woods:' Anabaptists, Ambitions, and a Northern Indiana Settlerscape, 1830–1841," in *Rooted and Grounded: Essays on Land and Christian Discipleship*, ed. Ryan D. Harker and Janeen Bertsche Johnson, Studies in Peace and Scripture 13 (Eugene, OR: Pickwick Publications, 2016).

43. John Thistle, "A Vast Inland Empire and the Last Great West: Remaking Society, Space and Environment in Early British Columbia," *Journal of Historical Geography* 37, no. 4 (2011).

44. Thistle, "A Vast Inland Empire and the Last Great West"; Ursula Lehmkuhl, "Good Land—Bad Land: Ecological Knowledge and the Settling of the Old Northwest, 1755–1805," *Settler Colonial Studies* 7, no. 2 (2017).

45. J. M. Bacon, "Settler Colonialism As Eco-Social Structure and the Production of Colonial Ecological Violence," *Environmental Sociology* 5, no. 1 (2019).

46. Whyte, "Settler Colonialism, Ecology, and Environmental Injustice," 125.

47. David A. Rossiter, "Negotiating Nature: Colonial Geographies and Environmental Politics in the Pacific Northwest," *Ethics, Place & Environment* 11, no. 2 (2008); Sean Robertson, "Natives Making Space: The *Softwood* Lumber Dispute and the Legal Geographies of Indigenous Property Rights," *Geoforum* 61 (May 2015); Robert A. Sauder, *The Yuma Reclamation Project: Irrigation, Indian Allotment, and Settlement along the Lower Colorado River* (Reno: University of Nevada Press, 2009); Wright, "Aboriginal Gillnet Fishers"; Dawn Hoogeveen, "Sub-Surface Property, Free-Entry Mineral Staking and Settler Colonialism in Canada," *Antipode* 47, no. 1 (2015); Esme G. Murdock, "Unsettling Reconciliation: Decolonial Methods For Transforming Social-Ecological Systems," *Environmental Values* 2, no. 5 (2018); Nick Estes, *Our History Is*

the Future: Standing Rock versus the Dakota Access Pipeline, and the Long Tradition of Indigenous Resistance (London: Verso, 2019).

48. Kenichi Matsui, *Native Peoples and Water Rights: Irrigation, Dams, and the Law in Western Canada*, McGill-Queen's Native and Northern Series 55 (Montreal and Ithaca, NY: McGill-Queen's University Press, 2009); Melanie K. Yazzie, "Unlimited Limitations: The Navajos' Winters Rights Deemed Worthless in the 2012 Navajo-Hopi Little Colorado River Settlement," *Wicazo Sa Review* 28 no. 1 (2013).

49. Jonathan Clapperton, "Naturalizing Race Relations: Conservation, Colonialism, and Spectacle at the Banff Indian Days," *Canadian Historical Review* 94, no. 3 (2013); Clint Carroll, "Native Enclosures: Tribal National Parks and the Progressive Politics of Environmental Stewardship in Indian Country," *Geoforum* 53 (2014); Michael Simpson and Jen Bagelman, "Decolonizing Urban Political Ecologies: The Production of Nature in Settler Colonial Cities," *Annals of the American Association of Geographers* 108, no. 2 (2018); Bianca Isaki, "State Conservation as Settler Colonial Governance at Ka'Ena Point, Hawai'i," *Environmental and Earth Law Journal* 3, no. 1 (2013).

50. Wolfe, *Settler Colonialism and the Transformation of Anthropology*, 163.

51. For engagements with this debate, see Kauanui, "'A Structure, Not an Event'"; Mark Rifkin, *Settler Common Sense: Queerness and Everyday Colonialism in the American Renaissance* (Minneapolis: University of Minnesota Press, 2014).

52. Roxanne Dunbar-Ortiz, *An Indigenous Peoples' History of the United States* (Boston: Beacon, 2014).

53. Patricia Nelson Limerick, *The Legacy of Conquest: The Unbroken Past of the American West* (New York: W. W. Norton, 1987); Patricia Nelson Limerick, *Something in the Soil: Legacies and Reckonings in the New West* (New York: W. W. Norton, 2000); Richard White, *"It's Your Misfortune and None of My Own": A New History of the American West* (Norman: University of Oklahoma Press, 1991); Walter L. Hixson, *American Settler Colonialism: A History* (New York: Palgrave Macmillan, 2013).

54. Jacoby, "The Broad Platform of Extermination"; Inwood and Bonds, "Property and Whiteness"; Raymund Paredes, "The Mexican Image in American Travel Literature, 1831–1969," *New Mexico Historical Review* 52, no. 1 (1977): 5–29; Martin Padget, "Travel, Exoticism, and the Writing of Region: Charles Fletcher Lummis and the 'Creation' of the Southwest," *Journal of the Southwest* 37, no. 3 (1995); Drinnon, *Facing West*.

55. Nathan F. Sayre, "Race, Nature, Nation, and Property in the Origins of Range Science," in *The Palgrave Handbook of Critical Physical Geography*, ed. Rebecca Love, Christine Biermann, and Stuart N. Lane (Cham: Springer, 2018); Marsha L. Weisiger, *Dreaming of Sheep in Navajo Country* (Seattle: University of Washington Press, 2009); Jake Kosek, *Understories: The Political Life of Forests in Northern New Mexico* (Durham, NC: Duke University Press, 2006); David Correia, "From Agropastoralism to Sustained Yield Forestry: Industrial Restructuring, Rural Change, and the Land-Grant Commons in Northern New Mexico," *Capitalism Nature Socialism* 16, no. 1 (2005); David Correia, "The Sustained Yield Forest Management Act and the Roots of Environmental Conflict in Northern New Mexico," *Geoforum* 38, no. 5 (2007).

56. Timothy P. Bowman, *Blood Oranges: Colonialism and Agriculture in the South Texas Borderlands* (College Station: Texas A&M University Press, 2016); Ignacio Martínez, "Settler Colonialism in New Spain and the Early Mexican Republic," in *The Routledge Handbook of the History of Settler Colonialism*, ed. Edward Cavanagh and Lorenzo Veracini (Abingdon and New York: Routledge, 2017); María Josefina

Saldaña-Portillo, "'How Many Mexicans [Is] a Horse Worth?' The League of United Latin American Citizens, Desegregation Cases, and Chicano Historiography," *South Atlantic Quarterly* 107, no. 4 (2008).

57. K. Maria D. Lane, "Engineering," in *The Sage Handbook of Historical Geography*, ed. Mona Domosh, Michael Heffernan, and Charles W. J. Withers (London: Sage, 2020).

58. K. Maria D. Lane, "Reading Boulder Dam: Landscape Alteration as National Transformation in 1930s America," *Aether* 11 (2013); K. Maria D. Lane, "Bridging the Florida Keys: Engineering an Environmental Transformation, 1904–1912," in *The American Environment Revisited: Environmental Historical Geographies of the United States*, ed. Geoffrey L. Buckley and Yolonda Youngs (Lanham, MD: Rowman & Littlefield, 2018).

59. Sheila Jasanoff and Sang-Hyun Kim, *Dreamscapes of Modernity: Sociotechnical Imaginaries and the Fabrication of Power* (Chicago: University of Chicago Press, 2015), 4; Jeffrey K. Stine and Joel Tarr, "At the Intersection of Histories: Technology and the Environment," *Technology and Culture* 39, no. 4 (1998); Sara B. Pritchard, "Toward an Environmental History of Technology," in *The Oxford Handbook of Environmental History*, ed. Andrew C. Isenberg (Oxford and New York: Oxford University Press, 2014); Edmund Russell et al., "The Nature of Power: Synthesizing the History of Technology and Environmental History," *Technology and Culture* 52, no. 2 (2011).

60. Paul Robbins, *Political Ecology: A Critical Introduction* (Malden, MA: Blackwell, 2004).

61. Karl Offen, "Historical Political Ecology: An Introduction," *Historical Geography* 32 (2004): 21.

62. For example, Christian Brannstrom, "What Kind of History for What Kind of Political Ecology?," *Historical Geography* 32 (2004).

63. Diana K. Davis, "Historical Political Ecology: On the Importance of Looking Back to Move Forward," *Geoforum* 40, no. 3 (2009).

64. Davis, "Historical Political Ecology," 286.

65. Ashley Carse, "Nature as Infrastructure: Making and Managing the Panama Canal Watershed," *Social Studies of Science* 42, no. 4 (2012); Jessica Budds, "Contested H_2O: Science, Policy and Politics in Water Resources Management in Chile," *Geoforum* 40, no. 3 (2009); Martha G. Bell, "Historical Political Ecology of Water: Access to Municipal Drinking Water in Colonial Lima, Peru (1578–1700)," *Professional Geographer* 67, no. 4 (2015); Erik Swyngedouw, "Technonatural Revolutions: The Scalar Politics of Franco's Hydro-social Dream for Spain, 1939–1975," *Transactions of the Institute of British Geographers* 32, no. 1 (2007); Jeffrey M. Banister and Stacie G. Widdifield, "The Debut of 'Modern Water' in Early 20th Century Mexico City: The Xochimilco Potable Waterworks," *Journal of Historical Geography* 46 (2014).

66. Sarah Whatmore, "Hybrid Geographies: Rethinking the 'Human' in Human Geography," in *Environment: Critical Essays in Human Geography*, ed. Kay Anderson and Bruce Braun (London: Routledge, 2008); Matthew W. Wilson, "Cyborg Geographies: Towards Hybrid Epistemologies," *Gender, Place and Culture* 16, no. 5 (2009); Donna Haraway, *Simians, Cyborgs, and Women: The Reinvention of Nature* (New York: Routledge, 2013); Paul S. Sutter, "The World with Us: The State of American Environmental History," *Journal of American History* 100, no. 1 (2013).

67. Rebecca Lave et al., "Intervention: Critical Physical Geography," *Canadian*

Geographer/Géographe canadien 58, no. 1 (2014): 3. Peter A. Walker, "Political Ecology: Where Is the Ecology?," *Progress in Human Geography* 29, no. 1 (2005). But see Tim Forsyth, *Critical Political Ecology: The Politics of Environmental Science* (London: Routledge, 2003), for an early call to engage in a critical political ecology that takes seriously the politics of environmental science and knowledge.

68. Lave et al., "Intervention."

69. Lave et al., "Intervention," 5.

70. Rebecca Lave, Christine Biermann, and Stuart N. Lane, *The Palgrave Handbook of Critical Physical Geography* (New York: Springer, 2018).

71. K. Maria D. Lane, "Commentary: Old and New," in "Interdisciplinary Research on Past Environments through the Lens of Historical-Critical Physical Geographies," special issue, *Historical Geography* 46 (2019).

72. Paul S. Sutter, "Nature's Agents or Agents of Empire?: Entomological Workers and Environmental Change during the Construction of the Panama Canal," *Isis* 98, no. 4 (2007).

73. David Delaney, *Nomospheric Investigations: The Spatial, the Legal and the Pragmatics of World-Making* (New York: Routledge, 2011); David F. Robinson, "Legal Geographies of Intellectual Property, 'Traditional' Knowledge, and Biodiversity: Experiencing Conventions, Laws, Customary Law, and Karma in Thailand," *Geographical Research* 51, no. 4 (2013).

74. Nicholas Blomley, *Law, Space, and the Geographies of Power* (New York: Guilford Press, 1994); Nicholas Blomley, David Delaney, and Richard T. Ford, eds., *The Legal Geographies Reader: Law, Power, and Space* (Oxford: Blackwell, 2001); Jane Holder and Carolyn Harrison, eds., *Law and Geography* (Oxford and New York: Oxford University Press, 2003).

75. Gary L. Thompson, Fred M. Shelley, and Chand Wije, eds., *Geography, Environment, and American Law* (Denver: University Press of Colorado, 1997).

76. Sheila Jasanoff, *Science at the Bar: Law, Science, and Technology in America* (Cambridge, MA: Harvard University Press, 1995); Delaney, *Nomospheric Investigations*.

77. David Delaney, *Law and Nature* (Cambridge: Cambridge University Press, 2003).

78. Melinda Harm Benson, "The *Tulare* Case: Water Rights, the Endangered Species Act, and the Fifth Amendment," *Environmental Law* 32, no. 3 (2002); Delaney, *Law and Nature*; Nicholas Blomley, "Simplification Is Complicated: Property, Nature, and the Rivers of Law," *Environment and Planning A* 40 (2008); Mark Zeitoun and J. A. Allan, "Applying Hegemony and Power Theory to Transboundary Water Analysis," *Water Policy* 10, no. S2 (2008); Melvin Woodhouse and Mark Zeitoun, "Hydro-Hegemony and International Water Law: Grappling with the Gaps of Power and Law," *Water Policy* 10, no. S2 (2008); Hari M. Osofsky, "The Role of Climate Change Litigation in Establishing the Scale of Energy Regulation," *Annals of the Association of American Geographers* 101, no. 4 (2011); Wendy Jepson, "Claiming Space, Claiming Water: Contested Legal Geographies of Water in South Texas," *Annals of the Association of American Geographers* 102, no. 3 (2012); Eleanor Andrews and James McCarthy, "Scale, Shale, and the State: Political Ecologies and Legal Geographies of Shale Gas Development in Pennsylvania," *Journal of Environmental Studies and Sciences* 4 (2014).

79. Hugo deVos, Rutgerd Boelens, and Rocio Bustamante, "Formal Law and Local Water Control in the Andean Region: A Fiercely Contested Field," *Water Resources*

Development 22, no. 1 (2006); John Agnew, "Waterpower: Politics and the Geography of Water Provision," *Annals of the Association of American Geographers* 101, no. 3 (2011); Robinson, "Legal Geographies of Intellectual Property."

80. Jepson, "Claiming Space, Claiming Water," 617. See also Eric P. Perramond, *Unsettled Waters: Rights, Law, and Identity in the American West* (Berkeley and Los Angeles: University of California Press, 2018).

81. Laura Benton, *A Search for Sovereignty: Law and Geography in European Empires, 1400–1900* (Cambridge: Cambridge University Press, 2010); Stephen Legg, "Legal Geographies and the State of Imperialism: Environments, Constitutions, and Violence," *Journal of Historical Geography* 37, no. 4 (2011); Elizabeth Kolsky, *Colonial Justice in British India: White Violence and the Rule of Law* (Cambridge: Cambridge University Press, 2010).

82. For an example of how the tricultural mythology constrains scholarly analysis, see D. W. Meinig, *Southwest: Three Peoples in Geographical Change, 1600–1970* (Oxford and New York: Oxford University Press, 1971). For a discussion of the very real ways a cultural imaginary produces space and the built environment, see Chris Wilson, *The Myth of Santa Fe: Creating a Modern Regional Tradition* (Albuquerque: University of New Mexico, 1997).

83. Daniel Tyler, "Anglo-American Penetration of the Southwest: The View from New Mexico," *Southwestern Historical Quarterly* 75, no. 3 (1972).

84. Refer to Juan Estevan Arellano, *Enduring Acequias: Wisdom of the Land, Knowledge of the Water* (Albuquerque: University of New Mexico Press, 2014), for a thoughtful rumination on the cultural intersections inherent in many terms he learned from childhood in the Embudo Valley.

85. Refer to chap. 2 for further discussion and citations to this literature.

86. This includes pure-blooded Spanish and Basque *peninsulares* (born in Spain) and *criollos* (born in the Americas); pure-blooded Indigenous peoples, either external to Spanish colonies or identified internally as *genízaros* who adopted Spanish language, religion, and custom (usually due to captivity); Africans, both enslaved and free; and many specific named combinations among all of these identities. See Martha Menchaca, *Recovering History, Constructing Race: The Indian, Black, and White Roots of Mexican Americans* (Austin: University of Texas Press, 2002), for a detailed discussion of scholarship on this topic.

87. Menchaca, *Recovering History, Constructing Race*, chap. 3. See also Ramón A. Gutiérrez, *When Jesus Came, the Corn Mothers Went Away: Marriage, Sexuality, and Power in New Mexico, 1500–1846* (Stanford, CA: Stanford University Press, 1991).

88. Phillip B. Gonzales, "Whither the Nuevomexicanos: The Career of a Southwestern Intellectual Discourse, 1907–2004," *Social Science Journal* 43, no. 2 (2006), refers to this prospect as "an intellectual fallacy" in his comprehensive discussion of the evolution of "Nuevomexicano" and related terms and concepts. See also John M. Nieto-Phillips, *The Language of Blood: The Making of Spanish-American Identity in New Mexico, 1880s–1930s* (Albuquerque: University of New Mexico Press, 2004); Laura E. Gómez, *Manifest Destinies: The Making of the Mexican American Race*, 2nd ed. (New York: New York University Press, 2018); Juan Martín Gallegos, "Reconstructing Identity/Revising Resistance: A History of Nuevomexicano/a Students at New Mexico Highlands University, 1910–1973" (Ph.D. diss., University of Arizona, 2013); Alvin O. Korte, *Nosotros: A Study of Everyday Meaning in Hispano New Mexico* (East Lansing: Michigan State University Press, 2012).

89. For example, Gómez, *Nuclear Nuevo México*; Sylvia Rodríguez, *Acequia: Water-Sharing, Sanctity, and Place* (Santa Fe, NM: School for Advanced Research Press, 2006); Arellano, *Enduring Acequias*.

90. For a compilation of both tender and critical examples, see Vanessa Fonseca-Chávez, Levi Romero, and Spencer R. Herrera, eds., *Querencia: Reflections on the New Mexico Homeland* (Albuquerque: University of New Mexico Press, 2020).

91. John Chávez, "The Chicano Homeland," in *The Multicultural Southwest: A Reader*, ed. A. Gabriel Meléndez et al. (Tucson: University of Arizona Press, 2001); Miguel Montiel, Tomás Atencio, and E. A. "Tony" Mares, *Resolana: Emerging Chicano Dialogues on Community and Globalization* (Tucson: University of Arizona Press, 2009); Fonseca-Chavez, Romero, and Herrera, *Querencia*.

92. Gómez, *Manifest Destinies*.

93. Gómez, *Manifest Destinies*; Paredes, *The Mexican Image*; Richard Melzer, "New Mexico in Caricature: Images of the Territory on the Eve of Statehood," *New Mexico Historical Review* 62, no. 4 (1987); Charles Montgomery, "Becoming 'Spanish-American': Race and Rhetoric in New Mexico Politics, 1880–1928," *Journal of American Ethnic History* 20, no. 4 (2001); Elinore M. Barrett, *The Spanish Colonial Settlement Landscapes of New Mexico, 1598–1680* (Albuquerque: University of New Mexico Press, 2012); Murrah-Mandril, *In the Mean Time*.

94. Michael J. Alarid, *Hispano Bastion: New Mexican Power in the Age of Manifest Destiny, 1837–1860* (Albuquerque: University of New Mexico Press, 2022); Montgomery, "Becoming 'Spanish-American.'"

95. Alarid, *Hispano Bastion* ; Gómez, *Manifest Destinies*.

96. Austin J. Miller, "Blackdom: Interpreting the Hidden History of New Mexico's Black Town" (master's thesis, University of New Mexico, 2018); Timothy E. Nelson, "The Significance of the Afro-Frontier in American History: Blackdom, Barratry, and Bawdyhouses in the Borderlands, 1900–1930" (Ph.D. diss., University of Texas at El Paso, 2015); Flora L. Price, "Forgotten Spaces and Resident Places: New Mexico Black Towns and Communities (1897–1930)" (Ph.D. diss., University of New Mexico, 2003).

97. For an extended view of New Mexico's cultural heritage, see A. Gabriel Meléndez et al., eds., *The Multicultural Southwest: A Reader* (Tucson: University of Arizona Press, 2001).

98. James Duncan and Derek Gregory, eds., *Writes of Passage: Reading Travel Writing* (London: Routledge, 1999), 121.

99. Mona Domosh, "The World Was Never Flat: Early Global Encounters and the Messiness of Empire," *Progress in Human Geography* 34, no. 4 (2010); Duncan and Gregory, *Writes of Passage*; Matthew Kurtz, "Situating Practices: The Archive and the File Cabinet," *Historical Geography* 29 (2001); Hayden Lorimer and Nick Spedding, "Locating Field Science: A Geographical Family Expedition to Glen Roy, Scotland," *British Journal for the History of Science* 38 (2005).

100. For example, Coulthard, "Subjects of Empire"; de Leeuw, Greenwood, and Lindsay, "Troubling Good Intentions."

101. Lianne C. Leddy, "*Dibaajimowinan* as Method: Environmental History, Indigenous Scholarship, and Balancing Sources," in *Methodological Challenges in Nature-Culture and Environmental History Research*, ed. Jocelyn Thorpe, Stephanie Rutherford, and L. Anders Sandberg (New York: Routledge, 2017); Simpson, "Anticolonial Strategies"; Smith, *Decolonizing Methodologies*; Kim TallBear, "Standing With and

Speaking as Faith: A Feminist-Indigenous Approach to Inquiry," in "Giving Back in Field Research," special issue, *Journal of Research Practice* 10, no. 2 (2014).

102. Laura Paskus, *At the Precipice: New Mexico's Changing Climate* (Albuquerque: University of New Mexico Press, 2020).

Chapter 2

1. Jorge Cañizares-Esguerra, *How to Write the History of the New World: Histories, Epistemologies, and Identities in the Eighteenth-Century Atlantic World* (Stanford, CA: Stanford University Press, 2001); Jennifer Nez Denetdale, *Reclaiming Diné History: The Legacies of Navajo Chief Manuelito and Juanita* (Tucson: University of Arizona Press, 2007).

2. "Trade," Museum Collections, accessed 7 July 2020, https://www.nps.gov/museum/exhibits/chcu/.

3. Ira G. Clark, *Water in New Mexico: A History of Its Management and Use* (Albuquerque: University of New Mexico Press, 1987).

4. Joseph P. Sánchez, Robert L. Spude, and Art Gómez, *New Mexico: A History* (Norman: University of Oklahoma Press, 2013).

5. Clark, *Water in New Mexico*; José A. Rivera, *Acequia Culture: Water, Land, and Community in the Southwest* (Albuquerque: University of New Mexico Press, 1998).

6. Sánchez, Spude, and Gómez, *New Mexico: A History*.

7. Fred M. Phillips, G. Emlen Hall, and Mary E. Black, *Reining in the Rio Grande: People, Land, and Water* (Albuquerque: University of New Mexico Press, 2011); Roxanne Dunbar-Ortiz, *Roots of Resistance: A History of Land Tenure in New Mexico* (Norman: University of Oklahoma Press, 2007).

8. Sánchez, Spude, and Gómez, *New Mexico: A History*.

9. Dunbar-Ortiz, *Roots of Resistance*.

10. Dunbar-Ortiz, *Roots of Resistance*.

11. William E. Doolittle, *Cultivated Landscapes of Native North America* (Oxford and New York: Oxford University Press, 2000).

12. Doolittle, *Cultivated Landscapes of Native North America*.

13. Clark, *Water in New Mexico*, 8.

14. Clark, *Water in New Mexico*.

15. Clark, *Water in New Mexico*.

16. Jack D. Forbes, *Apache, Navaho, and Spaniard*, Civilization of the American Indian 115 (Norman: University of Oklahoma Press, 1960); Meinig, *Southwest*.

17. Laura Bayer, Floyd Montoya, and the Pueblo of Santa Ana, *Santa Ana: The People, the Pueblo, and the History of Tamaya* (Albuquerque: University of New Mexico Press, 1994).

18. Many popular histories of New Mexico overlook the racial complexity of the original "Spanish" colony. Menchaca, *Recovering History, Constructing Race*, provides a detailed discussion of the racial and natal characteristics of those who participated in the Oñate-led entrada, noting that barely a quarter of the four hundred men in Oñate's party were recorded as white/Spanish during military inspections. Most of the remainder were recognized as *mestizo*, and Oñate himself was widely known at the time to be *mestizo* despite official records listing him as full-blooded Spanish. Indigenous, African, and *afromestizo* men were also present among the ranks of Oñate's group. See also Marc Simmons, *The Last Conquistador: Juan de Oñate and the Settling of the Far Southwest*, The Oklahoma Western Biographies 2

(Norman: University of Oklahoma Press, 1993); George P. Hammond and Agapito Rey, eds. And trans., *Don Juan de Oñate: Colonizer of New Mexico, 1595–1628; In Two Parts*, vol. 1, Coronado Cuarto Centennial Publications, 1540–1940, 5 and 6 (Albuquerque: University of New Mexico Press, 1953). For more on racial hierarchies and categories in colonial New Spain, and for discussion of the way racial and cultural norms migrated north with *mestizo* peoples and impacted racial politics in the United States, see Menchaca, *Recovering History, Constructing Race* and its detailed historical documentation. See also Gonzalo Aguirre Beltrán, "The Slave Trade in Mexico," *Hispanic American Historical Review* 24, no. 3 (1944), for a detailed history of West African presence in New Spain, first via slavery and later through *afromestizo* mestizaje among freedmen.

19. Dunbar-Ortiz, *Roots of Resistance*.
20. Sánchez, Spude, and Gómez, *New Mexico: A History*.
21. Richard L. Nostrand, *The Hispano Homeland* (Norman: University of Oklahoma Press, 1992).
22. Hammond and Rey, *Don Juan de Oñate*, vol. 1.
23. Sánchez, Spude, and Gómez, *New Mexico: A History*.
24. Barrett, *Spanish Colonial Settlement Landscapes*.
25. Alvar W. Carlson, *The Spanish-American Homeland: Four Centuries in New Mexico's Rio Arriba* (Baltimore, MD: Johns Hopkins University Press, 1990).
26. Barrett, *Spanish Colonial Settlement Landscapes*.
27. Barrett, *Spanish Colonial Settlement Landscapes*.
28. Hammond and Rey, *Don Juan de Oñate*, vol. 1; Barrett, *Spanish Colonial Settlement Landscapes*.
29. Hammond and Rey, *Don Juan de Oñate*, vol. 1.
30. Sánchez, Spude, and Gómez, *New Mexico: A History*, 49.
31. Dunbar-Ortiz, *Roots of Resistance*.
32. Barrett, *Spanish Colonial Settlement Landscapes*.
33. Peter Gerhard, *The North Frontier of New Spain* (Princeton, NJ: Princeton University Press, 1982); Elinore M. Barrett, *Conquest and Catastrophe: Changing Rio Grande Pueblo Settlement Patterns in the Sixteenth and Seventeenth Centuries* (Albuquerque: University of New Mexico Press, 2002).
34. Barrett, *Conquest and Catastrophe*, 80. See also Bayer, Montoya, and the Pueblo of Santa Ana, *Santa Ana*.
35. Dunbar-Ortiz, *Roots of Resistance*; Tracy L. Brown, *Pueblo Indians and Spanish Colonial Authority in Eighteenth-Century New Mexico* (Tucson: University of Arizona Press, 2013).
36. Dunbar-Ortiz, *Roots of Resistance*.
37. Brown, *Pueblo Indians and Spanish Colonial Authority in Eighteenth-Century New Mexico*.
38. Barrett, *Spanish Colonial Settlement Landscapes*.
39. Dunbar-Ortiz, *Roots of Resistance*.
40. J. Manuel Espinosa, *The Pueblo Indian Revolt of 1696 and the Franciscan Missions in New Mexico: Letters of the Missionaries and Related Documents* (Norman: University of Oklahoma Press, 1988).
41. Dunbar-Ortiz, *Roots of Resistance*.
42. Dunbar-Ortiz, *Roots of Resistance*, 46.
43. Barrett, *Spanish Colonial Settlement Landscapes*, 61, 164.
44. Sánchez, Spude, and Gómez, *New Mexico: A History*, 59.

45. Nostrand, *The Hispano Homeland*, 44; Dunbar-Ortiz, *Roots of Resistance*.
46. Carlson, *The Spanish-American Homeland*; Nostrand, *The Hispano Homeland*.
47. Dunbar-Ortiz, *Roots of Resistance*.
48. Nostrand, *The Hispano Homeland*.
49. Rodríguez, *Acequia*.
50. Anselmo F. Arellano, *The Acequia and Agricultural Tradition of New Mexico: Prehistoric through the Present* (Guadalupita, NM: Center for Land Grant Studies, 1986).
51. Thomas F. Glick, *Irrigation and Society in Medieval Valencia* (Cambridge, MA: Belknap Press of Harvard University Press, 1970); Clark, *Water in New Mexico*; Christopher S. Beekman, Phil C. Weigand, and John J. Pint, "Old World Irrigation Technology in a New World Context: Qanats in Spanish Colonial Western Mexico," *Antiquity* 73, no. 280 (1999). See also Arellano, *Enduring Acequias*, 24, for an account that claims to be "in no way a scholarly work" but that contains a wealth of wise and critical insights about the connections between New Mexico's acequia traditions and Spanish, Moorish, and Middle Eastern cultures.
52. Clark, *Water in New Mexico*; Rivera, *Acequia Culture*.
53. John O. Baxter, *Dividing New Mexico's Waters, 1700–1912* (Albuquerque: University of New Mexico Press, 1996).
54. Rivera, *Acequia Culture*.
55. Phillips, Hall, and Black, *Reining in the Rio Grande*.
56. Phillips, Hall, and Black, *Reining in the Rio Grande*.
57. Phillips, Hall, and Black, *Reining in the Rio Grande*, 44.
58. Clark, *Water in New Mexico*.
59. Phillips, Hall, and Black, *Reining in the Rio Grande*, 46.
60. Glick, *Irrigation and Society in Medieval Valencia*.
61. Malcolm Ebright, *Land Grants and Lawsuits in Northern New Mexico* (Albuquerque: University of New Mexico Press, 1994); Rivera, *Acequia Culture*.
62. Phillips, Hall, and Black, *Reining in the Rio Grande*, 46. See Rodríguez, *Acequia*, for the definitive ethnography of acequia culture and its connection to religious belief.
63. Rivera, *Acequia Culture*.
64. Rodríguez, *Acequia*. Refer to the section titled "Early Indigenous Geographies" for details on pre-Spanish irrigation practices.
65. Bayer, Montoya, and the Pueblo of Santa Ana, *Santa Ana*.
66. Rodríguez, *Acequia*, 13.
67. Phillips, Hall, and Black, *Reining in the Rio Grande*.
68. D. W. Meinig, *Atlantic America, 1492–1800*, vol. 1 of *The Shaping of America: A Geographical Perspective on 500 Years of History* (New Haven, CT: Yale University Press, 1986).
69. Rodríguez, *Acequia*.
70. Sánchez, Spude, and Gómez, *New Mexico: A History*.
71. Dunbar-Ortiz, *Roots of Resistance*, 70.
72. Malcolm Ebright, "Sharing the Shortages: Water Litigation and Regulation in Hispanic New Mexico, 1600–1850," *New Mexico Historical Review* 76, no. 1 (2001).
73. Alarid, *Hispano Bastion*. See also Maurilio E. Vigil, *Los Patrones: Profiles of Hispanic Leaders in New Mexican History* (Washington, DC: University Press of America, 1980); Manuel G. Gonzales and Thomas Joseph Price, *The Hispanic Elite of the Southwest*, Southwestern Studies 86 (El Paso: Texas Western Press, 1989); and Lynn I. Perrigo, *Hispanos: Historic Leaders in New Mexico* (Santa Fe, NM: Sunstone Press, 1985).

74. Alarid, *Hispano Bastion*, 6.
75. Pekka Hämäläinen, *The Comanche Empire* (New Haven, CT: Yale University Press, 2008).
76. Bayer, Montoya, and the Pueblo of Santa Ana, *Santa Ana*.
77. Meinig, *Southwest*.
78. Dunbar-Ortiz, *Roots of Resistance*.
79. Dunbar-Ortiz, *Roots of Resistance*.
80. Dunbar-Ortiz, *Roots of Resistance*; Alarid, *Hispano Bastion*.
81. Dunbar-Ortiz, *Roots of Resistance*.
82. Sánchez, Spude, and Gómez, *New Mexico: A History*.
83. Susan Calafate Boyle, *Los Capitalistas: Hispano Merchants and the Santa Fe Trade* (Albuquerque: University of New Mexico Press, 1997); Gómez, *Manifest Destinies*.
84. Gómez, *Manifest Destinies*.
85. Gómez, *Manifest Destinies*.
86. Richard Griswold del Castillo, *The Treaty of Guadalupe Hidalgo: A Legacy of Conflict* (Norman: University of Oklahoma Press, 1992).
87. Murrah-Mandril, *In the Mean Time*.
88. Gómez, *Manifest Destinies*, 48. See chap. 4 for further discussion of the Treaty of Guadalupe Hidalgo and its impacts in New Mexico.
89. Meinig, *Southwest*.
90. Meinig, *Southwest*.
91. Sánchez, Spude, and Gómez, *New Mexico: A History*. See Gómez, *Manifest Destinies*, for a discussion of how Nuevomexicano elites embraced claims of whiteness in order to curry favor among Anglos, with the overall effect of creating divisions among Nuevomexicanas/os and between Mexican/Pueblo peoples, which ultimately supported Anglo control and power.
92. Dunbar-Ortiz, *Roots of Resistance*. See Deena J. González, *Refusing the Favor: The Spanish-Mexican Women of Santa Fe, 1820–1880* (Oxford and New York: Oxford University Press, 1999), for a discussion of the way Anglo colonization impoverished even Nuevomexicano elites, focusing specifically on Nuevomexicana women.
93. Meinig, *Southwest*; Victor Westphall, *Mercedes Reales: Hispanic Land Grants of the Upper Rio Grande Region* (Albuquerque: University of New Mexico Press, 1983).
94. Sánchez, Spude, and Gómez, *New Mexico: A History*; Clark, *Water in New Mexico*.
95. del Castillo, *The Treaty of Guadalupe Hidalgo*.
96. Ebright, *Land Grants and Lawsuits in Northern New Mexico*.
97. Dunbar-Ortiz, *Roots of Resistance*.
98. Ebright, *Land Grants and Lawsuits in Northern New Mexico*.
99. Westphall, *Mercedes Reales*; G. Emlen Hall, *Four Leagues of Pecos: A Legal History of the Pecos Grant, 1800–1933* (Albuquerque: University of New Mexico Press, 1984); Kosek, *Understories*; David Correia, "Making Destiny Manifest: United States Territorial Expansion and the Dispossession of Two Mexican Property Claims in New Mexico, 1824–1899," *Journal of Historical Geography* 35, no. 1 (2009).
100. Ebright, *Land Grants and Lawsuits in Northern New Mexico*; Michael C. Meyer and Michael M. Brescia, "The Treaty of Guadalupe Hidalgo as a Living Document: Water and Land Use Issues in Northern New Mexico," *New Mexico Historical Review* 73, no. 4 (1998).
101. William deBuys, *Enchantment and Exploitation: The Life and Hard Times of a New Mexico Mountain Range* (Albuquerque: University of New Mexico Press,

1985); Correia, "Making Destiny Manifest"; David L. Caffey, *Chasing the Santa Fe Ring: Power and Privilege in Territorial New Mexico* (Albuquerque: University of New Mexico Press, 2014).

102. Phillips, Hall, and Black, *Reining in the Rio Grande*, 64.

103. Charles L. Briggs and John R. Van Ness, *Land, Water, and Culture: New Perspectives on Hispanic Land Grants*, 1st ed. (Albuquerque: University of New Mexico Press, 1987); Carlson, *The Spanish-American Homeland*.

104. Briggs and Van Ness, *Land, Water, and Culture*; María E. Montoya, *Translating Property: The Maxwell Land Grant and the Conflict over Land in the American West, 1840–1900* (Berkeley and Los Angeles: University of California Press, 2002); Phillips, Hall, and Black, *Reining in the Rio Grande*; Sánchez, Spude, and Gómez, *New Mexico: A History*.

105. Bayer, Montoya, and the Pueblo of Santa Ana, *Santa Ana*.

106. Bayer, Montoya, and the Pueblo of Santa Ana, *Santa Ana*.

107. Dunbar-Ortiz, *An Indigenous Peoples' History of the United States*.

108. Bayer, Montoya, and the Pueblo of Santa Ana, *Santa Ana*; Dunbar-Ortiz, *Roots of Resistance*.

109. Carlson, *The Spanish-American Homeland*.

110. Jacoby, "The Broad Platform of Extermination."

111. Sánchez, Spude, and Gómez, *New Mexico: A History*.

112. Janne Lahti, *Wars for Empire: Apaches, the United States, and the Southwest Borderlands* (Norman: University of Oklahoma Press, 2017).

113. Sánchez, Spude, and Gómez, *New Mexico: A History*.

114. Donald Worster, *Rivers of Empire: Water, Aridity, and the Growth of the American West* (New York: Pantheon Books, 1985); Limerick, *The Legacy of Conquest*; White, *"It's Your Misfortune and None of My Own"*; Gómez, *Manifest Destinies*.

115. Dunbar-Ortiz, *Roots of Resistance*.

116. Meinig, *Southwest*, 66.

117. Sánchez, Spude, and Gómez, *New Mexico: A History*.

118. Gómez, *Manifest Destinies*, 49.

119. Dunbar-Ortiz, *Roots of Resistance*.

120. Rodríguez, *Acequia*, 23.

121. Yolanda Leyva, "Monuments of Conformity: Commemorating and Protesting Oñate on the Border," *New Mexico Historical Review* 82, no. 3 (2007).

122. For example, Arellano, *Enduring Acequias*; Korte, *Nosotros*.

123. Sylvia Rodríguez, "The Hispano Homeland Debate Revisited," *Perspectives in Mexican American Studies* 3 (1992), provides an overview of the debate at its height. This debate is still ongoing. During the review process for this book, for example, one reviewer challenged my assertion that Nuevomexicano communities had ever been colonized, suggesting it was "not reflective of Indigenous narratives or understandings of the same history." A different reviewer objected to my discussion of Nuevomexicanos' indigeneity claims, arguing that scholars of color and Anglo authors present New Mexican history in different ways. Both reviews pushed me to revise my presentation of historical events, and they helped me better understand the deep importance of ongoing cultural studies scholarship in New Mexico.

124. Dunbar-Ortiz, *Roots of Resistance*, 72; Gómez, *Manifest Destinies*.

125. Melzer, "New Mexico in Caricature"; González, *Refusing the Favor*; Sánchez, Spude, and Gómez, *New Mexico: A History*.

126. Meléndez et al., *The Multicultural Southwest*.

127. Burl Noggle, "Anglo Observers of the Southwest Borderlands, 1825–1890: The Rise of a Concept," *Arizona and the West* 1, no. 2 (1959); Richard Francaviglia, "Elusive Land: Changing Geographic Images of the Southwest," in *Essays on the Changing Images of the Southwest*, ed. Richard Francaviglia and David Narrett (College Station: Texas A&M University Press, 1994); Nieto-Phillips, *The Language of Blood*; Marta Weigle, *Alluring New Mexico: Engineered Enchantment, 1821–2001* (Santa Fe: Museum of New Mexico Press, 2010).

128. Anthony P. Mora, *Border Dilemmas: Racial and National Uncertainties in New Mexico, 1848–1912* (Durham, NC: Duke University Press, 2011); Gómez, *Manifest Destinies*.

129. Phillips, Hall, and Black, *Reining in the Rio Grande*, 72.

130. All of this is from Phillips, Hall, and Black, *Reining in the Rio Grande*.

131. Phillips, Hall, and Black, *Reining in the Rio Grande*.

132. Jonathan B. Mabry and David A. Cleveland, "The Relevance of Indigenous Irrigation: A Comparative Analysis of Sustainability," in *Canals and Communities: Small-Scale Irrigation Systems*, ed. Jonathan B. Mabry (Tucson: University of Arizona Press, 1996).

133. Phillips, Hall, and Black, *Reining in the Rio Grande*.

134. Weisiger, *Dreaming of Sheep in Navajo Country*.

135. David Correia, "The Etiology of Rangeland Degradation in Northern New Mexico: A Critique of Establishment Explanations," *Southwestern Geographer* 8 (2004); Kosek, *Understories*.

136. Phillips, Hall, and Black, *Reining in the Rio Grande*.

137. Randall K. Wilson, "'Placing Nature': The Politics of Collaboration and Representation in the Struggle for La Sierra in San Luis, Colorado," *Ecumene* 6, no. 1 (1999); Correia, "From Agropastoralism to Sustained Yield Forestry"; Kosek, *Understories*; Correia, "The Sustained Yield Forest Management Act."

138. Carl Wilmsen, "Sustained Yield Recast: The Politics of Sustainability in Vallecitos, New Mexico," *Society and Natural Resources* 14, no. 3 (2001); Carl Wilmsen, "Maintaining the Environmental-Racial Order in Northern New Mexico," *Environment and Planning D: Society & Space* 25, no. 2 (2007).

139. Carlson, *The Spanish-American Homeland*, 87; Dunbar-Ortiz, *Roots of Resistance*, 4.

140. Rivera, *Acequia Culture*; Rodríguez, *Acequia*; Arellano, *Enduring Acequias*.

141. Nostrand, *The Hispano Homeland*; Phillip B. Gonzales, "Struggle for Survival: The Hispanic Land Grants of New Mexico, 1848–2001," *Agricultural History* 77, no. 2 (2003).

142. For example, Maya Kapoor, "Ancestral Pueblo Logging Practices Could Save New Mexico Pinelands," *High Country News*, 11 December 2017; Gómez, *Nuclear Nuevo México*.

Chapter 3

1. Robert Follansbee, *A History of the Water Resources Branch of the United States Geological Survey to June 30, 1919* (Washington, DC, 1939), 28.

2. Follansbee, *A History of the Water Resources Branch*; Arthur H. Frazier and Wilbur Heckler, *Embudo, New Mexico, Birthplace of Systematic Stream Gaging*, Geological Survey Professional Paper 778 (Washington, DC: U.S. Government Printing Office, 1972).

3. These two references constitute the only mentions of any interaction with local peoples in Newell's journals from the Embudo Camp, which he maintained daily during the nine o'clock hour. The Papers of Frederick Haynes Newell, Box 1, United States Library of Congress Manuscript Division.

4. Follansbee, *A History of the Water Resources Branch*.

5. Follansbee, *A History of the Water Resources Branch*, 36.

6. Follansbee, *A History of the Water Resources Branch*.

7. Follansbee, *A History of the Water Resources Branch*.

8. Follansbee, *A History of the Water Resources Branch*.

9. Follansbee, *A History of the Water Resources Branch*.

10. Donald J. Pisani, *Water, Land, and Law in the West: The Limits of Public Policy, 1850–1920* (Lawrence: University of Kansas Press, 1996), 191; Ian Tyrrell, *Crisis of the Wasteful Nation: Empire and Conservation in Theodore Roosevelt's America* (Chicago: University of Chicago Press, 2015).

11. Brian Balogh, "Scientific Forestry and the Roots of the Modern American State: Gifford Pinchot's Path to Progressive Reform," *Environmental History* 7, no. 2 (2002).

12. Samuel P. Hays, *Conservation and the Gospel of Efficiency: The Progressive Conservation Movement, 1890–1920* (originally published 1959; Pittsburgh, PA: University of Pittsburgh Press, 1999).

13. Tyrrell, *Crisis of the Wasteful Nation*.

14. In March 1889, the Embudo engineer Robert Robertson led an expedition to investigate hydrologic and agronomic practices in the Rio Grande valley south of Embudo. He reported in a letter to Newell that he saw evidence of irrigation and cultivation throughout the Española Valley, including near La Joya, San Ildefonso, San Juan, Santa Cruz, Pojoaque, and White Rock Cañon. Robertson reported that it was hard to evaluate soil fertility or irrigation functions since none of the land was under cultivation during the time of his trip. According to his observations, most fields appeared "bare and sterile" during the late winter season. Letter from Robert Robertson to F. H. Newell, 6 March 1889, Record Group 57, Water Resources Division, Powell Irrigation Survey and Hydrographic Records Concerning Field Operations, 1889–1890, Box 1, loose materials, Records of the US Geologic Survey, US National Archives and Records Administration. Other than Robertson's trip, camp documentation contains minimal evidence that engineers visited other areas in New Mexico except to set up stream gauges in the general vicinity of Embudo. The English-language newspaper *Santa Fe New Mexican* reported several times in 1888 and 1889 that USGS engineers were seen in Santa Fe, usually on official visits to meet with Territorial officials.

15. For a discussion of the rich acequia irrigation history in the Embudo valley, see Arellano, *Enduring Acequias*.

16. I use the term "white" in this chapter to reflect the broad racial dimensions of national-level Progressive politics. When referring to white people in New Mexico specifically, I return to the regionally specific term "Anglo," in accordance with my discussion of terminology from chap. 1.

17. One of the Embudo engineers, George Curtis, reported to Newell in 1889 that he had enlisted a "Scotch (?) Mining Engineer" who lived in Tres Piedras to help with stream gauging in that area. He mentioned contacting several other Anglo/white individuals for local assistance with gauge maintenance, but his letters never mentioned Nuevomexicano or Indigenous persons. Letter from George E. Curtis to

F. H. Newell, 20 February 1889, Record Group 57, Water Resources Division, Powell Irrigation Survey and Hydrographic, Records Concerning Field Operations, 1889–1890, Box 1, Folder 1, Records of the US Geologic Survey, US National Archives and Records Administration.

18. Pisani, *Water, Land, and Law in the West*, 185.

19. Pisani, *Water, Land, and Law in the West*.

20. Christian W. McMillen, "Rain, Ritual, and Reclamation: The Failure of Irrigation on the Zuni and Navajo Reservations, 1883–1914," *Western Historical Quarterly* 31, no. 4 (2000).

21. Tyrrell, *Crisis of the Wasteful Nation*.

22. Tyrrell, *Crisis of the Wasteful Nation*.

23. Tyrrell, *Crisis of the Wasteful Nation*, 15. See also Benjamin Heber Johnson, "Environment: Nature, Conservation, and the Progressive State," in *A Companion to the Gilded Age and Progressive Era*, ed. Christopher McKnight Nichols and Nancy C. Unger (Chichester: John Wiley & Sons, 2017).

24. Adam Rome, "What Really Matters in History? Environmental Perspectives on Modern America," *Environmental History* 7, no. 2 (2002); Bruce J. Schulman, "Governing Nature, Nurturing Government: Resource Management and the Development of the American State, 1900–1912," *Journal of Policy History* 17, no. 4 (2005); Sutter, "The World with Us."

25. Peter Walker and Louise Fortmann, "Whose Landscape? A Political Ecology of the 'Exurban' Sierra," *Cultural Geographies* 10, no. 4 (2003); Kevin Wehr, *America's Fight over Water: The Environmental and Political Effects of Large-Scale Water Systems* (New York: Routledge, 2004); Lane, "Reading Boulder Dam."

26. David E. Nye, "Technology, Nature, and American Origin Stories," *Environmental History* 8, no. 1 (2003); Wehr, *America's Fight over Water*.

27. Hays, *Conservation and the Gospel of Efficiency*; Donald J. Pisani, *To Reclaim a Divided West: Water, Law, and Public Policy, 1848–1902* (Albuquerque: University of New Mexico Press, 1992).

28. Hays, *Conservation and the Gospel of Efficiency*.

29. Johnson, "Environment: Nature, Conservation, and the Progressive State."

30. Hays, *Conservation and the Gospel of Efficiency*, xiii.

31. Matthew J. Liebmann et al., "Native American Depopulation, Reforestation, and Fire Regimes in the Southwest United States, 1492–1900 CE," *Proceedings of the National Academy of Sciences of the United States of America* 113, no. 6 (2016); Lee Klinger, "Ecological Evidence of Large-Scale Silviculture by California Indians," in *Unlearning the Language of Conquest: Scholars Expose Anti-Indianism in America*, ed. Four Arrows (Don Trent Jacobs) (Austin: University of Texas Press, 2006); Robin Wall Kimmerer and Frank Kanawha Lake, "The Role of Indigenous Burning in Land Management," *Journal of Forestry* 99, no. 11 (2001).

32. Nancy Langston, *Forest Dreams, Forest Nightmares: The Paradox of Old Growth in the Inland West* (Seattle: University of Washington Press, 1995).

33. Daniel T. Rodgers, *Atlantic Crossings: Social Politics in a Progressive Age* (Cambridge, MA: Belknap Press of Harvard University Press, 1998).

34. G. Emlen Hall, "The Forest Service and Western Water Rights: An Intimate Portrait of *United States v. New Mexico*," *Natural Resources Journal* 45, no. 4 (2005); Rutgerd Boelens and Paul H. Gelles, "Cultural Politics, Communal Resistance and Identity in Andean Irrigation Development," *Bulletin of Latin American Research* 24,

no. 3 (2005); Stephen N. Bretsen and Peter J. Hill, "Irrigation Institutions in the American West," *UCLA Journal of Environmental Law and Policy* 25, no. 2 (2007).

35. Michael C. Robinson, *Water for the West: The Bureau of Reclamation, 1902–1977* (Chicago: Public Works Historical Society, 1979); Mark Fiege, *Irrigated Eden: The Making of an Agricultural Landscape in the American West* (Seattle: University of Washington Press, 1999).

36. Pisani, *Water, Land, and Law in the West*.

37. Lane, "Reading Boulder Dam"; Chris Sneddon, Regis Barraud, and Marie-Anne Germaine, "Dam Removals and River Restoration in International Perspective," *Water Alternatives* 10, no. 3 (2017).

38. Asit K. Biswas, *History of Hydrology* (Amsterdam: North-Holland, 1970); Sorin Dumitrescu and Jaromir Nemec, "Hyrdology: A Look Back and a Look Forward," in *Three Centuries of Scientific Hydrology: Key Papers Submitted on the Occasion of the Celebration of the Tercentenary of Scientific Hydrology* (Paris: UNESCO-WMO/OMM-IAHS/AISH, 1974); Raymond L. Nace, "Development of Hydrology in North America," *Water International* 3, no. 3 (1978).

39. Follansbee, *A History of the Water Resources Branch*.

40. Follansbee, *A History of the Water Resources Branch*, 28.

41. Follansbee, *A History of the Water Resources Branch*.

42. Follansbee, *A History of the Water Resources Branch*, 91.

43. Robinson, *Water for the West*; Karen L. Smith, *The Magnificent Experiment: Building the Salt River Reclamation Project, 1890–1917* (Tucson: University of Arizona Press, 1986).

44. Schulman, "Governing Nature, Nurturing Government," 379.

45. Donald J. Pisani, *Water and American Government: The Reclamation Bureau, National Water Policy, and the West, 1902–1935* (Berkeley and Los Angeles: University of California Press, 2002).

46. Tyrrell, *Crisis of the Wasteful Nation*.

47. Robinson, *Water for the West*, 5.

48. Lane, "Reading Boulder Dam."

49. Pisani, *Water and American Government*, 2; originally from *Forestry and Irrigation* 9 (October 1903): 475–76.

50. Frederick Haynes Newell and Daniel William Murphy, *Principles of Irrigation Engineering: Arid Lands, Water Supply, Storage Works, Dams, Canals, Water Rights and Products*, 1st ed., 2nd impression (corrected) (New York: McGraw-Hill, 1913), 285–86.

51. Pisani, *Water and American Government*, 2; originally from F. H. Newell, *Irrigation in the United States* (New York: Thomas Y. Crowell, 1902), 406.

52. Rodgers, *Atlantic Crossings*; James L. Westcoat, Jr., "Wittfogel East and West: Changing Perspectives on Water Development in South Asia and the United States, 1670–2000," in *Cultural Encounters with the Environment: Enduring and Evolving Geographic Themes*, ed. Alexander B. Murphy, Douglas L. Johnson, and Viola Heaarmann (Lanham, MD: Rowman & Littlefield, 2000); Balogh, "Scientific Forestry and the Roots of the Modern American State"; Marilyn Lake, *Progressive New World: How Settler Colonialism and Transpacific Exchange Shaped American Reform* (Cambridge, MA: Harvard University Press, 2019).

53. Robert E. Rook, "An American in Palestine: Elwood Mead and Zionist Water Resource Planning, 1923–1936," *Arab Studies Quarterly* 22, no. 1 (2000); Tyrrell, *Crisis of the Wasteful Nation*, 101; Kornel S. Chang, review of *Progressive New World: How*

Settler Colonialism and Transpacific Exchange Shaped American Reform, by Marilyn Lake, *Labor: Studies in Working-Class History of the Americas* 17, no. 3 (2020): 143.

54. Pisani, *Water and American Government*.

55. Pisani, *Water and American Government*.

56. Smith, *The Magnificent Experiment*, 155.

57. This logic set the stage for a long century-plus of environmental racism. See Traci Brynne Voyles, *Wastelanding: Legacies of Uranium Mining in Navajo Country* (Minneapolis: University of Minnesota Press, 2015).

58. Daniel McCool, *Native Waters: Contemporary Indian Water Settlements and the Second Treaty Era* (Tucson: University of Arizona Press, 2002), 26.

59. Newell and Murphy, *Principles of Irrigation Engineering*, 265.

60. Donald J. Pisani, "Water Law and Localism in the West," *Halcyon* 14 (1992); Philippus Wester, "Capturing the Waters: The Hydraulic Mission in the Lerma-Chapala Basin, Mexico (1876–1976)," *Water History* 1, no. 1 (2009).

61. William E. Smythe, *The Conquest of Arid America*, revised ed. (1905; Seattle: University of Washington Press, 1969), 242.

62. Smythe, *The Conquest of Arid America*, 247.

63. Arthur Powell Davis, *Irrigation Works Constructed by the United States Government*, 1st ed. (New York: John Wiley & Sons, 1917).

64. Davis, *Irrigation Works Constructed by the United States Government*, 227.

65. Phillips, Hall, and Black, *Reining in the Rio Grande*.

66. Davis, *Irrigation Works Constructed by the United States Government*, 234–36.

67. Barbel Hannelore Schönfeld La Mar, "Water and Land in the Mesilla Valley, New Mexico: Reclamation and Its Effects on Property Ownership and Agricultural Land Use" (Ph.D. diss., University of Oregon, 1985).

68. Schönfeld La Mar, "Water and Land in the Mesilla Valley"; Daniel R. Beene and K. Maria D. Lane, "Unmappable Variables: GIS and The Complicated Historical Geography of Water in the Rio Grande Project," in *Historical Geography, GIScience and Textual Analysis: Landscapes of Time and Place*, ed. Charles Travis, Francis Ludlow, and Ferenc Gyuris (Cham: Springer Nature, 2020).

69. Donald J. Pisani, "The Dilemmas of Indian Water Policy, 1887–1928," in *Fluid Arguments: Five Centuries of Western Water Conflict*, ed. Char Miller (Tucson: University of Arizona Press, 2001).

70. Pisani, "The Dilemmas of Indian Water Policy," 82–83.

71. R. Douglas Hurt, *Indian Agriculture in America: Prehistory to the Present* (Lawrence: University Press of Kansas, 1987), 170.

72. Daniel McCool, "Winters Comes Home to Roost," in *Fluid Arguments: Five Centuries of Western Water Conflict*, ed. Char Miller (Tucson: University of Arizona Press, 2001), 120–21.

73. Weisiger, *Dreaming of Sheep in Navajo Country*.

74. Hurt, *Indian Agriculture in America*.

75. Pisani, *Water and American Government*, 155.

76. McMillen, "Rain, Ritual, and Reclamation."

77. Pisani, *Water and American Government*, 154.

78. Hurt, *Indian Agriculture in America*, 171.

79. Pisani, "The Dilemmas of Indian Water Policy," 83; David H. DeJong, *Stealing the Gila: The Pima Agricultural Economy and Water Deprivation, 1848–1921* (Tucson: University of Arizona Press, 2009).

80. Pisani, "The Dilemmas of Indian Water Policy."
81. Pisani, *Water and American Government*, 88.
82. McCool, *Native Waters*, 36.
83. Rivera, *Acequia Culture*, xix.
84. Gregory A. Hicks and Devon G. Peña, "Customary Practice and Community Governance in Implementing the Human Right to Water—The Case of the Acequia Communities of Colorado's Rio Culebra Watershed," *Willamette Journal of International Law and Dispute Resolution* 18, no. 2 (2010): 185.
85. Fonseca-Chávez, Romero, and Herrera, *Querencia*.
86. Smith, *The Magnificent Experiment*, 155.
87. Pisani, *Water and American Government*, 294, following James C. Scott, *Seeing like a State: How Certain Schemes to Improve the Human Condition Have Failed* (New Haven, CT: Yale University Press, 1998). See also Arun Agrawal, *Environmentality: Technologies of Government and the Making of Subjects* (Durham, NC: Duke University Press, 2005); Hays, *Conservation and the Gospel of Efficiency*.
88. Schulman, "Governing Nature, Nurturing Government"; Karen M. O'Neill, *Rivers by Design: State Power and the Origins of U.S. Flood Control* (Durham, NC: Duke University Press, 2006).
89. Tyrrell, *Crisis of the Wasteful Nation*.
90. Pisani, *Water and American Government*.
91. Jared Farmer, *Glen Canyon Dammed: Inventing Lake Powell and the Canyon Country* (Tucson: University of Arizona Press, 1999).
92. Donald Worster, *A River Running West: The Life of John Wesley Powell* (Oxford and New York: Oxford University Press, 2002).
93. Scott Kirsch, "John Wesley Powell and the Mapping of the Colorado Plateau, 1869–1879: Survey Science, Geographical Solutions, and the Economy of Environmental Values," *Annals of the Association of American Geographers* 92, no. 3 (2002).
94. For popularizations of Powell, see Marc Reisner, *Cadillac Desert: The American West and Its Disappearing Water* (New York: Penguin Books, 1986); Worster, *A River Running West*.
95. Wendy Nelson Espeland, "Bureaucratizing Democracy, Democratizing Bureacracy," *Law and Social Inquiry* 25, no. 4 (2000).
96. Andrew Curley, "Infrastructures as Colonial Beachheads: The Central Arizona Project and the Taking of Navajo Resources," *Environment and Planning D: Society and Space* 39, no. 3 (2021).

Chapter 4

1. Clark, *Water in New Mexico*, 24–25.
2. Ebright, *Land Grants and Lawsuits in Northern New Mexico*.
3. Frances Levine, "Dividing the Water: The Impact of Water Rights Adjudication on New Mexican Communities," *Journal of the Southwest* 32, no. 3 (1990).
4. Ebright, *Land Grants and Lawsuits in Northern New Mexico*; Correia, "Making Destiny Manifest"; David Correia, *Properties of Violence: Law and Land Grant Struggle in Northern New Mexico* (Athens: University of Georgia Press, 2013).
5. Ebright, "Sharing the Shortages."
6. David Schorr, *The Colorado Doctrine: Water Rights, Corporations, and Distributive Justice on the American Frontier*, (New Haven, CT: Yale University Press, 2012),

disagrees with the prevailing take on prior appropriation, arguing that the doctrine was actually meant to protect community rights by preventing speculative land purchases when buyers had no intention of developing water infrastructure.

7. Pisani, "Water Law and Localism in the West," 39.

8. Pisani, "Water Law and Localism in the West," 31.

9. Pisani, "Water Law and Localism in the West," 39.

10. Clark, *Water in New Mexico*, 24.

11. Rivera, *Acequia Culture*; Rodríguez, *Acequia*.

12. Clark, *Water in New Mexico*, 30.

13. Clark, *Water in New Mexico*.

14. Clark, *Water in New Mexico*.

15. Miguel A. Otero, *Report of the Governor of New Mexico to the Secretary of the Interior, for the Year Ending June 30, 1900* (Washington, DC: Government Printing Office, 1900), 229.

16. Otero, *Report of the Governor for 1900*, 227.

17. For more on the "heated but one-sided battle pitting the legislators from the three counties against the remainder of the assembly members," refer to Clark, *Water in New Mexico*, 100. Note 3 in chap. 8 of Clark's book provides a list of newspaper sources.

18. Pisani, *Water, Land, and Law in the West*.

19. An Act Creating the Office of Territorial Irrigation Engineer, To Promote Irrigation Development and Conserve the Waters of New Mexico for the Irrigation of Lands and for Other Purposes (A.H.B. 98), 1905 Acts of the Legislative Assembly of the Territory of New Mexico, Thirty-sixth Session (Santa Fe: New Mexican Printing Company, 1905), Chapter 102, Sec. 17, "Duties of Territorial Irrigation Engineer" (passed March 16, 1905).

20. An Act Creating the Office of Territorial Irrigation Engineer, Sec. 12, "Appointment. Term. Qualifications."

21. An Act Creating the Office of Territorial Irrigation Engineer, Sec. 17, "Duties of Territorial Irrigation Engineer."

22. An Act Creating the Office of Territorial Irrigation Engineer, Sec. 23, "Water Divisions."

23. An Act Creating the Office of Territorial Irrigation Engineer, Sec. 29, "Method and Manner of Adjudication of Water Rights by Board of Control," 280, and Sec. 27, "Duties of Irrigation Commissioner," 279.

24. An Act Creating the Office of Territorial Irrigation Engineer, Sec. 10, "Water Rights to Pass with Land Appurtenant Thereto. Right Held Subject to Local Custom and Rules," 273–74.

25. An Act Creating the Office of Territorial Irrigation Engineer, Sec. 10, "Water Rights to Pass with Land Appurtenant Thereto. Right Held Subject to Local Custom and Rules."

26. An Act Creating the Office of Territorial Irrigation Engineer, Sec. 8, "When Irrigation Works Exempt from taxation. Provisos," and Sec. 3, "Appeals. Provisos."

27. An Act Creating the Office of Territorial Irrigation Engineer, Sec. 37, "Appeals, Provisos."

28. An Act Creating the Office of Territorial Irrigation Engineer, Sec. 35, "Engineer to Make Examination, and Measurement of Streams and Diversion Marks," 281.

29. An Act Creating the Office of Territorial Irrigation Engineer, Sec. 12, "Appointment. Term. Qualifications."

30. H. J. Hagerman, *Report of the Governor of New Mexico to the Secretary of the Interior, for the Year Ended June 30, 1906* (Washington, DC: Government Printing Office, 1906), 90.

31. Phillips, Hall, and Black, *Reining in the Rio Grande*.

32. An Act to Conserve and Regulate the Use and Distribution of the Waters of New Mexico; to Create the Office of Territorial Engineer; to Create a Board of Water Commissioners, and for Other Purposes (H.B. 120), 1907 Acts of the Legislative Assembly of the Territory of New Mexico, Thirty-seventh Session (Santa Fe: The New Mexican Printing Company, 1907), Chapter 49, Sec. 1, "All Natural Waters in New Mexico Belong to Public" (passed March 19, 1907), 73.

33. An Act to Conserve and Regulate the Use and Distribution of the Waters of New Mexico, Sec. 4, "Creating Office of Territorial Engineer. How Appointed. Term of Office: Subject to Removal for Cause. Duties. Salary etc. Office, Where. Not to Engage in Private Practice, Except," 74.

34. An Act to Conserve and Regulate the Use and Distribution of the Waters of New Mexico, Sec. 9, "Fees to Be Received by Territorial Engineer."

35. An Act to Conserve and Regulate the Use and Distribution of the Waters of New Mexico, Sec. 18, "Engineer to Assist County Commissioners in Miscellaneous Work," and Sec. 19, "Engineer to Make Hydrographic Surveys," 79.

36. An Act to Conserve and Regulate the Use and Distribution of the Waters of New Mexico, Sec. 64, "Duties of Engineer in Cases of Appeal," 92.

37. An Act to Conserve and Regulate the Use and Distribution of the Waters of New Mexico, Sec. 14, "Engineer to Appoint Water Masters. Duties. Number."

38. An Act to Conserve and Regulate the Use and Distribution of the Waters of New Mexico, Sec. 16, "Rate of Pay for Water Master. How Paid," and Sec. 17, "Report of Water Master. To Whom and What to Consist Of."

39. An Act to Conserve and Regulate the Use and Distribution of the Waters of New Mexico, Sec. 15, "Appeal from Decision of Water Master. How Made and to Whom."

40. An Act to Conserve and Regulate the Use and Distribution of the Waters of New Mexico, Sec. 13, "Territory to Be Divided into Stream Systems."

41. An Act to Conserve and Regulate the Use and Distribution of the Waters of New Mexico, Sec. 3, "Who May Exercise Right of Eminent Domain to Acquire Rights-of-Way for Ditches, Etc. Engineers of U.S. Territory and Others May Enter upon Public and Private Lands, When. Liability for Damage."

42. An Act to Conserve and Regulate the Use and Distribution of the Waters of New Mexico, Sec. 3.

43. An Act to Conserve and Regulate the Use and Distribution of the Waters of New Mexico, Sec. 3.

44. An Act to Conserve and Regulate the Use and Distribution of the Waters of New Mexico, Sec. 19, 79.

45. An Act to Conserve and Regulate the Use and Distribution of the Waters of New Mexico, Sec. 20, "Attorney General to Institute Suit, When and for What Purpose. Proviso."

46. An Act to Conserve and Regulate the Use and Distribution of the Waters of

New Mexico, Sec. 2, "Beneficial Use Basis of Measurement of Right to Use Water. Rights to be Governed by Priority. When to Date."

47. An Act to Conserve and Regulate the Use and Distribution of the Waters of New Mexico, Sec. 44, "Water Appurtenant to Land Cannot Be Transferred. Proviso. Applicant to Publish Notice," and Sec. 45, "Method of Changing Use of Water Already Secured."

48. An Act to Conserve and Regulate the Use and Distribution of the Waters of New Mexico, Sec. 24, "Method of Making Application, etc., for Water Right. Engineer May Require Additional Information, When. Excess of Water," 81.

49. An Act to Conserve and Regulate the Use and Distribution of the Waters of New Mexico, Sec. 24. As interpreted by the courts, "beneficial" use almost always referred to economic productivity. Conservation of water to support river-dependent plant and animal species ("environmental flows") was not recognized as a beneficial use until the late twentieth century. Lawrence J. MacDonnell, "Return to the River: Environmental Flow Policy in the United States and Canada," *Journal of the American Water Resources Association* 45, no. 5 (2009); Consuelo Bokum, "Implementing the Public Welfare Requirement in New Mexico's Water Code," *Natural Resources Journal* 36, no. 4 (1996).

50. An Act to Conserve and Regulate the Use and Distribution of the Waters of New Mexico, Sec. 35, "Time May Be Extended. How and Length of Time," 85.

51. An Act to Conserve and Regulate the Use and Distribution of the Waters of New Mexico, Sec. 46, "Ditch Owners to Construct and Maintain Measuring Devices. Penalties for Disturbing Same," 87.

52. An Act to Conserve and Regulate the Use and Distribution of the Waters of New Mexico, Sec. 47, "Various Acts Constitute Misdemeanors. Engineer or Authorized Assistant May Make Arrest. Duties. Engineer and Assistants May Enter on Public and Private Property for Carrying Out Their Duties," 87; Sec. 48, "Unauthorized Use of Water a Misdemeanor"; Sec. 50, "Unlawful to Place or Maintain Obstructions in Ditch."

53. An Act to Conserve and Regulate the Use and Distribution of the Waters of New Mexico, Sec. 57, "Local Customs and Rules to Stand."

54. Clark, *Water in New Mexico*, 124.

55. John Shurts, *Indian Reserved Water Rights: The Winters Doctrine in Its Social and Legal Context, 1880s–1930s*, Legal History of the United States 8 (Norman: University of Oklahoma Press, 2000); McCool, *Native Waters*.

56. Andrew Curley, "Unsettling Indian Water Settlements: The Little Colorado River, the San Juan River, and Colonial Enclosures," *Antipode* 53, no. 3 (2019).

57. Critical geographic scholarship argues that the colonial underpinnings of *Winters* are reinforced every time Indigenous nations engage in legal settlements that use their water rights as bargaining chips. But recent decolonial activist efforts have successfully reframed and claimed *Winters* rights as part of Indigenous resurgence and nation-building. See Andrew Curley, "'Our Winters' Rights': Challenging Colonial Water Laws," *Global Environmental Politics* 19, no. 3 (2019).

58. Yazzie, "Unlimited Limitations"; Curley, "Unsettling Indian Water Settlements."

59. Melanie K. Yazzie and Cutchla Risling Baldy, "Introduction: Indigenous Peoples and the Politics of Water," *Decolonization: Indigeneity, Education & Society* 7, no. 1 (2018).

60. Baxter, *Dividing New Mexico's Waters*, 106.

61. Eric P. Perramond, "Water Governance in New Mexico: Adjudication, Law, and Geography," *Geoforum* 45 (March 2013); Perramond, *Unsettled Waters*.

Chapter 5

1. The Engineer's office submitted biennial reports in 1906, 1908, and 1910. The report that should have been submitted in 1912 (covering activities in 1911 and 1912) was never completed, owing both to the transition to statehood and to a leadership change in the Office of the Territorial Engineer.

2. Otero, *Report of the Governor for 1900*. The usage and meaning of the word "data" has shifted over the last three hundred years, but the modern concept was well established by the end of the nineteenth century. When reading this chapter's quotations, modern readers should employ their familiar understanding of "data" to mean empirical observations, tangible facts, or quantitative statistics. For a historical discussion of the word *data* and the concept underlying it, see Daniel Rosenberg, "Data as Word," *Historical Studies in the Natural Sciences* 48, no. 5 (2018).

3. For more on Otero's complicated position, see Murrah-Mandril, *In the Mean Time*, especially chap. 2, "The Land of Poco Tiempo." Otero, "a socialite and a politician [who was the] son of an elite Nuevomexicano and a southern belle," walked a complicated socioracial path. He came from a wealthy family aligned with Anglo economic and political interests, and he prioritized modernization in his political work, often adopting Progressive Era racist sentiments about Indigenous peoples. But his focus on modernization was oriented toward securing political enfranchisement for New Mexico, and he often pushed back against prevalent stereotypes that portrayed Nuevomexicanas/os as backward and incapable of modernization. Otero argued instead that corruption—perpetrated most often by Anglos, and fostered by the federal government's refusal to extend statehood to New Mexico—was the primary cause of the territory's underdevelopment. Murrah-Mandril, *In the Mean Time*, 49.

4. "Report of Commission on Irrigation and Water Rights," reprinted in Otero, *Report of the Governor for 1900*, 222.

5. "Report of Commission on Irrigation and Water Rights," reprinted in Otero, *Report of the Governor for 1900*, 224.

6. "Report of Commission on Irrigation and Water Rights," reprinted in Otero, *Report of the Governor for 1900*, 222.

7. Miguel A. Otero, *Report of the Governor of New Mexico to the Secretary of the Interior, 1903* (Washington, DC: Government Printing Office, 1903), 484.

8. "Report of the Commission on Irrigation," reprinted in Otero, *Report of the Governor of New Mexico, 1903*, 634.

9. Miguel A. Otero, *Report of the Governor of New Mexico to the Secretary of the Interior, 1905* (Washington, DC: Government Printing Office, 1905), 20.

10. As Murrah-Mandril notes, Otero's annual reports to the Secretary of the DOI during his nine-year stint as governor, from 1897 to 1906, included increasingly lengthy and passionate appeals for statehood as the years went by.

11. Otero, *Report of the Governor of New Mexico, 1905*, 174.

12. David M. White, *Report of the Irrigation Engineer for the Two Years Ending January 1, 1907*, Office of the Territorial Irrigation Engineer, Territory of New Mexico (Santa Fe, NM, 1907), 7.

13. Vernon L. Sullivan, *First Biennial Report of the Territorial Engineer to the Governor of New Mexico Including Water Supply*, Office of the Territorial Engineer, Territory of New Mexico (Santa Fe, NM, 1908), 10.

14. Sullivan, *First Biennial Report of the Territorial Engineer*, 31, 32.

15. Sullivan, *First Biennial Report of the Territorial Engineer*, 3.

16. I did not examine the USGS view of this arrangement in detail. Reports indicate that engineers from both agencies supported the federal-territorial cooperative agreement, and that they worked together effectively. But both agencies also complained about not having enough resources to carry out their own data collection independently.

17. George Curry, *Report of the Governor of New Mexico to the Secretary of the Interior, for the Fiscal Year ended June 30, 1908* (Washington, DC: Government Printing Office, 1908).

18. Sullivan, *First Biennial Report of the Territorial Engineer*, 15.

19. Sullivan, *First Biennial Report of the Territorial Engineer*, 9–10.

20. Sullivan, *First Biennial Report of the Territorial Engineer*, 1.

21. William J. Mills, *Report of the Governor of New Mexico to the Secretary of the Interior, for the Fiscal Year Ended June 30, 1910* (Washington, DC: Government Printing Office, 1910), 27.

22. Vernon L. Sullivan, *Second Biennial Report of the Territorial Engineer to the Governor of New Mexico Including Irrigation, Water Supply, Good Roads, Carey Act*, Office of the Territorial Engineer, Territory of New Mexico (Santa Fe, NM: New Mexican Printing Company, 1910), 21–22.

23. Sullivan, *Second Biennial Report of the Territorial Engineer*, 80.

24. Sullivan, *Second Biennial Report of the Territorial Engineer*, 80.

25. Bayer, Montoya, and the Pueblo of Santa Ana, *Santa Ana*; DeJong, *Stealing the Gila*; Rivera, *Acequia Culture*.

26. Miguel A. Otero, *Report of the Governor of New Mexico to the Secretary of the Interior, 1902* (Washington, DC: Government Printing Office, 1902), 6.

27. Otero, *Report of the Governor of New Mexico, 1902*, 6.

28. Otero, *Report of the Governor of New Mexico, 1905*, 12. Again, refer to Murrah-Mandril, *In the Mean Time*, for a discussion of Otero's commitment to technological modernization and social reform in service of political enfranchisement for New Mexico.

29. Otero, *Report of the Governor of New Mexico, 1903*, 330.

30. Otero, *Report of the Governor of New Mexico, 1903*, 309, citing an article by J. J. Vernon titled "Agriculture in New Mexico."

31. John B. Harper, "Report on Indian Irrigation Improvements," included in Miguel A. Otero, *Report of the Governor of New Mexico to the Secretary of the Interior, for the Year Ending June 30, 1901* (Washington, DC: Government Printing Office, 1901), 270.

32. John B. Harper, "Report of Superintendent of Irrigation on the Pueblo and Jicarilla Indian Reservations," included in Otero, *Report of the Governor of New Mexico, 1903*, 509.

33. Refer to Bayer, Montoya, and the Pueblo of Santa Ana, *Santa Ana*; Phillips, Hall, and Black, *Reining in the Rio Grande*.

34. E. M. Rowalt, *Soil Defense of Range and Farm Lands in the Southwest* (Washington, DC: United States Government Printing Office, 1939), 10.

35. Miguel A. Otero, *Report of the Governor of New Mexico to the Secretary of the Interior, 1904* (Washington, DC: Government Printing Office, 1904), 129.
36. Hagerman, *Report of the Governor of New Mexico for 1906*, 59.
37. Hagerman, *Report of the Governor of New Mexico for 1906*, 60.
38. Ralph Emerson Twitchell, *The Leading Facts of New Mexican History*, vol. 2 (Cedar Rapids, IA: Torch Press, 1911).
39. Otero, *Report of the Governor of New Mexico for 1901*, 259.
40. Fiege, *Irrigated Eden*.
41. *Report of the Governor of New Mexico for 1901*, 260.
42. For example, Derek Gregory, *Geographical Imaginations* (Oxford: Blackwell, 1994); Thongchai Winichakul, *Siam Mapped: A History of the Geo-Body of a Nation* (Honolulu: University of Hawai'i Press, 1994); Matthew Sparke, "A Map That Roared and an Original Atlas: Canada, Cartography, and the Narration of Nation," *Annals of the Association of American Geographers* 88, no. 3 (1998); Ryan, *The Cartographic Eye*; Mary Pat Brady, "'Full of Empty': Creating the Southwest as 'Terra Incognita,'" in *Nineteenth-Century Geographies: The Transformation of Space from the Victorian Age to the American Century*, ed. Helena Michie and Ronald R. Thomas (New Brunswick, NJ: Rutgers University Press, 2003), 251–64. Most of this literature builds on the ideas of Edward W. Said, *Orientalism* (New York: Pantheon Books, 1978).
43. Sullivan, *First Biennial Report of the Territorial Engineer*, 31.
44. Otero, *Report of the Governor of New Mexico, 1905*, 20.
45. Mills, *Report of the Governor of New Mexico, 1910*, 25–26.
46. Otero, *Report of the Governor of New Mexico, 1905*, 25.
47. Sullivan, *Second Biennial Report of the Territorial Engineer*, 126.
48. Sullivan, *Second Biennial Report of the Territorial Engineer*.
49. Sullivan, *First Biennial Report of the Territorial Engineer*, 15.
50. Otero, *Report of the Governor of New Mexico, 1905*.
51. Otero, *Report of the Governor of New Mexico for 1901*, 259.
52. Hagerman, *Report of the Governor of New Mexico for 1906*, 4.
53. Sullivan, *First Biennial Report of the Territorial Engineer*, 7.
54. Sullivan, *First Biennial Report of the Territorial Engineer*, 7.
55. Hagerman, *Report of the Governor of New Mexico for 1906*, 24.
56. Sullivan, *Second Biennial Report of the Territorial Engineer*, 95.
57. Otero, *Report of the Governor of New Mexico, 1905*, 7.
58. Otero, *Report of the Governor of New Mexico for 1901*, 259.
59. Sullivan, *First Biennial Report of the Territorial Engineer*, 43.
60. Sullivan, *Second Biennial Report of the Territorial Engineer*, 95.
61. Sullivan, *Second Biennial Report of the Territorial Engineer*, 97.
62. Sullivan, *Second Biennial Report of the Territorial Engineer*, 95.
63. Sullivan, *First Biennial Report of the Territorial Engineer*, 18.
64. Sullivan, *Second Biennial Report of the Territorial Engineer*, 94.
65. Young & Norton et al., Appellants v M.C. Hinderlider, Appellee, XV Paul A. F. Walter 666, No. 1328 (Supreme Court of the Territory of New Mexico 1910).
66. Hagerman, *Report of the Governor of New Mexico for 1906*, 90.
67. White, *Report of the Irrigation Engineer, 1907*, 7.
68. Hagerman, *Report of the Governor of New Mexico for 1906*, 26.
69. Otero, *Report of the Governor of New Mexico for 1901*, 270.
70. Otero, *Report of the Governor of New Mexico for 1901*, 271.

71. Otero, *Report of the Governor of New Mexico, 1905*, 24.
72. Otero, *Report of the Governor of New Mexico, 1905*, 21.
73. Vernon L. Sullivan, *Report on the Hondo Hydrographic Survey by the Territorial Engineer to the Court of the Sixth Judicial District of the Territory of New Mexico*, Territorial Engineer, Office of the Territorial Engineer, Territory of New Mexico (Santa Fe: New Mexico Printing Company, 1910), 95.
74. Sullivan, *First Biennial Report of the Territorial Engineer*, 63.
75. Sullivan, *First Biennial Report of the Territorial Engineer*, 63.
76. Sullivan, *First Biennial Report of the Territorial Engineer*, 64.
77. Otero, *Report of the Governor of New Mexico, 1905*, 22.
78. Sullivan, *Second Biennial Report of the Territorial Engineer*, 19.
79. Sullivan, *Second Biennial Report of the Territorial Engineer*, 19.
80. Sullivan, *Second Biennial Report of the Territorial Engineer*, 8, 19.
81. Sullivan, *First Biennial Report of the Territorial Engineer*, 64.
82. Sullivan, *First Biennial Report of the Territorial Engineer*, 12.
83. Sullivan, *Second Biennial Report of the Territorial Engineer*.
84. Sullivan, *Second Biennial Report of the Territorial Engineer*, 21–22. 16.
85. Sullivan, *First Biennial Report of the Territorial Engineer*, 7.
86. Hagerman, *Report of the Governor of New Mexico for 1906*, 26.

Chapter 6

1. Malcom Ebright and Rick Hendricks, *Pueblo Sovereignty: Indian Land and Water in New Mexico and Texas* (Norman: University of Oklahoma Press, 2019).
2. April L. Wilkinson, "A Framework for Understanding Tribal Courts and the Application of Fundamental Law: Through the Voices of Scholars in the Field of Tribal Justice," *Tribal Law Journal* 15, no. 1 (2014); Ada Pecos Melton, "Indigenous Justice Systems and Tribal Society," *Judicature* 79 (1995); Robert Yazzie, "Life Comes from It: Navajo Justice Concepts," *New Mexico Law Review* 24 (1994); Robert B. Porter, "Strengthening Tribal Sovereignty through Peacemaking: How the Anglo-American Legal Tradition Destroys Indigenous Societies," *Columbia Human Rights Law Review* 28, no. 2 (1996); Rudy Al James (ThlauGooYailthThlee—The First and Oldest Raven), "Traditional Native Justice: Restoration and Balance, not 'Punishment,'" in *Unlearning the Language of Conquest: Scholars Expose Anti-Indianism in America*, ed. Four Arrows (Don Trent Jacobs) (Austin: University of Texas Press, 2006).
3. This paragraph is based on Michael C. Meyer, *Water in the Hispanic Southwest: A Social and Legal History, 1550–1850* (Tucson: University of Arizona Press, 1996). See also José Ramón Remacha, "Traces of the Spanish Legal System in the USA," *New Mexico Historical Review* 69, no. 3 (1994).
4. Meyer, *Water in the Hispanic Southwest*.
5. Meyer, *Water in the Hispanic Southwest*.
6. Ebright, *Land Grants and Lawsuits in Northern New Mexico*, 62, 69.
7. Baxter, *Dividing New Mexico's Waters*, 44.
8. Baxter, *Dividing New Mexico's Waters*; Ebright, "Sharing the Shortages."
9. This paragraph is based on Baxter, *Dividing New Mexico's Waters*.
10. See Alarid, *Hispano Bastion*, for an analysis of how criminal cases in the new district court system reflected Nuevomexicano elites' social power during the American territorial period.

11. Baxter, *Dividing New Mexico's Waters*, 72.

12. Refer to chap. 4 for a discussion of the origins and implementation of this legislation.

13. David A. Reichard, "The Politics of Village Water Disputes in Northern New Mexico, 1882–1905," *Western Legal History* 9, no. 1 (1996).

14. Baxter, *Dividing New Mexico's Waters*, 84, 106.

15. Reichard, "The Politics of Village Water Disputes"; Martha E. Mulvany, "*State ex rel. Martinez v. City of Las Vegas*: The Misuse of History and Precedent in the Abolition of the Pueblo Water Rights Doctrine in New Mexico," *Natural Resources Journal* 45, no. 4 (2005).

16. Baxter, *Dividing New Mexico's Waters*.

17. For descriptions of historical cross-referencing to match New Mexican surnames with ethnicity as a painstaking and uncertain methodology, see Schönfeld La Mar, "Water and Land in the Mesilla Valley"; Nostrand, *The Hispano Homeland*.

Chapter 7

1. Wendy Nelson Espeland, "Legal Structure in Colonial Encounters: Bureaucratizing Culture and the Environment in the American Southwest," in *ABF Working Papers #9512* (Chicago: American Bar Foundation, 1996).

2. Historical details in this paragraph are drawn from Ralph Emerson Twitchell, "Rio Arriba County," in *The Leading Facts of New Mexican History* (Cedar Rapids, IA: Torch Press, 1917).

3. Meinig, *Atlantic America*; Nostrand, *The Hispano Homeland*.

4. Longer summaries of these two cases are provided in K. Maria D. Lane, "Water, Technology, and the Courtroom: Negotiating Reclamation Policy in Territorial New Mexico," *Journal of Historical Geography* 37, no. 3 (2011).

5. I use the name "San Juan Pueblo" throughout this account, but the pueblo restored its precolonial name in 2005 and is now known as Ohkay Owingeh.

6. The two sides disagreed on the date of the Acequia Nueva's initiation. The plaintiffs claimed it was constructed in 1892; the defendants protested it did not begin delivering water until 1895.

7. George Anton et al. vs Juan Bautista Talache et al. (decided 1904) Civil case no. 708, Collection 1973-017, Records of the United States Territorial and New Mexico District Courts for Rio Arriba County, Box no. 11, New Mexico State Records Center and Archives (hereinafter SRCA), Petition for civil injunction, 5 May 1903.

8. *George Anton et al. v. Juan Bautista Talache et al.*, Defendants' reply, undated.

9. *George Anton et al. v. Juan Bautista Talache et al.*, Plaintiff's Exhibit 5: affidavit by S. S. Filigonio Sanchez, 26 May 1903.

10. *George Anton et al. v. Juan Bautista Talache et al.*, Plaintiffs' reply, 24 May 1903.

11. *George Anton et al. v. Juan Bautista Talache et al.*, Petition and information, 14 March 1904.

12. *George Anton et al. v. Juan Bautista Talache et al.*, Petition and information, 14 March 1904.

13. Pueblo de San Juan v. Acequia Nueva et al. (decided 1905) Civil case no. 784, Collection 1973-017, Records of the United States Territorial and New Mexico District Courts for Rio Arriba County, Box no. 12, SRCA, Petition, undated.

14. *Pueblo de San Juan v. Acequia Nueva et al.*, Petition, undated.

15. *Pueblo de San Juan v. Acequia Nueva et al.*, Petition, undated.

16. *Pueblo de San Juan v. Acequia Nueva et al.*, Final ruling, 2 August 1905.

17. La Acequia de Los Garcias et al. v. La Acequia de Medio (decided 1905) Civil case no. 770, Collection 1973–017, Records of the United States Territorial and New Mexico District Courts for Rio Arriba County, Box no. 12, SRCA.

18. *Acequia de Los Garcias v. La Acequia de Medio*, Defendants' answer to show cause, 19 April 1905.

19. *Acequia de Los Garcias v. La Acequia de Medio*, Defendants' answer to show cause, 19 April 1905.

20. *Acequia de Los Garcias v. La Acequia de Medio*, Defendants' answer to show cause, 19 April 1905.

21. *Acequia de Los Garcias v. La Acequia de Medio*, Defendants' Exhibit A: affidavit by Robert R. Willison, 17 April 1905.

22. *Acequia de Los Garcias v. La Acequia de Medio*, Defendants' answer to show cause, 19 April 1905.

23. *Acequia de Los Garcias v. La Acequia de Medio*, Stipulation, 21 April 1905.

24. *Acequia de Los Garcias v. La Acequia de Medio*, Findings, judgment, and decree, 1 May 1905.

25. Ralph Emerson Twitchell, "Santa Fe County," in *The Leading Facts of New Mexican History* (Cedar Rapids, IA: Torch Press, 1917), 3. Other details in this paragraph are also drawn from this chapter.

26. Pollmann's name also appears incorrectly in some documents as "Pohlmann," even though his attorneys tried to correct the record multiple times. I use the correct spelling throughout this discussion.

27. Dockwiller's name appears incorrectly in the court record multiple times. Sometimes his first name is listed as "Alfonso," and his last name appears occasionally as "Dockweiler." These mistakes were sometimes corrected by hand but not always, despite his attorney's efforts.

28. Edward Miller v. Alphonso Dockwiller and Henry Pullman (decided 1903) Civil case no. 4064, Collection 1972–011, Records of the United States Territorial and New Mexico District Courts for Santa Fe County, Box no. 227, SRCA, Complaint, 4 May 1899.

29. *Miller v. Dockwiller and Pullman*, Miller affidavit, 13 May 1899.

30. *Miller v. Dockwiller and Pullman*, Pollmann affidavit, 15 May 1899.

31. Much to my dismay, this map is missing from the case file. Multiple other documents refer to it and confirm its importance as a key piece of evidence, but these textual descriptions do not provide a full understanding of the map's appearance or any details pertaining to it.

32. *Miller v. Dockwiller and Pullman*, Dockwiller affidavit, 17 May 1899.

33. *Miller v. Dockwiller and Pullman*, Pollmann affidavit, 15 May 1899.

34. *Miller v. Dockwiller and Pullman*, Miller affidavit, 17 May 1899.

35. *Miller v. Dockwiller and Pullman*, Weltmer affidavit, 16 May 1899; Rivenberg affidavit, 16 May 1899.

36. *Miller v. Dockwiller and Pullman*, Rivenberg affidavit, 16 May 1899.

37. *Miller v. Dockwiller and Pullman*, Affidavit/statement, May 19, 1899.

38. *Miller v. Dockwiller and Pullman*, Ysabel Ortega affidavit, 25 May 1899.

39. *Miller v. Dockwiller and Pullman*, Manuel Romero y Domingez affidavit, 25 May 1899.

40. Sadly, witness testimony transcripts were not preserved with the case file. Only a handful of sketch maps remain.

41. *Miller v. Dockwiller and Pullman*, Report of William H. Whiteman, Referee, 3 September 1900.

42. *Miller v. Dockwiller and Pullman*, Exceptions taken by the defendants to the report of W.H. Whiteman, referee, undated.

43. *Miller v. Dockwiller and Pullman*, Final ruling and injunction, 30 January 1903.

44. Historical details in this paragraph are drawn from Ralph Emerson Twitchell, "Sandoval County," in *The Leading Facts of New Mexican History* (Cedar Rapids, IA: Torch Press, 1917).

45. Justiniano Castillo v. the Atchison, Topeka and Santa Fe Railway Company (decided 1909) Civil case no. 177, Collection 1976-038, Records of the United States Territorial and New Mexico District Courts for Sandoval County, Box no. 4, SRCA, Instructions to jury, undated.

46. *Justiniano Castillo v. The AT&SF Railway Company*, Instructions to jury, undated, emphasis added.

47. Most of the documents in this case refer incorrectly to the Montano Grant (without the diacritical mark), but a few references use the name Montaño, so I have corrected it throughout.

48. Meinig, *Southwest*.

49. Rio Puerco Irrigation Company v. H. A. Jastro (decided 1912) Civil case no. 244, Collection 1976-038, Records of the United States Territorial and New Mexico District Courts for Sandoval County, Box no. 4, SRCA, Appellant's Exhibit E, 25 May 1911.

50. *Rio Puerco Irrigation Company v. Jastro*, Appellant's Exhibit E, 25 May 1911, 76.

51. *Rio Puerco Irrigation Company v. Jastro*, McChesney testimony in trial transcript, 15 February 1912.

52. *Rio Puerco Irrigation Company v. Jastro*, Appellee's Exhibit 2, Board of Water Commissioners ruling, 30 March 1911.

53. *Rio Puerco Irrigation Company v. Jastro*, Appellant's Exhibit D, Protest against applicants, filed by United States Reclamation Service, 19 December 1907.

54. *Rio Puerco Irrigation Company v. Jastro*, Appellee's Exhibit 2, Board of Water Commissioners ruling, 30 March 1911, 117.

55. *Rio Puerco Irrigation Company v. Jastro*, Appellee's Exhibit 2, Board of Water Commissioners ruling, 30 March 1911, 117.

56. *Rio Puerco Irrigation Company v. Jastro*, Appellee's Exhibit 2, Board of Water Commissioners ruling, 30 March 1911, 118

57. *Rio Puerco Irrigation Company v. Jastro*, McChesney testimony in trial transcript, 15 February 1912, 25.

58. *Rio Puerco Irrigation Company v. Jastro*, McChesney testimony in trial transcript, 15 February 1912, 25.

59. *Rio Puerco Irrigation Company v. Jastro*, Appellant's Exhibit G, Statement of P. E. Harroun, C.E., 27 January 1902.

60. H. A. Jastro v. Rio Puerco Irrigation Company (decided 1912) Civil case no. 245, Collection 1976-038, Records of the United States Territorial and New Mexico District Courts for Sandoval County, Box no. 4, SRCA, Final judgement, 2 May 1912.

61. Historical details here are based on Ralph Emerson Twitchell, "Bernalillo

County," in *The Leading Facts of New Mexican History* (Cedar Rapids, IA: Torch Press, 1917).

62. Algodones became part of the newly created Sandoval County in 1903, but the cases referenced here were filed when the villa was still part of Bernalillo County.

63. Pueblo de Santo Domingo v. Marcus C. de Baca et al. (decided 1899), Civil case no. 5283, Collection 1959–124, Records of the United States Territorial and New Mexico District Courts for Bernalillo County, Box no. 71, SRCA, Complaint and request for injunction, 10 April 1899.

64. The pueblo dropped its colonial name in 2010 and is now known by its original name, Kewa Pueblo. I use "Santo Domingo" throughout this account to accurately reference historical documents from that time.

65. *Pueblo de Santo Domingo v. Baca et al.*, Answer of defendants, 15 April 1899.

66. *Pueblo de Santo Domingo v. Baca et al.*, Motion for new trial, undated.

67. *Pueblo de Santo Domingo v. Baca et al.*, Complaint and request for injunction, 10 April 1899.

68. *Pueblo de Santo Domingo v. Baca et al.*, Motion for new trial, undated.

69. It is not clear from the case file whether the interpreter translated witness testimony given in Keres into Spanish or into English during the trial. All court documentation—both typed and handwritten—was recorded in English, which points toward the likelihood that witness testimony during the trial would have been translated into English. If so, this would have compounded the difficulty for Nuevomexicano participants from Peña Blanca. Many of them presumably spoke only Spanish and would have understood neither Keres nor English.

70. Court documents in this case do not use diacritical marks, but I confirmed by his signature that Gregorio García wrote his name with an accent. I have corrected the spelling throughout this narrative.

71. J.E. Matthews et al. v. Gregorio Garcia, Macedonia Herrera, and Guadalupe Nuanes (decided 1904), Civil case no. 6624, Collection 1959–124, Records of the United States Territorial and New Mexico District Courts for Bernalillo County, Box no. 85, SRCA, Certificate and Return to Peremptory Writ of Mandamus by Garcia and Herrera.

72. *Matthews et al. v. Garcia, Herrera, and Nuanes*, Certificate and Return to Peremptory Writ of Mandamus by Garcia and Herrera.

73. *Matthews et al. v. Garcia, Herrera, and Nuanes*, Certificate and Return of Guadalupe Nuanes to the Peremptory Writ, 2 August 1904.

74. *Matthews et al. v. Garcia, Herrera, and Nuanes*, Certificate and Return of Guadalupe Nuanes to the Peremptory Writ, 2 August 1904.

75. Martin P. Stamm and Naomi R. Stamm v. O. N. Marron et al., and the City of Albuquerque (decided 1899), Civil case no. 5346, Collection 1959–124, Records of the United States Territorial and New Mexico District Courts for Bernalillo County, Box no. 72, SRCA. The plaintiffs appealed the dismissal to the New Mexico Supreme Court, which directed the lower court to set aside the dismissal and rule in favor of the plaintiffs. The lower court then enjoined the City from maintaining the ditch on the plaintiffs' property in any manner other than by a covered flume of a certain size. The City was also forbidden to maintain the ditch and ordered to abate the nuisance caused by it.

76. City of Albuquerque v. Martin P. Stamm and Naomi R. Stamm (decided 1900),

Civil case no. 5519, Collection 1959-124, Records of the United States Territorial and New Mexico District Courts for Bernalillo County, Box no. 74, SRCA.

77. The City of Albuquerque v. The Los Griegos Community Ditch and Manuel R. Springer, Ambrosio Zamora and Gregorio Garcia, commissioners of said ditch; and the Albuquerque Community Ditch and John Mann, Susana Luna, and Antonio Jose Garcia, commissioners of said ditch (decided 1905), Civil case no. 6816, Collection 1959-124, Records of the United States Territorial and New Mexico District Courts for Bernalillo County, Box no. 87, SRCA.

78. Martin P. Stamm and Naomi R. Stamm v. The City of Albuquerque, Frank McKee Mayor, and Peter Hanley, A.W. Hayden, George P. Learned, Thomas Isherwood, Samuel Neustadt, George W. Harrison, Thomas N. Wilkerson, and John S. Beaven (decided 1906), Civil case no. 7143, Collection 1959-124, Records of the United States Territorial and New Mexico District Courts for Bernalillo County, Box no. 90, SRCA.

79. Frank H. Trotter v. Water Supply Company of Albuquerque (decided 1909), Civil case no. 8078, Collection 1959-124, Records of the United States Territorial and New Mexico District Courts for Bernalillo County, Box no. 99, SRCA; City of Albuquerque v. Water Supply Company of Albuquerque (decided 1909), Civil case no. 8091, Collection 1959-124, Records of the United States Territorial and New Mexico District Courts for Bernalillo County, Box no. 100, SRCA; Charles C. Braden v. Water Supply Company of Albuquerque (decided 1909), Civil case no. 8101, Collection 1959-124, Records of the United States Territorial and New Mexico District Courts for Bernalillo County, Box no. 100, SRCA; Water Supply Company of Albuquerque v. City of Albuquerque (decided 1911), Civil case no. 8432, Collection 1959-124, Records of the United States Territorial and New Mexico District Courts for Bernalillo County, Box no. 104, SRCA; James E. Matthews v. Water Supply Company of Albuquerque (decided 1912), Civil case no. 8891, Collection 1959-124, Records of the United States Territorial and New Mexico District Courts for Bernalillo County, Box no. 108, SRCA.

80. City of Albuquerque v. Antonio Garcia, Tomas Gurule, Tomas Apodaca, N. Metz, Manuel Sedillo, Gregorio Apodaca y Candelaria, Tomas G. Apodaca, Jose Salazar, William Bietz, Juan Padilla, Ignacio de Baca, Ignacio Compas, Sofia Vigil as Administratrix of the estate of Eslavio Vigil, and Eslavio Vigil, Delfino Vigil, Juan Vigil, Teresa Vigil, Sofia Vigil, and Emma Vigil, minor heirs of Eslavio Vigil, deceased, as individuals, and Antonio Garcia, Tomas Gurule, Tomas Apodaca, and N. Metz, as Ditch commissioners of the Contra Acequia running from the Barelas Ditch west to and through Barelas (decided 1911), Civil case no. 8596, Collection 1959-124, Records of the United States Territorial and New Mexico District Courts for Bernalillo County, Box no. 105, SRCA, Petition, 13 February 1911.

81. *City of Albuquerque v. Antonio Garcia et al.*, Petition, 13 February 1911.

82. *City of Albuquerque v. Antonio Garcia et al.*, Petition, 13 February 1911.

83. *City of Albuquerque v. Antonio Garcia et al.*, Exceptions of Defendant Tomás G. Apodaca to Findings of Board of Appraisers, undated.

84. *City of Albuquerque v. Antonio Garcia et al.*, Exceptions of Defendant Nick Metz to the Findings of the Board of Appraisers, undated.

85. *City of Albuquerque v. Antonio Garcia et al.*, Confirmation of the Report of the Appraisers, undated.

86. Ralph Emerson Twitchell, "Valencia County," in *The Leading Facts of New Mexican History* (Cedar Rapids, IA: Torch Press, 1917).

87. "Acequia de en Medio" is an unusual name (because of its back-to-back prepositions), but it appears consistently in all case documents, in both Spanish and English. One English-language document refers to the "Old Peralta, or De En Medio ditch," indicating it was originally named the Acequia de Peralta but was renamed. Jesus H. Sanchez v. Romulo Aragon, Francisco Aragon, Ramon Emilio Aragon, Diego Aragon, Gregorio Aragon, Margarita Aragon, Antonio Jose Aragon, and Jesus Sanchez y Alarid (decided 1899), Civil case no. 1419, Collection 1978–003, Records of the United States Territorial and New Mexico District Courts for Valencia County, Box no. 33, SRCA, Translation of Exhibit H, 27 February 1899.

88. This ditch name does not appear to have any relation to the "Picuris" place-name in northern New Mexico.

89. *Jesus H. Sanchez v. Romulo Aragon et al.*, Complaint, 25 July 1899.

90. *Jesus H. Sanchez v. Romulo Aragon et al.*, Plaintiff's reply, undated.

91. *Jesus H. Sanchez v. Romulo Aragon et al.*, Answer and Demurrer of all Defendants, 8 August 1899.

92. *Jesus H. Sanchez v. Romulo Aragon et al.*, Answer and Demurrer of all Defendants, 8 August 1899.

93. *Jesus H. Sanchez v. Romulo Aragon et al.*, Answer and Demurrer of all Defendants, 8 August 1899.

94. *Jesus H. Sanchez v. Romulo Aragon et al.*, Answer and Demurrer of all Defendants, 8 August 1899.

95. Frederick Tondre, Demetrio Vallejos, Andrew Sichler, Pascual Sais, and Justo Chaves v. Pueblo of Isleta (decided 1911), Civil case no. 8590, Collection 1959–124, Records of the United States Territorial and New Mexico District Courts for Bernalillo County, Box no. 105, SRCA, Petition, undated 1911.

96. *Frederick Tondre et al. v. Pueblo of Isleta*, Answer, 14 February 1911.

97. *Frederick Tondre et al. v. Pueblo of Isleta*, Reply, undated, did not specify any date for Huning's sale of the property, characterizing it only as "quite recently."

98. *Frederick Tondre et al. v. Pueblo of Isleta*, Reply, undated.

99. *Frederick Tondre et al. v. Pueblo of Isleta*, Petition, undated.

100. Pueblo de Isleta v. J. A. Pichard, Carlos Raff, Pablo Castillo, Lucas Sanchez, Antonio Garcia, Adolfo Didier, Richard Pohl, and Gavino Gilbert (decided 1911), Civil case no. 1749, Collection 1978–003, Records of the United States Territorial and New Mexico District Courts for Valencia County, Box no. 44, SRCA, Complaint, undated.

101. Historical details here are based on Ralph Emerson Twitchell, "Socorro County," in *The Leading Facts of New Mexican History* (Cedar Rapids, IA: Torch Press, 1917).

102. The case file does not delineate the exact location of the disputed spring and properties. Several springs carry the name "Horse Spring" or "Horse Springs" in what was then western Socorro County. Without knowing for sure which location the case refers to, I have narrowed it down to several similarly named springs in the watershed of the Gila River's West Fork, north of the Mogollon Mountains, in what is today part of Catron County.

103. George Belcher v. Montague Stevens and Augusta Helen Gorden Stevens (decided 1900), Civil case no. 3219, Collection 1976–031, Records of the United States Territorial and New Mexico District Courts for Socorro County, Box no. 120, SRCA, Complaint, 13 November 1899.

104. *Belcher v. Stevens and Stevens*, Answer, 24 January 1900.

105. *Belcher v. Stevens and Stevens*, Answer, 24 January 1900.

106. *Belcher v. Stevens and Stevens*, Final ruling, 24 February 1900.

107. Silvestre Esquibel, Leopoldo Contraras, Abran Barela, Alejo Gurule, and Fred Vasick, Trustees of the Grant of Cebilleta de la Joya v. The Atchison, Topeka, and Santa Fe Railway Company (decided 1909), Civil case no. 5368, Collection 1976-031, Records of the United States Territorial and New Mexico District Courts for Socorro County, Box no. 18068, SRCA, Complaint, 14 October 1909.

108. *Esquibel et al. v. AT&SF Railway*, Answer, 2 November 1909.

109. Historical details here are based on Ralph Emerson Twitchell, "Sierra County," in *The Leading Facts of New Mexican History* (Cedar Rapids, IA: Torch Press, 1917).

110. John B. McPherson v. Gabriel Chavez et al. (decided 1900), Civil case no. 779, Collection 1979-025, Records of the United States Territorial and New Mexico District Courts for Sierra County, Box no. 17291, SRCA, Demurrer, 14 April 1900.

111. *John B. McPherson v. Gabriel Chavez et al.*, Demurrer, 14 April 1900.

112. *John B. McPherson v. Gabriel Chavez et al.*, Sarah J. Benson affidavit, 30 March 1900.

113. *John B. McPherson v. Gabriel Chavez et al.*, Final decree, 12 December 1900.

114. Historical details here are based on Ralph Emerson Twitchell, " Doña Ana County," in *The Leading Facts of New Mexican History* (Cedar Rapids, IA: Torch Press, 1917).

115. Although private ditches did not resemble traditional acequias in terms of shared governance, territorial law by this time classified them as acequias, and people often used the term *acequia* in colloquial speech to refer to all ditches. In this particular case, the name/term was more than a colloquialism; many area irrigators assumed that the Palmer Acequia *did* operate like a traditional, communal acequia.

116. Case documents spell this name variously as "Ponsiano" or "Ponciano." Arrey himself signed documents with an "x" and therefore does not offer a correct spelling for the record.

117. Dona Ana 2366, Sarah Palmer and William Palmer, Jr., plaintiffs, v. Felix Otero (decided 1902), Civil case no. 2366, Collection 1976-015, Records of the United States Territorial and New Mexico District Courts for Doña Ana County, Box no. 41, SRCA, Palmer testimony in hearing transcript, 23 December 1902.

118. *Palmer and Palmer v. Otero*, Agapito Torres affidavit, 8 May 1901.

119. *Palmer and Palmer v. Otero*, Complaint, 12 April 1901.

120. *Palmer and Palmer v. Otero*, Pablo Mendoza affidavit, 8 May 1901; Tomás Gonzales affidavit, 10 May 1901.

121. *Palmer and Palmer v. Otero*, Gabaldon testimony in hearing transcript, 23 December 1902.

122. *Palmer and Palmer v. Otero*, Otero testimony in hearing transcript, 23 December 1902.

123. The only person whose testimony was *not* translated was Palmer's, and we know he spoke Spanish (and presumably could have testified in that language) because the record shows that he once objected to a specific turn of phrase an interpreter chose in rendering Otero's Spanish testimony into English.

124. *Palmer and Palmer v. Otero*, Otero testimony in hearing transcript, 23 December 1902.

125. *Palmer and Palmer v. Otero*, Otero testimony in hearing transcript, 23 December 1902.

126. The Arrey family leveraged their wealth into political control, and the town of Arrey is named after them.

127. The history of this patent is beyond the scope of this chapter, but presumably Arrey was able to claim the land on the basis of providing its water through the Arrey ContraAcequia. Nuevomexicano elites did manage to consolidate considerable wealth in some places during New Mexico's territorial era, but they nearly always did so at the expense of other Nuevomexicanas/os.

Chapter 8

1. Mark Kanazawa, *Golden Rules: The Origins of California Water Law in the Gold Rush* (Chicago: University of Chicago Press, 2015).

2. Estes, *Our History Is the Future*; Vine Deloria Jr., *Red Earth, White Lies: Native Americans and the Myth of Scientific Fact* (Golden, CO: Fulcrum, 1997).

3. Wilmsen, "Maintaining the Environmental-Racial Order in Northern New Mexico." See also Correia, "The Etiology of Rangeland Degradation in Northern New Mexico"; Correia, "From Agropastoralism to Sustained Yield Forestry"; Kosek, *Understories*.

4. The Office of the State Engineer maintains a list of all current and pending adjudications, with links to associated documents, accessed 19 May 2023, https://www.ose.state.nm.us/Legal/activeCases.php.

5. Perramond, *Unsettled Waters*.

6. Levine, "Dividing the Water."

7. Steven L. Danver, review of Bonnie G. Colby, John E. Thorsen, and Sarah Britton, eds., *Negotiating Tribal Water Rights: Fulfilling Promises in the Arid West*, *Journal of the West* 44, no. 4 (2005); John E. Thorson, Sarah Britton, and Bonnie G. Colby, eds., *Tribal Water Rights: Essays in Contemporary Law, Policy, and Economics* (Tucson: University of Arizona Press, 2006).

8. The New Mexico Acequia Association (NMAA) maintains a robust agenda of legislative priorities at "Legislative Updates," accessed 19 May 2023, https://lasacequias.org/legislative-updates/. NMAA priorities and talking points illustrate the range, complexity, and creativity involved in attempts to enact change within the current legal structure.

9. Ira Clark, "What Authority Should Reside in the State Engineer? New Mexico as a Case Study," *Natural Resources Journal* 32, no. 3 (1992).

10. Bruce Thomson and Scott Verhines, "New Mexico's Top Water Official Should Be a Licensed Engineer," Opinion, *Albuquerque Journal*, 3 February 2022, accessed 24 May 2023, https://www.abqjournal.com/2466858/new-mexicos-top-water-official-should-be-a-licensed-engineer.html.

11. An act relating to water; amending the eligibility requirements for the position of State Engineer to include geohydrologists, hydrologists, geologists and attorneys. H.B. 83, 55th NM Leg., 2d Sess., accessed 19 March 2022, https://www.nmlegis.gov/Sessions/22%20Regular/bills/house/HB0083.pdf. Representative Andrea Romero introduced this bill, but it never advanced beyond committee assignment.

12. For example, Red Nation, *The Red Deal: Indigenous Action to Save Our Earth* (Brooklyn, NY: Common Notions, 2021); Pueblo Action Alliance, "#Waterback Manifesto," 2021, accessed 19 March 2022, www.puebloactionalliance.org/water-back; New

Mexico Acequia Association, "Legislative Updates," accessed 27 May 2023, https://lasacequias.org/legislative-updates/.

13. Cajete, *Native Science*; Robin Wall Kimmerer, "The Fortress, the River and the Garden: A New Metaphor for Cultivating Mutualistic Relationship between Scientific and Traditional Ecological Knowledge," in *Contemporary Studies in Environmental and Indigenous Pedagogies: A Curricula [sic] of Stories and Place*, ed. Andrejs Kulnieks, Dan Roronhiakewen Longboat, and Kelly Young (Leiden: Brill, 2013).

14. Hicks and Peña, "Customary Practice and Community Governance," 188. See also Daniel McCool, "The River Commons: A New Era in U.S. Water Policy," *Texas Law Review* 83 (2005); Gibbs, "Just Add Water"; Hillary Hoffmann and Monte Mills, *A Third Way: Decolonizing the Laws of Indigenous Cultural Protection* (Cambridge: Cambridge University Press, 2020); Yazzie and Baldy, "Introduction: Indigenous Peoples and the Politics of Water"; Michelle Daigle, "Resurging through Kishiichiwan: The Spatial Politics of Indigenous Water Relations," *Decolonization: Indigeneity, Education & Society* 7 (2018).

15. Examples of this scholarship are cited throughout the book, including from authors such as Michael Alarid, Laura Gómez, Myrriah Gómez, Deena González, Felipe Gonzales, Enrique LaMadrid, Gabriel Meléndez, John Nieto-Phillips, Anna Nogar, Karen Roybal, Maurilio Vigil, and many more.

16. Sylvia Rodríguez, "Applied Research on Land and Water in New Mexico: A Critique," *Journal of the Southwest* 32, no. 3 (1990), 314.

17. The shooter, Steven Ray Baca, was not part of the militia, but militia members organized to protect him after he fired his weapon. I note that Baca's surname is of Nuevomexicano origin, but I was not able to find any information about his ethnic self-identification. Hannah Colton, "Protester Shot after Militiamen Raise Tensions at Oñate Monument," KUNM Radio, 2020, accessed 24 May 2023, https://www.kunm.org/local-news/2020-06-16/protester-shot-after-militiamen-raise-tensions-at-onate-monument; Matthew Reisen and Elise Kaplan, "City Removes Oñate statue after Monday's Violence," *Albuquerque Journal*, 16 June 2020, accessed 24 May 2023, https:www.abqjournal.com/news/local/city-removes-o-ate-statue-after-mondays-violence/article_e40199f4-dbc3-56c6-94f6-741bb09d79be.html. For an introduction to the complex identity politics that collide in memorials to Oñate, see Stan Alcorn, "Oñate's Foot," podcast audio, 99% Invisible, 46:23, 2018, accessed 19 May 2023, https://99percentinvisible.org/episode/onates-foot/.

Bibliography

Archival Sources

New Mexico Office of the State Engineer Library (Santa Fe, NM): Biennial Reports of the Territorial Irrigation Engineer, Biennial Reports of the Territorial Engineer.
New Mexico State Records Center and Archives (Santa Fe, NM): Records of the United States Territorial and New Mexico District Courts.
United States Library of Congress, Manuscript Division (Washington, DC): The Papers of Frederick Haynes Newell.
United States National Archives and Records Administration (Washington, DC): Records of the United States Geological Survey.

References Cited

Agnew, John. "Waterpower: Politics and the Geography of Water Provision." *Annals of the Association of American Geographers* 101, no. 3 (2011): 463–76.
Agrawal, Arun. *Environmentality: Technologies of Government and the Making of Subjects*. Durham, NC: Duke University Press, 2005.
Alarid, Michael J. *Hispano Bastion: New Mexican Power in the Age of Manifest Destiny, 1837–1860*. Albuquerque: University of New Mexico Press, 2022.
Alcorn, Stan. "Oñate's Foot." Podcast audio. 99% Invisible: 46 min., 23 sec., 2018. Accessed 27 May 2023. https://99percentinvisible.org/episode/onates-foot/.
Andrews, Eleanor, and James McCarthy. "Scale, Shale, and the State: Political Ecologies and Legal Geographies of Shale Gas Development in Pennsylvania." *Journal of Environmental Studies and Sciences* 4 (2014): 7–16.
Arellano, Anselmo F. *The Acequia and Agricultural Tradition of New Mexico: Prehistoric through the Present*. Guadalupita, NM: Center for Land Grant Studies, 1986.
Arellano, Juan Estevan. *Enduring Acequias: Wisdom of the Land, Knowledge of the Water*. Albuquerque: University of New Mexico Press, 2014.
Bacon, J. M. "Settler Colonialism as Eco-Social Structure and the Production of Colonial Ecological Violence." *Environmental Sociology* 5, no. 1 (2019): 59–69.
Balogh, Brian. "Scientific Forestry and the Roots of the Modern American State: Gifford Pinchot's Path to Progressive Reform." *Environmental History* 7, no. 2 (2002): 198–225.

Banister, Jeffrey M., and Stacie G. Widdifield. "The Debut of 'Modern Water' in Early 20th Century Mexico City: The Xochimilco Potable Waterworks." *Journal of Historical Geography* 46 (2014): 36–52.
Barker, Adam J. "The Contemporary Reality of Canadian Imperialism: Settler Colonialism and the Hybrid Colonial State." *American Indian Quarterly* 33, no. 3 (2009): 325–52.
———. "Locating Settler Colonialism." *Journal of Colonialism and Colonial History* 13, no. 3 (2012). Project MUSE database, doi:10.1353/cch.2012.0035.
Barrett, Elinore M. *Conquest and Catastrophe: Changing Rio Grande Pueblo Settlement Patterns in the Sixteenth and Seventeenth Centuries*. Albuquerque: University of New Mexico Press, 2002.
———. *The Spanish Colonial Settlement Landscapes of New Mexico, 1598–1680*. Albuquerque: University of New Mexico Press, 2012.
Bateman, Fiona, and Lionel Pilkington. *Studies in Settler Colonialism: Politics, Identity and Culture*. Basingstoke: Palgrave Macmillan, 2011.
Baxter, John O. *Dividing New Mexico's Waters, 1700–1912*. Albuquerque: University of New Mexico Press, 1996.
Bayer, Laura, Floyd Montoya, and the Pueblo of Santa Ana. *Santa Ana: The People, the Pueblo, and the History of Tamaya*. Albuquerque: University of New Mexico Press, 1994.
Beekman, Christopher S., Phil C. Weigand, and John J. Pint. "Old World Irrigation Technology in a New World Context: Qanats in Spanish Colonial Western Mexico." *Antiquity* 73, no. 280 (1999): 440–46.
Beene, Daniel R., and K. Maria D. Lane. "Unmappable Variables: GIS and the Complicated Historical Geography of Water in the Rio Grande Project." In *Historical Geography, GIScience and Textual Analysis: Landscapes of Time and Place*, edited by Charles Travis, Francis Ludlow, and Ferenc Gyuris, 163–77. Cham: Springer Nature, 2020.
Belich, James. *Replenishing the Earth: The Settler Revolution and the Rise of the Anglo-World, 1783–1939*. Oxford and New York: Oxford University Press, 2009.
Bell, Avril. *Relating Indigenous and Settler Identities: Beyond Domination*. London and New York: Palgrave Macmillan, 2014.
Bell, Morag, Robin Butlin, and Michael Heffernan, eds. *Geography and Imperialism, 1820–1940*. Manchester: Manchester University Press, 1995.
Bell, Martha G. "Historical Political Ecology of Water: Access to Municipal Drinking Water in Colonial Lima, Peru (1578–1700)." *Professional Geographer* 67, no. 4 (2015): 504–26.
Beltrán, Gonzalo Aguirre. "The Slave Trade in Mexico." *Hispanic American Historical Review* 24, no. 3 (1944): 412–31.
Benson, Melinda Harm. "The *Tulare* Case: Water Rights, the Endangered Species Act, and the Fifth Amendment." *Environmental Law* 32, no. 3 (2002): 551–87.
Benton, Laura. *A Search for Sovereignty: Law and Geography in European Empires, 1400–1900*. Cambridge: Cambridge University Press, 2010.
Biolsi, Thomas. "Imagined Geographies: Sovereignty, Indigenous Space, and American Indian Struggle." *American Ethnologist* 32, no. 2 (2005): 239–59.
Birch, Kean, and Fabian Muniesa, eds. *Assetization: Turning Things into Assets in Technoscientific Capitalism*. Cambridge, MA: MIT Press, 2020.
Biswas, Asit K. *History of Hydrology*. Amsterdam: North-Holland, 1970.

Blomley, Nicholas K. *Law, Space, and the Geographies of Power*. New York: Guilford Press, 1994.

———. "Simplification Is Complicated: Property, Nature, and the Rivers of Law." *Environment and Planning A* 40 (2008): 1825–42.

Blomley, Nicholas, David Delaney, and Richard T. Ford, eds. *The Legal Geographies Reader: Law, Power, and Space*. Oxford: Blackwell, 2001.

Boelens, Rutgerd, and Paul H. Gelles. "Cultural Politics, Communal Resistance and Identity in Andean Irrigation Development." *Bulletin of Latin American Research* 24, no. 3 (2005): 311–27.

Bokum, Consuelo. "Implementing the Public Welfare Requirement in New Mexico's Water Code." *Natural Resources Journal* 36, no. 4 (1996): 681–713.

Bowman, Timothy P. *Blood Oranges: Colonialism and Agriculture in the South Texas Borderlands*. College Station: Texas A&M University Press, 2016.

Boyle, Susan Calafate. *Los Capitalistas: Hispano Merchants and the Santa Fe Trade*. Albuquerque: University of New Mexico Press, 1997.

Brady, Mary Pat. "'Full of Empty': Creating the Southwest as 'Terra Incognita.'" In *Nineteenth-Century Geographies: The Transformation of Space from the Victorian Age to the American Century*, edited by Helena Michie and Ronald R. Thomas, 251–64. New Brunswick, NJ: Rutgers University Press, 2003.

Brannstrom, Christian. "What Kind of History for What Kind of Political Ecology?" *Historical Geography* 32 (2004): 71–87.

Braun, Bruce. "Colonialism's Afterlife: Vision and Visuality on the Northwest Coast." *Cultural Geographies* 9, no. 2 (2002): 202–47.

Braun, Bruce Willems. "Buried Epistemologies: The Politics of Nature in (Post) Colonial British Columbia." *Annals of the Association of American Geographers* 87, no. 1 (1997): 3–31.

Bretsen, Stephen N., and Peter J. Hill. "Irrigation Institutions in the American West." *UCLA Journal of Environmental Law and Policy* 25, no. 2 (2007): 283–331.

Briggs, Charles L., and John R. Van Ness. *Land, Water, and Culture: New Perspectives on Hispanic Land Grants*. 1st ed. Albuquerque: University of New Mexico Press, 1987.

Brown, Tracy L. *Pueblo Indians and Spanish Colonial Authority in Eighteenth-Century New Mexico*. Tucson: University of Arizona Press, 2013.

Budds, Jessica. "Contested H_2O: Science, Policy and Politics in Water Resources Management in Chile." *Geoforum* 40, no. 3 (2009): 418–30.

Burke, Peter. *What Is the History of Knowledge?* Cambridge: Polity Press, 2016.

Burow, Paul Berne, Samara Brock, and Michael R. Dove. "Unsettling the Land: Indigeneity, Ontology, and Hybridity in Settler Colonialism." *Environment and Society* 9, no. 1 (2018): 57–74.

Byrd, Jodi A. *The Transit of Empire: Indigenous Critiques of Colonialism*. Minneapolis: University of Minnesota Press, 2011.

Caffey, David L. *Chasing the Santa Fe Ring: Power and Privilege in Territorial New Mexico*. Albuquerque: University of New Mexico Press, 2014.

Cajete, Gregory. *Native Science: Natural Laws of Interdependence*. Santa Fe, NM: Clear Light, 2000.

Cañizares-Esguerra, Jorge. *How to Write the History of the New World: Histories, Epistemologies, and Identities in the Eighteenth-Century Atlantic World*. Stanford, CA: Stanford University Press, 2001.

Carey, Mark, M. Jackson, Alessandro Antonello, and Jaclyn Rushing. "Glaciers, Gender, and Science: A Feminist Glaciology Framework for Global Environmental Change Research." *Progress in Human Geography* 40, no. 6 (2016): 770–93.

Carlson, Alvar W. *The Spanish-American Homeland: Four Centuries in New Mexico's Rio Arriba*. Baltimore, MD: Johns Hopkins University Press, 1990.

Carroll, Clint. "Native Enclosures: Tribal National Parks and the Progressive Politics of Environmental Stewardship in Indian Country." *Geoforum* 53 (2014): 31–40.

Carse, Ashley. "Nature as Infrastructure: Making and Managing the Panama Canal Watershed." *Social Studies of Science* 42, no. 4 (2012): 539–63.

Chang, Kornel S. Review of *Progressive New World: How Settler Colonialism and Transpacific Exchange Shaped American Reform*, by Marilyn Lake. *Labor: Studies in Working-Class History of the Americas* 17, no. 3 (2020): 142–44.

Clapperton, Jonathan. "Naturalizing Race Relations: Conservation, Colonialism, and Spectacle at the Banff Indian Days." *Canadian Historical Review* 94, no. 3 (2013): 349–79.

Clark, Ira. "What Authority Should Reside in the State Engineer? New Mexico as a Case Study." *Natural Resources Journal* 32, no. 3 (1992): 467–86.

Clark, Ira G. *Water in New Mexico: A History of Its Management and Use*. Albuquerque: University of New Mexico Press, 1987.

Clayton, Daniel. "The Question of Making Native Space" [guest editorial]. *BC Studies: The British Columbian Quarterly* 138–39 (Summer–Autumn 2003): 5–11.

Colton, Hannah. "Protester Shot after Militiamen Raise Tensions at Oñate Monument." KUNM Radio, 2020. Accessed 24 May 2023. https://www.kunm.org/local-news/2020-06-16/protester-shot-after-militiamen-raise-tensions-at-onate-monument.

Coombs, Annie E., ed. *Rethinking Settler Colonialism: History and Memory in Australia, Canada, Aotearoa New Zealand and South Africa*. Manchester: Manchester University Press, 2006.

Correia, David. "The Etiology of Rangeland Degradation in Northern New Mexico: A Critique of Establishment Explanations." *Southwestern Geographer* 8 (2004): 35–63.

———. "From Agropastoralism to Sustained Yield Forestry: Industrial Restructuring, Rural Change, and the Land-Grant Commons in Northern New Mexico." *Capitalism Nature Socialism* 16, no. 1 (2005): 25–44.

———. "Making Destiny Manifest: United States Territorial Expansion and the Dispossession of Two Mexican Property Claims in New Mexico, 1824–1899." *Journal of Historical Geography* 35, no. 1 (2009): 87–103.

———. *Properties of Violence: Law and Land Grant Struggle in Northern New Mexico*. Athens: University of Georgia Press, 2013.

———. "The Sustained Yield Forest Management Act and the Roots of Environmental Conflict in Northern New Mexico." *Geoforum* 38, no. 5 (2007): 1040–51.

Coulthard, Glen S. "Subjects of Empire: Indigenous Peoples and the 'Politics of Recognition' in Canada." *Contemporary Political Theory* 6, no. 4 (2007): 437–60.

Cox, Shaphan, Christina Birdsall-Jones, Roy Jones, Thor Kerr, and Steve Mickler. "Indigenous Persistence and Entitlement: Noongar Occupations in Central Perth, 1988–1989 and 2012." *Journal of Historical Geography* 54 (2016): 13–23.

Curley, Andrew. "Infrastructures as Colonial Beachheads: The Central Arizona Project and the Taking of Navajo Resources." *Environment and Planning D: Society and Space* 39, no. 3 (2021): 387–404.

———."'Our Winters' Rights': Challenging Colonial Water Laws." *Global Environmental Politics* 19, no. 3 (2019): 57–76.

———. "Unsettling Indian Water Settlements: The Little Colorado River, the San Juan River, and Colonial Enclosures." *Antipode* 53, no. 3 (2019): 705–23.

Curry, George. *Report of the Governor of New Mexico to the Secretary of the Interior, for the Fiscal Year Ended June 30, 1908.* Washington, DC: Government Printing Office, 1908.

Daigle, Michelle. "Resurging through Kishiichiwan: The Spatial Politics of Indigenous Water Relations." *Decolonization: Indigeneity, Education & Society* 7 (2018): 159–72.

Dalley, Hamish. "The Deaths of Settler Colonialism: Extinction as a Metaphor of Decolonization in Contemporary Settler Literature." *Settler Colonial Studies* 8, no. 1 (2018): 30–46.

Danver, Steven L. Review of Bonnie G. Colby, John E. Thorsen, and Sarah Britton, eds., *Negotiating Tribal Water Rights: Fulfilling Promises in the Arid West*. *Journal of the West* 44, no. 4 (2005): 91–92.

Daston, Lorraine. "The History of Science and the History of Knowledge." *KNOW: A Journal on the Formation of Knowledge* 1, no. 1 (2017): 131–54.

Davies, Gail. "Mobilizing Experimental Life: Spaces of Becoming with Mutant Mice." *Theory, Culture & Society* 30, nos. 7–8 (2013): 129–53.

Davis, Arthur Powell. *Irrigation Works Constructed by the United States Government*. 1st ed. New York: John Wiley & Sons, 1917.

Davis, Diana K. "Historical Political Ecology: On the Importance of Looking Back to Move Forward." *Geoforum* 40, no. 3 (2009): 285–86.

de Leeuw, Sarah. "Alice through the Looking Glass: Emotion, Personal Connection, and Reading Colonial Archives along the Grain." *Journal of Historical Geography* 38, no. 3 (2012): 273–81.

de Leeuw, Sarah, Margo Greenwood, and Nicole Lindsay. "Troubling Good Intentions." *Settler Colonial Studies* 3, nos. 3–4 (2013): 381–94.

deBuys, William. *Enchantment and Exploitation: The Life and Hard Times of a New Mexico Mountain Range*. Albuquerque: University of New Mexico Press, 1985.

DeJong, David H. *Stealing the Gila: The Pima Agricultural Economy and Water Deprivation, 1848–1921*. Tucson: University of Arizona Press, 2009.

del Castillo, Richard Griswold. *The Treaty of Guadalupe Hidalgo: A Legacy of Conflict*. Norman: University of Oklahoma Press, 1992.

Delaney, David. *Law and Nature*. Cambridge: Cambridge University Press, 2003.

———. *Nomospheric Investigations: The Spatial, the Legal and the Pragmatics of World-Making*. New York: Routledge, 2011.

Delbourgo, James. "The Knowing World: A New Global History of Science." *History of Science* 57, no. 3 (2019): 373–99.

Deloria, Vine, Jr. *Red Earth, White Lies: Native Americans and the Myth of Scientific Fact*. Golden, CO: Fulcrum, 1997.

Denetdale, Jennifer Nez. *Reclaiming Diné History: The Legacies of Navajo Chief Manuelito and Juanita*. Tucson: University of Arizona Press, 2007.

deVos, Hugo, Rutgerd Boelens, and Rocio Bustamante. "Formal Law and Local Water Control in the Andean Region: A Fiercely Contested Field." *Water Resources Development* 22, no. 1 (2006): 37–48.

Dippie, Brian W. *The Vanishing American: White Attitudes and U.S. Indian Policy*. Middletown, CT: Wesleyan University Press, 1982.

Domosh, Mona. "The World Was Never Flat: Early Global Encounters and the Messiness of Empire." *Progress in Human Geography* 34, no. 4 (2010): 419–35.

Donovan, Amy, and Clive Oppenheimer. "At the Mercy of the Mountain? Field Stations and the Culture of Volcanology." *Environment and Planning A* 47, no. 1 (2015): 156–71.

Doolittle, William E. *Cultivated Landscapes of Native North America*. Oxford and New York: Oxford University Press, 2000.

Drayton, Richard Harry. *Nature's Government: Science, Imperial Britain, and the "Improvement" of the World*. New Haven, CT: Yale University Press, 2000.

Drinnon, Richard. *Facing West: The Metaphysics of Indian-Hating and Empire-Building*. Minneapolis: University of Minnesota Press, 1980.

Driver, Felix. *Geography Militant: Cultures of Exploration and Empire*. Oxford: Blackwell, 2001.

Dumitrescu, Sorin, and Jaromir Nemec. "Hyrdology: A Look Back and a Look Forward." In *Three Centuries of Scientific Hydrology: Key Papers Submitted on the Occasion of the Celebration of the Tercentenary of Scientific Hydrology*, 16–20. Paris: UNESCO-WMO/OMM-IAHS/AISH, 1974.

Dunbar-Ortiz, Roxanne. *An Indigenous Peoples' History of the United States*. Boston: Beacon, 2014.

———. *Roots of Resistance: A History of Land Tenure in New Mexico*. Norman: University of Oklahoma Press, 2007.

Duncan, James, and Derek Gregory, eds. *Writes of Passage: Reading Travel Writing*. London: Routledge, 1999.

Dupré, John. "Metaphysical Disorder and Scientific Disunity." In *The Disunity of Science: Boundaries, Contexts, and Power*, edited by Peter Galison and David J. Stump, 101–17. Stanford, CA: Stanford University Press, 1996.

Ebright, Malcolm. *Land Grants and Lawsuits in Northern New Mexico*. Albuquerque: University of New Mexico Press, 1994.

———. "Sharing the Shortages: Water Litigation and Regulation in Hispanic New Mexico, 1600–1850." *New Mexico Historical Review* 76, no. 1 (2001): 3–45.

Ebright, Malcom, and Rick Hendricks. *Pueblo Sovereignty: Indian Land and Water in New Mexico and Texas*. Norman: University of Oklahoma Press, 2019.

Edmonds, Penelope. "Unpacking Settler Colonialism's Urban Strategies: Indigenous Peoples in Victoria, British Columbia, and the Transition to a Settler-Colonial City." *Urban History Review/Revue d'histoire urbaine* 38, no. 2 (2010): 4–20.

Edney, Matthew H. *Mapping an Empire: The Geographical Construction of British India, 1765–1843*. Chicago: University of Chicago Press, 1997.

Egan, Brian, and Jessica Place. "Minding the Gaps: Property, Geography, and Indigenous Peoples in Canada." *Geoforum* 44, no. 1 (2013): 129–38.

Elkins, Caroline, and Susan Pederson, eds. *Settler Colonialism in the Twentieth Century: Projects, Practices, Legacies*. New York: Routledge, 2005.

Espeland, Wendy Nelson. "Bureaucratizing Democracy, Democratizing Bureaucracy." *Law and Social Inquiry* 25, no. 4 (2000): 1077–109.

———. "Legal Structure in Colonial Encounters: Bureaucratizing Culture and the Environment in the American Southwest." In *Abf Working Papers #9512*, 1–34. Chicago: American Bar Foundation, 1996.

Espinosa, J. Manuel. *The Pueblo Indian Revolt of 1696 and the Franciscan Missions in New Mexico: Letters of the Missionaries and Related Documents*. Norman: University of Oklahoma Press, 1988.

Estes, Nick. *Our History Is the Future: Standing Rock versus the Dakota Access Pipeline, and the Long Tradition of Indigenous Resistance*. London: Verso, 2019.

Farmer, Jared. *Glen Canyon Dammed: Inventing Lake Powell and the Canyon Country*. Tucson: University of Arizona Press, 1999.

Fiege, Mark. *Irrigated Eden: The Making of an Agricultural Landscape in the American West*. Seattle: University of Washington Press, 1999.

Finnegan, Diarmid A. "Finding a Scientific Voice: Performing Science, Space and Speech in the 19th Century." *Transactions of the Institute of British Geographers* 42, no. 2 (2017): 192–205.

Follansbee, Robert. *A History of the Water Resources Branch of the United States Geological Survey to June 30, 1919*. Washington, DC, 1939.

Fonseca-Chávez, Vanessa, Levi Romero, and Spencer R. Herrera, eds. *Querencia: Reflections on the New Mexico Homeland*. Albuquerque: University of New Mexico Press, 2020.

Forbes, Jack D. *Apache, Navaho, and Spaniard*. Civilization of the American Indian 115. Norman: University of Oklahoma Press, 1960.

Forsyth, Tim. *Critical Political Ecology: The Politics of Environmental Science*. London: Routledge, 2003.

Francaviglia, Richard. "Elusive Land: Changing Geographic Images of the Southwest." In *Essays on the Changing Images of the Southwest*, edited by Richard Francaviglia and David Narrett, 8–39. College Station: Texas A&M University Press, 1994.

Frazier, Arthur H., and Wilbur Heckler. *Embudo, New Mexico, Birthplace of Systematic Stream Gaging*. Geological Survey Professional Paper 778. Washington, DC: U.S. Government Printing Office, 1972.

Gallegos, Juan Martín. "Reconstructing Identity/Revising Resistance: A History of Nuevomexicano/a Students at New Mexico Highlands University, 1910–1973." Ph.D. diss., University of Arizona, 2013.

Gascoigne, John. *Science and the State*. Cambridge: Cambridge University Press, 2019.

Gerhard, Peter. *The North Frontier of New Spain*. Princeton, NJ: Princeton University Press, 1982.

Gibbs, Leah M. "Just Add Water: Colonisation, Water Governance, and the Australian Inland." *Environment and Planning A* 41, no. 12 (2009): 2964–83.

Glick, Thomas F. *Irrigation and Society in Medieval Valencia*. Cambridge, MA: Belknap Press of Harvard University Press, 1970.

Godlewska, Anne, and Neil Smith. *Geography and Empire*. Oxford: Blackwell, 1994.

Goeman, Mishuana. "The Tools of a Cartographic Poet: Unmapping Settler Colonialism in Joy Harjo's Poetry." *Settler Colonial Studies* 2, no. 2 (2012): 89–112.

Goldstein, Alyosha, and Alex Lubin, eds. "Settler Colonialism." Special issue, *South Atlantic Quarterly* 107, no. 4 (2008).

Gómez, Laura E. *Manifest Destinies: The Making of the Mexican American Race*. 2nd ed. New York: New York University Press, 2018.

Gómez, Myrriah. *Nuclear Nuevo México: Colonialism and the Effects of the Nuclear Industrial Complex on Nuevomexicanos*. Tucson: University of Arizona Press, 2022.

Gonzales, Manuel G., and Thomas Joseph Price. *The Hispanic Elite of the Southwest*. Southwestern Studies 86. El Paso: Texas Western Press, 1989.

Gonzales, Phillip B. "Struggle for Survival: The Hispanic Land Grants of New Mexico, 1848–2001." *Agricultural History* 77, no. 2 (2003): 293–324.

———. "Whither the Nuevomexicanos: The Career of a Southwestern Intellectual Discourse, 1907–2004." *Social Science Journal* 43, no. 2 (2006): 273–86.

González, Deena J. *Refusing the Favor: The Spanish-Mexican Women of Santa Fe, 1820–1880*. Oxford and New York: Oxford University Press, 1999.

Gordon, Neve, and Moriel Ram. "Ethnic Cleansing and the Formation of Settler Colonial Geographies." *Political Geography* 53 (July 2016): 20–29.

Greenhough, Beth. "Citizenship, Care and Companionship: Approaching Geographies of Health and Bioscience." *Progress in Human Geography* 35, no. 2 (2011): 153–71.

———. "Tales of an Island-Laboratory: Defining the Field in Geography and Science Studies." *Transactions of the Institute of British Geographers* 31, no. 2 (2006): 224–37.

Gregory, Derek. *Geographical Imaginations*. Oxford: Blackwell, 1994.

Griffiths, Tom, and Libby Robin, eds. *Ecology and Empire: Environmental History of Settler Societies*. Edinburgh: Keele University Press, 1997.

Gutiérrez, Ramón A. *When Jesus Came, the Corn Mothers Went Away: Marriage, Sexuality, and Power in New Mexico, 1500–1846*. Stanford, CA: Stanford University Press, 1991.

Hagerman, H. J. *Report of the Governor of New Mexico to the Secretary of the Interior, for the Year Ended June 30, 1906*. Washington, DC: Government Printing Office, 1906.

Hall, G. Emlen. "The Forest Service and Western Water Rights: An Intimate Portrait of *United States v. New Mexico*." *Natural Resources Journal* 45, no. 4 (2005): 979–1051.

———. *Four Leagues of Pecos: A Legal History of the Pecos Grant, 1800–1933*. Albuquerque: University of New Mexico Press, 1984.

Hämäläinen, Pekka. *The Comanche Empire*. New Haven, CT: Yale University Press, 2008.

Hammond, George P., and Agapito Rey, eds. and trans. *Don Juan de Oñate: Colonizer of New Mexico, 1595–1628; In Two Parts*. Vol. 1. Coronado Cuarto Centennial Publications, 1540–1940, 5 and 6. Albuquerque: University of New Mexico Press, 1953.

Hannah, Matthew G. *Governmentality and the Mastery of Territory in Nineteenth-Century America*. Cambridge: Cambridge University Press, 2000.

———. "Space and Social Control in the Administration of the Oglala Lakota ('Sioux'), 1871–1879." *Journal of Historical Geography* 19, no. 4 (1993): 412–32.

Hansen, Karen V., Ken Chih-Yan Sun, and Debra Osnowitz. "Immigrants as Settler Colonists: Boundary Work between Dakota Indians and White Immigrant Settlers." *Ethnic and Racial Studies* 40, no. 11 (2017): 1919–38.

Haraway, Donna. *Simians, Cyborgs, and Women: The Reinvention of Nature*. New York: Routledge, 2013.

Harley, J. B. "Maps, Knowledge, and Power." In *The Iconography of Landscape: Essays on the Symbolic Representation, Design and Use of Past Environments*, edited by Denis Cosgrove and Stephen Daniels, 277–312. Cambridge: Cambridge University Press, 1988.

Harris, Cole. *Making Native Space: Colonialism, Resistance and Reserves in British Columbia*. Vancouver: University of British Columbia Press, 2002.

Hays, Samuel P. *Conservation and the Gospel of Efficiency: The Progressive Conservation Movement, 1890–1920*. Originally published 1959. Pittsburgh, PA: University of Pittsburgh Press, 1999.

Henke, Christopher R., and Thomas F. Gieryn. "Sites of Scientific Practice: The Enduring Importance of Place." In *New Handbook of Science and Technology Studies*, edited by Edward J. Hackett, Olga Amsterdamska, Michael Lynch, and Judy Wajcman, 353–76. Cambridge, MA: MIT Press, 2008.

Hicks, Gregory A., and Devon G. Peña. "Customary Practice and Community Governance in Implementing the Human Right to Water—The Case of the Acequia Communities of Colorado's Rio Culebra Watershed." *Willamette Journal of International Law and Dispute Resolution* 18, no. 2 (2010): 185–210.

Hixson, Walter L. *American Settler Colonialism: A History*. New York: Palgrave Macmillan, 2013.

Hoffmann, Hillary, and Monte Mills. *A Third Way: Decolonizing the Laws of Indigenous Cultural Protection*. Cambridge: Cambridge University Press, 2020.

Holder, Jane, and Carolyn Harrison, eds. *Law and Geography*. Oxford and New York: Oxford University Press, 2003.

Hoogeveen, Dawn. "Sub-Surface Property, Free-Entry Mineral Staking and Settler Colonialism in Canada." *Antipode* 47, no. 1 (2015): 121–38.

Hunt, Dallas, and Shaun A. Stevenson. "Decolonizing Geographies of Power: Indigenous Digital Counter-Mapping Practices on Turtle Island." *Settler Colonial Studies* 7, no. 3 (2017): 372–92.

Hurt, R. Douglas. *Indian Agriculture in America: Prehistory to the Present*. Lawrence: University Press of Kansas, 1987.

Inwood, Joshua, and Anne Bonds. "Confronting White Supremacy and a Militaristic Pedagogy in the U.S. Settler Colonial State." *Annals of the American Association of Geographers* 106, no. 3 (2016): 521–29.

Inwood, Joshua F. J., and Anne Bonds. "Property and Whiteness: The Oregon Standoff and the Contradictions of the U.S. Settler State." *Space and Polity* 21, no. 3 (2017): 253–68.

Isaki, Bianca. "State Conservation as Settler Colonial Governance at Kaʻena Point, Hawaiʻi." *Environmental and Earth Law Journal* 3, no. 1 (2013): 57–125.

Jacoby, Karl. "The Broad Platform of Extermination." In *North American Borderlands: Rewriting Histories*, edited by Brian DeLay, 284–304. New York: Routledge, 2013.

Jasanoff, Sheila. *The Fifth Branch: Science Advisers as Policymakers*. Cambridge, MA: Harvard University Press, 1990.

———. *Science at the Bar: Law, Science, and Technology in America*. Cambridge, MA: Harvard University Press, 1995, 1995.

———, ed. *States of Knowledge: The Co-Production of Science and the Social Order*. London: Routledge, 2004.

Jasanoff, Sheila, and Sang-Hyun Kim. *Dreamscapes of Modernity: Sociotechnical Imaginaries and the Fabrication of Power*. Chicago: University of Chicago Press, 2015.

Jepson, Wendy. "Claiming Space, Claiming Water: Contested Legal Geographies of

Water in South Texas." *Annals of the Association of American Geographers* 102, no. 3 (2012): 614–31.

Johnson, Benjamin. "Environment: Nature, Conservation, and the Progressive State." In *A Companion to the Gilded Age and Progressive Era*, edited by Christopher McKnight Nichols and Nancy C. Unger, 71–83. Chichester: John Wiley & Sons, 2017.

Kanazawa, Mark. *Golden Rules: The Origins of California Water Law in the Gold Rush*. Chicago: University of Chicago Press, 2015.

Kapoor, Maya. "Ancestral Pueblo Logging Practices Could Save New Mexico Pinelands." *High Country News*, 11 December 2017.

Kauanui, J. Kēhaulani. "'A Structure, Not an Event': Settler Colonialism and Enduring Indigeneity." *Lateral* 5, no. 1 (2016): 1–8.

Kiernan, Ben. *Blood and Soil: A World History of Genocide and Extermination from Sparta to Darfur*. New Haven, CT: Yale University Press, 2007.

Kimmerer, Robin Wall "The Fortress, the River and the Garden: A New Metaphor for Cultivating Mutualistic Relationship between Scientific and Traditional Ecological Knowledge." In *Contemporary Studies in Environmental and Indigenous Pedagogies: A Curricula [sic] of Stories and Place*, edited by Andrejs Kulnieks, Dan Roronhiakewen Longboat, and Kelly Young, 49–76. Leiden: Brill, 2013.

Kimmerer, Robin Wall, and Frank Kanawha Lake. "The Role of Indigenous Burning in Land Management." *Journal of Forestry* 99, no. 11 (2001): 36–41.

Kirsch, Scott. "John Wesley Powell and the Mapping of the Colorado Plateau, 1869–1879: Survey Science, Geographical Solutions, and the Economy of Environmental Values." *Annals of the Association of American Geographers* 92, no. 3 (2002): 548–72.

Klinger, Lee. "Ecological Evidence of Large-Scale Silviculture by California Indians." In *Unlearning the Language of Conquest: Scholars Expose Anti-Indianism in America*, edited by Four Arrows (Don Trent Jacobs), 153–65. Austin: University of Texas Press, 2006.

Kolsky, Elizabeth. *Colonial Justice in British India: White Violence and the Rule of Law*. Cambridge: Cambridge University Press, 2010.

Korte, Alvin O. *Nosotros: A Study of Everyday Meaning in Hispano New Mexico*. East Lansing: Michigan State University Press, 2012.

Kosek, Jake. *Understories: The Political Life of Forests in Northern New Mexico*. Durham, NC: Duke University Press, 2006.

Kurtz, Matthew. "Situating Practices: The Archive and the File Cabinet." *Historical Geography* 29 (2001): 26–37.

Laforge, Julia M. L., and Stéphane M. McLachlan. "Environmentality on the Canadian Prairies: Settler-Farmer Subjectivities and Agri-Environmental Objects." *Antipode* 50, no. 2 (2018): 359–83.

Lahti, Janne. *Wars for Empire: Apaches, the United States, and the Southwest Borderlands*. Norman: University of Oklahoma Press, 2017.

Lake, Marilyn. *Progressive New World: How Settler Colonialism and Transpacific Exchange Shaped American Reform*. Cambridge, MA: Harvard University Press, 2019.

Lane, K. Maria D. "Bridging the Florida Keys: Engineering an Environmental Transformation, 1904–1912." In *The American Environment Revisited: Environmental Historical Geographies of the United States*, edited by Geoffrey L. Buckley and Yolonda Youngs, 235–54. Lanham, MD: Rowman & Littlefield, 2018.

———. "Commentary: Old and New." In "Interdisciplinary Research on Past Environments through the Lens of Historical-Critical Physical Geographies," special issue, *Historical Geography* 46 (2019): 151–59.

———. "Engineering." In *The Sage Handbook of Historical Geography*, edited by Mona Domosh, Michael Heffernan, and Charles W. J. Withers, 698–719. London: Sage, 2020.

———. "Reading Boulder Dam: Landscape Alteration as National Transformation in 1930s America." *Aether* 11 (2013): 102–26.

———. "Water, Technology, and the Courtroom: Negotiating Reclamation Policy in Territorial New Mexico." *Journal of Historical Geography* 37, no. 3 (2011): 300–311.

Langston, Nancy. *Forest Dreams, Forest Nightmares: The Paradox of Old Growth in the Inland West*. Seattle: University of Washington Press, 1995.

Latour, Bruno. *Science in Action: How to Follow Scientists and Engineers through Society*. Milton Keynes: Open University Press, 1987.

Lave, Rebecca, Christine Biermann, and Stuart N. Lane. *The Palgrave Handbook of Critical Physical Geography*. New York: Springer, 2018.

Lave, Rebecca, Matthew W. Wilson, Elizabeth S. Barron, et al. "Intervention: Critical Physical Geography." *Canadian Geographer/Géographe canadien* 58, no. 1 (2014): 1–10.

Leddy, Lianne C. "*Dibaajimowinan* as Method: Environmental History, Indigenous Scholarship, and Balancing Sources." In *Methodological Challenges in Nature-Culture and Environmental History Research*, edited by Jocelyn Thorpe, Stephanie Rutherford, and L. Anders Sandberg, 93–104. New York: Routledge, 2017.

Legg, Stephen. "Legal Geographies and the State of Imperialism: Environments, Constitutions, and Violence." *Journal of Historical Geography* 37, no. 4 (2011): 505–8.

Lehman, Jessica. "Making an Anthropocene Ocean: Synoptic Geographies of the International Geophysical Year (1957–1958)." *Annals of the American Association of Geographers* 110, no. 3 (2020): 606–22.

Lehmkuhl, Ursula. "Good Land—Bad Land: Ecological Knowledge and the Settling of the Old Northwest, 1755–1805." *Settler Colonial Studies* 7, no. 2 (2017): 141–63.

Levine, Frances. "Dividing the Water: The Impact of Water Rights Adjudication on New Mexican Communities." *Journal of the Southwest* 32, no. 3 (1990): 268–77.

Leyva, Yolanda. "Monuments of Conformity: Commemorating and Protesting Oñate on the Border." *New Mexico Historical Review* 82, no. 3 (2007): 343–67.

Liebmann, Matthew J., Joshua Farella, Christopher I. Roos, Adam Stack, Sarah Martini, and Thomas W. Swetnam. "Native American Depopulation, Reforestation, and Fire Regimes in the Southwest United States, 1492–1900 CE." *Proceedings of the National Academy of Sciences of the United States of America* 113, no. 6 (2016): E696–E704.

Limerick, Patricia Nelson. *The Legacy of Conquest: The Unbroken Past of the American West*. New York: W. W. Norton, 1987.

———. *Something in the Soil: Legacies and Reckonings in the New West*. New York: W. W. Norton, 2000.

Livingstone, David N. *Dealing with Darwin: Place, Politics, and Rhetoric in Religious Engagements with Evolution*. Baltimore, MD: Johns Hopkins University Press, 2014.

———. "Putting Geography in Its Place." *Australian Geographical Studies* 38, no. 1 (2000): 1–9.
———. "The Spaces of Knowledge: Contributions towards a Historical Geography of Science." *Environment and Planning D: Society and Space* 13, no. 1 (1995): 5–34.
Lorimer, Hayden, and Nick Spedding. "Locating Field Science: A Geographical Family Expedition to Glen Roy, Scotland." *British Journal for the History of Science* 38 (2005): 13–33.
Mabry, Jonathan B., and David A. Cleveland. "The Relevance of Indigenous Irrigation: A Comparative Analysis of Sustainability." In *Canals and Communities: Small-Scale Irrigation Systems*, edited by Jonathan B. Mabry, 227–60. Tucson: University of Arizona Press, 1996.
MacDonnell, Lawrence J. "Return to the River: Environmental Flow Policy in the United States and Canada." *Journal of the American Water Resources Association* 45, no. 5 (2009): 1087–99.
Maddison, Sarah, Tom Clark, and Ravi de Costa, eds. *The Limits of Settler Colonial Reconciliation: Non-Indigenous People and the Responsibility to Engage*. Singapore: Springer Nature, 2016.
Mahony, Martin, and Mike Hulme. "Epistemic Geographies of Climate Change: Science, Space and Politics." *Progress in Human Geography* 42, no. 3 (2018): 395–424.
Manning, Susan M. "Contrasting Colonisations: (Re)Storying Newfoundland/ Ktaqmkuk as Place." *Settler Colonial Studies* 8, no. 3 (2018): 314–31.
Mar, Tracey Banivanua, and Penelope Edmonds, eds. *Making Settler Colonial Space: Perspectives on Race, Place and Identity*. Basingstoke: Palgrave Macmillan, 2010.
Martínez, Ignacio. "Settler Colonialism in New Spain and the Early Mexican Republic." In *The Routledge Handbook of the History of Settler Colonialism*, edited by Edward Cavanagh and Lorenzo Veracini, 109–24. Abingdon and New York: Routledge, 2017.
Matsui, Kenichi. *Native Peoples and Water Rights: Irrigation, Dams, and the Law in Western Canada*. McGill-Queen's Native and Northern Series 55. Montreal and Ithaca, NY: McGill-Queen's University Press, 2009.
Mawani, Renisa. "Law, Settler Colonialism, and 'the Forgotten Space' of Maritime Worlds." *Annual Review of Law and Social Science* 12 (2016): 107–31.
Mayhew, Robert J., and Charles W. J. Withers. *Geographies of Knowledge: Science, Scale, and Spatiality in the Nineteenth Century*. Baltimore, MD: Johns Hopkins University Press, 2020.
McClellan, James. *Colonialism and Science: Saint Domingue in the Old Regimes*. Chicago: University of Chicago Press, 2010.
McCool, Daniel. *Native Waters: Contemporary Indian Water Settlements and the Second Treaty Era*. Tucson: University of Arizona Press, 2002.
———. "The River Commons: A New Era in U.S. Water Policy." *Texas Law Review* 83 (2005): 1903–27.
———. "Winters Comes Home to Roost." In *Fluid Arguments: Five Centuries of Western Water Conflict*, edited by Char Miller, 120–38. Tucson: University of Arizona Press, 2001.
McMillen, Christian W. "Rain, Ritual, and Reclamation: The Failure of Irrigation on the Zuni and Navajo Reservations, 1883–1914." *Western Historical Quarterly* 31, no. 4 (2000): 435–56.

Meeks, Eric V. "The Tohono O'odham, Wage Labor, and Resistant Adaptation, 1900–1930." *Western Historical Quarterly* 34, no. 4 (2003): 469–90.
Meinig, D. W. *Atlantic America, 1492–1800*. Vol. 1 of *The Shaping of America: A Geographical Perspective on 500 Years of History*. New Haven, CT: Yale University Press, 1986.
———. *Southwest: Three Peoples in Geographical Change, 1600–1970*. Oxford and New York: Oxford University Press, 1971.
Meléndez, A. Gabriel, M. Jane Young, Patricia Moore, and Patrick Pynes, eds. *The Multicultural Southwest: A Reader*. Tucson: University of Arizona Press, 2001.
Melton, Ada Pecos. "Indigenous Justice Systems and Tribal Society." *Judicature* 79, no. 3 (1995): 126–33.
Melzer, Richard. "New Mexico in Caricature: Images of the Territory on the Eve of Statehood." *New Mexico Historical Review* 62, no. 4 (1987): 335–60.
Menchaca, Martha. *Recovering History, Constructing Race: The Indian, Black, and White Roots of Mexican Americans*. Austin: University of Texas Press, 2002.
Meusburger, Peter, Derek Gregory, and Laura Suarsana. *Geographies of Knowledge and Power*. Knowledge and Space 7. Heidelberg and New York: Springer, 2015.
Meyer, Michael C. *Water in the Hispanic Southwest : A Social and Legal History, 1550–1850*. Tucson: University of Arizona Press, 1996. 1984.
Meyer, Michael C., and Michael M. Brescia. "The Treaty of Guadalupe Hidalgo as a Living Document: Water and Land Use Issues in Northern New Mexico." *New Mexico Historical Review* 73, no. 4 (1998): 321–45.
Miller, Austin J. "Blackdom: Interpreting the Hidden History of New Mexico's Black Town." Master's thesis, University of New Mexico, 2018.
Miller, D. Ezra. "'But It Is Nothing except Woods': Anabaptists, Ambitions, and a Northern Indiana Settlerscape, 1830–1841." In *Rooted and Grounded: Essays on Land and Christian Discipleship*, edited by Ryan D. Harker and Janeen Bertsche Johnson, 208–17. Studies in Peace and Scripture 13. Eugene, OR: Pickwick Publications, 2016.
Mills, William J. *Report of the Governor of New Mexico to the Secretary of the Interior, for the Fiscal Year Ended June 30, 1910*. Washington, DC: Government Printing Office, 1910.
Montgomery, Charles. "Becoming 'Spanish-American': Race and Rhetoric in New Mexico Politics, 1880–1928." *Journal of American Ethnic History* 20, no. 4 (2001): 59–84.
Montiel, Miguel, Tomás Atencio, and E. A. "Tony" Mares. *Resolana: Emerging Chicano Dialogues on Community and Globalization*. Tucson: University of Arizona Press, 2009.
Montoya, María E. *Translating Property: The Maxwell Land Grant and the Conflict over Land in the American West, 1840–1900*. Berkeley and Los Angeles: University of California Press, 2002.
Mora, Anthony P. *Border Dilemmas: Racial and National Uncertainties in New Mexico, 1848–1912*. Durham, NC: Duke University Press, 2011.
Mulvany, Martha E. "*State ex rel. Martinez v. City of Las Vegas*: The Misuse of History and Precedent in the Abolition of the Pueblo Water Rights Doctrine in New Mexico." *Natural Resources Journal* 45, no. 4 (2005): 1089–1116.
Murdock, Esme G. "Unsettling Reconciliation: Decolonial Methods for Transforming Social-Ecological Systems." *Environmental Values* 27, no. 5 (2018): 513–33.

Murrah-Mandril, Erin. *In the Mean Time: Temporal Colonization and the Mexican American Literary Tradition.* Lincoln: University of Nebraska Press, 2020.

Nace, Raymond L. "Development of Hydrology in North America." *Water International* 3, no. 3 (1978): 20–26.

Naylor, Simon. "Introduction: Historical Geographies of Science—Places, Contexts, Cartographies." In "Historical Geographies of Science," [special issue,] *British Journal for the History of Science* 38, no. 1 (2005): 1–12.

———. *Regionalizing Science: Placing Knowledges in Victorian England.* London: Pickering & Chatto, 2010.

Neale, Timothy, and Stephen Turner. "Other People's Country: Law, Water, Entitlement." *Settler Colonial Studies* 5, no. 4 (2015): 277–81.

Nelson, Timothy E. "The Significance of the Afro-Frontier in American History: Blackdom, Barratry, and Bawdyhouses in the Borderlands, 1900–1930." Ph.D. diss., University of Texas at El Paso, 2015.

New Mexico Acequia Association. "Legislative Updates." Accessed 19 May 2023. https://lasacequias.org/legislative-updates/.

Newell, Frederick Haynes, and Daniel William Murphy. *Principles of Irrigation Engineering: Arid Lands, Water Supply, Storage Works, Dams, Canals, Water Rights and Products.* 1st ed., 2nd impression (corrected). New York: McGraw-Hill, 1913.

Nieto-Phillips, John M. *The Language of Blood: The Making of Spanish-American Identity in New Mexico, 1880s–1930s.* Albuquerque: University of New Mexico Press, 2004.

Noggle, Burl. "Anglo Observers of the Southwest Borderlands, 1825–1890: The Rise of a Concept." *Arizona and the West* 1, no. 2 (1959): 105–31.

Norman, Emma S. "Indigenous Space, Scalar Politics and Water Governance in the Salish Sea Basin." In *Negotiating Water Governance: Why the Politics of Scale Matter,* edited by Emma S. Norman, Christina Cook, and Alice Cohen, 281–98. London and New York: Routledge, 2016.

Nostrand, Richard L. *The Hispano Homeland.* Norman: University of Oklahoma Press, 1992.

Nye, David E. "Technology, Nature, and American Origin Stories." *Environmental History* 8, no. 1 (2003): 8–24.

Offen, Karl. "Historical Political Ecology: An Introduction." *Historical Geography* 32 (2004): 19–42.

O'Neill, Karen M. *Rivers by Design: State Power and the Origins of U.S. Flood Control.* Durham, NC: Duke University Press, 2006.

Osofsky, Hari M. "The Role of Climate Change Litigation in Establishing the Scale of Energy Regulation." *Annals of the Association of American Geographers* 101, no. 4 (2011): 775–82.

Östling, Johan, David Larsson Heidenblad, Erling Sandmo, Anna Nilsson Hammar, and Kari H. Nordberg. "The History of Knowledge and the Circulation of Knowledge: An Introduction." In *Circulation of Knowledge: Explorations in the History of Knowledge,* edited by Johan Östling, Erling Sandmo, David Larsson Heidenblad, Anna Nilsson Hammar, and Kari H. Nordberg, 9–33. Lund: Nordic Academic Press, 2018.

O'Sullivan, Tanya. *Geographies of City Science: Urban Life and Origin Debates in Late Victorian Dublin.* Pittsburgh, PA: University of Pittsburgh Press, 2019.

Otero, Miguel A. *Report of the Governor of New Mexico to the Secretary of the Interior, for the Year Ending June 30, 1900*. Washington, DC: Government Printing Office, 1900.

———. *Report of the Governor of New Mexico to the Secretary of the Interior, for the Year Ending June 30, 1901*. Washington, DC: Government Printing Office, 1901.

———. *Report of the Governor of New Mexico to the Secretary of the Interior, 1902*. Washington, DC: Government Printing Office, 1902.

———. *Report of the Governor of New Mexico to the Secretary of the Interior, 1903*. Washington, DC: Government Printing Office, 1903.

———. *Report of the Governor of New Mexico to the Secretary of the Interior, 1904*. Washington, DC: Government Printing Office, 1904.

———. *Report of the Governor of New Mexico to the Secretary of the Interior, 1905*. Washington, DC: Government Printing Office, 1905.

Padget, Martin. "Travel, Exoticism, and the Writing of Region: Charles Fletcher Lummis and the 'Creation' of the Southwest." *Journal of the Southwest* 37, no. 3 (1995): 421–49.

Paredes, Raymund. "The Mexican Image in American Travel Literature, 1831–1869." *New Mexico Historical Review* 52, no. 1 (1977): 5–29.

Parrinello, Giacomo, Etienne S. Benson, and Wilko Graf von Hardenberg. "Estimated Truths: Water, Science, and the Politics of Approximation." *Journal of Historical Geography* 68 (April 2020): 3–10.

Paskus, Laura. *At the Precipice: New Mexico's Changing Climate*. Albuquerque: University of New Mexico Press, 2020.

Pearson, David. *The Politics of Ethnicity in Settler Societies: States of Unease*. Basingstoke and New York: Palgrave, 2001.

Perramond, Eric P. *Unsettled Waters: Rights, Law, and Identity in the American West*. Berkeley and Los Angeles: University of California Press, 2018.

———. "Water Governance in New Mexico: Adjudication, Law, and Geography." *Geoforum* 45 (March 2013): 83–93.

Perrigo, Lynn I. *Hispanos: Historic Leaders in New Mexico*. Santa Fe, NM: Sunstone Press, 1985.

Phillips, Fred M., G. Emlen Hall, and Mary E. Black. *Reining in the Rio Grande: People, Land, and Water*. Albuquerque: University of New Mexico Press, 2011.

Pisani, Donald J. "The Dilemmas of Indian Water Policy, 1887–1928." In *Fluid Arguments: Five Centuries of Western Water Conflict*, edited by Char Miller, 78–94. Tucson: University of Arizona Press, 2001.

———. *To Reclaim a Divided West: Water, Law, and Public Policy, 1848–1902*. Albuquerque: University of New Mexico Press, 1992.

———. *Water and American Government: The Reclamation Bureau, National Water Policy, and the West, 1902–1935*. Berkeley and Los Angeles: University of California Press, 2002.

———. *Water, Land, and Law in the West: The Limits of Public Policy, 1850–1920*. Lawrence: University of Kansas Press, 1996.

———. "Water Law and Localism in the West." *Halcyon* 14 (1992): 33–55.

Porter, Robert B. "Strengthening Tribal Sovereignty through Peacemaking: How the Anglo-American Legal Tradition Destroys Indigenous Societies." *Columbia Human Rights Law Review* 28, no. 2 (1996): 235–305.

Powell, Richard C. "Geographies of Science: Histories, Localities, Practices, Futures." *Progress in Human Geography* 31, no. 3 (2007): 309–29.

——. *Studying Arctic Fields: Cultures, Practices, and Environmental Sciences.* Montreal and Ithaca, NY: McGill-Queen's University Press, 2017.

Price, Flora L. "Forgotten Spaces and Resident Places: New Mexico Black Towns and Communities (1897–1930)." Ph.D. diss., University of New Mexico, 2003.

Pritchard, Sara B. "Toward an Environmental History of Technology." In *The Oxford Handbook of Environmental History*, edited by Andrew C. Isenberg, 227–58. Oxford and New York: Oxford University Press, 2014.

Pueblo Action Alliance. "#Waterback Manifesto," 2021. Accessed 19 March 2022. www.puebloactionalliance.org/water-back.

Raby, Megan. "'Slash-and-Burn Ecology': Field Science as Land Use." *History of Science* 57, no. 4 (2019): 441–68.

Red Nation. *The Red Deal: Indigenous Action to Save Our Earth.* Brooklyn, NY: Common Notions, 2021.

Regan, Paulette. *Unsettling the Settler Within: Indian Residential Schools, Truth Telling, and Reconciliation in Canada.* Vancouver: University of British Columbia Press, 2010.

Reichard, David A. "The Politics of Village Water Disputes in Northern New Mexico, 1882–1905." *Western Legal History* 9, no. 1 (1996): 8–33.

Reisen, Matthew, and Elise Kaplan. "City Removes Oñate Statue after Monday's Violence." *Albuquerque Journal*, 16 June 2020. Accessed 24 May 2023. https://www.abqjournal.com/news/local/city-removes-o-ate-statue-after-mondays-violence/article_e40199f4-dbc3-56c6-94f6-741bb09d79be.html.

Reisner, Marc. *Cadillac Desert: The American West and Its Disappearing Water.* New York: Penguin Books, 1986.

Renn, Jürgen. *The Evolution of Knowledge: Rethinking Science for the Anthropocene.* Princeton, NJ: Princeton University Press, 2020.

Rifkin, Mark. *Settler Common Sense: Queerness and Everyday Colonialism in the American Renaissance.* Minneapolis: University of Minnesota Press, 2014.

Rivera, José A. *Acequia Culture: Water, Land, and Community in the Southwest.* Albuquerque: University of New Mexico Press, 1998.

Robbins, Paul. *Political Ecology: A Critical Introduction.* Malden, MA: Blackwell, 2004.

Robertson, Sean. "Natives Making Space: The *Softwood* Lumber Dispute and the Legal Geographies of Indigenous Property Rights." *Geoforum* 61 (May 2015): 138–47.

Robinson, David F. "Legal Geographies of Intellectual Property, 'Traditional' Knowledge, and Biodiversity: Experiencing Conventions, Laws, Customary Law, and Karma in Thailand." *Geographical Research* 51, no. 4 (2013): 375–86.

Robinson, Michael C. *Water for the West: The Bureau of Reclamation, 1902–1977.* Chicago: Public Works Historical Society, 1979.

Rodgers, Daniel T. *Atlantic Crossings: Social Politics in a Progressive Age.* Cambridge, MA: Belknap Press of Harvard University Press, 1998.

Rodríguez, Sylvia. *Acequia: Water-Sharing, Sanctity, and Place.* Santa Fe, NM: School for Advanced Research Press, 2006.

——. "Applied Research on Land and Water in New Mexico: A Critique." *Journal of the Southwest* 32, no. 3 (1990): 300–315.

——. "The Hispano Homeland Debate Revisited." *Perspectives in Mexican American Studies* 3 (1992): 95–114.

Rome, Adam. "What Really Matters in History? Environmental Perspectives on Modern America." *Environmental History* 7, no. 2 (2002): 303–18.
Rook, Robert E. "An American in Palestine: Elwood Mead and Zionist Water Resource Planning, 1923–1936." *Arab Studies Quarterly* 22, no. 1 (2000): 71–89.
Rosenberg, Daniel. "Data as Word." *Historical Studies in the Natural Sciences* 48, no. 5 (2018): 557–67.
Rossiter, David A. "Lessons in Possession: Colonial Resource Geographies in Practice on Vancouver Island, 1859–1865." *Journal of Historical Geography* 33, no. 4 (2007): 770–90.
———. "Negotiating Nature: Colonial Geographies and Environmental Politics in the Pacific Northwest." *Ethics, Place & Environment* 11, no. 2 (2008): 113–28.
Rowalt, E. M. *Soil Defense of Range and Farm Lands in the Southwest*. Washington, DC: United States Government Printing Office, 1939.
Russell, Edmund, James Allison, Thomas Finger, John K. Brown, Brian Balogh, and W. Bernard Carlson. "The Nature of Power: Synthesizing the History of Technology and Environmental History." *Technology and Culture* 52, no. 2 (2011): 246–59.
Ryan, Simon. *The Cartographic Eye: How Explorers Saw Australia*. Cambridge: Cambridge University Press, 1996.
Said, Edward W. *Orientalism*. New York: Pantheon Books, 1978.
Saldaña-Portillo, María Josefina. "'How Many Mexicans [Is] a Horse Worth?' The League of United Latin American Citizens, Desegregation Cases, and Chicano Historiography." *South Atlantic Quarterly* 107, no. 4 (2008): 809–31.
Sánchez, Joseph P., Robert L. Spude, and Art Gómez. *New Mexico: A History*. Norman: University of Oklahoma Press, 2013.
Sauder, Robert A. *The Yuma Reclamation Project: Irrigation, Indian Allotment, and Settlement along the Lower Colorado River*. Reno: University of Nevada Press, 2009.
Sayre, Nathan F. "Race, Nature, Nation, and Property in the Origins of Range Science." In *The Palgrave Handbook of Critical Physical Geography*, edited by Rebecca Lave, Christine Biermann, and Stuart N. Lane, 339–56. Cham: Springer, 2018.
Schmidt, Jeremy J. "Bureaucratic Territory: First Nations, Private Property, and 'Turn-Key' Colonialism in Canada." *Annals of the American Association of Geographers* 108, no. 4 (2018): 1–16.
Schönfeld La Mar, Barbel Hannelore. "Water and Land in the Mesilla Valley, New Mexico: Reclamation and Its Effects on Property Ownership and Agricultural Land Use." Ph.D. diss., University of Oregon, 1985.
Schorr, David. *The Colorado Doctrine: Water Rights, Corporations, and Distributive Justice on the American Frontier*. New Haven, CT: Yale University Press, 2012.
Schulman, Bruce J. "Governing Nature, Nurturing Government: Resource Management and the Development of the American State, 1900–1912." *Journal of Policy History* 17, no. 4 (2005): 375–403.
Scott, James C. *Seeing like a State: How Certain Schemes to Improve the Human Condition Have Failed*. New Haven, CT: Yale University Press, 1998.
Shapin, Steven. "Placing the View from Nowhere: Historical and Sociological Problems in the Location of Science." *Transactions of the Institute of British Geographers* 23, no. 1 (1998): 5–12.
Shurts, John. *Indian Reserved Water Rights: The Winters Doctrine in Its Social and*

Legal Context, 1880s–1930s, Legal History of the United States 8. Norman: University of Oklahoma Press, 2000.

Simmons, Marc. *The Last Conquistador: Juan de Oñate and the Settling of the Far Southwest*. The Oklahoma Western Biographies 2. Norman: University of Oklahoma Press, 1991.

Simpson, Audra. "Settlement's Secret." *Cultural Anthropology* 26, no. 2 (2011): 205–17.

Simpson, Leanne R. "Anticolonial Strategies for the Recovery and Maintenance of Indigenous Knowledge." In "The Recovery of Indigenous Knowledge," special issue, *American Indian Quarterly* 28, nos. 3–4 (2004): 373–84.

Simpson, Michael, and Jen Bagelman. "Decolonizing Urban Political Ecologies: The Production of Nature in Settler Colonial Cities." *Annals of the American Association of Geographers* 108, no. 2 (2018): 558–68.

Smith, Crosbie, and Jon Agar. *Making Space for Science: Territorial Themes in the Shaping of Knowledge*. New York: St. Martin's Press, 1998.

Smith, Karen L. *The Magnificent Experiment: Building the Salt River Reclamation Project, 1890–1917*. Tucson: University of Arizona Press, 1986.

Smith, Linda Tuhiwai. *Decolonizing Methodologies: Research and Indigenous Peoples*. London: Zed Books, 2012.

Smythe, William E. *The Conquest of Arid America*. Originally published 1905. Revised ed. Seattle: University of Washington Press, 1969.

Sneddon, Chris S., Regis Barraud, and Marie-Anne Germaine. "Dam Removals and River Restoration in International Perspective." *Water Alternatives* 10, no. 3 (2017): 648–54.

Snelgrove, Corey, Rita Kaur Dhamoon, and Jeff Corntassel. "Unsettling Settler Colonialism: The Discourse and Politics of Settlers, and Solidarity with Indigenous Nations." *Decolonization: Indigeneity, Education & Society* 3, no. 2 (2014): 1–32.

Sparke, Matthew. "A Map That Roared and an Original Atlas: Canada, Cartography, and the Narration of Nation." *Annals of the Association of American Geographers* 88, no. 3 (1998): 463–95.

Stanley, Anna. "Resilient Settler Colonialism: 'Responsible Resource Development,' 'Flow-through' Financing, and the Risk Management of Indigenous Sovereignty in Canada." *Environment and Planning A* 48, no. 12 (2016): 2422–42.

Steinman, Erich. "Settler Colonial Power and the American Indian Sovereignty Movement: Forms of Domination, Strategies of Transformation." *American Journal of Sociology* 117, no. 4 (2012): 1073–1130.

Stine, Jeffrey K., and Joel Tarr. "At the Intersection of Histories: Technology and the Environment." *Technology and Culture* 39, no. 4 (1998): 601–40.

Sullivan, Vernon L. *First Biennial Report of the Territorial Engineer to the Governor of New Mexico Including Water Supply*. Office of the Territorial Engineer, Territory of New Mexico. Albuquerque, NM: Albuquerque Morning Journal, 1908.

———. *Report on the Hondo Hydrographic Survey by the Territorial Engineer to the Court of the Sixth Judicial District of the Territory of New Mexico*. Territorial Engineer, Office of the Territorial Engineer, Territory of New Mexico. Santa Fe: New Mexican Printing Company, 1910.

———. *Second Biennial Report of the Territorial Engineer to the Governor of New Mexico Including Irrigation, Water Supply, Good Roads, Carey Act*. Office of the

Territorial Engineer, Territory of New Mexico. Santa Fe: New Mexican Printing Company, 1910.

Sutter, Paul S. "Nature's Agents or Agents of Empire? Entomological Workers and Environmental Change During the Construction of the Panama Canal." *Isis* 98, no. 4 (2007): 724–54.

———. "The World with Us: The State of American Environmental History." *Journal of American History* 100, no. 1 (2013): 94–119.

Swyngedouw, Erik. "Technonatural Revolutions: The Scalar Politics of Franco's Hydro-Social Dream for Spain, 1939–1975." *Transactions of the Institute of British Geographers* 32, no. 1 (2007): 9–28.

TallBear, Kim. "Standing With and Speaking as Faith: A Feminist-Indigenous Approach to Inquiry." In "Giving Back in Field Research," special issue, *Journal of Research Practice* 10, no. 2 (2014). Accessed 22 May 2023. http://jrp.icaap.org/index.php/jrp/article/view/405/371.

TallBear, Kimberly. *Native American DNA: Tribal Belonging and the False Promise of Genetic Science*. Minneapolis: University of Minnesota Press, 2013.

Temper, Leah. "Blocking Pipelines, Unsettling Environmental Justice: From Rights of Nature to Responsibility to Territory." *Local Environment* 24, no. 2 (2019): 94–112.

Thistle, John. "A Vast Inland Empire and the Last Great West: Remaking Society, Space and Environment in Early British Columbia." *Journal of Historical Geography* 37, no. 4 (2011): 418–28.

Thompson, Gary L., Fred M. Shelley, and Chand Wije, eds. *Geography, Environment, and American Law*. Denver: University Press of Colorado, 1997.

Thomson, Bruce, and Scott Verhines. "New Mexico's Top Water Official Should Be a Licensed Engineer." *Albuquerque Journal*, 3 February 2022. Accessed 24 May 2023. https://www.abqjournal.com/2466858/new-mexicos-top-water-official-should-be-a-licensed-engineer.html.

Thorson, John E., Sarah Britton, and Bonnie G. Colby, eds. *Tribal Water Rights: Essays in Contemporary Law, Policy, and Economics*. Tucson: University of Arizona Press, 2006.

Tofa, Matalena. "Incomplete Reconciliations: A History of Settling Grievances in Taranaki, New Zealand." *Journal of Historical Geography* 46 (October 2014): 26–35.

"Trade." Museum Collections of the Chaco Culture National Historical Park. Accessed 7 July 2020. https://www.nps.gov/museum/exhibits/chcu/.

Twitchell, Ralph Emerson. *The Leading Facts of New Mexican History*. Vol. 2. Cedar Rapids, IA: Torch Press, 1911.

———. "Bernalillo County." In *The Leading Facts of New Mexican History*, 3–62. Cedar Rapids, IA: Torch Press, 1917.

———. "Doña Ana County." In *The Leading Facts of New Mexican History*, 185–223. Cedar Rapids, IA: Torch Press, 1917.

———. "Rio Arriba County." In *The Leading Facts of New Mexican History*, 505–48. Cedar Rapids, IA: Torch Press, 1917.

———. "Sandoval County." In *The Leading Facts of New Mexican History*, 106–72. Cedar Rapids, IA: Torch Press, 1917.

———. "Santa Fe County." In *The Leading Facts of New Mexican History*, 4–105. Cedar Rapids, IA: Torch Press, 1917.

———. "Sierra County." In *The Leading Facts of New Mexican History*, 263–81. Cedar Rapids, IA: Torch Press, 1917.

———. "Socorro County." In *The Leading Facts of New Mexican History*, 282–394. Cedar Rapids, IA: Torch Press, 1917.

———. "Valencia County." In *The Leading Facts of New Mexican History*, 1–86. Cedar Rapids, IA: Torch Press, 1917.

Tyfield, David, Rebecca Lave, Samuel Randalls, and Charles Thorpe, eds. *The Routledge Handbook of the Political Economy of Science*. Abingdon and New York: Routledge, 2017.

Tyler, Daniel. "Anglo-American Penetration of the Southwest: The View from New Mexico." *Southwestern Historical Quarterly* 75, no. 3 (1972): 325–38.

Tyrrell, Ian. *Crisis of the Wasteful Nation: Empire and Conservation in Theodore Roosevelt's America*. Chicago: University of Chicago Press, 2015.

Veracini, Lorenzo. *Settler Colonialism: A Theoretical Overview*. Basingstoke and New York: Palgrave Macmillan, 2010.

———. "Introducing *Settler Colonial Studies*." *Settler Colonial Studies* 1, no. 1 (2011): 1–12.

Verburgt, Lukas M. "The History of Knowledge and the Future History of Ignorance." *KNOW: A Journal on the Formation of Knowledge* 4, no. 1 (2020): 1–24.

Vigil, Maurilio E. *Los Patrones: Profiles of Hispanic Leaders in New Mexican History*. Washington, DC: University Press of America, 1980.

Vimalassery, Manu, Juliana Hu Pegues, and Alyosha Goldstein. "Introduction: On Colonial Unknowing." *Theory & Event* 19, no. 4 (2016). Accessed 14 March 2019. https://muse.jhu.edu/article/633283.

Vitale, Patrick S. "Making Science Suburban: The Suburbanization of Industrial Research and the Invention of 'Research Man.'" *Environment and Planning A* 49, no. 12 (2017): 2813–34.

Voyles, Traci Brynne. *The Settler Sea: California's Salton Sea and the Consequences of Colonialism*. Lincoln: University of Nebraska Press, 2022.

———. *Wastelanding: Legacies of Uranium Mining in Navajo Country*. Minneapolis: University of Minnesota Press, 2015.

Walker, Peter, and Louise Fortmann. "Whose Landscape? A Political Ecology of the 'Exurban' Sierra." *Cultural Geographies* 10, no. 4 (2003): 469–91.

Walker, Peter A. "Political Ecology: Where Is the Ecology?" *Progress in Human Geography* 29, no. 1 (2005): 73–82.

Watson, Annette, and Orville Huntington. "Transgressions of the Man on the Moon: Climate Change, Indigenous Expertise, and the Posthumanist Ethics of Place and Space." *GeoJournal* 79, no. 6 (2014): 721–36.

Wehr, Kevin. *America's Fight over Water: The Environmental and Political Effects of Large-Scale Water Systems*. New York: Routledge, 2004.

Weigle, Marta. *Alluring New Mexico: Engineered Enchantment, 1821–2001*. Santa Fe: Museum of New Mexico Press, 2010.

Weisiger, Marsha L. *Dreaming of Sheep in Navajo Country*. Seattle: University of Washington Press, 2009.

Westcoat, James L., Jr. "Wittfogel East and West: Changing Perspectives on Water Development in South Asia and the United States, 1670–2000." In *Cultural Encounters with the Environment: Enduring and Evolving Geographic Themes*, edited by Alexander B. Murphy, Douglas L. Johnson, and Viola Heaarmann, 109–32. Lanham, MD: Rowman & Littlefield, 2000.

Wester, Philippus. "Capturing the Waters: The Hydraulic Mission in the Lerma-Chapala Basin, Mexico (1876–1976)." *Water History* 1, no. 1 (2009): 9–29.

Westphall, Victor. *Mercedes Reales: Hispanic Land Grants of the Upper Rio Grande Region*. Albuquerque: University of New Mexico Press, 1983.

Whatmore, Sarah. "Hybrid Geographies: Rethinking the 'Human' in Human Geography." In *Environment: Critical Essays in Human Geography*, edited by Kay Anderson and Bruce Braun. London: Routledge, 2008.

White, David M. *Report of the Irrigation Engineer for the Two Years Ending January 1, 1907*. Office of the Territorial Irrigation Engineer, Territory of New Mexico. Santa Fe, NM, 1907.

White, Richard. *The Roots of Dependency Subsistence, Environment, and Social Change among the Choctaws, Pawnees, and Navajos*. Lincoln: University of Nebraska Press, 1988.

———. *"It's Your Misfortune and None of My Own": A New History of the American West*. Norman: University of Oklahoma Press, 1991.

Whyte, Kyle. "Settler Colonialism, Ecology, and Environmental Injustice." *Environment and Society* 9, no. 1 (2018): 125–44.

Wilkinson, April L. "A Framework for Understanding Tribal Courts and the Application of Fundamental Law: Through the Voices of Scholars in the Field of Tribal Justice." *Tribal Law Journal* 15, no. 1 (2014–15): Article 3.

Williams, Jerry, ed. *New Mexico in Maps*. 2nd ed. Albuquerque: University of New Mexico Press, 1986.

Williams, Robert A., Jr. *The American Indian in Western Legal Thought: The Discourses of Conquest*. Oxford and New York: Oxford University Press, 1990.

Wilmsen, Carl. "Sustained Yield Recast: The Politics of Sustainability in Vallecitos, New Mexico." *Society and Natural Resources* 14, no. 3 (2001): 193–207.

———. "Maintaining the Environmental-Racial Order in Northern New Mexico." *Environment and Planning D: Society and Space* 25, no. 2 (2007).

Wilson, Chris. *The Myth of Santa Fe: Creating a Modern Regional Tradition*. Albuquerque: University of New Mexico Press, 1997.

Wilson, Matthew W. "Cyborg Geographies: Towards Hybrid Epistemologies." *Gender, Place & Culture* 16, no. 5 (2009): 499–516.

Wilson, Randall K. "'Placing Nature': The Politics of Collaboration and Representation in the Struggle for La Sierra in San Luis, Colorado." *Ecumene* 6, no. 1 (1999): 1–28.

Winichakul, Thongchai. *Siam Mapped: A History of the Geo-Body of a Nation*. Honolulu: University of Hawai'i Press, 1994.

Wolfe, Patrick. "Settler Colonialism and the Elimination of the Native." *Journal of Genocide Research* 8, no. 4 (2006): 387–409.

———. *Settler Colonialism and the Transformation of Anthropology: The Politics and Poetics of an Ethnographic Event*. London: Cassell, 1999.

Woodhouse, Melvin, and Mark Zeitoun. "Hydro-Hegemony and International Water Law: Grappling with the Gaps of Power and Law." *Water Policy* 10, no. S2 (2008): 103–19.

Worster, Donald. *A River Running West: The Life of John Wesley Powell*. Oxford and New York: Oxford University Press, 2002.

———. *Rivers of Empire: Water, Aridity, and the Growth of the American West*. New York: Pantheon Books, 1985.

Wright, Miriam. "Aboriginal Gillnet Fishers, Science, and the State: Salmon Fisheries Management on the Nass and Skeena Rivers, British Columbia, 1951–1961." *Journal of Canadian Studies* 44, no. 1 (2010): 5–35.

Yazzie, Melanie K. "Unlimited Limitations: The Navajos' *Winters* Rights Deemed Worthless in the 2012 Navajo-Hopi Little Colorado River Settlement." *Wicazo Sa Review* 28, no. 1 (2013): 26–37.

Yazzie, Melanie K., and Cutchla Risling Baldy. "Introduction: Indigenous Peoples and the Politics of Water." *Decolonization: Indigeneity, Education & Society* 7, no. 1 (2018): 1–18.

Yazzie, Robert. "Life Comes from It: Navajo Justice Concepts." *New Mexico Law Review* 24 (1994): 175–90.

Zeitoun, Mark, and J. A. Allan. "Applying Hegemony and Power Theory to Transboundary Water Analysis." *Water Policy* 10, no. S2 (2008): 3–12.

Zwierlein, Cornel. *The Dark Side of Knowledge: Histories of Ignorance, 1400 to 1800*. Leiden: Brill, 2016.

Index

The letter *t* following a page number denotes a table, and the letter *f* denotes a figure.

Abbott, Ira, 176, 182–83
acequia culture, 34–37, 226n62
acequias: administration and governance, 34, 35, 36, 74, 77, 79, 89, 118–19, 134, 144, 145, 167, 173, 185; cultural importance, 36, 49, 68–69, 77, 210, 226n62; definition, 34, 77–78; disputes involving, 145–52, 154–58, 169–77, 179–84, 196–202; elections, 125t, 134, 159, 168; and expertise, 69, 78, 98; history, 34, 226n51; infrastructure, 34–35, 38, 77, 145; labor requirement, 35, 77, 178, 197; legal status, 36, 74, 76–78, 82–83, 249n8; locations in New Mexico, 35, 55, 144, 153, 159, 167, 178, 185, 230n15; maintenance, 35, 37, 69, 77, 134, 197; participants (*see* mayordomos; New Mexico, government institutions and officials: acequia commissions; parciantes); private vs. public, 77–78, 154, 158, 193–94, 199–200, 202, 248n115; relationship to Indigenous irrigation, 34, 36–37; subsistence orientation, 35–37, 50, 64, 78, 153; terminology, 34–36. *See also* water rights
acequias in New Mexico: Acequia de Belen, 182–83; Acequia de en Medio, 179–80, 247n87; Acequia del Medio, 149–52; Acequia de los Garcias, 149–52; Acequia de Picurie, 179–80, 247n88; Acequia de Santo Domingo, 169–70; Acequia en Media, 154; Acequia los Charcos, 182; Acequia los Lentes, 181–84; Acequia Nuestra Señora de Belen de la Ladera, 182–83; Acequia Nueva, 145–48; Los Griegos and Los Candelarias Acequia, 171–74; Palmer Acequia, 196–202; San Ysidro Acequia Madre, 196, 197, 200
"acequiazation," 37
Acoma Pueblo, 31
adjudication of water rights, 79, 82, 83, 84, 86, 90, 112, 118, 205, 208. *See also* courts; law
agriculture: alfalfa, 77, 106, 154, 160, 176, 178, 180, 185, 192, 198; as basis for Anglo settlement, 41, 63, 84, 89, 101–4, 184, 191, 205; beans, 36, 37, 180, 198; cereals, 178, 180; commercial vs. subsistence, 38, 39, 43, 64, 67–68, 69, 71, 72, 73, 77–78, 111; corn, 26, 37, 101, 180, 198; cotton, 31, 37, 177; and environmental change, 10, 47–50, 72; fruits, 37, 105–6, 144, 153, 154, 155, 156, 157, 176, 192; grains, 29, 31, 154, 177; grapes, 185, 154; history of in New Mexico, 15, 27–29, 31, 34–37; livestock grazing, 10, 32, 42, 47, 48, 67, 77, 162, 186–87; strawberries, 155; vegetables, 37, 154–55, 176,

agriculture (continued) 177; wheat, 37, 180, 198. *See also* agronomy; dry farming; irrigation; soils

agronomy, 91, 93, 98, 125t

Alamogordo basin, 103

Albuquerque, city of: flooding, 48; history, 2–3, 29, 34, 167–68; Spanish plaza vs. Anglo new town, 174; 2020 protest, 211–12; water disputes, 171–77, 245–46nn75–80; water system, 1–2, 174–75

Albuquerque Foundry and Machine Shop, 174

Albuquerque Land & Irrigation Company, 130, 168

Albuquerque Water Supply Company, 174

alcalde, 37, 118

alfalfa (crop), 77, 106, 154, 160, 176, 178, 180, 185, 192, 198

Algodones, village of, 158, 160, 168, 245n62

alkali, 183. *See also* salinization (of soils)

alluvial fans, 177

"American Indian," 15

Americanization, 46–49, 97, 113–15, 205, 206

Anglo-Americans (Anglos): as beneficiaries of reclamation policy, 63–66, 73, 205–6; dominance in legal system, 77–78, 89–90, 120–21, 141–43, 144, 159, 168, 179, 193, 206; elevated as experts, 20, 55, 61–63, 69–71, 97–101, 138–39, 205, 206; and environmental change, 46–49, 57–58, 63, 72, 143, 162, 179, 181, 205; ignorance of aridlands agriculture, 4, 91, 97, 102–4, 107–11, 113, 114, 166, 205–6; population growth in New Mexico, 18, 20, 39, 50, 73, 112–13, 120, 123, 167, 184–85; role in commercial agriculture, 40–41, 46–47, 76, 88, 104–5, 204, 208; settlement impact on non-Anglos, 4, 6, 21, 39, 40–46, 59, 71–72, 74–75, 79, 141–43, 154, 177–78, 193, 206–7; use of term, 15; in water disputes, 127–33, 138–39. *See also* Dutch settlers; ethnicity: ethnic relations; German settlers; race; settler colonialism

Angostura Arroyo, 160–61

Antonio Gutierrez land grant, 182

Apaches, 24, 29, 32, 44–45, 98, 99, 178, 184, 194

Apodaca, Tomás, 176

aquaculture, 154, 156

Archuleta, Taofilo, 148

aridity, 4, 5, 19, 24–26, 47, 51, 52, 70, 75, 105, 109–11

Arizona, state of, 24, 26, 27

Arrey, Ponsiano, 198, 200, 202, 249n126

AT&SF (Atchison, Topeka and Santa Fe) railroad, 111, 153, 159, 160–62, 167, 174, 178, 186, 187–90

Australia, 61, 71

ayuntamientos, 118

bajadas, 177

Barelas Ditch, 174–77

beans (crop), 36, 37, 180, 198

beavers, 162, 166

Belcher, George, 186–87

Belen, town of, 178, 182–84, 188

beneficial use, and water rights, 68, 75, 84, 107. *See also* water rights

Bernabe M. Montaño land grant, 162–67

Bernalillo, village of, 158, 159, 160

Bernalillo County, 79, 162, 167–68, 177, 185

Bernalillo District Court, 129t, 133t, 134, 135, 139t, 168, 172, 183–84

BIA (Bureau of Indian Affairs), 66–69

Bietz, William, 176

Black Range, 191

Blueher, Herman, 176

boosterism, 46–47, 61, 64, 78, 97, 102, 111, 120, 186, 191

border, U.S.-Mexico, 38, 65, 194, 195

Bosque Redondo, 44–45

breakwaters, 149–52

Bureau of Indian Affairs (BIA), 66–69

Bureau of Reclamation, 71, 112

Camino Real (de Tierra Adentro), 40, 153, 167

"Campbell method," 102

Canadian River, 26, 97, 102, 104, 123
capitalism, 46, 49–50, 58, 84, 89, 90, 95, 104–7, 108, 112, 114, 120–21, 203
Carey Act, 47, 94
Carlsbad, town of, 64
Carlsbad Project, 65
cartography, 6, 8, 59, 80, 93, 97, 137, 143, 144, 149
cash crops, 67, 153, 185, 196, 198, 200, 202
cash economy, 39, 40–41, 45, 48, 67, 70
Castillo, Justiniano, 160
Catron County, 186
Cebilleta de la Joya land grant, 187–90
cereal (crop), 178, 180. *See also* grain (crop)
cession, Mexican. *See* Mexican cession
Chaco Canyon, 26–27
Chaco Phenomenon, 26
Chama River. *See* Rio Chama
"chickenpark," 176
Chihuahuan Desert, 24, 194
Civil War, U.S., 44, 46, 55, 57
climate crisis, 19, 90, 210, 211
Cochiti Pueblo, 99, 158
colonialism, American. *See* Americanization; Anglo-Americans (Anglos); Indian policy, U.S.; settler colonialism
colonialism, settler. *See* settler colonialism
colonialism, Spanish. *See* acequia culture; land grants in New Mexico; mestizaje; Oñate, Juan de; Pueblo Revolt; settler colonialism
Colorado, state of, 2, 27, 47, 65, 94, 97, 123, 144
Colorado Plateau, 24, 26, 27, 29, 44
Colorado River, 2, 177
Comanches, 24, 29, 38, 44, 45
commons, 43, 47, 74
condemnations, 44, 125t, 130, 134–35, 153, 168, 175–77, 182–83
Congress, U.S., 17, 47, 52, 54, 57, 59–60, 159, 195, 205
conquistadores, 47
Continental Divide, 2, 24
contra acequias, 34, 174–77, 198–99
copper, 47. *See also* mining

corn (crop), 26, 37, 101, 180, 198
Coronado, Vásquez de, 29
corporations: in water disputes, 116, 128t, 129–30t, 131t, 132t, 137, 138, 159, 162, 179, 185, 203, 208; water rights of, 78, 86
Corrales, village of, 158
cotton (crop), 31, 37, 177
Court of Private Land Claims, U.S., 41, 43, 163
courts: adjudication of water rights, 79, 82, 83, 84, 86, 90, 112, 118, 205, 208; dispossession of non-Anglo lands, 43, 44, 45; dominated by Anglos, 77–78, 89–90, 120–21, 141–43, 144, 159, 168, 179, 193, 206; history of in New Mexico, 117–21; personnel, 21, 118–20; production of knowledge, 21, 56–57, 79; recognition of maps as evidence, 83, 149–52, 155–56, 189–90; relation to territorial engineer's office, 84–85, 92, 95–96, 106–7, 112, 136; rulings on environmental questions, 139–40, 143, 160, 161–62, 165–67, 172–73, 178, 180–81, 185–86, 187, 190, 195, 206; scientific argumentation and evidence, 81, 95, 136–39, 143, 157, 190; and settler colonialism, 7, 21, 143, 202–3, 206; use of interpreters, 170–71, 200–201, 248n123; water disputes in New Mexico, 116–40, 141–203. *See also* condemnations; Court of Private Land Claims, U.S.; Supreme Court, New Mexico; Supreme Court, U.S.; *Winters v. United States*
CPG. *See* critical physical geography
CPLC. *See* Court of Private Land Claims, U.S.
critical physical geography, 13
Culebra Range, 52
cultural imperialism, 90, 205
current meter. *See* stream gauging
Curry, George, 95, 96

dams: beaver, 162, 166; checkdams, 26, 29; disputes concerning, 148–52, 162–67, 186–87; engineering work

dams (continued)
  on, 81, 87, 92, 109, 110, 112; environmental impacts of, 63, 65; failures, 64–65, 67, 99, 110, 164; as federal projects, 59, 65–66, 71, 191, 195; as settler infrastructure, 11, 65–66, 78, 114, 164–67, 185; as symbol of progress, 56, 58–59, 65, 191. *See also* Indian Irrigation Service (IIS); reclamation projects in New Mexico; Reclamation Service, U.S.
data: concept of, 238n2; as focus of political ecology, 12; reliability, 93, 94; science, 93–97; for stream gauging, 53, 59–60, 93, 95 (*see also* stream gauging); systematic collection of, 57, 85–86, 93–97, 112; used for Anglo settlement, 21, 57, 93–97, 99, 113, 114; value in court, 95–96, 106, 113, 117, 125t, 137t, 143, 202–3
debt, 39, 64
decolonization, 5, 11, 15, 18–19, 88, 212, 237n57
deforestation, 10, 48–49, 50, 56
Denver, city of, 53
Denver and Rio Grande railroad, 52
Department of Interior, U.S., 92, 100, 163
desagüe, 34, 145–46
Desert Land Act, 47
diacritics, 17, 143
Dietz, William, 176
Diné, 15, 24, 29, 44–45
displacement: through court system, 141–42, 144–203, 206; through environmental change, 10–11, 48–49, 63; as goal of settler colonialism, 3, 6, 7, 18–19, 23, 59, 62, 93, 211; role of science and expertise in, 3, 11, 20, 52, 55, 58, 62, 69, 70–71, 113–15; via water management, 6, 20, 21–22, 50, 61–62, 70–71, 82–83, 93, 206
dispossession: as central to settler colonialism, 6, 7, 32, 40, 43, 208–9, 211; through court system, 7, 21, 41, 45, 121, 141, 203; through environmental damage, 47, 162–63; role of science in, 3–4, 5–6, 22, 204–7; via water management, 8, 20, 50, 208
dispute resolution: under American territorial law, 119–21; Indigenous practices for, 117; under Mexican law, 38, 118–19; under Spanish colonial law, 117–18
Dockwiller, Alphonso, 154–58
Doña Ana County, 191, 194–96, 200
Doña Ana District Court, 130t, 133, 133t, 134, 135, 139t, 196–202
"double colonization," 45
dry farming, 27, 101, 102–3, 110
Duran, Luciano, 196, 198, 200, 202
Dutch settlers, 155, 156, 158

efficiency: enforced by engineers, 89, 105, 107, 109; as expertise, 70, 80; in irrigation projects, 20, 64, 82, 83, 106, 110, 114; as Progressive governance, 57, 62, 80, 100, 205; regulatory, 107, 111–13; and settler colonialism, 204–5. *See also* waste prevention
Elephant Butte Dam and Reservoir, 65–66, 165, 191, 195
El Paso, village of, 33, 48, 194
Embudo, 52, 55, 222n84; USGS training camp, 52–54, 58, 59, 62, 69, 70, 71, 87, 148, 230n3, 230n14
eminent domain, 80, 84, 86. *See also* condemnations
engineering: agencies, 11–12, 20–21, 73, 74, 80–87; Anglo dominance of, 55, 57, 62–63, 66; claimed to be apolitical, 14, 57, 60, 69, 72; credibility in court disputes, 149–50, 164–66, 184; duties of territorial engineers, 81, 84–85, 87; efficiency, 63, 89, 104–7, 109; environmental impacts of, 4–5, 10–11, 22, 48–49, 51–52, 57–58, 63–66, 72, 139–40, 202–5, 207; expertise, 20, 51, 60, 66–67, 68, 82, 92, 97–101, 209; government programs in, 3, 4, 51, 52, 54, 56–57, 58–63, 72, 205–6; of irrigation projects, 51, 54, 63, 80–88, 94, 97–101, 104; as knowledge work, 11–12, 14, 21, 51–52, 55, 57, 69, 70–72, 81, 87, 91–115; and modernist

INDEX

science, 11–12, 51, 57, 81, 83, 141, 205–6; and Progressive governance, 20, 51, 55, 56–57, 61, 62, 69–70, 93, 101, 107, 111–13, 204; role in displacing non-Anglos, 59, 63–64, 70–71, 78, 207, 211; support for new settlers and speculators, 48, 58, 61, 86–87, 101–4, 205–6; as tool of settler colonialism, 3, 4, 5–6, 8, 10–12, 19, 20–21, 51, 59, 61, 91–93, 105, 113–15, 143, 204, 206, 208–10. *See also* hydrography; New Mexico, government institutions and officials: Office of the State Engineer; New Mexico, government institutions and officials: Office of the Territorial (Irrigation) Engineer; permits, water; reclamation policy; stream gauging; territorial engineer, New Mexico; territorial irrigation engineer, New Mexico

Enlightenment, 8, 14

environmental change, 5, 8, 10–11, 46–50, 57–58, 63, 72, 143, 162, 179, 181, 205

environmental damage and disaster, 4–5, 10–11, 22, 48–49, 51–52, 57–58, 63–66, 72, 139–40, 202–5, 207

environmental futures, 5, 19, 209, 212

environmental governance, 51, 56–57, 71–72

environmental justice, 50, 212

environmental knowledge, 4–5, 6, 8, 10–11, 12–14, 17, 21–22, 69, 70–71, 113–15, 206. *See also* knowledge

environmental management: and Americanization, 46–49, 97, 113–15, 205, 206; and Anglo settlement, 10, 46–49, 57–58, 63, 143, 205; based on modernist philosophy, 9–10, 51–52, 70–71; conflicts over, 10–11, 116–17, 134, 137–40; conservation projects and policy, 11, 56–57, 61–63; decolonial possibilities for, 5, 88; focus of human-environment scholarship, 12–14; in New Mexico, 5, 8, 11, 44, 48–49, 63–64, 72, 162, 179, 181; in Progressive agenda, 20, 51–52, 56–58, 61–63, 71–72, 204–5, 207; scientific policy for, 5–6, 56–57, 93–97, 208–9, 210; and settler colonialism, 4–5, 10–12, 21, 46–50, 51–52, 57–58, 63–66, 72, 89–90, 139–40, 202–5, 209–10. *See also* environmental change; environmental knowledge; expertise; reclamation policy

environmental-management states, 56, 71

environmental-racial order, 208

environmental science, 10, 13

erosion, 125t, 140, 164, 166, 188–89

Española, city of, 144

Española Valley, 230n14

Estancia basin, 103

ethnic cleansing, 7, 43–46

ethnicity: Americanization and, 46–49, 97, 113–15, 205, 206; in court disputes, 117, 120, 123, 126, 127–33, 138, 143; ethnic relations, 5, 21, 43, 45–46, 57, 79, 123, 140, 143, 153–54, 158, 173, 177, 211; in historical records, 126; and New Mexico's tricultural myth, 14–15, 17, 222n82; terminology for, 14–18. *See also* Anglo-Americans (Anglos); ethnic cleansing; genízaros; genocide; Indigenous groups in New Mexico; mestizaje; Nuevomexicanas/os; Pueblo nations of New Mexico; race

expertise: based on race and ethnicity, 4, 51, 58, 62–63, 66–68, 69–71, 90, 139, 204–6; based on science and quantification, 4, 6, 21, 56, 59, 70, 80–81, 91, 114; claimed to be apolitical, 51, 57, 61, 71–72; as colonial tool, 20, 51–52, 61, 69, 104, 138–39, 141, 204–6, 209; in engineering, 20, 51, 60, 66–67, 68, 82, 92, 97–101, 209; focus of political ecology, 12; presumed for Anglos, 20, 55, 61–63, 69–71, 97–101, 138–39, 205, 206; and Progressivism, 20, 51, 55–58, 69–71, 80, 114, 204–6; in reclamation policy, 60–61, 69–71; as tool for devaluing nonscientific knowledge, 52, 61, 62, 98–101; used in water disputes, 21, 116, 139–40, 149. *See also* environmental-management states

278 INDEX

"Fall" bill, 79–80
fisheries, 10
flooding: damage from, 3, 5, 10, 31, 48, 67, 99, 125t, 148–52, 160–67, 178, 179, 186, 188–90, 192–94; as irrigation method, 27, 65, 109; and irrigation projects, 47–49, 65, 103, 146–48; natural cycles in New Mexico, 2, 5, 26, 28, 35, 103, 111, 167, 195
forests: deforestation, 10, 47, 48–49, 50, 56, 58, 195; forestry, 10, 47, 58; lumber, 31; national, 43, 56; of New Mexico, 26, 31, 41; Progressive policy for, 61, 208
Forest Service, U.S., 49
Four Corners, 27, 45
Freeman, W. B., 95, 97
fruit (crop), 37, 105–6, 144, 153, 154, 155, 156, 157, 176, 192

Gadsden Purchase, 194
Garcia, Alejandrino, 147
García, Gregorio, 171–73
Garfield, town of, 196, 201
General Land Office, New Mexico, 162
genízaros, 33, 37, 207
genocide, 7, 44, 45, 207
geographical imagination, 101
geographies, hybrid, 12–13, 14
geographies of science, 3, 6, 8–12, 207
geography, critical physical, 13
geography, historical, 3, 6, 7–8, 13, 14, 18, 206–8
geography, history of, 101
geography, human-environment, 12–14
geography, knowledge of, 101–4
geography, legal, 6, 13–14, 116–26
geography of New Mexico. *See* New Mexico, history and geography
Geological Survey, U.S., 52, 54, 59, 60, 87, 95, 96–97, 112, 148
German settlers, 184
Gila River, 26, 123, 186, 191
governance: of acequia systems, 34–37, 50, 69, 74, 76–77, 79, 89, 144–45, 167, 172; based on scientific expertise, 20, 51–52, 54, 57, 58, 69–71, 78;

environmental, 51, 56–57, 71–72; Progressive vision for, 20, 51–52, 57–58, 69–71, 73–74, 89; Pueblo, 170–71; transitions in New Mexico, 118–20; of water, 20, 100, 125t, 133t, 134, 144–45, 173, 210. *See also* environmental-racial order
grain (crop), 29, 31, 154, 177
Grant County, 192
grapes (crop), 185, 154
grazing, livestock, 10, 32, 42, 47, 48, 67, 77, 162, 186–87. *See also* overgrazing
Great Plains, 24, 26, 46
groundwater, 1–4, 103, 104, 105, 123, 125t, 139t, 191, 209
Guadalupe Hidalgo, Treaty of, 4, 39–40, 41, 43, 74
Gulf of Mexico, 26

haciendas, 32, 33, 144, 177–78
Hagerman, Herbert, 100–101, 104, 114
Harper, John, 99–100
Harris, Cole, 3–4
Harroun, Philip, 164, 166
Hatch, village of, 196
Herrera, Macedonio, 171–73
Hillsborough (Hillsboro), town of, 191–94
Hispano. *See* ethnicity: terminology for; Nuevomexicanas/os
historical geography. *See* geography, historical
Hohokam, 26–27
Holt, H. B., 198, 201
Homestead Act, 47, 138
homesteading, 43, 47, 63, 102, 159, 185–86, 194, 196, 198, 199, 202
Hondo Creek, 64, 95, 97, 110
Hondo Hydrographic Survey, 97, 106
Hopi, 24
Horse Springs, 186–87
human-environment geography, 12–14
Huning, Louis, 182
hybrid geographies, 12–13, 14
Hydrographic Branch, U.S. Geological Survey, 60
hydrography: government program, 59–60, 97; hydrographers as experts, 54,

55, 205; as support for settlement, 99, 112; surveys, 85–86, 92, 93–97, 106–7, 112, 113. *See also* Hondo Hydrographic Survey; Rayado Hydrographic Survey; stream gauging

hydrology: conditions, 26, 47–48, 59, 63, 65, 97–98, 99, 116, 165; disputes, 125t, 137t, 139, 139t, 141, 155, 161, 206; expertise, 61, 91, 92–93, 114, 205, 209; history of, 59; knowledge of, 5, 8, 9, 21, 37, 52, 54, 71, 107–11, 207; survey and mapping, 20, 26, 80, 190

hydropower, 105

ignorance, 4, 55, 57, 70, 91, 99, 107–11, 113, 114, 166, 205–6

IIS (Indian Irrigation Service), 66–68, 108

imagination, geographical, 101

Indian Affairs, Bureau of, 66–69

Indian Irrigation Service (IIS), 66–68, 108

Indian policy, U.S., 43–45

Indigenous groups in New Mexico: ancestral Puebloans, 24; Apaches, 24, 29, 32, 44–45, 98, 99, 178, 184, 194; Basketmaker peoples, 26; Chaco Phenomenon, 26–27; Comanches, 24, 29, 38, 44, 45; Diné, 15, 24, 29, 44–45; genízaros, 33, 37, 107; Mogollon culture, 26–27; Pueblos (*see* Pueblo nations of New Mexico); Utes, 29, 45

Indigenous scholars, 4–5, 18, 23, 210

Indigenous sovereignty, 4, 7, 11, 43, 67, 184

Indigenous studies, 11. *See also* decolonization

Interior, U.S. Department of, 92, 100, 163

Interior, U.S. Secretary of, 65, 92, 94, 95, 97, 98, 101, 104, 105, 109

intersectionality, 8, 16

irrigation: communal management of, 28–29, 37, 49, 72, 74, 78–79, 82, 117, 120, 135, 167; disputes over, 145–48, 154–58, 162–67, 169–73, 179–81, 186–87, 191–94, 196–202; engineering, 54, 63, 80–88, 94, 97–101, 104; environmental and social impacts of, 10, 47–49, 51, 58, 63–69, 99, 204–5; Indigenous approaches to, in Spanish era, 36–37; integral to settler colonialism, 19–20, 21–22, 23, 49–51, 52, 61, 63, 66, 68, 73, 88–90, 91, 97–101, 108, 114–15, 204, 205–6, 210; intensification by Anglo settlers, 10, 47, 49–50, 63, 72, 75–76, 81, 89–90, 200, 202; knowledge, 62, 93–97, 101–4, 107–11, 206; precolonial history of, 26–29; Progressive programs for (*see* reclamation policy); promoted as economic development, 41, 46–47, 48–49, 61, 64, 68, 75, 77, 78, 91, 97, 102, 111, 120, 191, 200, 203; scientific approach to, 51, 52–53, 54, 58–63, 61, 81, 104 (*see also* expertise); Spanish colonial approach to, 30, 32, 34–37; for subsistence vs. profit, 63, 72, 73, 89–90, 104–7, 120, 204. *See also* acequia culture; acequias; dams; engineering: of irrigation projects; Indian Irrigation Service (IIS); Irrigation Survey, U.S.; permits, water; reclamation policy; Reclamation Service, U.S.; water rights

Irrigation and Water Rights, Commission on, 79, 82, 91, 92, 93

Irrigation Survey, U.S., 54, 59

Isleta Pueblo, 15, 167, 178, 179, 181–84

Jastro, H. A., 162–67

Jemez Mountains, 158

Jemez Pueblo, 158

Jemez River, 26

Kansas City, 38

Kearney Code, 119

Keres (language), 170, 245n69

Kewa (Santo Domingo) Pueblo, 15, 158, 169–71, 245n64

Kline ditch, 106

knowledge: of agronomy, 111–12; coproduced with landscape, 12–13; of data science, 93–97; of engineering, 97–101; as focus of scholarship, 8–14; of geography, 101–4; of hydrography,

knowledge (continued)
92–97; of hydrology, 107–11; ignorance and, 4, 55, 57, 70, 91, 99, 107–11, 113, 114, 166, 205–6; and imperialism, 61–62, 71; Indigenous, 37, 52, 108; local, 9, 55, 57; of markets, 104–7; needed for irrigation, 62, 93–97, 101–4, 107–11, 206; networks of, 34, 52, 91, 92–93; Nuevomexicano, 49, 69, 70; politics of, 3, 4, 14; and power, 9, 13; produced by scientists and engineers, 5, 8, 11–12, 14, 21, 51–52, 55, 57, 69, 71–72, 81, 87; produced through law and courts, 4, 14, 21, 56–57, 79, 116–17, 123, 125, 125t, 137–40, 143, 144, 190, 202–4, 206; of public administration, 111–13; racialized, 8, 52, 61, 62, 69–70, 98–101, 108–9, 113–15; structures of, 5–6, 12–13, 21, 91, 92–93, 113–15; as tool of settler colonialism, 3, 4–5, 6, 7–8, 10–11, 12–13, 17, 21–22, 61, 69, 70–71, 91, 93, 113–15, 143, 206. *See also* environmental knowledge; expertise; geographical imagination

La Joya, town of, 145, 187–90, 230n14
land grants in New Mexico, 33, 38, 41–43, 50, 74
Las Cruces, town of, 194, 195, 201
law: American system of, 14, 41, 73, 74, 76, 89, 119; analysis of legal disputes, 121–26; coproduced with space, 13–14; dispute resolution, 119–21, 206; dominance of Anglo-Americans in legal system, 77–78, 89–90, 120–21, 141–43, 144, 159, 168, 179, 193, 206; and environmental knowledge, 4, 14, 21, 116–17, 123, 125, 125t, 137–40, 143, 144, 190, 202–3, 206; formal vs. customary, 36, 37, 38, 74, 117, 118; incompatibility of different legal traditions, 74, 75–76, 89; Indigenous dispute resolution and, 117, 121, 206; judicial interpretation, 74, 118; legal status of acequias, 36, 74, 76–78, 82–83, 249n8; Mexican system of, 38, 76, 77, 119, 206; and Progressivism, 60, 73–74, 80–81, 89–90, 91, 205; property rights, 7, 33, 40, 41, 43, 47, 72, 74, 100, 121, 206; role in settler colonialism, 45, 47, 52, 73–76, 89–90, 91, 107, 202; and science, 13–14, 87; social relations and, 13–14; Spanish system of, 31, 36, 76, 77, 119, 206; in territorial New Mexico, 41, 50, 73–90; water policy, 20, 73–90, 93–94, 95–96, 205. *See also* adjudication of water rights; commons; Court of Private Land Claims, U.S.; Kearney Code; land grants in New Mexico; legal geography; New Mexico, laws of; prior appropriation doctrine; riparian rights doctrine; Treaty of Guadalupe Hidalgo; water rights
legal geography, 6, 13–14, 116–26
Leland, Charles, 187, 192
Lewis, Charles, 163–64
Livingstone, David, 9
Llano Estacado, 24
Loma Parda, village of, 201, 202
Los Griegos and Los Candelarias Acequia, 171–74
Los Lentes, village of, 181–84
Los Lunas, town of, 178

management, environmental. *See* environmental management
management, water. *See* acequia culture; acequias; dams; engineering: of irrigation projects; environmental management; governance: of water; irrigation; permits, water; reclamation policy; water rights
Manzano Mountains, 178
Maxwell, town of, 103
mayordomos, 34–37, 38, 77, 78, 81, 82, 89, 112, 118, 119
McFie, John, 147–48, 150, 152, 157–58
McPherson, John, 191–94
Mead, Elwood, 79
Mechem, Merritt, 184, 189, 190
Mesa Verde, 27
Mesilla, village of, 194
Mesilla Valley, 41, 65, 191, 194, 195
mestizaje, 8, 16, 17, 33, 34, 37, 46, 126, 207, 224n18. *See also* genízaros

INDEX 281

Metcalf, W. P., 176
Metz, Nick, 176–77
Mexican-American War, 39–40
Mexican cession, 4, 39–40, 43, 74, 119, 158, 162, 169
Mexico, Republic of, 37–40, 65, 194
Mexico City, 32, 37
Miller, Edward, 154–58
Mills, William, 96
Mimbres basin, 103
Mimbres River, 26
mining, 10, 11, 29, 31, 33, 47, 50, 56, 107, 166, 184, 190–91, 193
modernity, 11, 13, 56, 57, 72
Mogollon culture, 26–27
Mogollon Mountains, 24, 247n102
Morrill Act, 47

Navajo Nation, 15, 67–68, 98
Navy, U.S., 53
neoliberalism, 12–13
Newell, Frederick, 52–53, 55, 59–63, 71, 230n3, 230n14, 230n17
Newlands, Francis, 60
New Mexico, government institutions and officials: acequia commissions, 36, 77–78, 82; attorney general, 86; board of control, 81, 82, 85, 88; cabildos, 36, 118; Commission on Irrigation and Water Rights, 79, 82, 91, 92, 93; district courts, 85, 116, 120–21; governor, 38, 78, 92, 118; jueces de paz, 119; mayordomos, 34–37, 38, 77, 78, 81, 82, 89, 112, 118, 119; Office of the State Engineer, 90, 208–9, 210, 212; Office of the Territorial (Irrigation) Engineer, 20, 80, 84, 105, 108, 111, 113, 114, 136, 164, 207; prefectos, 119; probate judges, 119–20, 121, 123, 126, 128; Special Attorney for the Pueblo Indians of New Mexico, U.S., 100; Supreme Court, 82, 107, 177, 183, 184; territorial assembly, 41, 45, 73, 77–78, 93, 95, 208; territorial engineer, 84–85, 86–87, 95–96, 99, 102–3, 105–6, 107, 109, 110, 112, 114; territorial irrigation engineer, 84, 94, 101, 108; water masters, 85, 87

New Mexico, history and geography: acequias, 34, 226n51; agriculture, 15, 27–29, 31, 34–37; Americanization, 46–49, 97, 113–15, 205, 206; booster industry, 41, 46–47, 61, 64, 75, 77, 78, 91, 97, 102, 111, 191; cultural history, 23–24, 26–46; economic development, 97–98, 99, 100, 102, 104, 120, 143, 200; environmental geography, 24–26, 31, 46–49; land grants, 33, 38, 41–43, 50, 74; land speculation, 64, 75, 76, 78–79, 84, 86–87; legal history, 73–90, 117–21, 200; Mexican period, 37–40, 118–19; modernization, 93, 238n3; precolonial period, 19, 26–29, 117; Spanish colonial period, 19, 23, 29–37, 117–18; statehood, 17, 21, 40, 46, 50, 72, 78, 90, 92, 93, 94, 97, 184, 205; territorial period, 12, 39–50, 73–90, 119–21, 202–3. See also acequia culture; acequias; Anglo-Americans (Anglos); Camino Real (de Tierra Adentro); displacement; dispossession; environmental change; environmental damage and disaster; ethnicity; homesteading; Indigenous groups in New Mexico; irrigation; Nuevomexicanas/os; Pueblo nations of New Mexico; reclamation projects in New Mexico; "Santa Fe Ring"; Santa Fe Trail; settler colonialism; tricultural myth
New Mexico, laws of: 1882 water law, 78; 1887 water law, 78; 1897 water law, 79, 82, 93; 1903 water bills, 79–80; 1905 water law, 80–83; 1907 water law, 73, 83–88; evolution of modern water law, 20, 73, 76–90; Kearney Code, 119; legal transitions, 75–76, 116–21, 144
New Mexico College of Agriculture and Mechanic Arts, 96
New Mexico State Records Center and Archive, 122, 126
New Mexico State University, 96
New Mexico Town Company, 167
"New West" history, 11
New York, 162, 163, 164

New Zealand, 6, 71
Nicanora Ditch, 106
Nuanes, Guadalupe, 171–73
Nuevomexicanas/os: activism of, 16, 210, 211–12; as both colonizers and colonized, 8, 20, 23, 40, 203, 204; core settlement areas, 34, 38, 99; displaced by Anglos, 5–6, 20, 63–65, 72, 83, 90, 203, 206–7, 211; elites, 17, 40, 45, 68, 93, 118–19, 120, 138, 227n91, 238n3; indigeneity claims, 46, 144, 228n123; knowledge, 49, 69, 70, 98; land-based communities, 41, 46, 49, 77, 207; participation in New Mexico territorial assembly, 41, 45, 77; place-based lifeways, 16, 49, 70, 89, 117, 207; racial complexity, 8, 17, 46, 227n91, 228n123; use of term, 16–18; in water disputes, 118–19, 120–21, 127–33, 206. *See also* acequia culture; commons; environmental-racial order; land grants in New Mexico; mestizaje; Otero, Miguel; settler colonialism

Ohkay Owingeh (San Juan) Pueblo, 30–31, 242n5
Oñate, Juan de, 29–32, 211, 224n18
Ortega bill, 79–80
Otero, Felix, 196–202
Otero, Miguel, 93–95, 97–98, 99, 100–101, 102, 104, 105, 109, 110, 238n3
overgrazing, 48–49

Pacific Ocean, 26, 212
Palmer, William, 196–202
Palmer Acequia, 196–202
parciantes, 34, 98, 118, 179
Parker, Frank, 192–93, 198, 201
Pecos Pueblo, 27
Pecos River, 26, 38, 41, 44, 95, 97, 102, 104, 106
Pecos valley, 64, 79, 103, 104, 110, 114
Peña Blanca, village of, 158, 159, 169–71
Percha Creek, 191–92
permits, water, 73, 80–81, 82, 83, 86, 87, 94, 97, 112, 205
Philippines, 104

Pisani, Donald, 76
"placelessness," 9, 10, 57, 141, 207
place names, 15, 122, 143, 242n5, 245n64
Plaza Alcalde, town of, 145
political ecology, 12, 14
Pollmann, Henry, 154–58
Ponsiano Arrey lateral, 196, 200
Portales basin, 103
poststructuralism, 5, 12
Powell, John Wesley, 52, 54, 59, 60, 71
Preemption Act, 47
prior appropriation doctrine, 75–76, 84, 89, 107, 136, 234n6
Progressive Party, 51, 55, 69, 73
Progressivism: apolitical claims of, 51, 57, 61, 71–72; conservation, 56, 57, 58, 60, 61; contradictions, 57–58, 62–63, 72; efficiency, 20, 56, 57, 62, 70, 80, 100, 109, 113, 205; elevation of science and engineering, 20, 51, 55, 56–57, 61, 69–70, 93, 101, 107; environmental management agenda, 20, 51–52, 56–58, 61–63, 71–72, 204–5, 207; expansion of government bureaucracy, 20, 55, 57, 70–71, 72; and expertise, 20, 51, 55–58, 69–71, 80, 91, 114, 204–6; focus on American West, 20, 55–57; global competition, 56, 61–62; law and policy, 60, 73–74, 80–81, 89–90, 91, 205; modernist beliefs and vision, 51, 56, 57, 66, 141; and profit, 61–62; and racism, 20, 55, 56, 57–58, 62–63, 70–71, 98, 100, 112, 205; and settler colonialism, 20, 51–52, 55, 58, 61–62, 69–71, 74, 80, 93, 98, 112, 205; social reform, 55–56, 58, 60, 66–69, 207. *See also* environmental damage and disaster; environmental-management states; governance; Reclamation Act; reclamation policy; Roosevelt, Theodore
Pueblo nations of New Mexico: Acoma, 31; Cochiti, 99, 158; communal organization, 26–27; irrigation history, 27–29; Isleta, 15, 167, 178, 179, 181–84; Jemez, 158; original vs. colonial names, 15; Pecos, 27; relation to ancient peoples, 26–27; relation to

nomadic groups, 27, 29; Sandia, 167; San Felipe, 158; San Gabriel (Yunque Owingeh), 31; San Ildefonso, 99, 230n14; San Juan (Ohkay Owingeh), 30–31, 242n5; Santa Ana (Tamaya), 158, 160; Santo Domingo (Kewa), 15, 158, 169–71, 245n64; Tesuque Pueblo, 157–58; Tiwa, 2; Zia, 158; Zuni, 27, 67–68

Pueblo Revolt, 33, 144, 178

Puerco River, 26, 159, 162–67

Puerto Rico, 104

race: as basis of settler colonialism, 7, 8, 17, 47, 50, 68, 112, 204, 207–8; expertise based on, 4, 51, 58, 62–63, 66–68, 69–71, 90, 139, 204–6; interracial identity (see mestizaje); and knowledge, 4, 5, 9, 17; racial injustice, 22, 211–12; racialization of colonized peoples, 4, 7, 15–18, 71; racial politics, 10, 11, 58; racism inherent in Progressivism, 20, 55, 56, 57–58, 62–63, 70–71, 98, 100, 112, 205; relations in independent Mexico, 37–38; relations in Spanish colony, 16, 29, 31, 45, 224n18; relations in territorial American colony, 5, 7, 39, 45–46, 49; and science, 70–71, 107–8, 204; terminology, 14–18; and water policy, 4, 5, 8, 62–63, 64, 70, 100; and whiteness, 7, 15–17, 19, 39, 69–71, 139, 205, 227n91, 230n16; and white supremacy, 7–8, 55, 60, 63, 69–71, 205, 208. See also Americanization; Anglo-Americans (Anglos); environmental-racial order; ethnicity; mestizaje; Nuevomexicanas/os

railroads, 5, 41, 45, 47, 52, 86, 95, 120, 143, 159, 167, 184. See also AT&SF (Atchison, Topeka and Santa Fe) railroad

Ranchitos, village of, 145

Rayado Hydrographic Survey, 107

Rayado stream, 97

Raynolds, Herbert, 165, 166

Reclamation, U.S. Bureau of, 71, 112

Reclamation Act, 54, 60, 73, 80

reclamation policy: apolitical claims of, 51, 57, 61, 71–72; contradictions, 57, 58, 62, 107–11; efficiency as goal, 20, 63–64, 109–11, 204, 205; environmental impacts of, 51, 63–64, 65; failures, 62, 64–65, 66–68, 99, 110, 164; federal projects, 59, 65–66, 71, 191, 195; financial model, 54, 60, 62; irrigation congresses, 61–62; knowledge exchange among settler nations, 61–62, 71; in law, 20, 73–90, 93–94, 95–96, 205; led by experts, 20, 52, 60–61, 69–71, 209; marquee project for Progressives, 51; public popularity, 62; racism, 4, 5, 8, 62–63, 64, 70, 100; in science and engineering, 52–53, 58–63, 81; social impacts of, 65–69; as tool of settler colonialism, 49, 51, 63–69, 72. See also dams; displacement; dispossession; expertise; Indian Irrigation Service (IIS); law: water policy; Progressivism; Reclamation Act; reclamation projects in New Mexico; Reclamation Service, U.S.; Reclamation Survey

reclamation projects in New Mexico: Carlsbad Project, 65; Elephant Butte Dam and Reservoir, 65, 165, 191, 195; Hondo Creek project, 64; Pecos valley project, 64; Rio Grande Project, 65, 191, 195; Zuni Reservoir, 67, 100. See also Indian Irrigation Service (IIS); Reclamation Service, U.S.

Reclamation Service, U.S., 49, 60, 62, 64, 66, 68, 69, 70, 79, 80, 81, 112, 165, 191, 195

Reclamation Survey, 94, 96

Red River, 26

repartimiento, 32, 118

resilience, Indigenous, 10, 31, 49

resilience, Nuevomexicano, 23, 63

rights, water. See water rights

Rincon Valley, 65, 191, 195

Rio Abajo. See under Rio Grande

Rio Arriba. See under Rio Grande

Rio Arriba County, 144–52

Rio Arriba District Court, 129t, 130, 133t, 135, 139t

Rio Chama, 2, 21, 26, 30, 123, 143, 144, 145, 152

Rio de las Truchas, 149, 150f, 152
Rio de Tesuque, 154–57
Rio Grande: aggradation, 47–48; Chama–Rio Grande corridor, 21, 30, 123, 126, 127f, 132, 143, 144, 206; flooding, 47–48, 49, 103, 179, 182, 185, 188–90; floodplains, 2, 24, 28, 35, 103, 159, 160, 174, 179, 185, 194; headwaters, 2, 24, 26, 123, 195; lower valley of, 165, 194, 195, 199; main stem, 1–2, 21, 23, 26, 35, 153, 158; middle valley of, 2, 33, 35, 48, 90, 130, 167, 168, 169, 171, 177, 181, 184, 188–90; Rio Abajo, 31, 34, 35; Rio Arriba, 31, 32, 34, 35, 47; seasonal flow of, 2, 3, 53–54, 65, 97, 103, 149, 160, 167, 169, 171, 185–86, 188–90; settlement history, 2, 26, 27, 29–34, 40, 48, 99, 109, 130, 160, 167, 174, 177, 202, 207; tributaries, 35, 65, 123, 145, 149–50, 153, 158, 165–66, 207; valley, 3, 23, 47, 72, 109, 130, 161; watershed, 5, 16, 19, 34, 70, 116. *See also* dams; Embudo; Rio Grande Project; salinization (of soils)
Rio Grande Project, 65, 191, 195
Rio Puerco, 26, 159, 162–67
Rio Puerco Irrigation Company, 162–67
Rio Salado, 26
riparian rights doctrine, 75
Rocky Mountains, 24, 29, 96
Rodríguez, Sylvia, 210–11
Roosevelt, Theodore, 56, 60, 61, 79, 100

salinization (of soils), 10, 48, 63, 65–66
Salt River, 26, 27
Sanchez, Jesus, 179–81
Sanchez y Alarid, Jesus, 179–81
Sandia Mountains, 2
Sandia Pueblo, 167
Sandoval County, 158–67
San Felipe Pueblo, 158
San Gabriel (Yunque Owingeh) Pueblo, 31
Sangre de Cristo Mountains, 149
San Ildefonso Pueblo, 99, 230n14
San Juan (Ohkay Owingeh) Pueblo, 30–31

San Juan Mountains, 52
San Juan River, 2, 26–27, 38, 104, 119, 123
San Marcial, village of, 188
Santa Ana (Tamaya) Pueblo, 158, 160
Santa Fe, village of, 32, 34, 38, 39, 74, 76, 122, 153, 164
Santa Fe County, 134, 135, 152–58, 167
"Santa Fe Ring," 43
Santa Fe Trail, 38–39, 40, 153, 178
Santo Domingo (Kewa) Pueblo, 15, 158, 169–71, 245n64
San Ysidro, village of, 158
San Ysidro Acequia Madre, 196, 197, 200
science: assumed "placelessness," 9, 57, 141, 148, 171; basis of expertise, 4, 6, 21, 56, 59, 70, 80–81, 91, 114; claimed to be apolitical, 51, 57, 61, 71–72; and engineering, 4, 10, 14, 20, 54, 69, 72, 93, 107; as evidence in court, 81, 95, 136–39, 140, 143, 157, 190; geographies of, 3, 6, 8–10; government-sponsored, 3, 52, 54, 57, 60–61, 69; impossibility of objectivity, 9–10, 51, 69, 71–72, 205, 209; and law, 13–14, 143; modernist, 8–9, 11–12, 51–52, 57, 80, 141, 143, 209, 210; and Progressivism, 20, 51, 55, 56–57, 61, 69–70, 93, 101, 107; and racism, 70–71, 107–8, 204; in reclamation policy, 51, 52–53, 54, 58–63, 81, 104; role in displacement, 11, 20, 52, 55, 58, 62, 69, 70–71, 113–15; role in dispossession, 3–4, 5–6, 22, 204–7; and settler colonialism, 3, 4, 5–6, 8, 10–12, 19, 20–21, 51, 59, 91–93, 105, 113–15, 143, 204, 206, 209–10. *See also* agronomy; cartography; critical physical geography; data: science; environmental science; hydrography; hydrology; knowledge; reclamation policy: in science and engineering; soils: science; stream gauging; STS (science and technology studies); technoscience
scientific expeditions, 53, 57
Secretary of the Interior, U.S., 65, 92, 94, 95, 97, 98, 101, 104, 105, 109
settler colonialism: Anglo entry into

New Mexico, 19–20, 23, 40–46; boosterism in New Mexico, 41, 46–47, 61, 64, 75, 77, 78, 91, 97, 102, 111, 191; and capitalism, 49–50, 68, 73, 104–7, 108, 112, 114; complicity of scholars in, 18–19, 23, 211; cultural identity and erasure, 8, 16, 23, 46–47, 49–50, 206–7; and economic control, 45–46, 47, 50; enacted by courts, 7, 21, 116–17, 143, 202–3, 205, 206; and engineering expertise, 20, 51–52, 61, 69, 104, 138–39, 141, 204–6, 209; and environmental change, 10–11, 46–49, 63, 162–63; and environmental knowledge, 3, 4–5, 7–8, 10–11, 12–14, 17, 21–22, 61, 69, 70–71, 91, 93, 113–15, 143, 206; expertise as tool for, 20, 52, 61, 141, 204–6; vs. extractive colonialism, 6, 11, 14; knowledge exchange among settler nations, 61–62, 71; through law, 45, 47, 52, 73–76, 89–90, 91, 107, 202; noble savage myth, 47; in North America, 6–7; and place names, 15, 242n5, 245n64; and Progressivism, 20, 51–52, 55, 58, 61–62, 69–71, 74, 80, 93, 98, 112, 205; and race relations, 16, 17, 29, 31, 45, 224n18; and racialization of colonized peoples, 4, 7, 15–18, 71; racism as basis of, 7, 8, 17, 47, 50, 68, 112, 204, 207–8; and reclamation policy, 63–69; resistance to, 4, 23, 31, 32–33, 38, 44, 50, 143, 207; through science and engineering, 3, 4, 5–6, 8, 10–12, 19, 20–21, 51, 59, 91–93, 105, 113–15, 143, 204, 206, 209–10; self-perpetuation, 6, 7, 11, 72, 207–8, 210; "settlerscapes," 10; Spanish entry into New Mexico, 19, 23, 29–34; as structure not event, 5, 6, 11, 207; in water policy, 19–20, 21–22, 23, 49–51, 52, 61, 63, 66, 68, 73, 88–90, 91, 97–101, 108, 114–15, 204, 205–6, 210. See also decolonization; displacement; dispossession; "double colonization"; ethnic cleansing; genocide; sovereignty; violence

"settlerscapes," 10
Sierra County, 190–91
Sierra Diablo, 191
Sierra District Court, 130t, 133t, 134, 135, 139t, 191–94
Silver City, town of, 191, 201
sinkholes, 97
Smythe, William, 64
"socionatures," 13
sociotechnical imaginary, 12
Socorro, town of, 184
Socorro County, 79, 184–86
Socorro District Court, 130t, 133t, 134, 139t, 185, 186–90
Soil Conservation Service, U.S., 49
soils: degradation, 10, 56, 63, 166; and duty of water, 105–6; fertility, 61, 64, 96, 187–88; moisture, 101, 102–3, 107, 109 (see also "Campbell method"); salinization, 10, 48, 63, 65–66; science, 101, 103, 107–8, 111
sovereignty: Indigenous, 4, 7, 11, 43, 67, 184; transitions in New Mexico, 10, 37–40, 74, 90, 194
Springer, Manuel, 172, 176
Springer project, 103
State Engineer, New Mexico Office of, 90, 208–9, 210, 212
Stevens, Helen, 186–87
Stevens, Montague, 186–87
St. Louis, city of, 38
strawberries (crop), 155
stream gauging, 53–54, 59–60, 87, 95–97, 114. See also Embudo: USGS training camp; hydrography
STS (science and technology studies), 8–9
subsistence: agriculture, 21, 34, 38, 63, 64, 67, 77, 99; vs. commercial activities, 39, 40, 41, 43, 46, 50, 58, 63, 68, 72, 73, 78, 89–90, 98, 104–7, 111, 120, 204, 206, 207; communities' resilience to settler colonialism, 64, 65, 78, 116, 203–4, 208; strategies and activities, 10, 15, 27, 49
Sullivan, Vernon, 87, 95–97, 102–3, 104, 106–7, 110–13

Supreme Court, New Mexico, 82, 107, 177, 183, 184
Supreme Court, U.S., 74, 88
surveying: and court disputes, 124t, 137t, 149, 152, 171, 181, 184, 188, 189f, 190, 192; by irrigation engineers, 80–81, 84–85, 86–87, 92, 103; land, 93; legal rights of surveyors, 85–86; scientific, 114, 119, 137, 205. *See also* hydrography: surveys; hydrology: survey and mapping; Irrigation Survey, U.S.; Reclamation Survey; scientific expeditions; Surveyor General, U.S.; Topographic Survey, USGS; USGS (United States Geological Survey)
Surveyor General, U.S., 162

Tamaya (Santa Ana) Pueblo, 158, 160
Tapia, Anastacio, 172–73
technoscience, 4, 101
Territorial (Irrigation) Engineer, New Mexico Office of, 20, 80, 84, 105, 108, 111, 113, 114, 136, 164, 207. *See also* State Engineer, New Mexico Office of
territorial engineer, New Mexico, 84–85, 86–87, 95–96, 99, 102–3, 105–6, 107, 109, 110, 112, 114
territorial irrigation engineer, New Mexico, 84, 94, 101, 108
Tesuque Pueblo, 157–58
Tesuque River, 154–57
Texas, state of, 24, 39, 65, 123, 177, 191, 194
Timber Culture Act, 47
Topographic Survey, USGS, 59–60, 96
Torrance County, 178
Torres, Agapito, 197
transhumance, 144
Treaty of Guadalupe Hidalgo, 4, 39–40, 41, 43, 74
tricultural myth, 14–15, 17
Truchas, Rio de las, 145, 150f, 152

underflow. *See* groundwater
University of New Mexico, 18
USGS (United States Geological Survey), 52, 54, 59, 60, 87, 95, 96–97, 112, 148
Utah, state of, 27
Utes, 29, 45

Valencia, partido of, 177–78
Valencia County, 177–79, 181–83, 185
Valencia District Court, 129t, 133t, 135, 138, 139t, 178–79, 183
Vargas, Diego de, 33
vegetables (crop), 37, 154–55, 176, 177
violence: American colonial, 7, 11, 19, 23, 29, 31, 39, 45, 52; Spanish colonial, 8, 19, 23, 29, 31

Washington, D.C., 97
waste prevention, 55–56, 57, 81, 106, 109–13, 205
water management. *See* acequia culture; acequias; dams; engineering: of irrigation projects; governance: of water; irrigation; permits, water; reclamation policy; water rights
water policy. *See* reclamation policy
water rights: centralized management by engineers, 72, 84, 97, 107; communitarian vs. individualistic, 74, 76; disputed in court, 113, 116–18, 125t, 128, 133t, 136, 138, 147–48, 154–58, 165, 170, 177, 179, 181–82, 185–86; Indigenous, 88, 100; and land speculation, 64, 75, 76, 78–79, 84, 86–87; state vs. federal jurisdiction, 74, 75. *See also* acequia culture; adjudication of water rights; beneficial use, and water rights; condemnations; Irrigation and Water Rights, Commission on; permits, water; prior appropriation doctrine; riparian rights doctrine
water sampling, 52, 96
Weather Bureau, U.S., 96
wells, groundwater, 2, 64, 101, 103, 104, 105
wheat (crop), 37, 180, 198
White, David, 83, 94, 95, 108
Whiteman, William, 157
whiteness. *See* race: and whiteness

white supremacy. *See* race: and white supremacy
Williams, J. B., 53, 54
Wilson, Charles, 196–98
wing-dam, 150, 151f
Winters v. United States, 88
Wolfe, Patrick, 11

Yunque Owingeh (San Gabriel) Pueblo, 31

Zia Pueblo, 158
Zuni Pueblo, 27, 67–68
Zuni Reservoir, 100

www.ingramcontent.com/pod-product-compliance
Lightning Source LLC
Chambersburg PA
CBHW022039290426
44109CB00014B/909